always up to date

The law changes, but Nolo is always on top of it! We offer several ways to make sure you and your Nolo products are always up to date:

1 **Nolo's Legal Updater**
We'll send you an email whenever a new edition of your book is published! Sign up at **www.nolo.com/legalupdater**.

2 **Updates @ Nolo.com**
Check **www.nolo.com/update** to find recent changes in the law that affect the current edition of your book.

3 **Nolo Customer Service**
To make sure that this edition of the book is the most recent one, call us at **800-728-3555** and ask one of our friendly customer service representatives.
Or find out at **www.nolo.com**.

3rd edition

The Manager's Legal Handbook

By Attorneys Lisa Guerin and Amy DelPo

Third Edition	NOVEMBER 2005
Editors	STEPHANIE BORNSTEIN
	LISA GUERIN
Cover Design	TONI IHARA
Book Design	TERRI HEARSH
Proofreading	JOE SADUSKY
Index	ELLEN SHERRON
Printing	CONSOLIDATED PRINTERS, INC.

Guerin, Lisa, 1964–
    Manager's legal handbook / by Lisa Guerin & Amy DelPo
        p. cm.
    Rev. ed. of: Everyday employment law. 2nd ed. 2004.
    ISBN 1-4133-0366-8 (alk. paper)
    1. Labor laws and legislation--United States--Popular works. 2. Labor contract--United
States--Popular works. 3. Employee rights--United States--Popular works. 4.
Executives--United States--Handbooks, manuals, etc. I. DelPo, Amy 1967– II. Guerin,
Lisa, 1964- Everyday employment law. III. Title

    KF3455.Z9G84 2005
    344.7301--dc22

                                                                    2005051821

Quanity sales: For information on bulk purchases or corporate premium sales, please
contact the Special Sales Department. For academic sales or textbook adoptions, ask for
Academic Sales. 800-955-4775, Nolo, 950 Parker Street, Berkeley, CA 94710.

Acknowledgments

The authors would like to thank:

On the first edition, our wonderful editor, Shannon Miehe, whose sense of humor, organizational skills, lightning-fast speed, and careful editing made working on this book a pleasure.

On subsequent editions, our editor and friend, Stephanie Bornstein, who helped transform the book into a must-have legal guide for managers.

Mary Randolph, Jake Warner, and Janet Portman, all of whom helped us figure out how to organize this material—and how to avoid the dreaded "scope creep."

Ella Hirst, for meticulously researching and compiling the state charts.

Stan Jacobsen, for his research help and ever-positive attitude.

John M. True, III, formerly of Leonard Carder, LLP, in Oakland, California, for writing some of the privacy material and helping out with the information on unions.

Philip Monrad, also of Leonard Carder, for his generous help with the unions chapter.

Table of Contents

3 Discrimination

4 Personnel Basics

5 Time Off

Appendix

Resources

Index

INTRODUCTION

Navigating the Maze of Employment Law

Some managers learn the hard way that good intentions aren't enough. In these days of burgeoning employment laws, regulations, and lawsuits, successfully and safely managing workers (employees and independent contractors alike) requires a whole lot more than just following your instincts. Lawmakers and courts have created a complicated web of dos and don'ts that covers the entire spectrum of workplace issues, from hiring and firing to discrimination and harassment. If you are a supervisor, manager, or human resources specialist, you've got to learn how to navigate this legal maze—or risk serious trouble for your company and yourself.

Fortunately, learning what you need to know to manage workers on a daily basis doesn't have to be time-consuming or difficult—or even unpleasant. This book distills these complicated issues down to the basics, providing the most important information you need to know when you walk into your workplace every day.

How to Use This Book

This book gives you the information you need to deal with many common workplace concerns and issues. Each chapter focuses on a specific employment law topic—such as hiring, compensation and hours, privacy in the workplace, and so on—and breaks that subject down into the issues managers are most likely to face.

Of course, every company is different and every manager has different areas of responsibility and expertise. Although this book explains the legal rules that apply to managers and companies alike, not every manager will have the authority to make ultimate decisions on matters of policy or serious personnel matters, such as firing and layoffs. We provide this information to give you some legal background that will help you understand your role in the process, as your company defines it.

Each chapter includes:

- **Frequently Asked Questions (FAQs).** We introduce you to the chapter topic through quick answers to questions that managers and employers commonly face.
- **Articles.** We break down the chapter's topic into a series of separate articles, so that you can get right to the information you need. That way, you can focus only on the rules that apply to the situation at hand without having to wade through an entire book looking for your answer.
- **50-State Charts.** We provide you with a summary of information on your state's legal requirements where necessary, in addition to the federal law covered in the chapter.
- **Lessons From the Real World.** Learn from the failures and victories of companies that have been taken to court by their employees.
- **Legal Dos and Don'ts.** We provide a handful of strategies to follow—and

traps to avoid—as you implement the information in each chapter.

- **Test Your Knowledge.** Find out how well you understand each topic by taking our quiz at the end of each chapter.

You can read through the entire book at once, pick and choose among chapters of special interest to your company, or use the book as a desk reference by consulting particular articles as issues come up. No matter how you use the book, the basic information we provide will help answer your most common employment questions.

Additional Resources

Although most managers will rarely need more information than what we provide here, you might occasionally have a problem that requires you to seek additional help. We alert you to those potential trouble spots and point you toward resources that can give you the extra information you need.

The appendix (at the end of the book) contains a list of resources you can consult for more information. These resources include:

- Contact information for the federal agencies that enforce federal workplace laws, including the Equal Employment Opportunity Commission (EEOC), the Occupational Health and Safety Administration (OSHA), the Department of Labor (DOL), and the Federal Trade Commission (FTC).
- Contact information for the state agencies that enforce state workplace laws, including a list of state departments of labor and state fair employment offices.
- A list of Internet resources, including government agencies and private organizations whose websites provide helpful information about the topics we cover here.
- A list of Nolo's employment and human resources titles, including books that will help you investigate workplace problems, evaluate employee performance, create legally sound independent contractor agreements, draft an employee handbook, and much more. ■

1

Hiring

Hiring can be a tough task for managers. It's challenging enough to find the right hire for the job—someone with the skills, attitude, personality, and other important qualities to be a success at your company. When you add legal concerns to the mix, hiring can seem like a truly daunting responsibility.

But you cannot ignore your legal obligations when hiring new employees. Federal and state employment laws reach beyond just current employees; many also protect those who apply for jobs by, for example, prohibiting discriminatory job postings, putting limits on the information you can gather in a background check, or outlawing certain kinds of applicant screening tests. What's more, the things you say and do during the hiring process could come back to haunt you and your company later, particularly if an employee claims that you offered a job contract or promised job security.

The good news is that following sensible and careful hiring practices will keep your company out of immediate legal trouble, help you find the most qualified employees, and—by screening out problem employees from the get-go—help prevent management headaches and possible lawsuits down the road.

This chapter explains the legal ins and outs of hiring, including practical advice on how to find, interview, and seal the deal with your lucky new hire.

Frequently Asked Questions About Hiring

■ **Do I have to advertise open positions?**

No. Although federal, state, and local governments typically have to post openings, private companies don't. Nonetheless, there are some very good reasons to advertise:

- You can choose from a larger pool of applicants, which increases your odds of finding a great person for the job.
- You avoid unintentional discrimination. (For example, if you rely solely on word of mouth when looking for applicants and you only know people of your race or ethnicity, then your hiring process may be discriminatory—even though that is not your intention.)
- You can avoid the appearance of nepotism or favoritism. If you hire your friends, family members, or neighbors to come work for you, the employees who currently report to you may think you'll play favorites. By posting open positions and choosing your hires from a broad range of

Frequently Asked Questions About Hiring (continued)

applicants, you can show your reports that you hire—and manage—on merit alone. (For advice on effective and legal job advertisements, see "Advertisements," below.)

■ **Are there questions I cannot ask during a job interview?**

Yes. For example, you may not ask whether an applicant has a disability, what country an applicant comes from, and, in some states, whether an applicant has ever been arrested. (To learn what questions you can and cannot ask an applicant during an interview, see "Interviews," below.)

■ **Are there things I shouldn't say when I'm trying to convince a really strong applicant to take a job?**

Absolutely. Although you'll be tempted to sell your company during a job interview, don't overdo it. If you exaggerate—or out-and-out lie—about the position, the company's prospects, or other important facts, and the applicant takes the job based on your statements, that employee can sue the company if your statements turn out to be false or overly optimistic. (For more information on statements to avoid when hiring, see "Making Promises," below.)

■ **Can I ask whether an applicant has a disability?**

No. The Americans With Disabilities Act (ADA) prohibits you from asking whether an applicant has a disability. Instead, you should focus your interview questions on the applicant's abilities—for example, you may ask whether and how an applicant would perform each essential job function. If you know that an applicant has a disability (because it is obvious or the applicant has told you about it), you may ask whether the applicant will need an accommodation to perform the job. (For more on avoiding disability discrimination when hiring, see "Applicants With Disabilities," below.)

■ **Can I ask every applicant to take a lie detector test?**

No. The Employee Polygraph Protection Act (EPPA) prohibits lie detector tests from being required by all but a few types of employers—those that provide certain types of security services or manufacture pharmaceuticals, for example. (For more information on what tests you can—and can't—ask applicants to take, see "Testing Applicants," below.)

Frequently Asked Questions About Hiring (continued)

■ **Can I run background checks on applicants?**

It depends on the information you plan to collect. You can check information that is relevant to the job for which you are considering hiring the worker. However, state and federal laws restrict you from gathering or using certain types of records. If you are considering running a background check, your best strategy is to ask applicants to consent to the check in advance, in writing. (See "Background Checks," below, for more information.)

■ **Can I hire teenagers to do clerical work?**

Generally, yes. Teenagers who are at least 16 years old may work unlimited hours in any profession that the government has not deemed hazardous. You can also hire younger teens, although the law restricts how many hours they may work. (For more information on hiring teenagers, see "Young Workers," below.)

■ **If I want to offer someone a job, do I have to do it in writing?**

There is no law that governs how you offer someone a job. You can do it over the phone, with a formal letter, or using smoke signals, if you'd like. However, you should probably send written offer letters just to make sure potential hires understand exactly what you are offering. Offer letters aren't without their pitfalls, however, so be careful what you write. (To learn how to write a legally safe offer letter, see "Offer Letters," below.)

■ **When I hire someone, should I use a written contract?**

It depends on the circumstances. The law does not require you to use a written employment contract and, for the most part, you probably won't want to. However, there may be times when writing a contract is a good idea—for example, if you want the employee to make a long-term commitment to the company. (To learn about when you should and should not use an employment contract, see "Written Employment Contracts," below.)

Advertisements

Although most "help wanted" ads contain only a handful of words, using the wrong sort of words can land your company in legal trouble. Any job requirement that discriminates against applicants based on a characteristic protected by law (for example, race or gender) violates federal law and the laws of many states. (To learn which characteristics are protected by federal and state law, see Chapter 3.)

Some off-limits topics are obvious—most managers know that an ad can't state "only white males need apply." But companies can get into trouble by posting an ad that discriminates on a more subtle level—and they may not even realize it until it's too late.

For example, let's say you want to hire a technician for your company's information systems department. Almost all of the technician's day would be spent at a computer. On occasion, however, technicians at your company have to install new equipment, which might require them to carry computers, monitors, printers, and so on. Should you write an ad saying that you are looking for someone who can lift at least 50 pounds? Well, that kind of requirement would screen out applicants with certain disabilities, as well as disproportionate numbers of women. Because the lifting is only occasional and could be accomplished by other means—using machinery, for example—including such a requirement in your ad could be discriminatory.

Similarly, watch for words or descriptions that imply you have a discriminatory preference. For example, let's say you are looking for someone to do odd jobs around your office, from answering phones to filing to typing. Your ad can say that you are looking for an "office worker," but if you say you are looking for a "girl Friday," it implies that you are only looking for women—and therefore that you would discriminate against male applicants. The same precaution applies to terms like "handyman" or "waiter."

So what can you say? If you follow two basic rules, you should steer clear of trouble:

- **Focus on the essential functions of the job.** In other words, only ask for the skills or characteristics that the job absolutely requires. For example, if you are looking for someone to proofread magazine articles, you probably don't need someone with a college science degree—unless, of course, your magazine is a professional scientific journal where someone might need such a specialized education. If there is an up-to-date job description for the position, you can use it to focus the ad appropriately.

- **Pay attention to the literal meaning of the words you use.** This is particularly important with the suffix "-man"—as in "salesman," "repairman," and so on (try "salesperson" and "general repair person" instead), or gendered positions such as "waiter" (use "server" or "waitperson" instead). It is also important to be cautious when using words that refer to age. For example, if you want someone who is energetic with a lot of fresh ideas, you might want to say in your ad "looking for worker with a youthful attitude." But if you do, you are expressing an age preference—which is discriminatory and illegal.

Interviews

The spontaneous and unpredictable nature of the job interview makes it rife with traps, even for managers with the best of intentions. Well-meaning, innocent comments could be construed by an applicant as prejudicial or could be used later by an unhappy applicant as the basis of a discrimination lawsuit.

For example, let's say an applicant grew up near your home town and attended the same high school as you and your siblings. You might naturally want to ask when the applicant graduated, as a way to find out whether you know people in common. The problem is, the answer will necessarily reveal the applicant's age—and if the applicant is at least 40 years old, this could be part of a discrimination claim if you later offer the job to someone else.

On the other hand, you don't want to get so hung up on every word you say that you defeat the purpose of the interview: to learn about the applicant's skills and experience so you can choose

the best-qualified candidate for the position.

Here are some tips that will help you stay out of legal trouble while also getting the information you need to make the right choice:

- **Don't ask about any characteristic that the law prohibits you from considering in making your decision.** (To learn about these protected characteristics, see Chapter 3.) For example, you can't base your hiring decisions on an applicant's religious beliefs or national origin, so you shouldn't be asking about those things in your interviews. In "Pre-Employment Inquiries," at the end of this chapter, we give you some ideas on how to get information while staying within the bounds of the law.

- **Respect the applicant's privacy.** Although federal law does not require you to do so, many state laws and rules of etiquette do. For example, asking applicants in California about their sexual fantasies (yes—that actually happened in a real life case) violates their state-protected right to privacy. (For more information on privacy in the workplace, see Chapter 6.)

- **If an applicant raises a delicate subject, it's usually best to skirt the issue.** Unless the topic is directly related to the position—for example, the applicant reveals that he or she has a disability and will need an accommodation to perform the job—politely steer the conversation in another direction. Although it might seem a bit awkward, you'll be better off in the long run if you don't take the applicant's comments as an invitation to start a long conversation about, for example, relationship troubles or political beliefs.

- **Ask open-ended questions to get the candidate talking.** There's a big difference between a closed question—such as "How many supervisory positions have you held?"—and an open one—such as "Tell me about your most recent experience supervising others." The more open your questions, the more you invite the candidate to talk. This will not only give you the factual information you need to make a decision, but will also let you see how well applicants carry themselves, think on their feet, and so on.

- **Ask behavioral questions, if possible.** It can be tough to find out whether applicants have important, yet some-what intangible qualifications, such as problem-solving skills or the ability to work well as part of a team. If you just come out and ask, all but the most dim-witted applicants are going to know the correct answer. ("Are you good at solving problems?" "You bet!") On the other hand, if you ask about specific instances in which the applicant had to use that skill, you're more likely to get a helpful response. To find out about a candidate's problem-solving skills,

for example, you could say, "Tell me about a problem you recently faced in your current position and how you handled it."

- **Focus on what the job really requires.** Use the job description for the position (if you have one) to script some interview questions that will help you find out if the applicant has the necessary skills and experience. If you don't have a job description, create a list of the essential tasks the employee you hire will have to perform, then craft questions that will help you figure out whether the applicant can meet these requirements. Remember, the law absolutely allows you to ask questions that directly relate to the job you are trying to fill.

- **Cover similar ground with each applicant.** You can't ask exactly the same questions of each applicant, nor should you. After all, you don't want to miss the opportunity an interview offers to ask follow-up questions spontaneously or delve more deeply into particular topics. On the other hand, you should try to cover the same basic topics and general questions with each applicant. This will help you compare candidates when it's time to choose your hire; it will also help you avoid claims of discrimi-nation by applicants who don't get the job.

Making Promises

A common mistake managers make during hiring is to exaggerate about the prospects of the business ("We're expanding like wild fire—those stock options will be worth millions in no time!") or about the security of the job ("We never fire anybody; if you do good work, you'll have a job for life!"). Lots of companies and managers embellish when they're trying to sell an especially desirable applicant on a job. No harm in that, right?

Wrong. If you tell a prospective employee something about a job, you'd better be able to back it up. If the employee takes the job in part because of what you said, then that employee can turn around and sue if your promises or statements later prove false. Courts sometimes decide that a promise or statement you make to a prospective employee turns into a contract if the employee accepts the job offer because of what you said. If the position doesn't live up to your statements, your company has broken the contract—and might have to pay damages to the employee.

It's easy to avoid making inflated promises if you follow one simple rule: Tell the truth. After all, job applicants are trying to figure out whether the job will fit with their career goals, skills, and lives outside the workplace. They deserve to know the truth so they can make the right decision.

This strategy will not only keep you out of legal trouble, but also increase your chances of finding an employee who is right for the job and for your business. No one wants a disgruntled employee on the payroll. If you've told the applicant the truth and he or she still wants the job, then you've probably found a good fit.

Here are a few rules that will help you avoid common promise pitfalls:

- **Don't make predictions about your company's financial future.** Even if you honestly believe that your company is headed for the Fortune 500, keep your optimism to yourself. If the applicant asks about the company's prospects, stick to the facts—and if you make any statements about what the future might bring, clearly identify them as hopes, not predictions. For example, you might say, "Our business has doubled in each of the last three years, and we're hoping that growth trend will continue," but you shouldn't say, "We'll be the industry leader by this time next year."

- **Don't estimate the future value of stock options.** Let's face it: You simply can't know what your company's stock options will be worth in the future. It's fine to explain the stock option program to applicants and to tell them that you hope the options will be valuable, but don't say things like, "When these options vest, we'll all be millionaires!"

- **Don't say anything that might limit your right to make personnel decisions in the future.** If you tell an applicant that your company fires workers only for poor performance, this will limit your ability to terminate that person for any other reason—such as personality conflicts or economic downturns—if he or she accepts the job. Similarly, if you promise pay increases at regular intervals, the employee could hold you to that promise, even if your company's financials or the employee's perform-ance doesn't warrant a raise.

- **If layoffs are likely, say so.** If your com-pany is considering staff reductions and there is even a remote chance that the applicant you are interview-ing might lose that new job as a re-sult, disclose this before the applicant accepts the job. Otherwise, you may find your company slapped with a lawsuit—especially if the employee left a secure job elsewhere to come work for your company. Of course, this strategy might make it difficult to find new employees, but it really isn't fair (or legal) to hire people on false pretenses.

- **Be accurate in describing the position.** Don't exaggerate the job require-ments to land an applicant—and don't play bait and switch by offering an applicant one job, then placing him or her in another. It may not matter much to you who does what, but it will matter a lot to the employee. An employee who accepts the posi-tion based on statements that turn out to be false will have grounds for a lawsuit.

Lessons From the Real World

A California company paid the price for intensely recruiting an employee with promises it couldn't keep. Rykoff-Sexton, Inc., promised Andrew Lazar job security, significant pay increases, an eventual executive position, and a bright future with a company that was financially strong. Lazar took the bait and left a lucrative job in New York City, his home of 40 years.

Although Lazar excelled in his new job, the pay increases and bonuses never came. Eventually, Rykoff fired Lazar because of a "reorganization."

Lazar sued and won. He argued to the California Supreme Court that Rykoff should have to keep the promises it used to recruit him, and the court agreed. The court decided that Rykoff's broken promises amounted to fraud because it knew the promises were untrue when it made them.

Lazar v. Rykoff-Sexton, Inc., 12 Cal.4th 631, 909 P.2d 981, 49 Cal.Rptr.2d 377 (1996).

Applicants With Disabilities

Of all the antidiscrimination laws, none confuses managers more than the Americans With Disabilities Act (ADA), 42 U.S.C. §§ 12101-12213, especially when it comes to hiring. Managers want to find out if the person they hire can actually perform the job but often aren't sure how to explore this issue without running afoul of the law. (For information on how the ADA applies to existing employees, see "Disability" in Chapter 3.)

If you remember one simple rule, you'll be in good shape: You can ask candidates about their abilities, but not about their disabilities. This means that you can ask how an applicant plans to perform each function of the job, but you cannot ask whether the applicant has any disabilities that will prevent him or her from performing each function of the job.

One way to ensure that you stay within the rules is to attach a detailed job description to the application or describe the job duties to the applicant during the job interview. Then ask how the applicant plans to perform the job. This approach gives applicants an opportunity to talk about their qualifications and strengths. It also gives them a chance to let you know whether they might need reasonable accommodations to do the job.

Some other rules to keep in mind:

- If you have no reason to believe that the applicant has a disability, you cannot ask whether the applicant will need an accommodation to perform the job.
- If you know that the applicant has a disability (for example, the disability is obvious or the applicant has told you about it), you can ask about accommodations.

The U.S. Equal Employment Opportunity Commission (EEOC) is the federal agency that enforces the ADA. According to the EEOC, you should never ask the following questions in a job interview or on a job application:

- Have you ever had or been treated for any of the following conditions or diseases? (Followed by a checklist of various diseases or conditions.)
- List any conditions or diseases for which you have been treated in the past three years.
- Have you ever been hospitalized? If so, for what condition?
- Have you ever been treated by a psychologist or psychiatrist? If so, for what?
- Have you ever been treated for any mental condition?
- Do you suffer from any health-related condition that might prevent you from performing this job?
- Have you had any major illnesses in the past five years?
- How many days were you absent from work because of illness last year? (You may, however, tell the applicant what your attendance requirements are and then ask whether the applicant will be able to meet those requirements.)
- Do you have any physical defects that preclude you from doing certain types of things?
- Do you have any disabilities or impairments that might affect your ability to do the job?

- Are you taking any prescribed drugs?
- Have you ever been treated for drug addiction or alcoholism?
- Have you ever filed a workers' compensation claim?

According to the EEOC, you may ask the following questions in a job interview:

- Can you perform all of the job functions?
- How would you perform the job functions? (Note that if you want to ask an applicant this question, you should ask it of all applicants.)
- Can you meet the job's attendance requirements?
- What are your professional certifications and licenses?
- Do you currently use illegal drugs?

Testing Applicants

Many companies like to use preemployment tests as a way to screen out applicants who are not suitable for a job. These tests include skills tests, aptitude tests, psychological tests, personality tests, honesty tests, medical tests, and drug tests.

Although you are allowed to do some testing of applicants, both state and federal law impose numerous restrictions on what you can do. These restrictions are often vague and open to contradictory interpretations. As a result, you should only use tests that are absolutely necessary and, unless the test is as basic as a typing

test, you should consider consulting with a lawyer before administering the test to make sure that it will pass legal muster in your state.

Avoiding Disability Discrimination

For all tests—including those described below—you must take care to avoid discriminating against applicants who are protected by the Americans With Disabilities Act (ADA). (For information on the ADA, see Chapter 3.) To ensure that a test does not unfairly screen out people with disabilities, it must accurately measure people's skills, not their disabilities. For example:

- Avoid testing mental, sensory, manual, or speaking skills unless they are job-related. For example, even though a typing test is a manual test that will screen out people who cannot use their hands, it is acceptable if you are filling a job for a typist.
- Accommodate people with disabilities by giving them a test that is "disability neutral" whenever possible. For example, if you are giving a written test to applicants for a sales position to test their knowledge of sales techniques, you can offer to read the test to a blind applicant. This is a reasonable accommodation because sight is not required for the job, but it is required to take the test.

Skills Tests

Skills tests range from something as simple as a typing test to something as complicated as an architectural drafting test. Generally speaking, these tests are legal as long as they genuinely test a skill necessary to perform the job, don't violate the ADA (see above), and don't unfairly exclude anyone based on a protected characteristic.

Aptitude, Psychological, and Personality Tests

Some companies use written tests—often in a multiple choice format—to learn about an applicant's general abilities, personality, and/or work style. However, using these tests leaves you vulnerable to various types of lawsuits. For example:

- A multiple choice aptitude test may discriminate against minority applicants or female applicants because it really reflects test-taking ability rather than actual job skills. (Studies have shown that some aptitude tests are biased against women and minority test takers.)
- A personality test can be even riskier. Such a test may invade a person's privacy by inquiring into topics that are personal in nature, such as sexual preferences or religious beliefs. (Many states specifically protect a person's right to privacy—even from inquiries by employers.) In addition, these tests can lead to a

discrimination lawsuit. For example, if you decide not to hire someone based on his or her answers to questions dealing with religious issues, the applicant could argue that you discriminated based on his or her religion. (For more about discrimination, see Chapter 3.)

- Psychological and personality tests are treated like medical tests (see below) when they ask for answers that would indicate whether the applicant has a mental disorder or impairment. If they do, they will be governed by the Americans With Disabilities Act (ADA) and all of its restrictions. (For more on hiring and the ADA, see "Applicants With Disabilities," above.)

If you decide to use one of these types of tests, proceed with extreme caution. Make sure that the test has been screened scientifically for validity and that it genuinely correlates to necessary job skills. Review the test carefully for any questions that may intrude into an applicant's privacy. And, depending on the complexity and purpose of the test you use, your company may need to hire an expert to interpret the results.

Lie Detector and Honesty Tests

The federal Employee Polygraph Protection Act, 29 U.S.C. §§ 2001 and following, generally prohibits employers from requiring applicants to take a lie detector test or from asking applicants about the results of previous lie detector tests. The law contains a few narrowly defined exceptions for certain types of employers, including those that provide armored car, alarm, or guard services, and those that manufacture, distribute, or dispense pharmaceuticals.

Even though no federal law specifically outlaws written honesty tests, these tests sometimes violate federal and state laws that protect against discrimination and violations of privacy. Plus, the tests can be unreliable.

Some states have adopted their own rules about polygraph tests—and some of these rules are even stricter than the federal law. To find out what your state requires, see "Employee Polygraph Examination Laws," at the end of this chapter.

Medical Tests

Medical testing is tricky. To avoid violating the Americans With Disabilities Act, you shouldn't ask for an applicant's medical history or conduct any medical exam before you make a job offer.

However, once you decide to offer the applicant a job, you can make the offer conditional on the applicant passing a medical exam. Just make sure that you require the exam for all entering employees doing the same job. If you only require people whom you believe or know to have disabilities to take the exam, you will be violating the Americans With Disabilities Act.

Drug Tests

The laws on drug testing vary widely from state to state. Some states allow them only for jobs involving public safety; some states allow them only for drivers; some states allow them for any occupation; some states don't allow them at all. Consult "State Drug and Alcohol Testing Laws," at the end of this chapter, for information on your state's rules.

Lessons From the Real World

The Rent-A-Center company was forced to pay $2.1 million to settle a class action lawsuit after requiring job applicants to take a 502-question, true-or-false personality test that inquired into applicants' sexual preferences, religious beliefs, and political beliefs, among other things.

The test asked applicants to answer true or false to questions such as "Many of my dreams are about sex matters," "I am strongly attracted to members of my own sex," and "I believe there is a God."

Applicants sued, arguing that the test violated their right to privacy and discriminated against them based on religion and sexual preference. As their attorney said, they couldn't see any reason why Rent-A-Center would need to know such highly personal information.

The company ponied up $2.1 million in a settlement deal to avoid a trial on the case.

Michael Joe, "Rent-A-Center Settles Invasion of Privacy Suit," *The Recorder*, (July 11, 2000).

Background Checks

When you are making hiring decisions, you might need a bit more information than applicants provide. After all, some folks—surveys estimate between 30% and 40% of applicants—give false or incomplete information in employment applications. And workers probably don't want you to know certain facts about their past that might disqualify them from getting a job. Generally, it's good policy to do a little checking before making a job offer.

However, you do not have an unfettered right to dig into applicants' personal affairs. Workers have a right to privacy in certain personal matters, a right they can enforce by suing your company if you pry too deeply. How can you avoid crossing this line? Here are a few tips to keep in mind:

- **Make sure your inquiries are related to the job.** If you decide to do a background check, stick to information that is relevant to the job for which you are considering the worker. For example, if you are hiring a security guard who will carry a weapon and be responsible for large amounts of cash, you might reasonably check for past criminal convictions. If you are hiring a seasonal farm worker, however, a criminal background check is probably unnecessary.

- **Ask for consent.** You are on safest legal ground if you ask the applicant, in writing, to consent to a background check. Explain clearly what you plan to check and how you will gather information. This gives applicants a chance to take themselves out of the running if there are things they don't want you to know. It also prevents applicants from later claiming invasion of privacy. If an applicant refuses to consent to a reasonable request for information, you may legally decide not to hire the worker on that basis.

- **Be reasonable.** Managers can get their employers into legal trouble if they engage in background check overkill. You will not need to perform an extensive background check on every applicant. Even if you decide to check, you probably won't need to get into excessive detail for every position. If you find yourself questioning neighbors, ordering credit checks, and performing exhaustive searches of public records every time you hire a clerk or counterperson, you need to scale your efforts back.

In addition to these general considerations, specific rules apply to certain types of information:

- **School records.** Under federal law and the law of some states, educational records—including transcripts, recommendations, and financial information—are confidential. Because of these laws, most schools will not release records without the consent of the student. And some schools will only release records directly to the student.
- **Credit reports.** Under the Fair Credit Reporting Act, (FCRA) 15 U.S.C.

§ 1681, employers must get an employee's written consent before seeking that employee's credit report. Many companies routinely include a request for such consent in their employment applications. If you decide not to hire or promote someone based on information in the credit report, you must provide a copy of the report and let the applicant know of his or her right to challenge the report under the FCRA. Some states have more stringent rules limiting the use of credit reports.

- **Bankruptcies.** Federal law prohibits discriminating against applicants because they have filed for bankruptcy. This means that you cannot decide not to hire someone simply because he or she has declared bankruptcy in the past.
- **Criminal records.** The law varies from state to state on whether, and to what extent, a private employer may consider an applicant's criminal history in making hiring decisions. Some states don't allow you to ask about arrests (as opposed to convictions), convictions that occurred well in the past, juvenile crimes, or sealed records. Some states allow you to consider convictions only if the crimes are relevant to the job. And some states allow you to consider criminal history only for certain positions: nurses, child care workers, private detectives, and other jobs requiring licenses, for example.

Because of this variation among the states, you should consult with a lawyer or do further legal research on the law of your state before digging into an applicant's criminal past.

- **Workers' compensation records.** You may consider information contained in the public record from a workers' compensation appeal in making a job decision only if the applicant's injury might interfere with his or her ability to perform required duties.

- **Other medical records.** Under the Americans With Disabilities Act, you may inquire about an applicant's ability to perform specific job duties only; you may not request medical records. Companies cannot make job decisions (on hiring or promotion, for example) based on an applicant's disability, as long as the employee can do the job, with or without a reasonable accommodation. Some states also have laws protecting the confidentiality of medical records.

- **Records of military service.** Members and former members of the armed forces have a right to privacy in their service records. These records may be released only under limited circumstances, and consent is generally required. However, the military may disclose name, rank, salary, duty assignments, awards, and duty status without the member's consent.

- **Driving records.** You should check the driving record of any employee whose job will require large amounts of driving (delivery persons or bus drivers, for example). These records are available, sometimes for a small fee, from the state's motor vehicles department.

Young Workers

Many jobs around an office and in a business are perfect for younger workers. For example, if you need someone to photocopy documents for an hour or two a day, a high school student who comes in after school might be just what you are looking for. The student gets experience and extra pocket money, and your company gets someone who is willing to work just a few hours a week on the cheap.

The history of child labor in this country isn't quite so benign, however. Children once worked long hours in hazardous jobs—such as manufacturing and mining—for very little money. They didn't attend school, and they often suffered serious—even fatal—health problems.

To protect child workers, the federal and state governments passed laws regulating the type of work children can do, the number of hours they can work, and the types of businesses that can employ them.

Before you hire any worker younger than 18, you should check both federal and state law. We describe the federal law here. To find out about your state child labor law, contact your state department of labor.

The Fair Labor Standards Act (FLSA), 29 U.S.C. §§ 2201 and following, is the federal law that governs child labor. Virtually all employees and businesses must follow the FLSA, although a handful of businesses, including small farms, are not required to. To find out about exceptions to FLSA requirements, refer to the website of the U.S. Department of Labor—the federal agency that enforces the FLSA—at www .dol.gov.

Hazardous Jobs

According to the U.S. Department of Labor, workers younger than 18 may never perform the following types of hazardous jobs (some exceptions are made for apprentices and students):

- manufacturing or storing explosives
- driving a motor vehicle and being an outside helper on a motor vehicle
- coal or other mining
- logging and sawmilling
- anything involving power-driven, wood-working machines
- anything involving exposure to radioactive substances and ionizing radiations
- anything involving power-driven hoisting equipment
- anything involving power-driven metal-forming, punching, and shearing machines

- meat packing or processing (including anything involving power-driven meat slicing machines)
- anything involving power-driven bakery machines
- anything involving power-driven paper products machines
- manufacturing brick, tile, and related products
- anything involving power-driven circular saws, band saws, and guillotine shears
- wrecking, demolition, and ship-breaking operations
- roofing and work performed on or near roofs, including installing or working on antennas and rooftop appliances, and
- excavation operations.

Agricultural Jobs

If you own or operate a farm or other type of agricultural business, the following child labor rules apply to you:

- You may hire a worker who is 16 years or older for any work, whether hazardous or not, for unlimited hours.
- You may hire a worker who is 14 or 15 years old for any nonhazardous work outside of school hours.
- You may hire a worker who is 12 or 13 years old for any nonhazardous work outside of school hours if the child's parents work on the same farm or if you have their written consent.

• You may hire a worker who is 10 or 11 years old if you've been granted a waiver by the U.S. Department of Labor to employ the youngster as a hand harvest laborer for no more than eight weeks in any calendar year.

• If you own or operate the farm, you can hire your own children to do any kind of work on the farm, regardless of their ages.

Nonagricultural Jobs

If you seek to hire a youngster for work that is nonagricultural, the following rules apply:

• You may hire a worker who is 18 years or older for any job, hazardous or not, for unlimited hours.

• A worker who will do job-related driving on public roads must be at least 17 years old, must have a valid driver's license, and must not have any moving violations.

• You may hire a worker who is 16 or 17 years old for any nonhazardous job, for unlimited hours.

• You may hire a worker who is 14 or 15 years old outside school hours in various nonmanufacturing, nonmining, and nonhazardous jobs, but some restrictions apply. The teen cannot work more than three hours on a school day, 18 hours in a school week, eight hours on a nonschool day, or 40 hours in a nonschool week. Also, the work cannot begin

before 7 a.m. or end after 7 p.m., except from June 1 through Labor Day, when evening hours are extended to 9 p.m.

Offer Letters

When it comes to offer letters, keep them short and sweet. The same rules that apply to job interviews apply to offer letters: Stick to the facts and don't make promises you can't keep. Applicants might some day try to turn an offer letter into a contract that sets the terms and conditions of the job or limits your company's right to fire or discipline them.

Avoid using language that makes promises or assurances about the employment relationship. For example, if you tell the applicant "We look forward to a long and happy relationship with you" or "We think you have a bright future at this company," the applicant might assume that you're offering more than the normal "at-will" employment—and that you can't end the employment relationship without a good reason. If you want to fire the employee in the future, these words might come back to haunt you.

Similarly, don't specify job duties, benefits, pay schedules, vacation/sick leave, or any other benefit you might want to change in the future. The employee might argue that your letter created a contract and try to hold the company to it.

So what can you say? You might want to:

• congratulate the applicant

- confirm the job title
- name the applicant's supervisor
- state the starting salary, and
- establish a start date.

In addition, if you haven't or won't offer the applicant a written contract for employment (the vast majority of employees don't have written employment contracts), confirm in writing that employment is at will—meaning that there is no employment contract and you can fire the employee at any time for any reason that isn't illegal.

For more about written employment contracts, see "Written Employment Contracts," below. For more about at-will employment, see "At-Will Employment" in Chapter 4.

Written Employment Contracts

A written employment contract is a document that an employer and an employee sign, setting forth the terms of their relationship with each other. In addition to clearly describing what the employee is going to do for the employer (the job) and what the employer is going to do for the employee (the salary), the contract can address many other issues, including:

- the duration of the job (for example, one year, two years, or indefinitely)
- the specifics of the employee's responsibilities
- the employee's benefits (for example, health insurance, vacation leave, or disability leave)
- grounds for termination

- limitations on the employee's ability to compete with your company once the employee leaves
- protection of company trade secrets and client lists
- who will own the employee's work product (for example, if the employee writes books or invents gadgets for your company), and
- a method for resolving any disputes between the employee and the company.

Written employment contracts have distinct advantages and disadvantages that you should consider carefully before committing your company to the terms of such a contract.

Advantages

Employment contracts can make sense if you want or need to control the employee's ability to quit. For example, if the employee is a high-level manager or executive, or if the employee is especially valuable to the company (such as the secretary who is the organizational backbone of the office), then a contract can protect the company against the sudden, unexpected loss of the employee. It can lock the employee into a specific term (for example, two years), or it can require the employee to provide enough notice to allow your company to find and train a suitable replacement (for example, 90 days' notice instead of two weeks' notice).

Employment contracts can also protect your company if the employee will learn or have access to confidential and sensitive business information. You can insert confidentiality clauses into the contract that prevent the employee from disclosing this information or using it for personal gain. (For more on this topic, see "Nondisclosure Agreements" in Chapter 10.)

Similarly, a contract can prevent employees from competing against your company after they move on to other pursuits. (For more on this topic, see "Noncompete Agreements" in Chapter 10.)

Sometimes, you can use an employment contract as a way to entice a highly skilled individual to accept a job offer. Job security and beneficial terms often sweeten the deal enough for a highly desirable applicant who is on the fence to join your team.

Finally, an employment contract can give the company greater control over the employee. If you specify the standards for the employee's performance and grounds for termination, you may have an easier time terminating an employee who doesn't live up to those standards.

Disadvantages

An employment contract is a two-way street: Just as the contract requires the worker to stay for a certain period of time, it limits your company's right to fire the worker for the same period. Your company won't have the ability to alter the terms of the employment as its business needs change. To alter the terms, you'll have to renegotiate the contract and offer the employee some new benefit in exchange for the alteration to make the new agreement binding. And, no matter what you offer, the employee is free to reject any proposed new terms. These factors can make the renegotiation process time-consuming and complicated.

For example, let's say you sign a two-year contract with a new employee. If, six months later, you decide you don't need the employee after all, you can't terminate the relationship. If you do, you will set your company up for a breach of contract lawsuit. Similarly, if you promised benefits in the contract, the company can't stop paying for them before the term is up without breaching the contract and risking a lawsuit.

Another disadvantage of employment contracts is that they always contain an unwritten obligation, imposed by law, to deal fairly with the employee. In legal terms, this is called the "covenant of good faith and fair dealing." If you treat an employee with whom you have signed a contract in a way that seems unfair, your company may end up in court. By contrast, this obligation does not arise with employees who don't have contracts. Indeed, as long as you don't violate any law—such as the antidiscrimination laws (see Chapter 3), wage and hour laws (see Chapter 2), or health and safety laws (see Chapter 7)—you can generally treat those employees as you wish.

Checklist: First Day Paperwork

When your new hire shows up on the first day of work, there will be lots to do—and plenty of forms to be completed. Use this checklist to make sure you don't forget any important paperwork. (Of course, your company may not use every form on this list—or may have come up with additional paperwork of its own—so make sure you modify this checklist if necessary.)

Required Government Paperwork

☐ USCIS Form I-9, Employment Eligibility Verification. The federal government requires employers to complete this form verifying that new hires are eligible to work in the United States. Get more information at www.uscis.gov.

☐ IRS Form W-4, Withholding Allowance Certificate. New employees use this form to tell your company how much income tax to withhold from their paychecks. Go to www.irs.gov for information.

☐ New hire reporting information. Employers must provide information on new employees to a state agency, which uses it to find parents who owe child support. For information on your state's requirements, go to www.acf.dhhs.gov.

Company Forms

☐ Signed offer letter or employment contract.

☐ Employee handbook acknowledgment form (see Chapter 4).

☐ Acknowledgment of company email policy (see Chapter 6).

☐ Benefits paperwork, such as enrollment forms.

☐ Emergency contact information.

☐ Acknowledgment of receiving company property, such as a cell phone, car, or laptop computer to be used offsite.

Legal Dos and Don'ts: Hiring

Do:

- **Focus on the essential elements of the job.** You can avoid problems with antidiscrimination and privacy laws by remembering your hiring goal: to find an applicant who can do the job well. Keeping your eyes on this prize will stop you from delving into an applicant's personal affairs, religious beliefs, medical conditions, or other forbidden topics.

- **Use written contracts sparingly.** A written contract is a great way to seal the deal with a stellar applicant whom you want to retain. It's also a fast track to the court house if used with an employee whom you might have to fire or lay off.

- **Put your offer in writing.** No law requires you to use written offer letters, but they're an easy and effective way to make sure the applicant knows exactly what the job entails. And if you are offering an at-will position, an offer letter spelling that out will help you document your intentions.

Don't:

- **Shade the truth.** Always be honest when dealing with job applicants. Someone who accepts a job based on your false statements about the job can ask a court to hold the company to your promises—or to pay for your misrepresentations.

- **Get too personal.** Privacy laws differ from state to state, but you'll always be on shaky legal ground if you delve into an applicant's personal life.

- **Test unless you really need to—and you've cleared the test with a lawyer.** The law of testing is changing all the time, which makes it a ripe source of lawsuits for invasion of privacy, disability discrimination, and more. The good news is that the vast majority of companies can make sound hiring decisions without resorting to testing.

Test Your Knowledge

Questions

1. You should ask every applicant exactly the same questions when interviewing for a position. ☐ True ☐ False

2. You may ask disabled applicants whether and how they could perform the essential functions of the position. ☐ True ☐ False

3. It's best to ask only about verifiable facts during an interview, such as where an applicant works or what positions he or she has held. ☐ True ☐ False

4. You can make promises to an applicant during the hiring process, as long as employees at your company have to sign an at-will agreement. ☐ True ☐ False

5. If an applicant brings up his or her religion, it's okay to ask questions and state your opinions about it. ☐ True ☐ False

6. A company can require all applicants to take a personality test. ☐ True ☐ False

7. You have the right to look at an applicant's credit report when making hiring decisions. ☐ True ☐ False

8. It's a good idea to send an offer letter to successful applicants. ☐ True ☐ False

9. A company should never offer applicants a written employment contract. ☐ True ☐ False

10. Antidiscrimination laws and other workplace restrictions apply only to employees, not to job applicants. ☐ True ☐ False

Answers

1. False. Although you should cover the same basic ground with every applicant, you shouldn't script the entire interview. Otherwise, you'll miss opportunities to follow up on issues applicants raise and delve more deeply into areas of interest or concern.

2. True. Although there are some limits on what you can ask about disabilities, you are entitled to find out whether the applicant can do the job.

3. False. You should certainly find out what positions an applicant has held, but the most informative questions are open-ended queries that invite the applicant to talk about his or her experience and skills.

4. False. An at-will agreement is not a silver bullet, especially if an applicant left a good position to come to work for your company based on your false statements. If you entice someone with promises that won't come true, you will have an unhappy employee—and perhaps a lawsuit—on your hands.

5. False. Even if an employee brings up a delicate topic, it's best to simply move on. If you get into a discussion and say something that the employee finds distasteful or biased, the fact that the employee raised the issue in the first place won't save you from a discrimination claim.

6. The answer depends on the test, how it's administered, what it measures, and what you use it for. Courts have found that some personality tests are unnecessarily invasive and violate applicants' rights to privacy.

7. True, but only if you get the applicant's consent. Many companies ask all applicants to consent to a credit check in their job application.

8. True. You can use the offer letter to set forth the basic terms of the job and let future employees know that they will be working at will, if that's your company's policy.

9. False. Written employment contracts should be the exception rather than the rule, but there are circumstances when it makes sense to use one.

10. False. Antidiscrimination laws apply to every stage of the employment relationship, including "help wanted" ads, applications, interviews, and actually selecting your new hire.

Preemployment Inquiries

Subject	Lawful Preemployment Inquiries	Unlawful Preemployment Inquiries
Name	Applicant's full name. Have you ever worked for this company under a different name? Is any additional information relative to a different name necessary to check work record? If yes, explain.	Original name of an applicant whose name has been changed by court order or otherwise. Applicant's maiden name.
Address or Duration of Residence	How long have you been a resident of this state or city?	
Birthplace	None	Birthplace of applicant. Birthplace of applicant's parents, spouse, or other close relatives. Requirements that applicant submit birth certificate, naturalization, or baptismal record.
Age	Are you 18 years old or older? This question may be asked only for the purpose of determining whether applicants are of legal age for employment.	How old are you? What is your date of birth?
Religion or Creed	None	Inquiry into an applicant's religious denomination, religious affiliations, church, parish, pastor, or religious holidays observed.
Race or Color	None	Complexion or color of skin. Inquiry regarding applicant's race.
Photograph	None	Any requirement for a photograph prior to hire.
Height	None	Inquiry regarding applicant's height (unless you have a legitimate business reason).
Weight	None	Inquiry regarding applicant's weight (unless you have a legitimate business reason).
Marital Status	Is your spouse employed by this employer?	Requirement that an applicant provide any information regarding marital status or children. Are you single or married? Do you have any children? Is your spouse employed? What is your spouse's name?

Preemployment Inquiries (continued)

Subject	Lawful Preemployment Inquiries	Unlawful Preemployment Inquiries
Gender	None	Mr., Miss, or Mrs. or an inquiry regarding gender.
		Inquiry as to ability or plans to reproduce or advocacy of any form of birth control.
		Requirement that women be given pelvic examinations.
Disability	These [provide applicant with list] are the essential functions of the job. How would you perform them?	Inquiries regarding an individual's physical or mental condition which are not directly related to the requirements of a specific job and which are used as a factor in making employment decisions in a way which is contrary to the provisions or purposes of the Civil Rights Act.
Citizenship	Are you legally authorized to work in the United States on a full-time basis?	Questions about subjects below are unlawful, but the applicant may be required to reveal some of this information as part of the federal I-9 process:
		Country of citizenship.
		Whether an applicant is a naturalized or native-born citizen; the date when the applicant acquired citizenship.
		Requirement that an applicant produce naturalization papers or first papers.
		Whether applicant's parents or spouse are naturalized or native-born citizens of the United States: the date when such parent or spouse acquired citizenship.
National Origin	Inquiry into language applicant speaks and writes fluently.	Inquiry into applicant's lineage, ancestry, national origin, descent, parentage, or nationality unless part of the federal I-9 process in determining employment eligibility.
		Nationality of applicant's parents or spouse.
		Inquiry into how applicant acquired ability to read, write, or speak a foreign language.
Education	Inquiry into the academic, vocational, or professional education of an applicant and public and private schools attended.	

Preemployment Inquiries (continued)		
Subject	**Lawful Preemployment Inquiries**	**Unlawful Preemployment Inquiries**
Experience	Inquiry into work experience. Inquiry into countries applicant has visited.	
Arrests	Have you ever been convicted of a crime? Are there any felony charges pending against you?	Inquiry regarding arrests which did not result in conviction (except for law enforcement agencies).
Relatives	Names of applicant's relatives already employed by this company.	Address of any relative of applicant, other than address (within the United States) of applicant's father and mother, husband or wife, and minor dependent children.
Notice in Case of Emergency	Name and address of person to be notified in case of accident or emergency.	Name and address of nearest relative to be notified in case of accident or emergency.
Organizations	Inquiry into the organizations of which an applicant is a member, excluding organizations the name or character of which indicates the race, color, religion, national origin, or ancestry of its members.	List of all clubs, societies, and lodges to which the applicant belongs.

Employee Polygraph Examination Laws

Alaska

Alaska Stat. § 23.10.037

Employers covered: All

What's prohibited: Employer may not suggest, request, or require that employee or applicant take a lie detector test.

California

Cal. Lab. Code § 432.2

Employers covered: All

What's prohibited: Employer may not demand or require that employee or applicant take a lie detector test.

What's allowed: Employer may request a test, if applicant is advised in writing of legal right to refuse to take it.

Connecticut

Conn. Gen. Stat. Ann. § 31-51g

Employers covered: All, including employment agencies.

What's prohibited: Employer may not request or require that employee or applicant take a lie detector test.

Delaware

Del. Code Ann. tit. 19, § 704

Employers covered: All

What's prohibited: Employer may not suggest, request, or require that employee or applicant take a lie detector test in order to obtain or continue employment.

District of Columbia

D.C. Code Ann. §§ 32-901 to 32-903

Employers covered: All

What's prohibited: Employer may not administer, have administered, use, or accept the results of any polygraph examination.

Hawaii

Haw. Rev. Stat. § 378-26.5

Employers covered: All

What's prohibited: Employer may not require employee or applicant to take lie detector test.

What's allowed: Employer may request test if current or prospective employee is told, orally and in writing, that refusing to take test will not result in being fired or hurt chances of getting job.

Idaho

Idaho Code § 44-903

Employers covered: All

What's prohibited: Employer may not require an employee or applicant to take a lie detector test.

Illinois

225 Ill. Comp. Stat. § 430/14.1

Employers covered: All

What's prohibited: Unless directly related to employment, examination may not include questions about:

- political, religious, or labor-related beliefs, affiliations, or lawful activities
- beliefs or opinions on racial matters, or
- sexual preferences or activity.

Iowa

Iowa Code § 730.4

Employers covered: All

What's prohibited: Employer may not request, require, administer, or attempt or threaten to administer a lie detector test; may not request or require that employee or applicant sign waiver of any action prohibited by this law.

Maine

Me. Rev. Stat. Ann. tit. 32, § 7166

Employers covered: All

Employee Polygraph Examination Laws (continued)

What's prohibited: Employer may not request, require, suggest, or administer a lie detector test.

What's allowed: Employee may voluntarily request a test if these conditions are met:
- results cannot be used against employee
- employer must give employee a copy of the law when employee requests test, and
- test must be recorded or employee's witness must be present during the test, or both.

Maryland

Md. Code Ann. [Lab. & Empl.] § 3-702

Employers covered: All

What's prohibited: Employer may not require or demand that employee or applicant take a lie detector test.

What's required: All employment applications must include specified notice that no person can be required to take a lie detector test as a condition of obtaining or continuing employment; must include space for applicant to sign and acknowledge notice.

Massachusetts

Mass. Gen. Laws ch. 149, § 19B

Employers covered: All

What's prohibited: Employer may not request, require, or administer a lie detector test.

What's required: All employment applications must include specified notice that it is unlawful to require a lie detector test as a condition of obtaining or continuing employment.

Michigan

Mich. Comp. Laws §§ 37.203, 338.1719

Employers covered: All

What's prohibited: Employer may not request, require, administer, or attempt or threaten to administer a lie detector test; may not request or require that employee or applicant sign waiver of

any action prohibited by this law.

What's allowed: Employee may voluntarily request a test if these conditions are met:
- before taking test employee is given copy of the law
- employee is given copies of test results and reports
- no questions asked about sexual practices; marital relationship; or political, religious, or labor or union affiliations, unless questions are relevant to areas under examination, and
- examiner informs employee
  - of all questions that will be asked
  - of right to accept, refuse, or stop test at any time
  - that employee is not required to answer questions or give information, and
  - that information volunteered could be used against employee or made available to employer, unless otherwise agreed to in writing.

Minnesota

Minn. Stat. Ann. §§ 181.75, 181.76

Employers covered: All

What's prohibited: Employer may not directly or indirectly solicit or require an applicant or employee to take a lie detector test.

What's allowed: Employee may request a test, but only if employer informs employee that test is voluntary. Results of voluntary test may be given only to those authorized by employee.

Montana

Mont. Code Ann. § 39-2-304

What's prohibited: Employer may not require an employee or applicant to take a lie detector test.

Nebraska

Neb. Rev. Stat. § 81-1932

Employers covered: All

Employee Polygraph Examination Laws (continued)

What's prohibited: Employer may not require an employee or applicant to take a lie detector test.

What's allowed: Employer may request that test be taken, but only if these conditions are met:

- no questions asked about sexual practices; marital relationship; or political, religious, or labor or union affiliations
- examinee is given written and oral notice that test is voluntary and may be discontinued at any time
- examinee signs form stating that test is being taken voluntarily
- prospective employees are asked only job-related questions and are not singled out for testing in a discriminatory manner
- employee requested to take test only in connection with a specific investigation
- results of test are not the sole reason for terminating employment, and
- all questions and responses are kept on file by the employer for at least one year.

Nevada

Nev. Rev. Stat. Ann. §§ 613.480 to 613.510

Employers covered: All

Exceptions: Manufacturers or distributors of controlled substances; providers or designers of security systems and personnel; ongoing investigation.

What's prohibited: Employer may not directly or indirectly require, request, suggest, or cause a lie detector test to be taken; may not use, accept, refer to, or ask about the results of any test. May not take adverse employment action solely on the basis of test results or a refusal to take test.

What's allowed: Nevada law allows testing in the same limited circumstances as the federal EPPA, with similar rules and restrictions on when and how the test is given.

New Jersey

N.J. Stat. Ann. § 2C:40A-1

Employers covered: All

Exceptions: Employers that deal with controlled dangerous substances.

What's prohibited: Employer may not influence, request, or require applicant or employee to take a lie detector test.

What's allowed: Employers who are allowed to test must observe these rules:

- job must require direct access to controlled substance
- test limited to preceding 5 years
- questions must be work-related or pertain to improper handling, use, or illegal sale of legally distributed controlled dangerous substances
- test taker has right to legal counsel
- written copy of test results must be given to test taker upon request
- test information may not be released to any other employer or person, and
- employee or prospective employee must be informed of right to present results of a second independently administered test prior to any personnel decision being made.

New York

N.Y. Lab. Law §§ 733 to 739

Employers covered: All

What's prohibited: Employer may not require, request, suggest, permit, or use results of a lie detector test.

Oregon

Or. Rev. Stat. Ann. §§ 659.840, 659A.300

Employers covered: All

What's prohibited: Employer may not require an employee or applicant to take a lie detector test.

Employee Polygraph Examination Laws (continued)

Pennsylvania

18 Pa. Cons. Stat. Ann. § 7321

Employers covered: All

Exceptions: Employers with positions that have access to narcotics or dangerous drugs.

What's prohibited: Employer may not require an employee or applicant to take a lie detector test.

Rhode Island

R.I. Gen. Laws §§ 28-6.1-1 to 28-6.1-4

Employers covered: All

What's prohibited: Employer may not request, require, subject, nor directly or indirectly cause an employee or applicant to take a lie detector test.

Tennessee

Tenn. Code Ann. §§ 62-27-123, 62-27-128

Employers covered: All

What's prohibited: Employer may not take any personnel action based solely upon the results of a polygraph examination. No questions may be asked about:

- religious, political, or labor-related beliefs, affiliations, or lawful activities
- beliefs or opinions about racial matters
- sexual preferences or activities
- disabilities covered by the Americans With Disabilities Act, or
- activities that occurred more than 5 years before the examination, except for felony convictions and violations of the state drug control act.

(Exception: Examination is part of an investigation of illegal activity in one of the above subject areas.)

What's required: Prospective examinee must be told if examiner is a law enforcement or court official and informed that any illegal activity disclosed may be used against examinee. Must

receive and sign a written notice of rights including:

- right to refuse to take the test or to answer any question
- right to terminate examination at any time
- right to request an audio recording of examination and pretest interview, and
- right to request examination results within 30 days of taking it.

Vermont

Vt. Stat. Ann. tit. 21, §§ 494 to 494e

Employers covered: All

Exceptions: Employers whose primary business is sale of precious metals, gems, or jewelry; whose business includes manufacture or sale of regulated drugs and applicant's position requires contact with drugs; employers authorized by federal law to require a test.

What's prohibited: Employer may not request, require, administer, or attempt or threaten to administer a lie detector test. May not request or require that employee or applicant sign waiver of any action prohibited by state law. May not discriminate against employee who files a complaint of violation of laws.

When testing is allowed, no questions may be asked about:

- political, religious, or labor union affiliations
- sexual practices, social habits, or marital relationship (unless clearly related to job performance), or
- any matters unrelated to job performance.

What's required: Prior to taking test examinee must receive a copy of state laws and a copy of all questions to be asked. Must be told that any information disclosed could be used against examinee or made available to employer, unless there is a signed written agreement to the contrary. Examinee must be informed of rights including:

Employee Polygraph Examination Laws (continued)

- right to accept or refuse to take examination
- right to refuse to answer any questions or give any information
- right to stop examination at any time, and
- right to a copy of examination results and of any reports given to employer.

Virginia

Va. Code Ann. § 40.1-51.4:3

Employers covered: All

What's prohibited: Employer may not require an applicant to answer questions about sexual activities in a polygraph test, unless the sexual activity resulted in a conviction for violation of state law.

What's required: Any record of examination results must be destroyed or maintained on a confidential basis, open to inspection only upon agreement of the employee.

Washington

Wash. Rev. Code Ann. § 49.44.120

Employers covered: All

Exceptions: Applicant or employee who manufactures, distributes, or dispenses controlled substances, or who works in a sensitive position directly involving national security.

What's prohibited: Employer may not require, directly or indirectly, that an employee or applicant take a lie detector test.

West Virginia

W. Va. Code §§ 21-5-5a to 21-5-5d

Employers covered: All

Exceptions: Employees or applicants with direct access to controlled substances.

What's prohibited: Employer may not require or request, directly or indirectly, that an employee or applicant take a lie detector test; may not knowingly use the results of a lie detector test.

Wisconsin

Wis. Stat. Ann. § 111.37

Employers covered: All

Exceptions: Manufacturers or distributors of controlled substances; providers or designers of security systems and personnel; ongoing investigation.

What's prohibited: Employer may not directly or indirectly require, request, suggest, or cause an applicant or employee to take a lie detector test; may not use, accept, refer to, or inquire about the results of a test. May not take adverse employment action solely on the basis of test results or a refusal to take test. May not discriminate or retaliate against employee who files a complaint of violation of laws.

What's allowed: Wisconsin law allows testing in the same limited circumstances as the federal EPPA, with similar rules and restrictions on when and how the test is given.

Current as of February 2005

State Drug and Alcohol Testing Laws

Note: The states of Colorado, Delaware, District of Columbia, Kansas, Kentucky, Massachusetts, Michigan, Missouri, Nevada, New Hampshire, New Jersey, New Mexico, New York, Pennsylvania, South Dakota, Texas, Washington, West Virginia, Wisconsin, and Wyoming are not included in this chart because they do not have specific drug and alcohol testing laws governing private employers. Additional laws may apply. Check with your state department of labor for more information. (See "Departments of Labor," in the appendix.)

Alabama

Ala. Code §§ 25-5-330 to 25-5-340

Employers affected: Employers who establish a drug-free workplace program to qualify for a workers' compensation rate discount.

Testing applicants: Must test upon conditional offer of employment. Must test all new hires. Job ads must include notice that drug and alcohol testing required.

Testing employees: Random testing permitted. Must test after an accident that results in lost work time. Must also test upon reasonable suspicion; reasons for suspicion must be documented and made available to employee upon request.

Employee rights: Employees have 5 days to contest or explain a positive test result. Employer must have an employee assistance program or maintain a resource file of outside programs.

Notice and policy requirements: All employees must have written notice of drug policy. Must give 60 days' advance notice before implementing testing program. Policy must state consequences of refusing to take test or testing positive.

Drug-free workplace program: Yes.

Alaska

Alaska Stat. §§ 23.10.600 and following

Employers affected: Voluntary for employers with one or more full-time employees. (There is no state-mandated drug and alcohol testing.)

Testing employees: Employer may test:
- for any job-related purpose
- to maintain productivity and safety
- as part of an accident investigation, or
- upon reasonable suspicion.

Employee rights: Employer must provide written test results within 5 working days. Employee has 10 working days to request opportunity to explain positive test results; employer must grant request within 72 hours or before taking any adverse employment action.

Notice and policy requirements: Before implementing a testing program employer must distribute a written drug policy to all employees and must give 30 days' advance notice. Policy must state consequences of a positive test or refusal to submit to testing.

Arizona

Ariz. Rev. Stat. §§ 23-493 and following

Employers affected: Employers with one or more full-time employees.

Testing applicants: Employer must inform prospective hires that they will undergo drug testing as a condition of employment.

Testing employees: Employees are subject to random and scheduled tests:
- for any job-related purpose
- to maintain productivity and safety, or
- upon reasonable suspicion.

Employee rights: Policy must inform employees of their right to explain positive results.

Notice and policy requirements: Before conducting tests employer must give employees a copy of the written policy. Policy must state the consequences of a positive test or refusal to submit to testing.

Drug-free workplace program: Yes.

State Drug and Alcohol Testing Laws (continued)

Arkansas

Ark. Code Ann. §§ 11-14-105 to 11-14-112

Employers affected: Employers who establish a drug-free workplace program to qualify for a workers' compensation rate discount.

Testing applicants: Must test upon conditional offer of employment. Job ads must include notice that drug and alcohol testing required.

Testing employees: Employer must test any employee:
- on reasonable suspicion of drug use
- as part of a routine fitness-for-duty medical exam
- after an accident that results in injury, or
- as follow-up to a required rehabilitation program.

Employee rights: Employer may not refuse to hire applicant or take adverse personnel action against an employee on the basis of a single positive test that has not been verified by a confirmation test. An applicant or employee has 5 days after receiving test results to contest or explain them.

Notice and policy requirements: Employer must give all employees a written statement of drug policy and must give 60 days' advance notice before implementing program.

Drug-free workplace program: Yes.

California

Cal. Lab. Code §§ 1025, 1026

Employers affected: No provisions for private employer testing. An employer with 25 or more employees must reasonably accommodate an employee who wants to enter a treatment program. Employer is not, however, required to provide paid leave. Employer may fire or refuse to hire an employee whose drug or alcohol use interferes with job duties or workplace safety.

Employee rights: Employer must safeguard privacy of employee who enters treatment program.

Connecticut

Conn. Gen. Stat. Ann. §§ 31-51t to 31-51bb

Employers affected: All.

Testing applicants: Employer must inform job applicants in writing that drug testing is required as a condition of employment.

Testing employees: Employer may test:
- when there is reasonable suspicion that employee is under the influence of drugs or alcohol and job performance is or could be impaired
- when authorized by federal law
- when employee's position is dangerous or safety-sensitive, or
- as part of a voluntary employee assistance program.

Employee rights: Employer may not take any adverse personnel action on the basis of a single positive test that has not been verified by a confirmation test.

Florida

Fla. Stat. Ann. §§ 440.101 to 440.102

Employers affected: Employers who establish a drug-free workplace program to qualify for a workers' compensation rate discount.

Testing applicants: Must inform job applicants that drug and alcohol testing is required as a condition of employment.

Testing employees: Must test any employee:
- on reasonable suspicion of drug use
- as part of a routine fitness-for-duty medical exam, or
- as part of a required rehabilitation program.

Employee rights: Employees who voluntarily seek treatment for substance abuse cannot be fired, disciplined, or discriminated against,

State Drug and Alcohol Testing Laws (continued)

unless they have tested positive or have been in treatment in the past. All employees have the right to explain positive results within 5 days. Employer may not take any adverse personnel action on the basis of an initial positive result that has not been verified by a confirmation test.

Notice and policy requirements: Prior to implementing testing, employer must give 60 days' advance notice and must give employees written copy of drug policy.

Drug-free workplace program: Yes.

Georgia
Ga. Code Ann. §§ 34-9-410 to 34-9-421

Employers affected: Employers who establish a drug-free workplace program to qualify for a workers' compensation rate discount.

Testing applicants: Applicants are required to submit to a substance abuse test after they have been offered employment.

Testing employees: Must test any employee:
- on reasonable suspicion of drug use
- as part of a routine fitness-for-duty medical exam, or
- as part of a required rehabilitation program.

Employee rights: Employees have 5 days to explain or contest a positive result. Employer must have an employee assistance program or maintain a resource file of outside programs.

Notice and policy requirements: Employer must give applicants and employees notice of testing and must give 60 days' notice before implementing program. All employees must receive a written policy statement; policy must state the consequences of refusing to submit to a drug test or of testing positive.

Drug-free workplace program: Yes.

Hawaii
Haw. Rev. Stat. §§ 329B-1 and following

Employers affected: All.

Testing applicants: Same conditions as current employees.

Testing employees: Employer may test employees only if these conditions are met:
- employer pays all costs including confirming test
- tests are performed by a licensed laboratory
- employee receives a list of the substances being tested for
- there is a form for disclosing medicines and legal drugs, and
- the results are kept confidential.

Idaho
Idaho Code §§ 72-1701 to 72-1714

Employers affected: Voluntary for all private employers.

Testing applicants: Employer may test as a condition of hiring.

Testing employees: May test as a condition of continued employment.

An employer who follows drug-free workplace guidelines may fire employees who refuse to submit to testing or who test positive for drugs or alcohol. Employees will be fired for misconduct and denied unemployment benefits.

Employee rights: An employee or applicant who receives notice of a positive test may request a retest within 7 working days. If the retest results are negative, the employer must pay for the cost; if they are positive, the employee must pay.

Drug-free workplace program: Yes (compliance is optional).

Illinois
775 Ill. Comp. Stat. § 5/2-104(C)(3)

Employers affected: Employers with 15 or more employees.

Testing employees: Statute does not "encourage,

State Drug and Alcohol Testing Laws (continued)

prohibit, or authorize" drug testing, but employers may test employees who have been in rehabilitation.

Indiana

Ind. Code Ann. §§ 22-9-5-6(b), 22-9-5-24

Employers affected: Employers with 15 or more employees.

Testing employees: Employer may prohibit all employees from using or being under the influence of alcohol and illegal drugs. Employer may test employees who have been in rehabilitation. Employee may be held to the same standards as other employees, even if the unsatisfactory job performance or behavior is due to drug use or alcoholism.

Iowa

Iowa Code § 730.5

Employers affected: Employers with one or more full-time employees.

Testing applicants: Employer may test as a condition of hiring.

Testing employees: Employer may test employees:
- as a condition of continued employment
- upon reasonable suspicion
- during and after rehabilitation, or
- following an accident that caused a reportable injury or more than $1,000 property damage.

Employee rights: Employee has 7 days to request a retest. Employers with 50 or more employees must provide rehabilitation for any employee who has worked for at least one year and has not previously violated the substance abuse policy; no adverse action may be taken if employee successfully completes rehabilitation. Employer must have an employee assistance program or maintain a resource file of outside programs.

Drug-free workplace program: Yes (compliance is optional).

Louisiana

La. Rev. Stat. Ann. §§ 49:1001 and following

Employers affected: Employers with one or more full-time employees. (Does not apply to oil drilling, exploration, or production.)

Testing applicants: Employer may require all applicants to submit to drug and alcohol test. Employer does not have to confirm a positive result of a preemployment drug screen but must offer the applicant the opportunity to pay for a confirmation test and a review by a medical review officer.

Employee rights: Except for a preemployment test, employer may not take adverse personnel action on the basis of an initial screen. Employees with confirmed positive results have 7 working days to request access to all records relating to the drug test. Employer may allow employee to undergo rehabilitation without termination of employment.

Maine

Me. Rev. Stat. Ann. tit. 26, §§ 681 to 690

Employers affected: Employers with one or more full-time employees. (Law does not require or encourage employers to conduct substance abuse testing.)

Testing applicants: Employer may require applicant to take a drug test only if offered employment or placed on an eligibility list.

Testing employees: Employer may test based upon probable cause but may not base belief on a single accident; must document the facts and give employee a copy. May test when:
- there could be an unreasonable threat to the health and safety of coworkers or the public, or
- an employee returns to work following a positive test.

State Drug and Alcohol Testing Laws (continued)

Employee rights: Employee who tests positive has 3 days to explain or contest results. Employee must be given an opportunity to participate in a rehabilitation program for up to 6 months; an employer with more than 20 full-time employees must pay for half of any out-of-pocket costs. After successfully completing the program, employee is entitled to return to previous job with full pay and benefits.

Notice and policy requirements: All employers must have a written policy approved by the state department of labor. Policy must be distributed to each employee at least 30 days before it takes effect. Any changes to policy require 60 days' advance notice. An employer with more than 20 full-time employees must have an employee assistance program certified by the state office of substance abuse before implementing a testing program.

Maryland

Md. Code Ann., [Health-Gen.] § 17-214

Employers affected: Law applies to all employers.

Testing applicants: May use preliminary screening to test applicant. If initial result is positive, may make job offer conditional on confirmation of test results.

Testing employees: Employer may require substance abuse testing for legitimate business purposes only.

Employee rights: The sample must be tested by a certified laboratory; at the time of testing employee may request laboratory's name and address. An employee who tests positive must be given:

- a copy of the test results
- a copy of the employer's written drug and alcohol policy
- a written notice of any adverse action employer intends to take, and

- a statement of employee's right to an independent confirmation test at own expense.

Minnesota

Minn. Stat. Ann. §§ 181.950 to 181.957

Employers affected: Employers with one or more full-time employees. (Employers are not required to test.)

Testing applicants: Employers may require applicants to submit to a drug or alcohol test only after they have been given a job offer and have seen a written notice of testing policy. May only test if required of all applicants for same position.

Testing employees: Employers may require drug or alcohol testing only according to a written testing policy. Testing may be done if there is a reasonable suspicion that employee:

- is under the influence of drugs or alcohol
- has violated drug and alcohol policy
- has been involved in an accident, or
- has sustained or caused another employee to sustain a personal injury.

    Random tests permitted only for employees in safety-sensitive positions. With two weeks' notice, employers may also test as part of an annual routine physical exam.

Employee rights: If test is positive, employee has 3 days to explain the results; employee must notify employer within 5 days of intention to obtain a retest. Employer may not discharge employee for a first-time positive test without offering counseling or rehabilitation; employee who refuses or does not complete program successfully may be discharged.

Notice and policy requirements: Employees must be given a written notice of testing policy which includes consequences of refusing to take test or having a positive test result. Two weeks'

State Drug and Alcohol Testing Laws (continued)

notice required before testing as part of an annual routine physical exam.

Mississippi

Miss. Code Ann. §§ 71-7-1 and following, 71-3-205 and following

Employers affected: Employers with one or more full-time employees. Employers who establish a drug-free workplace program to qualify for a workers' compensation rate discount must implement testing procedures.

Testing applicants: May test all applicants as part of employment application process. Employer may request a signed statement that applicant has read and understands the drug and alcohol testing policy or notice. (Must test applicants if drug-free workplace.)

Testing employees: May require drug and alcohol testing of all employees:
- on reasonable suspicion
- as part of a routinely scheduled fitness-for-duty medical examination
- as a follow-up to a rehabilitation program, or
- if they have tested positive within the previous 12 months.

Employee rights: Employer must inform an employee in writing within 5 working days of receipt of a positive confirmed test result; employee may request and receive a copy of the test result report. Employee has 10 working days after receiving notice to explain the positive test results. Private employer who elects to establish a drug-free workplace program must have an employee assistance program or maintain a resource file of outside programs.

Notice and policy requirements: 30 days before implementing testing program employer must give employees written notice of drug and alcohol policy which includes consequences:
- of a positive confirmed result

- of refusing to take test, and
- of other violations of the policy.

Drug-free workplace program: Yes.

Montana

Mont. Code Ann. §§ 39-2-205 to 39-2-211

Employers affected: Employers with one or more employees.

Testing applicants: May test as a condition of hire.

Testing employees: Employees may be tested:
- on reasonable suspicion
- after involvement in an accident that causes personal injury or more than $1,500 property damage
- as a follow-up to a previous positive test, or
- as a follow-up to treatment or a rehabilitation program.

Employer may conduct random tests as long as there is an established date and all personnel are subject to testing.

Employer may require an employee who tests positive to undergo treatment as a condition of continued employment.

Employee rights: After a positive result, employee may request additional confirmation by an independent laboratory; if the results are negative, employer must pay the test costs.

Notice and policy requirements: Written policy must be available for review 60 days before testing.

Nebraska

Neb. Rev. Stat. §§ 48-1901 and following

Employers affected: Employers with 6 or more full-time and part-time employees.

Testing employees: Employer may require employees to submit to drug or alcohol testing and may discipline or discharge any employee who refuses.

State Drug and Alcohol Testing Laws (continued)

Employee rights: Employer may not take adverse action on the basis of an initial positive result unless it is confirmed according to state and federal guidelines.

North Carolina

N.C. Gen. Stat. §§ 95-230 to 95-235

Employers affected: Law applies to all employers.

Testing employees: Employer must preserve samples for at least 90 days after confirmed test results are released.

Employee rights: Employee has right to retest a confirmed positive sample at own expense.

North Dakota

N.D. Cent. Code § 34-01-15

Employers affected: Any employer who requires a medical exam as a condition of hire or continued employment may include a drug or alcohol test.

Testing employees: Employer may test following an accident or injury that will result in a workers' compensation claim, if employer has a mandatory policy of testing under these circumstances, or if employer or physician has reasonable grounds to suspect injury was caused by impairment due to alcohol or drug use.

Ohio

Ohio Admin. Code §§ 4123-17-58, 4123-17-58.1

Employers affected: Employers who establish a drug-free workplace program to qualify for a workers' compensation rate discount.

Testing applicants: Must test all applicants and new hires within 90 days of employment.

Testing employees: Must test employees:
- on reasonable suspicion
- following a return to work after a positive test
- after an accident which results in an injury requiring offsite medical attention or property damage over limit specified in drug and alcohol policy, or

- at random to meet requirements for greater discounts.

Employee rights: Employer must have an employee assistance plan. Employer must offer health care coverage which includes chemical dependency counseling and treatment.

Notice and policy requirements: Policy must state consequences for refusing to submit to testing or for violating guidelines. Policy must include a commitment to rehabilitation.

Drug-free workplace program: Yes.

Oklahoma

Okla. Stat. Ann. tit. 40, §§ 551 to 565

Employers affected: Employers with one or more employees. (Drug or alcohol testing not required or encouraged.)

Testing applicants: Employer may test applicants as a condition of employment and may refuse to hire applicant who refuses to undergo test or has a confirmed positive result.

Testing employees: Before requiring testing, employer must provide an employee assistance program. Random testing is allowed. May test employees:
- on reasonable suspicion
- after an accident resulting in injury or property damage over $500
- as part of a routine fitness-for-duty examination, or
- as follow-up to a rehabilitation program.

Employee rights: Employee has right to retest a positive result at own expense; if the confirmation test is negative, employer must reimburse costs.

Notice and policy requirements: Before requiring testing, employer must:
- adopt a written policy
- give a copy to each employee and to any applicant offered a job, and

State Drug and Alcohol Testing Laws (continued)

• allow 30 days' notice.

Oregon

Or. Rev. Stat. §§ 659.840, 659A.300, 438.435

Employers affected: Law applies to all employers.

Testing applicants: Unless there is reasonable suspicion that an applicant is under the influence of alcohol, no employer may require a breathalyzer test as a condition of employment. Employer is not prohibited from conducting a test if applicant consents.

Testing employees: Unless there is reasonable suspicion that an employee is under the influence of alcohol, no employer may require a breathalyzer or blood alcohol test as a condition of continuing employment. Employer is not prohibited from conducting a test if employee consents.

Employee rights: No action may be taken based on the results of an on-site drug test without a confirming test performed according to state health division regulations. Upon written request, test results will be reported to the employee.

Rhode Island

R.I. Gen. Laws §§ 28-6.5-1 to 28-6.5-2

Employers affected: Law applies to all employers.

Testing employees: May require employee to submit to a drug test only if there are reasonable grounds, based on specific observations, to believe employee is using controlled substances that are impairing job performance.

Employee rights: Employee who tests positive may have the sample retested at employer's expense and must be given opportunity to explain or refute results. Employee may not be terminated on the basis of a positive result

but must be referred to a licensed substance abuse professional. After referral, employer may require additional testing and may terminate employee if test results are positive.

South Carolina

S.C. Code Ann. §§ 41-1-15, 38-73-500

Employers affected: Employers who establish a drug-free workplace program to qualify for a workers' compensation rate discount.

Testing employees: Must conduct random testing among all employees. Must conduct a follow-up test within 30 minutes of the first test.

Employee rights: Employee must receive positive test results in writing within 24 hours.

Notice and policy requirements: Employer must notify all employees of the drug-free workplace program at the time it is established or at the time of hiring, whichever is earlier. Program must include a policy statement that balances respect for individuals with the need to maintain a safe, drug-free environment.

Drug-free workplace program: Yes.

Tennessee

Tenn. Code Ann. §§ 50-9-101 and following

Employers affected: Employers who establish a drug-free workplace program to qualify for a workers' compensation rate discount.

Testing applicants: Must test applicants upon conditional offer of employment. Job ads must include notice that drug and alcohol testing is required.

Testing employees: Employer must test upon reasonable suspicion; must document behavior on which the suspicion is based within 24 hours or before test results are released, whichever is earlier; and must give a copy to the employee upon request. Employer must test employees:

• who are in safety-sensitive positions

State Drug and Alcohol Testing Laws (continued)

- as part of a routine fitness-for-duty medical exam
- after an accident that results in injury, or
- as a follow-up to a required rehabilitation program.

Employee rights: Employee has the right to explain or contest a positive result within 5 days. Employee may not be fired, disciplined, or discriminated against for voluntarily seeking treatment unless employee has previously tested positive or been in a rehabilitation program.

Notice and policy requirements: Before implementing testing program, employer must provide 60 days' notice and must give all employees a written drug and alcohol policy statement.

Drug-free workplace program: Yes.

Utah

Utah Code Ann. §§ 34-38-1 to 34-38-15

Employers affected: Employers with one or more employees.

Testing applicants: Employer may test any applicant for drugs or alcohol as long as management also submits to periodic testing.

Testing employees: Employer may test employee for drugs or alcohol as long as management also submits to periodic testing. Employer may also require testing to:

- investigate an accident or theft
- maintain employee or public safety, or
- ensure productivity, quality, or security.

Employee rights: Employer may suspend, discipline, discharge, or require treatment on the basis of a confirmed positive test result.

Notice and policy requirements: Testing must be conducted according to a written policy that has been distributed to employees and is available for review by prospective employees.

Vermont

Vt. Stat. Ann. tit. 21, §§ 511 and following

Employers affected: Employers with one or more employees.

Testing applicants: Employer may not test applicants for drugs or alcohol unless there is a job offer conditional on a negative test result and applicant is given written notice of the testing procedure and a list of the drugs to be tested for.

Testing employees: Random testing not permitted unless required by federal law. Employer may not require testing unless:

- there is probable cause to believe an employee is using or is under the influence
- employer has an employee assistance program which provides rehabilitation, and
- employee who tests positive and agrees to enter employee assistance program is not terminated.

Employee rights: Employer must contract with a medical review officer who will review all test results and keep them confidential. Medical review officer is to contact employee or applicant to explain a positive test result. Employee or applicant has right to an independent retest at own expense. Employee who successfully completes employee assistance program may not be terminated, although employee may be suspended for up to 3 months to complete program. Employee who tests positive after completing treatment may be fired.

Virginia

Va. Code Ann. § 65.2-813.2

Employers affected: Employers who establish drug-free workplace programs to qualify for workers' compensation insurance discount.

Drug-free workplace program: State law gives insurers the authority to establish guidelines and criteria for testing.

Current as of February 2005

State Laws on Employee Arrest and Conviction Records

The following chart summarizes state laws and regulations on whether an employer can get access to an employee's or prospective employee's past arrests or convictions. It includes citations to statutes and agency websites, as available.

Many states allow or require private sector employers to run background checks on workers, particularly in fields like child care, elder care, home health care, private schools, private security, and the investment industry. Criminal background checks usually consist of sending the applicant's name (and sometimes fingerprints) to the state police or to the FBI. State law may forbid hiring people with certain kinds of prior convictions, depending on the kind of job or license involved.

Federal law allows the states to establish procedures for requesting a nationwide background check to find out if a person has been "convicted of a crime that bears upon the [person's] fitness to have responsibility for the safety and well-being of children, the elderly, or individuals with disabilities." (42 U.S.C.A. § 5119a(a)(1).)

If your state isn't listed in this chart, then it doesn't have a general statute on whether private sector employers can find out about arrests or convictions. There might be a law about your particular industry, though.

It's always a good idea to consult your state's nondiscrimination enforcement agency or labor department to see what kinds of questions you can ask. The agency guidelines are designed to help employers comply with state and federal law. For further information, contact your state's agency, listed in the appendix.

Alaska

Agency guidelines for preemployment inquiries: Alaska Department of Labor and Workforce Development, Alaska Employer Handbook, "Pre-Employment Questioning," at www.labor.state.ak.us/employer/aeh.pdf.

Arizona

Ariz. Rev. Stat. § 13-904(E)

Rights of employees and applicants: Unless the offense has a reasonable relationship to the occupation, an occupational license may not be denied solely on the basis of a felony or misdemeanor conviction.

California

Cal. Lab. Code § 432.7

Rules for employers:
- **Arrest records.** May not ask about an arrest that did not lead to conviction; may not ask about pretrial or post-trial diversion program. May ask about arrest if prospective employee is awaiting trial.
- **Convictions.** May ask about conviction even if no sentence is imposed.

Agency guidelines for preemployment inquiries: Department of Fair Employment and Housing, "Pre-Employment Inquiry Guidelines," DFEH-161 at www.dfeh.ca.gov/Publications/DFEH%20161.pdf.

Colorado

Colo. Rev. Stat. §§ 24-72-308 (IIfI), 8-3-108(m)

Rules for employers: May not inquire about arrest for civil or military disobedience unless it resulted in conviction.

Rights of employees and applicants: May not be required to disclose any information in a sealed record; may answer questions about arrests or convictions as though they had not occurred.

Agency guidelines for preemployment inquiries: Colorado Civil Rights Division, Publications, "Preventing Job Discrimination," at www.dora.state.co.us/civil-rights/publications/jobdiscrim2001.pdf.

State Laws on Employee Arrest and Conviction Records (continued)

Connecticut

Conn. Gen. Stat. Ann. §§ 46a-79 to 46a-80, 31-51i

Rules for employers: State policy encourages hiring qualified applicants with criminal records. If an employment application form contains any question concerning criminal history, it must include the following notice in clear and conspicuous language: "The applicant is not required to disclose the existence of any arrest, criminal charge, or conviction, the records of which have been erased." Employer may not disclose information about a job applicant's criminal history except to members of the personnel department or person(s) in charge of hiring or conducting the interview.

Rights of employees and applicants: May not be asked to disclose information about a criminal record that has been erased; may answer any question as though arrest or conviction never took place. May not be discriminated against in hiring or continued employment on the basis of an erased criminal record.

Delaware

Del. Code Ann. tit. 11, § 4374(e)

Rights of employees and applicants: Do not have to disclose an arrest record that has been expunged.

District of Columbia

D.C. Code Ann. § 2-1402.66

Rules for employers:
- **Arrest records.** May not obtain or inquire into arrest record.
- **Convictions.** May obtain record of convictions occurring within the last 10 years.

Florida

Fla. Stat. Ann. § 112.011

Rights of employees and applicants: May not be disqualified to practice or pursue any occupation or profession that requires a license, permit, or certificate because of a prior conviction, unless it was for a felony or first-degree misdemeanor and is directly related to the specific line of work.

Georgia

Ga. Code Ann. §§ 35-3-34, 42-8-62 to 42-8-63

Rules for employers: In order to obtain a criminal record from the state Crime Information Center, employer must supply the individual's fingerprints or signed consent. If an adverse employment decision is made on the basis of the record, must disclose all information in the record to the employee or applicant and tell how it affected the decision.

Rights of employees and applicants: Probation for a first offense is not a conviction; may not be disqualified for employment once probation is completed.

Hawaii

Haw. Rev. Stat. §§ 378-2.to 378-2.5, 831-3.2

Rules for employers:
- **Arrest records.** It is a violation of law for any employer to refuse to hire, to discharge, or to discriminate in terms of compensation, conditions, or privileges of employment because of a person's arrest or court record.
- **Convictions.** May inquire into a conviction only after making a conditional offer of employment, provided it has a rational relation to job. May not examine any convictions over 10 years old.

Rights of employees and applicants: If an arrest or conviction has been expunged, may state that no record exists and may respond to questions as a person with no record would respond.

Agency guidelines for preemployment inquiries: Hawaii Civil Rights Commission, "Guide to Pre-Employment Inquiries," at www.state.hi.us/hcrc/brochures.html.

State Laws on Employee Arrest and Conviction Records (continued)

Idaho

Agency guidelines for preemployment inquiries: Idaho Human Rights Commission, "Pre-Employment Inquiries," at www2.state.id.us/ihrc/preemp21.htm.

Illinois

775 Ill. Comp. Stat. § 5/2-103

Rules for employers: It is a civil rights violation to ask about an arrest or criminal history record that has been expunged or sealed, or to use the fact of an arrest or criminal history record as a basis for refusing to hire or to renew employment. Law does not prohibit employer from using other means to find out if person actually engaged in conduct for which they were arrested.

Kansas

Kan. Stat. Ann. §§ 12-4516(g), 21-4619(h), 22-4710

Rules for employers: Cannot inspect or inquire into criminal record unless employee or applicant signs a release. Employers can require access to criminal records in specific businesses.

Rights of employees and applicants: If arrest, conviction, or diversion record is expunged, do not have to disclose any information about it.

Agency guidelines for preemployment inquiries: Kansas Human Rights Commission, "Guidelines on Equal Employment Practices: Preventing Discrimination in Hiring," at www.khrc.net/hiring.html.

Louisiana

La. Rev. Stat. Ann. § 37:2950

Rights of employees and applicants: Prior conviction cannot be used as a basis to deny employment or an occupational or professional license, unless conviction is for a felony and directly relates to the job or license being sought.

Special situations: Protection does not apply to medical, engineering and architecture, or funeral and embalming licenses.

Maine

Me. Rev. Stat. Ann. tit. 5, § 5301; tit. 28-A, § 703-A; Code Me. R. 94-348 Ch. 3, § 3.06(B)(7)

Rights of employees and applicants: A conviction is not an automatic bar to obtaining an occupational or professional license. Only convictions that directly relate to the profession or occupation, that include dishonesty or false statements, that are subject to imprisonment for more than 1 year, or that involve sexual misconduct on the part of a licensee may be considered.

Maryland

Md. Code Ann. [Crim. Proc.], § 10-109; Md. Regs. Code 09.01.10.02

Rules for employers: May not inquire about any criminal charges that have been expunged. May not use a refusal to disclose information as basis for not hiring an applicant.

Rights of employees and applicants: Need not refer to or give any information about an expunged charge. A professional or occupational license may not be refused or revoked simply because of a conviction; agency must consider the nature of the crime and its relation to the occupation or profession; the conviction's relevance to the applicant's fitness and qualifications; when conviction occurred and other convictions, if any; and the applicant's behavior before and after conviction.

Massachusetts

Mass. Gen. Laws ch. 151B, § 4; ch. 276, § 100A; Mass. Regs. Code tit. 804, § 3.02

Rules for employers: If job application has a question about prior arrests or convictions, it must state that an applicant with a sealed record is entitled to answer, "No record."

State Laws on Employee Arrest and Conviction Records (continued)

- **Arrest records.** May not ask about arrests that did not result in conviction.
- **Convictions.** May obtain record of convictions occurring within the last 10 years. May not ask about first-time convictions for drunkenness, simple assault, speeding, minor traffic violations, or disturbing the peace; may not ask about misdemeanor convictions 5 or more years old.

Rights of employees and applicants: If criminal record is sealed, may answer, "No record" to any inquiry about past arrests or convictions.

Agency guidelines for preemployment inquiries: Massachusetts Commission Against Discrimination, "Discrimination on the Basis of Criminal Record," at www.state.ma.us/mcad/crimrec.html.

Michigan

Mich. Comp. Laws § 37.2205a

Rules for employers: May not request information on any arrests or misdemeanor charges that did not result in conviction.

Rights of employees and applicants: Employees or applicants are not making a false statement if they fail to disclose information they have a civil right to withhold.

Agency guidelines for preemployment inquiries: Michigan Civil Rights Commission, "Pre-Employment Inquiry Guide," at www.michigan.gov/documents/pre-employment_inquery_guide_13019_7.pdf.

Minnesota

Minn. Stat. Ann. §§ 364.01 to 364.03

Rules for employers: State policy encourages the rehabilitation of criminal offenders; employment opportunity is considered essential to rehabilitation.

Rights of employees and applicants: No one can be disqualified from pursuing or practicing an occupation that requires a license, unless the crime directly relates to the occupation. Agency may consider the nature and seriousness of the crime and its relation to the applicant's fitness for the occupation. Even if the crime does relate to the occupation, a person who provides evidence of rehabilitation and present fitness cannot be disqualified.

Agency guidelines for preemployment inquiries: Minnesota Department of Human Rights, "Hiring, Job Interviews and the Minnesota Human Rights Act," at www.humanrights.state.mn.us/employer_hiring.html.

Missouri

Agency guidelines for preemployment inquiries: Commission on Human Rights, Missouri Department of Labor and Industrial Relations, "Pre-Employment Inquiries," at www.dolir.state.mo.us/hr/interview.htm.

Nebraska

Neb. Rev. Stat. § 29-3523

Rules for employers: May not obtain access to information regarding arrests that do not lead to conviction.

Nevada

Nev. Rev. Stat. Ann. §§ 179.301, 179A.100(3)

Rules for employers: May obtain a prospective employee's criminal history record only if it includes convictions or a pending charge, including parole or probation.

Special situations: State Gaming Board may inquire into sealed recoreds to see if conviction relates to gaming.

Agency guidelines for preemployment inquiries: Nevada Equal Rights Commission, "Pre-Employment Inquiry Guide," at http://detr.state.nv.us/nerc/nerc_preemp.htm.

State Laws on Employee Arrest and Conviction Records (continued)

New Hampshire

N.H. Rev. Stat. Ann. § 651:5 (Xc); N.H. Code Admin. R. Hum 405.03

Rules for employers: May ask about a previous criminal record only if question substantially follows this wording: "Have you ever been arrested for or convicted of a crime that has not been annulled by a court?"

- **Arrest records.** It is unlawful discrimination for an employer to ask about an arrest record, to have a job requirement that applicant have no arrest record, or to use information about an arrest record to make a hiring decision, unless it is a business necessity. It is unlawful discrimination to ask about arrest record if it has the purpose or effect of discouraging applicants of a particular racial or national origin group.

New Jersey

N.J. Stat. Ann. §§ 5:5-34.1, 5:12-89 to 5:12-91, 32:23-86; N.J. Admin. Code tit. 13, §§ 59-1.2, 59-1.6

Rules for employers: May obtain information about convictions and pending arrests or charges to determine the subject's qualifications for employment. Employers must certify that they will provide sufficient time for applicant to challenge, correct, or complete record, and will not presume guilt for any pending charges or court actions.

Rights of employees and applicants: Applicant who is disqualified for employment based on criminal record must be given adequate notice and reasonable time to confirm or deny accuracy of information.

Special situations: There are specific rules for casino employees, longshoremen and related occupations, horse racing, and other gaming industry jobs.

New Mexico

Criminal Offender Employment Act, N.M. Stat. Ann. 28-2-1 to 28-2-6

For a license, permit, or other authority to engage in any regulated trade, business, or profession, a regulating agency may consider convictions for felonies and for misdemeanors involving moral turpitude. Such convictions cannot be an automatic bar to authority to practice in the regulated field, though.

New York

N.Y. Correct. Law §§ 750 to 754; N.Y. Exec. Law § 296(16)

Rules for employers:

- **Arrest records.** It is unlawful discrimination to ask about any arrests or charges that did not result in conviction, unless they are currently pending.
- **Convictions.** Employers with 10 or more employees may not deny employment based on a conviction unless it relates directly to the job or would be an "unreasonable" risk to property or to public or individual safety.

Rights of employees and applicants: Upon request, applicant must be given, within 30 days, a written statement of the reasons why employment was denied.

Agency guidelines for preemployment inquiries: New York State Division of Human Rights, "Recommendations on Employment Inquiries," at www.nysdhr.com/employment.html.

North Dakota

N.D. Cent. Code § 12-60-16.6

Rules for employers: May obtain records of convictions or of criminal charges (adults only) occurring in the past year.

Agency guidelines for preemployment inquiries: North Dakota Department of Labor, Human

State Laws on Employee Arrest and Conviction Records (continued)

Rights Division, "Employment Applications and Interviews," www.state.nd.us/labor/publications/docs/brochures/005.pdf.

Ohio

Ohio Rev. Code Ann. §§ 2151.358 (I), 2953.33

Rules for employers: May not inquire into any sealed convictions or sealed bail forfeitures, unless question has a direct and substantial relation to job.

Rights of employees and applicants: May not be asked about arrest records that are expunged; may respond to inquiry as though arrest did not occur.

Oklahoma

Okla. Stat. Ann. tit. 22, § 19(F)

Rules for employers: May not inquire into any criminal record that has been expunged.

Rights of employees and applicants: If record is expunged, may state that no criminal action ever occurred. May not be denied employment for refusing to disclose sealed criminal record information.

Oregon

Or. Rev. Stat. §§ 181.555 to 181.560, 659A.030

Rules for employers: Before requesting information, employer must notify employee or applicant; when submitting request, must tell State Police Department when and how person was notified. May not discriminate against an applicant or current employee on the basis of an expunged juvenile record unless there is a "bona fide occupational qualification."

- **Arrest records.** May request information about arrest records less than 1 year old that have not resulted in acquittal or have not been dismissed.
- **Convictions.** May request information about conviction records.

Rights of employees and applicants: Before State Police Department releases any criminal record information, it must notify employee or applicant and provide a copy of all information that will be sent to employer. Notice must include protections under federal civil rights law and the procedure for challenging information in the record. Record may not be released until 14 days after notice is sent.

Pennsylvania

18 Pa. Cons. Stat. Ann. § 9125

Rules for employers: May consider felony and misdemeanor convictions only if they directly relate to person's suitability for the job.

Rights of employees and applicants: Must be informed in writing if refusal to hire is based on criminal record information.

Agency guidelines for preemployment inquiries: Pennsylvania Human Relations Commission, Publications, "Pre-Employment Inquiries," at http://sites.state.pa.us/PA_Exec/PHRC/publications/literature/Pre-Employ%20QandA%READ.pdf.

Rhode Island

R.I. Gen. Laws §§ 12-1.3-4, 28-5-7 (7)

Rules for employers:
- **Arrest records.** It is unlawful to include on an application form or to ask as part of an interview if the applicant has ever been arrested or charged with any crime.
- **Convictions.** May ask if applicant has been convicted of a crime.

Rights of employees and applicants: Do not have to disclose any conviction that has been expunged.

South Dakota

Agency guidelines for preemployment inquiries: South Dakota Division of Human

State Laws on Employee Arrest and Conviction Records (continued)

Rights, "Pre-employment Inquiry Guide," at www.state.sd.us/dol/boards/preemplo.htm suggests that an employer shouldn't ask or check into arrests or convictions if they are not substantially related to the job.

Texas

Tex. Health & Safety Code Ann. §§ 765.001 and following; Tex. Gov't. Code Ann. § 411.118

Special situations: A criminal background check is permitted upon a conditional offer of employment in a private "residential dwelling project," which includes a condominium, apartment building, hotel, motel, or bed and breakfast, where the employee may be reasonably required to have access to residential units. Applicant must give written consent to release of criminal record information.

Utah

Utah Admin. R. 606-2 (V)

Rules for employers: Utah Labor Division Anti-Discrimination Rules, Rule R606-2. "Pre-Employment Inquiry Guide," at www.rules.utah. gov/publicat/code/r606/r606-002.htm.

- **Arrest records**. It is not permissible to ask about arrests.
- **Convictions.** Asking about felony convictions is permitted but is not advisable unless related to job.

Vermont

Vt. Stat. Ann. tit. 20, § 2056c

Rules for employers: Only employers who provide care for children, the elderly, and the disabled or who run postsecondary schools with residential facilities may obtain criminal record information from the state Criminal Information Center. May obtain record only after a conditional offer of employment is made and applicant has given written authorization on a

signed, notarized release form.

Rights of employees and applicants: Release form must advise applicant of right to appeal any of the findings in the record.

Virginia

Va. Code Ann. § 19.2-392.4

Rules for employers: May not require an applicant to disclose information about any criminal charge that has been expunged.

Rights of employees and applicants: Need not refer to any expunged charges if asked about criminal record.

Washington

Wash. Rev. Code Ann. §§ 43.43.815, 9.94A.640(3), 9.96.060(3), 9.96A.020; Wash. Admin. Code 162-12-140

Rules for employers:
- **Arrest records.** Employer who asks about arrests must ask whether the charges are still pending, have been dismissed, or led to conviction.
- **Convictions.** Employer who obtains a conviction record must notify employee within 30 days of receiving it and must allow the employee to examine it. May make an employment decision based on a conviction only if it is less than 10 years old and the crime involves behavior that would adversely affect job performance.

Rights of employees and applicants: If a conviction record is cleared or vacated, may answer questions as though the conviction never occurred. A person convicted of a felony cannot be refused an occupational license unless the conviction is less than 10 years old and the felony relates specifically to the occupation or business.

Special situations: Employers are entitled to

State Laws on Employee Arrest and Conviction Records (continued)

obtain complete criminal record information for positions that require bonding, or that have access to trade secrets, confidential or proprietary business information, money, or items of value.

West Virginia

Agency guidelines for preemployment inquiries: Bureau of Employment Programs, "Pre-employment Inquiries Technical Assistance Guide," at www.wvbep.org/bep/Bepeeo/empinqu.htm. The state's website says that employers can only make inquiries about convictions directly related to the job. Consider the nature and recentness of the conviction and evidence of rehabilitation. Include a disclaimer that a conviction is not necessarily a bar to employment.

Wisconsin

Wis. Stat. Ann. §§ 111.31 to 111.335

Rules for employers: It is a violation of state civil rights law to discriminate against an employee on the basis of a prior arrest or conviction record.

- **Arrest records.** May not ask about arrests unless there are pending charges.
- **Convictions.** May not ask about convictions unless charges substantially relate to job.

Special situations: Employers are entitled to obtain complete criminal record information for positions that require bonding and for burglar alarm installers.

Agency guidelines for preemployment inquiries: Wisconsin Department of Workforce Development, Civil Rights Division Publications, "Fair Hiring & Avoiding Loaded Interview Questions," at www.dwd.state.wi.us/dwd/publications/212A/ERD-4825-PWEB.pdf.

Current as of February 2005

2

Compensation and Hours

No matter how much you encourage creativity, camaraderie, and good cheer in your team or department, you know that employees don't show up every day for the sheer fun of it—they do so to get paid (as, probably, do you). Pay is, perhaps, the most basic part of the employment relationship: Employees are paid in return for their labor. Despite the simplicity of this exchange, however, the legal rules governing pay and work can get pretty complicated. And managers—who often have to participate in setting pay levels, deciding whether employees should receive overtime, and figuring out how to pay employees who travel for business, among other things—can easily get caught in the middle.

This chapter covers some compensation basics, including:

- setting pay levels
- the minimum wage
- overtime
- paying for on-call and travel time
- flexible work schedules
- deductions and wage garnishments
- equal pay for men and women, and
- record keeping requirements.

While not every manager will need to know the information in this chapter, it provides valuable information if you work in human resources, payroll or otherwise have to deal with compensation issues; you have some input into the pay levels of those who report to you; or you assign or approve employee schedules (including such issues as overtime, business trips, flextime, and so on) for which you'd like to know the legal rules. (And this chapter may also answer some of your questions about your own paycheck.)

Frequently Asked Questions About Compensation and Hours

How should I decide what to pay people?

Here are five steps to help you set pay for any given position: (1) clearly define the job you are paying for and the level of talent necessary to do it well; (2) examine your or your company's budget to determine what you can afford to pay; (3) look internally at what others in your company are being paid for similar jobs, (4) gather external information on what other companies pay for similar jobs; and (5) find out the job candidate's pay requirements. (For an explanation of these five steps, see "Deciding What to Pay People," below.)

Do we have to pay the minimum wage to employees who receive tips?

It depends. Under federal law, as long as an employee regularly earns at least $30 per month in tips, the employee can be paid as little as $2.13 an hour. However,

Frequently Asked Questions About Compensation and Hours (continued)

that amount plus the tips the employee actually earns must add up to at least the federal minimum wage. If the employee's total earnings fall short of the minimum wage, the employer must make up the difference. And some states, including California, don't allow employers to pay tipped employees less than the state minimum wage. (For more information on minimum wage laws, see "The Minimum Wage," below.)

■ **Are managers entitled to overtime pay?**

As long as they earn at least $455 a week and actually manage people, probably not. Under federal law, executive, professional, and administrative employees are not entitled to overtime pay. (For more, see "Overtime," below.)

■ **If an employee goes on an overnight business trip, do we have to pay for every hour the employee spends away from home—even hours spent sleeping or eating?**

No. You must pay for the hours the employee actually spends working, of course. You also have to pay for travel time, but only if the employee travels during his or her regularly working hours. (These are the rules for overnight trips; the rules for one-day trips are different. For the full story, see "Travel Time," below.)

■ **Are employees entitled to be paid for on-call time, even if they don't have to stay at work?**

Employees are entitled to be paid for every on-call hour spent at the worksite. If employees aren't required to remain at the workplace, they are entitled to be paid for on-call time only if they are significantly restricted during those hours. (For more on paying for on-call time, see "On-Call Time," below.)

■ **If I allow one or a few workers to work on a flexible schedule, do I have to allow everyone to do so?**

No. Certain positions are better suited for flexible schedules than others. As long as you do not base your decision on who can work a flexible schedule on an illegal reason, such as discriminating in who gets the benefit based on race, gender, or age (and you stay within the bounds of overtime laws), you can allow only some workers to work flextime. (For more information, see "Flexible Work Schedules," below.)

Frequently Asked Questions About Compensation and Hours (continued)

■ **Can I put an exempt employee on unpaid suspension while I investigate a claim that he sexually harassed a coworker?**

It depends on your company's written policy. If you dock an exempt employee's pay, you risk making that employee nonexempt—and, therefore, entitled to earn overtime—unless an exception applies. Employers are allows to put exempt employees on unpaid suspension for violating workplace conduct rules, but only if the employer has a written policy regarding such suspensions that applies to all employees. (For more information, see "Pay Docking and Unpaid Suspensions," below.)

■ **Can we deduct money from a worker's paycheck to repay a cash advance?**

The answer is yes under the federal law, as long as you don't withhold so much money that the employee is effectively earning less than the minimum wage. But some states don't allow employers to make these kinds of deductions. (For more on withholding pay, see "Garnishments," below.)

■ **Are female employees entitled to be paid as much as male employees— even if their jobs are different?**

No. Under the Equal Pay Act, men and women are entitled to equal pay for doing the same work. But if men and women's job duties differ, equal pay is not required. (For more on the Equal Pay Act, see "Equal Pay," below.)

■ **Can I get rid of employees' payroll records once they quit or are fired?**

No. Federal law requires employers to keep certain records—including records on wages, hours, deductions, overtime, and pay dates—for each of its workers. You have to keep these records for three years, even if the worker leaves your company. (For more information on these rules, see "Record Keeping Requirements," below.)

The Fair Labor Standards Act

The Fair Labor Standards Act (FLSA), 29 U.S.C. §§ 201 and following, is the primary federal law governing wages and hours. The FLSA sets the federal minimum wage; establishes rules for overtime pay, child labor, and paycheck deductions; and requires businesses to keep certain records showing the pay and hours of their workers.

Not every company is subject to the FLSA, although most are. Generally, a business is covered if it has $500,000 or more in annual sales. Smaller companies will still be covered if their employees work in what Congress calls "interstate commerce." Most employees are covered—engaging in interstate commerce includes making phone calls to or from another state, sending mail out of state, or handling goods that have come from or will go to another state. And the wage and hour rules also apply to employees who work out of their homes.

Certain types of workers are not protected by the FLSA—that is, they are not entitled to the minimum wage or overtime pay. These include:

- independent contractors (only employees are covered by the FLSA—for more information about independent contractors, see Chapter 9)
- outside salespeople (a salesperson who works a route, for example)
- certain computer specialists (systems analysts, programmers, and software engineers who earn at least $27.63 per hour)
- employees of seasonal amusement or recreational businesses (such as ski resorts or county fairs)
- employees of certain small newspapers and newspaper deliverers
- workers engaged in fishing operations
- employees who work on small farms, and
- certain switchboard operators.

Many states also have their own wage and hour laws, including some that provide workers with more protections than the FLSA—and place more obligations on companies. To make things a bit trickier, a business must follow whichever rule (state or federal) gives its workers more protection. It may have to abide by a patchwork of laws, applying a minimum federal standard in some areas and a more protective state standard in others. For example, if your company does business in a state that requires a higher minimum wage but sets lower standards for child labor, it will have to follow the state minimum wage law while applying the stricter federal child labor rules.

To find out more about your state's law—and about how it compares to federal law—contact your state labor department. (Contact information is available in the appendix.)

Deciding What to Pay People

While the bulk of this chapter covers the rules of wage and hour law, we begin with the most basic compensation question first: How do you figure out what to pay for which jobs? And what if the jobs are similar but require different levels of experience or skill? The following sections provide you with a method and the tools you need to craft compensation packages that pay fairly for the work done and, hopefully, attract employees who will do the job well.

Steps to Determine What to Pay

While there are many shifting variables to consider when determining pay, the process by which you consider these variables can be summed up in five steps:

Step 1: Clearly define the job you are paying for and the level of talent necessary to do it well.

Step 2: Examine your own budget to determine what you can afford to pay.

Step 3: Look internally at what others in your company are being paid for similar jobs (to achieve "internal equity").

Step 4: Gather external information on what other companies pay for similar jobs (called "external market data"). To do this, you may wish to gather both quantitative data—for example, surveys—and qualitative or anecdotal data—for

example, asking those in your professional network what they pay or finding out what your job applicants have been earning.

Step 5: Find out the job candidate's pay requirements.

Think of this process as having five different factors, all of which need to be considered before making your own determination.

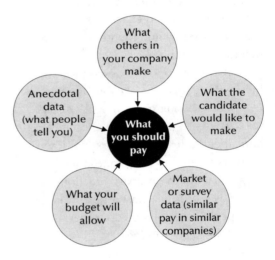

At first glance, you may be wondering if you really need to do all of this work to set pay. Do not fear: We take you through this process step by step (although not all of the steps may pertain to you or your workplace). While doing this work may take a little time, it will be time well spent: You will be able to attract better candidates and justify your pay requests to your employees and management. And, the pay you determine will be fair and appropriate.

Define the Job

First and foremost, until you understand precisely what it is that you are paying for, you cannot begin to know what you should pay. Spending a few minutes up front to clearly define the job will help enormously as you figure out what to pay. Each type of job could conceivably have many different levels or requirements that you compensate differently. Your best bet is to capture the job exactly as you know it to be currently and then begin your pay determination there.

Start with a good job description. (For help writing this, see *The Job Description Handbook*, by Margaret M. Mader-Clark (Nolo)). If you do not have a job description, spend a few minutes jotting down answers to the following questions:

- What are the primary functions of this job? What must a person in this position absolutely do to get this job done successfully?
- What other responsibilities does the job have? Might you add any responsibilities in the near future?
- What skills and abilities are necessary to do this job? Are there any special requirements needed, such as licenses, certificates, or certain educational requirements?
- Are there any special characteristics of this job to consider—for example, strange work hours, significant travel, being on call, dangerous or undesirable job duties?

Once you have a clear understanding of the position, you are ready to begin setting the pay. It's a good idea to write this down so you can refer back to the document should anyone question your process for establishing pay.

Examine Your Budget

Of course, one of the biggest determinants of what you will pay an employee is how much your business can afford to pay. After clarifying the job description, this is the first thing to consider when hiring or promoting someone into a position. Deciding how much you can afford to pay will differ depending on the type of company you work for:

- **Small businesses.** Small business owners typically know exactly what their constraints are when setting pay. Often, while they would like to hire more senior or managerial-level candidates, their budgets only allow for hiring entry-level employees.
- **Private companies.** Privately held companies vary in their level of sophistication around compensation structures. Get familiar with your company's approach and make sure that you are on the same page as your company's finance and human resources departments when getting ready to set a pay package.
- **Public companies.** Publicly owned companies are more likely to have formal compensation structures and even people to help you determine

pay. Nevertheless, be prepared with a clear definition of the job, an understanding of whether your position has been budgeted for, and what that budget includes—for example, whether it covers just the salary or fringe benefits or bonuses as well.

With your budget number in hand, you now have the "top line" of what you can pay someone—an amount of compensation that you cannot exceed (although your company may have a process to do so if it's absolutely necessary). You can now move on to figure out where, from the top line down, you should set your pay.

Consider What Others in Your Company Make

Paying fairly across like positions within a company—known as "internal equity"—can be a loaded issue for many workplaces. How many times have you heard complaints about a new hire making more than someone who has been there for five years? It's a good idea to generate a report that shows the title, level, and compensation of similarly situated employees (you don't need their names for this exercise). Then, look for and consider the following:

- **Current pay levels.** What are people in similar positions within your company making? Keep in mind that positions need not be exactly the same or even in the same job

family to be considered in an internal equity study. For instance, if you are hiring a Director of Marketing, it's helpful to understand compensation of not only other marketing directors at your company, but directors in other corporate functions as well. It is also a good idea to consider the pay of those directly below or above the position. Compression (pay that is too close to the level above or below) can lead to future problems when it comes time to give someone a raise.

- **Starting pay levels.** What did people in these similar positions make when they first started (and how long ago was that)?

- **Education or experience levels.** The newcomer may have much more experience than your other employees, which may warrant more pay. If so, be prepared to justify the higher pay, because employees may very well learn what their coworkers are making.

- **Requirements of the job.** You may have added responsibilities to the position, making it different from an existing position. For example, if you are hiring an International Sales Manager to open a new sales branch for India, his or her position may be very different from the other six Sales Managers on your staff. While their titles may be the same, the other six all came to work for existing businesses and were not responsible for opening their own sales branches. This is a significant difference in the requirements of the job (as well as the experience necessary to do that job successfully) that could warrant higher pay.

Studying internal equity can be complex; don't let it become anything more than a guideline to help you set pay for a particular job. You may ultimately decide to hire at a compensation level well above or below what others are currently making, but as long as you can clearly explain the differences in the job requirements or tasks, you should be able to justify the difference.

Gather External Market Data

Next, gather what is called "external market data" by finding out what other companies pay employees in the same or similar positions to the one you are trying to fill. There are two main sources for this data—surveys and anecdotal information—both of which have advantages and disadvantages. Surveys provide concrete quantitative data across a broad spectrum, but unfortunately tend to stale so quickly that, by the time they are published, they are already outdated (although the Internet is helping to alleviate this problem). Qualitative anecdotal data suffers from not being very scientific and tapping into a smaller pool of information, but can be even more relevant because of its freshness—learning what people earn right now.

Surveys. A quick Web search can often provide fairly decent external market data on a whole variety of positions. Try visiting www.salaryexpert.com or other job websites like Monster (www.monster.com) and Jobs.com (www.jobs.com). When looking at survey information on these websites, you will see that most of the information is broken up into a few different pieces:

- **Geographical information.** Pay will always vary based on supply and demand and that, of course, varies by geography. Auto mechanics are more prevalent in Detroit than in New York City. As such, the average salary for an auto mechanic will be different in each.
- **Level of the job.** This is where your job definition will come in handy. Typically there are about three levels listed for any job: entry, mid, and high. Titles used to define these three levels vary—for example, hiring for an "Associate," "Junior," or "Senior" position (as in "Associate Clerk") or hiring for the position plus a "1," "2," or "3" (as in "Clerk 2"), and so on. Be sure to look for data that matches the proper job level—the same level as the job for which you are setting pay.
- **Industry.** The industry or type of industry also helps to determine pay for any given position. Fast growing industries, such as high tech or biotech, typically pay more than well-established industries, such as shipping and manufacturing. Pay

is often a function of supply and demand: In newer industries, you may be required to pay more for new skill sets (such as computer programming), whereas in more established industries, there are usually more people with the proper training to choose from.

Take any survey information you find with a grain of salt. As mentioned above, it may be outdated and it may not be a direct match with your position. But like internal equity, it can provide another guideline to help you set pay; use it as such, not as an absolute.

Anecdotal information. While surveys may seem scientific and important, often the freshest data will come from professional organizations, colleagues in your field, and even the candidates interested in the position themselves. Anecdotal information you glean from speaking to people can also be more relevant than survey data, because it is usually more targeted and a better match to the position you are filling.

You can gather anecdotal information from a number of different sources. At meetings of professional organizations to which you belong, check in with your peers to find out what they are currently paying people. Also, read organizational newsletters and websites, especially if they list classifieds for open positions; often a "Help Wanted" ad will list a salary range for an open position.

You can also get such information from applicants who come in to interview for the position. It's a fair question to ask them not only their current salary, but also their future salary requirements.

Understand the Candidate's Requirements

By looking at your budget, you determined the top line of what you can pay for a given position. Internal equity and external market data gave you some parameters for what you should pay to be competitive. The last piece of the puzzle is finding out what the job candidate will accept. This is the bottom line of what you can pay.

Once you narrow the pool of applicants down to one or two real candidates for the position, you will need to ask the candidates both what they made in their last position (which you may have done in gathering anecdotal information from all of the applicants in the previous step) and what the lowest pay range they would accept from you for the new position (don't phrase it this way, of course!). To make such a question sound better and not seem like you are trying to lowball the candidate, ask a question such as, "What pay would seem reasonable to you if you were to join us?" With a stroke of good luck, this number will be below your top line number and within your other guidelines. Often, however, you will need to massage the numbers and use some creative techniques (as described below) to come up with a compensation package that is acceptable to both the candidate and your company.

Putting It All Together

After going through all five steps, how do you turn all of this information into a pay package? In a perfect world, your top line is higher than your bottom line and the candidate and you agree to something in between. If this is not the case, consider the following creative techniques for making the numbers work:

- Establish base pay that reasonably falls within these parameters, but allows for pay increases in the future.
- Offer bonuses or variable pay based on performance on top of the base pay. Bonuses can be short-term (at signing or after 90 days), mid-term (after six months or at annual performance appraisals), or long-term (designed to retain an employee). Make sure you communicate the entire compensation package to the candidate, not just the base pay.
- If you are a public company that offers stock to your employees, negotiate how much stock the candidate will get.
- You can often make up differences in what a candidate would like to make and what you can afford by offering noncash compensation, such as enhanced vacation benefits, paid maternity or paternity leave, or educational assistance.

All of these elements can be part of a compensation package—and most of them will require different levels of company approval, so check your policies before offering them. If you are creative with the different tools your company has to offer and can tailor the compensation package to the individual, you should be able to hire your chosen candidate.

The Minimum Wage

Many managers will never have to worry about the minimum wage. However, if you supervise low-wage or tipped employees, you participate in determining compensation, or you implement your company's pay program (for example, you work in human resources or payroll), you need to know the basic rules.

Federal law requires employers to pay employees a minimum wage (currently $5.15 per hour). However, each state may impose a higher minimum wage requirement—and many do. The federal law is always the minimum—that is, a company must pay the higher amount, whether it's state or federal. For information on your state's minimum wage requirements, see "State Minimum Wage Laws for Regular and Tipped Employees", at the end of this chapter.

How It's Paid

Even employees who aren't paid by the hour are entitled to the minimum wage.

In other words, although the minimum wage is an hourly standard, employees don't have to be paid by the hour for the minimum wage requirement to kick in. Employees entitled to the minimum wage may receive a salary, commission, wages plus tips, or piece rate, as long as the total amount paid divided by the total number of hours worked by the employee equals at least the minimum wage.

Living Wage Laws

Some cities and counties have passed "living wage" ordinances, requiring certain businesses to pay their workers more than the federal or state minimum wage. The living wage rate is usually calculated by figuring out how much a full-time worker would have to make to support a family of four at or above the poverty line in that geographic area. Some living wage laws also require employers to provide certain benefits or allow employers to pay a lower wage if they already provide benefits.

City and county governments often impose these requirements in areas where the cost of living has skyrocketed beyond that of the rest of the country (such as San Francisco and New York). If your company does business in an area with a high cost of living, there is more likely to be a living wage law.

Many of these laws cover only companies that have contracts with, or receive subsidies from, the state or county, but some apply more broadly to private employers in the area. Check city or county ordinances (or consult a local attorney) for information about local living wage laws.

Minimum Wage for Younger Workers

Under federal law, younger workers—workers under the age of 20—may be paid a lower minimum wage for a few months. These workers are entitled to at least $4.25 an hour during their first 90 days of employment. (Note that these are calendar days—including weekends and holidays—not days that the employee actually works.) Workers who reach their twentieth birthday are entitled to the standard minimum wage, even if they have not yet put in 90 days at your company.

Some states don't allow a youth minimum wage. In these states, younger workers are entitled to the same minimum wage as anyone else.

Employees Who Receive Other Types of Compensation

Under federal law and the laws of some states, companies may be allowed to pay less than the minimum wage to employees who receive other types of compensation. For example, if your company provides room and board to employees, the company can deduct money from their paychecks as reimbursement—even if they'll end up with less than the minimum wage for that pay period—as long as the employee agrees to this arrangement in writing. See "Garnishments," below, for more information.

Some employers are also entitled to a "tip credit" under federal law. A company has to pay only $2.13 an hour to employees who make at least $30 per month in tips. However, if the employee's wage plus actual earned tips does not add up to the minimum wage for each pay period, the employer must pay the difference. And some states—including California—do not allow employers to take a tip credit. California employers must pay tipped employees the minimum wage, regardless of how generous their customers are.

Overtime

Federal and state laws require most employers to pay overtime. The overtime premium is 50% of the employee's usual hourly wage. This means an employee who works overtime must be paid "time and a half"—the employee's usual hourly wage plus the 50% overtime premium—for every overtime hour worked.

These laws contain many exceptions, so not all employees are entitled to overtime. Employees who are eligible for overtime are called "nonexempt" employees, and those who are not eligible for overtime are called "exempt" employees. The laws are a bit confusing—and misclassifying employees can be a very costly mistake if your company faces a lawsuit or a government audit. Because this is an area

where a lot of managers get in trouble, it's worth taking some time to learn the rules.

Weekly Versus Daily Standard

Federal law and the laws of most states impose a weekly overtime standard, which means that nonexempt employees are entitled to overtime for every hour more than 40 that they work in a week, regardless of how many hours they work in a day. For example, Alex is a nonexempt employee who works 12 hours on Monday and six hours on Tuesday (and doesn't work any more hours in the week). He is not entitled to receive overtime under the weekly overtime standard, even though he worked more than eight hours on Monday.

California and a handful of other states have a daily overtime standard, which means that nonexempt employees are entitled to overtime for every hour more than eight that they work in a day and every hour more than 40 that they work in a week. Let's take Alex from the paragraph above. In a daily overtime state, he would be entitled to overtime pay for the four extra hours he worked on Monday, even though he didn't even come close to working 40 hours in the week.

Which Employees Are Entitled to Overtime

If a business is covered by either the FLSA or a state overtime law, then all of its employees are entitled to overtime unless they are exempt—that is, unless they fit into an exception to the overtime rules.

Probably the most common—and confusing—exceptions to the overtime laws are for so-called "white collar" workers. Employees who the law defines as "administrative, executive, or professional" need not be paid overtime. To be considered such, employees must be paid on a salary basis and must spend most of their time performing job duties that require the use of discretion and independent judgment.

An employee who is paid on a salary basis must earn at least $455 per week and must receive the same salary every week, regardless of how many hours the employee works or the quantity or quality of the work the employee does. There are a few circumstances in which a salaried worker may be paid less than his or her full salary for a week—for example, if the employee takes unpaid time off under the Family and Medical Leave Act. Generally, however, if an employer docks an employee's pay (for not meeting a sales target, for example), then the employee is not paid on a salary basis and is entitled to overtime. (For more information, see "Pay Docking and Unpaid Suspensions," below.)

Not every employee who earns $455 or more per week is exempt from overtime. The employee must also be performing certain types of work—generally, work that requires an advanced degree, is managerial or supervisory in nature, or requires the employee to make relatively high-level business decisions. Here are the basic requirements for the administrative, executive, and professional exemptions:

- An administrative employee must perform office or other nonmanual work that is directly related to the management or business operations of the employer or its customers and must exercise discretion and independent judgment regarding significant issues.

- An executive employee's primary duty must be managing the employer's enterprise or a recognized division or department of that enterprise; the employee must regularly supervise at least two full-time employees (or the equivalent) and must have the authority to hire and fire or have significant input into hiring and firing decisions.

- A professional employee's primary duty must either be performing work that requires advanced knowledge in the field of science or learning, of a type that is usually attained through an advanced course of study; or performing work that requires invention, imagination, originality, or talent in a recognized creative or artistic field.

Classification Rules for White Collar Employees

Administrative Employee

Does employee earn at least $455 per week on a salary basis? — **No**

↓ **Yes**

Is employee's main duty office or other nonmanual work that directly relates to the management or general business operations of the company or its customers? — **No**

↓ **Yes**

Does the employee's primary duty include exercising discretion and independent judgment on significant matters? — **No**

↓ **Yes**

Exempt   **Not exempt**

Executive Employee

Does employee earn at least $455 per week on a salary basis? — **No**

↓ **Yes**

Is employee's primary duty to manage the company or a recognized subdivision or department within the company? — **No**

↓ **Yes**

Does employee regularly supervise at least two full-time employees? — **No**

↓ **Yes**

Does employee have authority to hire or fire or have significant input into hiring, firing, and other personnel decisions? — **No**

↓ **Yes**

Exempt   **Not exempt**

Classification Rules for White Collar Employees (continued)

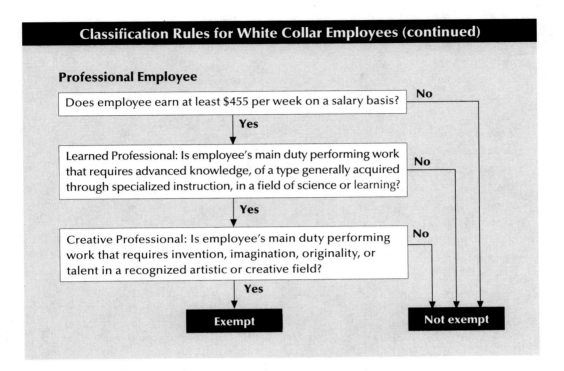

Professional Employee

Does employee earn at least $455 per week on a salary basis?

Yes → **No** →

Learned Professional: Is employee's main duty performing work that requires advanced knowledge, of a type generally acquired through specialized instruction, in a field of science or learning?

Yes → **No** →

Creative Professional: Is employee's main duty performing work that requires invention, imagination, originality, or talent in a recognized artistic or creative field?

Yes → **No** →

Exempt

Not exempt

Lessons From the Real World

Rose Bell and her coworkers worked as insurance adjusters for Farmers Insurance Exchange. All day long, for an average of 50 hours a week, they adjusted insurance claims—inspecting damaged property and cars and calculating how much Farmers would (or would not) pay to its customers to cover their losses.

Farmers didn't pay its adjusters any overtime. Instead, it classified them as exempt administrative workers, claiming that they routinely exercised independent judgment and discretion in doing their jobs. When Bell brought a class action lawsuit against Farmers, however, the judge did not agree.

The judge found that the adjusters did not fall under the administrative exemption because they did not perform specialized work related to the company's business policies. Instead, they were "production workers"— workers whose primary duty is to perform the very service or create the very product that the employer is in business to provide. Farmers Insurance Exchange existed, as a corporate entity, to adjust insurance claims. The claims adjusters' job was to adjust these claims. They did not administer Farmers' business affairs, set company policy, or perform management-related tasks. In other words, they were not exempt administrative employees.

A jury ordered Farmers to pay a whopping $90 million to the class of claims adjusters for their unpaid overtime hours—and this figure doesn't include what Farmers will have to pay in interest, attorney fees (for itself and for the class of employees), and court costs.

Bell v. Farmers Insurance Exchange, 87 Cal.App.4th 805 (2001); Lisa Girion, "Massive Award in Overtime Lawsuit," *Los Angeles Times* (July 11, 2001).

Compensatory Time Might Not Be Legal

Some companies adopt a policy of giving their employees compensatory, or "comp," time—an hour off at some later date for every extra hour worked—instead of paying them overtime. But, as many managers are surprised to learn, these policies are generally illegal under federal law, at least for private employers (state and local governments can offer comp time, in certain circumstances). The reason? They preclude employees from collecting an overtime premium—the extra pay to which they are entitled for working more than a set number of hours. (The overtime premium is 50% of the employee's usual hourly wage, so an employee who works overtime must be paid "time and a half," or the employee's usual hourly wage plus the 50% overtime premium, for every overtime hour worked.)

All of this means that if you wish to give your employees time off instead of money for extra hours worked, you cannot simply establish an hour-for-hour policy (that is, telling the employee to take an hour off for every hour of overtime worked). You may be able to handle this by adjusting an employee's hours during a pay period so that the amount of the employee's paycheck takes into account the overtime premium, yet remains constant. To make the math come out right, the employee must take an hour and a half off for every extra hour worked.

For example, if an employee who generally earns $1,600 every two weeks (or $20 an hour) works an extra 10 hours during the first week of the pay period, the employee is entitled to $300 in overtime pay—10 hours multiplied by one-and-a-half times the employee's hourly rate, or $30. If the employee took 15 hours off in the second week of the pay period, however, his or her paycheck would remain the same: The employee would receive $300 in overtime pay, but would be docked $300 (15 hours multiplied by $20 an hour) for the time not worked.

Travel Time

Employees who are paid by the hour and/or are entitled to overtime pay also have the right to be paid for some hours they spend traveling for work. If your reports routinely travel as part of their jobs or go on business trips that take them out of the area, you'll need to be able to figure out whether (and how much) they are entitled to be paid for this time.

Although employees are not entitled to pay for time spent commuting to and from work, they must be paid for travel time that is part of the job. If, for example, employees are required to go out on service calls, the time spent traveling to and from the customers must be paid. Also, if employees are required to take employer-provided transportation from a central location to the worksite, they may have to be paid for this time.

Even if an employee's job does not ordinarily involve travel, an employee who is required to come to the workplace at odd hours to deal with emergency situations may be entitled to pay. For example, if a mechanic works a regular 9-to-5 schedule but is sometimes called in during the night shift to repair equipment that has broken down, the mechanic is entitled to be paid for those extra hours.

Special rules apply to employees who occasionally travel to another location for business. The rules depend on whether the trip includes an overnight stay.

One-Day Trips

If you send an employee on a one-day business trip, the employee is entitled to pay for hours spent in transit. For example, if an employee has to drive two hours each way to get to an out-of-town business meeting, the company must pay for the four hours of total travel time. However, if the employee goes straight from home to the meeting, the company can deduct the time it would otherwise have taken the employee to commute to work.

Pay for Travel Time: One-Day Trip

Time spent traveling	_____
Minus usual commute time	– _____
Equals compensable travel time	= _____

EXAMPLE: It usually takes Polly about ½ hour each way to commute to the office. You send her to a business meeting in a city that's two hours away. Polly doesn't come into the office at all that day but instead drives from her home straight to the meeting and straight home again afterwards. She is entitled to three hours of paid travel time in addition to the time she spends working:

	4 hours travel time
-	1 hour usual commute time
=	3 hours compensable travel time

Overnight Trips

When an employee spends more than a day out of town, the rules are different. Of course, the employee must be paid for all of the time he or she spends actually working. However, whether the employee is entitled to pay for time spent in transit depends on when the travel takes place. Employees are entitled to pay for time spent traveling only during the hours when they regularly work (the period of the day they regularly work). However, they are entitled to be paid for weekend travel that takes place during these hours, even if they ordinarily work Monday through Friday.

Pay for Travel Time: Overnight Trip

Time spent traveling	_____
Minus travel time outside usual work hours	– _____
Equals compensable travel time	= _____

EXAMPLE: You send Polly to attend a three-day business conference out of town. Her usual schedule is 9 a.m. to 5 p.m., Monday through Friday. She leaves her home to head for the airport at 5 a.m. Wednesday morning and arrives at the conference in time for the 9 a.m. orientation. Because the conference ends late on Friday, she returns home Saturday morning, catching an 8 a.m. flight and pulling into her driveway at home by noon. Of course, Polly is entitled to pay for all of the hours she actually spends at the conference, even if it goes beyond her regularly scheduled hours. In addition, she is entitled to three hours of travel time.

```
    8 hours travel time
    5 hours of travel outside usual
-   work hours
_____
=  3 hours compensable travel time
```

On-Call Time

Under federal law, employees are entitled to be paid for time that their employer controls and that benefits their employer. Generally, this includes time that the employee cannot spend as he or she wishes, even if that time is not spent working. For example, an employee who has to cover the phones while eating lunch is entitled to be paid for that time, even if the phones aren't ringing.

If employees are required to stay on company premises or at a customer's location while waiting for a work assignment, they are entitled to be paid even if they do not spend that time actually working. For example, a mechanic who knits a sweater while waiting for a customer to arrive, a corporate trainer who must wait for the client to gather employees and set up equipment, or a secretary who does a crossword puzzle while waiting for an assignment is entitled to be paid for that time.

If employees must be on-call elsewhere, they are entitled to be paid for those hours over which they have little or no control and which they cannot use for their own enjoyment or benefit. If you place significant restrictions on an employee who is on call, that employee should be paid. There are few hard-and-fast rules in this area—but, generally, the more constraints on an employee, the more likely he or she should be paid.

Here are some factors a court or agency might consider when deciding this issue:

- **How many calls an employee gets while on call.** The more calls an employee has to respond to, the more likely he or she is entitled to pay, particularly if any of the calls require the employee to report to work or give immediate advice or guidance over the phone.
- **How long an employee has to respond after a call.** If employees are required to report in immediately after being paged, for example, they have a better argument that they should be paid for their time.

Lessons From the Real World

Shelly Reimer was a nurse at Dakota Heartland Health Systems. She and her coworkers were required to spend some time "on call." They did not have to be at the workplace during this time, but they had to be reachable by cell phone, beeper, or regular phone; had to be able to report to the hospital within 20 minutes of getting called; and had to refrain from drinking alcohol or using "mind-altering" drugs or medications while on call. Dakota Heartland paid the nurses less than the minimum wage for time spent on call.

Reimer and her coworkers sued, arguing that they were entitled to regular pay for the time they spent on call. But the court disagreed. Finding that the restrictions placed on nurses were minimal, the court noted that they "could play sports, work at home, go shopping, or visit friends and neighbors" while on call. The court also found that nurses typically were not called in more than once per shift and that once a nurse was called in to work, she was paid at her regular rate. Because nurses were free to engage in a variety of activities, and because they were called in relatively rarely, the court found that their time was not spent for the benefit of Dakota Heartland and did not have to be compensated at regular rates. *Reimer v. Dakota Heartland Health Systems*, Case No. 00-2413 (8th Cir. July 16, 2001).

- **Where an employee can go while on call.** Employees who must stay within a limited distance of work are more likely to be entitled to compensation.
- **What employees can do while on call.** The more rules imposed on on-call workers, such as a ban on alcohol or a requirement that they respond quickly and in person to calls (which can be difficult if the employee is out running or taking the kids to school), the more likely it is that they are entitled to pay for this time.

Flexible Work Schedules

As we all know, it can sometimes seem impossible to work full time during business hours and simultaneously meet our family and other personal obligations—whether they be caring for a child, helping an elderly parent, or taking care of our own health needs. More and more companies are starting to respond to their workers' needs for flexibility by allowing employees to work flexible schedules or what is often referred to as "flextime."

Helping employees to meet their family or personal needs can pay off for the company as well. Allowing employees to work flexible schedules can reduce distractions on the job and increase worker productivity, loyalty, and job satisfaction, which in turn reduces turnover and related costs. This section describes flextime and its legality; for more on other types of personnel policies that can help employees balance work and family, see "Family-Friendly Workplace Policies" in Chapter 4.

Flextime Defined

Generally speaking, an employee who works on a flexible schedule still works full time but simply does his or her work during what may not be considered normal business hours. This means that instead of working 9:00 a.m. to 5:00 p.m., an employee may, for example, work 7:00 a.m. to 3:00 p.m. to be home to provide care for his or her children after school, work 11:00 a.m. to 7:00 p.m. in order to take an elderly parent to morning physical therapy, or work 8:00 a.m. to 6:00 p.m. four days a week to have a full day off to care for his or her infant. (Other types of work arrangements such as working part time or job sharing are discussed in "Family-Friendly Workplace Policies" in Chapter 4.)

Flextime is not the same thing as compensatory or "comp" time: In comp time, an employee works overtime—beyond his or her regular work hours—in order to earn additional time off—a practice which may raise legal questions. (See "Compensatory Time Might Not Be Legal," above.) Flextime, on the other hand, is a policy whereby your company allows its workers to work a regular eight-hour day or forty-hour week, just not requiring the work to be done during normal business hours.

Is Flextime Legal?

On the whole, flextime is perfectly legal, with two caveats. First, if any employee wants to work more than eight hours in one day, your company must be careful to follow any state overtime laws that apply. Under federal law, an employee who works no more than 40 hours in a week, regardless of how many hours he or she works per day, has not worked overtime and is not entitled to overtime pay. So, for example, an employee who works four 10-hour days and then has three days off need not be paid overtime. However, some states have laws that provide a daily overtime standard—meaning that workers are entitled to overtime if they work more than a set number of hours in a day, even if they ultimately work fewer than 40 hours in a week.

So, if you allow a worker to work more than the set number of hours per day, you might have to pay overtime unless the law explicitly allows you and your employees to agree on an alternative workweek. California, Colorado, and Connecticut are among the states that have a daily overtime standard. To find out the rules in your state, including whether you and your employees can arrange an alternative workweek schedule, contact your state labor department. (See the appendix for contact information.)

Second, as with any employment benefit your company may establish, you cannot discriminate unlawfully based on race, gender, religion, age, disability, or any other protected characteristic in how you administer the benefit. This does not mean that you must let all workers work a flexible schedule if you let any worker do so; it just means that you cannot decide who has access to the benefit based on some impermissible characteristic. Obviously, certain jobs are more suited to working a flexible schedule. For example, jobs that do not need to be done during business hours or that do not require the worker to be present when other employees are present—such as editing books or accounting—may allow a flexible schedule, whereas jobs that must be done while the business is open—such as reception or computer support for employees—may not. Also, if appropriate flextime may be used as a reasonable accommodation for an employee with a disability. (See "Disability," in chapter 3, for more reasonable accommodations.)

If your company chooses to institute flexible work schedules, however, you could hear some grumbling from those not allowed to work flexible hours. To reduce the chances of this happening, you will want to establish clear, consistent policies that can be administered fairly and will not inspire employees to cry foul—or discrimination. For more on establishing personnel policies in general, see Chapter 4. For more information on instituting flexible work schedules, contact any of the number of organizations that work on such issues, including research organizations like the Families and Work Institute (www.familiesandwork.org), and

consulting groups such as Catalyst (www.catalyst.org) and Winning Workplaces (www.winningworkplaces.com).

Pay Docking and Unpaid Suspensions

Some managers discipline employees by docking their pay or putting them on unpaid suspension for violating workplace rules. However, this type of policy can create big problems if the employee whose pay is reduced is exempt from overtime—that is, the employee is not entitled to overtime pay because he or she is paid on a salary basis and generally has to exercise a certain degree of responsibility and discretion in doing the job.

What's Wrong With Docking Pay?

To qualify as exempt, employees have to be paid a set amount each pay period, without any reductions based on the quantity or quality of work they do. If you dock their pay, you may inadvertently make them nonexempt employees and thereby entitle them to overtime. As you might guess, the money saved by docking the employee's salary could be far exceeded by the money the company could have to pay out in overtime.

Under federal law, exempt employees—those who are not entitled to overtime—must earn at least $455 per week (or $23,660 per year). To be exempt, employees must be paid on a salary basis. (For more information see "Overtime Pay," below.) This means that all or some of the employee's salary is a fixed amount that doesn't depend on how many hours they work, how much work they accomplish, or the quality of their work. As long as employees do some work during the week, they are entitled to their full weekly pay, unless the time they take off falls into one of the exceptions described below.

Permissible Salary Deductions

Employers may make salary deductions (without jeopardizing the employee's exempt status) for one or more full days an employee takes off for the following reasons:

- to handle personal affairs
- to go on unpaid family or medical leave under the Family and Medical Leave Act (see Chapter 5 for information on this law)
- for disability or illness, if the employer has a plan (such as disability insurance or sick leave) that compensates employees for this time off
- to serve on a jury, as a witness, or on temporary military leave, but the employer may deduct only any amount that the employee receives as jury or witness fees or as military pay
- during the employee's first or last week of work, if the employee does not work a full week
- as a penalty imposed in good faith for infractions of safety rules of major significance (rules that prevent

serious danger in the workplace or to other employees), or

- to serve an unpaid disciplinary suspension imposed in good faith for infractions of workplace conduct rules, but only if the employer has a written policy regarding such suspensions that applies to all employees.

Penalties for Improper Deductions

A company that makes improper deductions from a salaried employee's pay can get into big trouble. However, the law contains a "safe harbor" provision, which offers some protection if you make improper deductions inadvertently.

Actual Practice of Improper Deductions

A company will be penalized if it has an "actual practice" of making improper deductions. Among the factors a court or government agency will consider when making this determination are:

- the number of improper deductions
- the time period during which the deductions were made
- how many employees were subjected to improper salary deductions and where those employees worked
- how many managers were responsible for taking improper deductions and where those managers worked, and
- whether the company has a clearly communicated policy that either

permits or prohibits improper deductions.

A company that has an actual practice of making improper deductions will lose the overtime exemption for all employees who work in the job classification(s) for which the deductions were made and who work for the same managers responsible for making the deductions. In other words, if you make improper deductions, your company will have to pay overtime (if earned by the employees) to everyone who reports to you and holds the same position as the employee whose pay you docked.

Safe Harbor Protections

A company will not be subject to the penalties noted above if:

- any improper deductions were either isolated or inadvertent, and the company reimburses the employees for the money improperly withheld, or
- the company has a clearly communicated policy prohibiting improper deductions (including a complaint procedure), reimburses employees for the money improperly withheld, and makes a good faith effort to comply with the law in the future.

Garnishments

A company may be legally obligated to deduct money from a worker's paycheck to satisfy certain debts—for example child support or tax debts. In addition, you might be allowed to deduct money to satisfy the worker's debt to the company— for a cash advance, for example. However, except in very limited circumstances, an employer is not allowed to withhold so much money that a worker's pay falls below the required minimum wage.

Wage Garnishment, Child Support Orders, and Tax Debts

If you receive a court order or notice from a government agency requiring you to withhold money from a worker's paycheck, simply follow the instructions in the documents. Generally, an employer may be required to deduct money from a worker's paycheck in three situations:

- **Wage garnishments.** A court might order your company to withhold money to satisfy certain debts, including student loan debts, alimony or spousal support, or money owed to someone who won a lawsuit against the worker. This type of order is called a wage "attachment" or "garnishment." The paperwork you receive from the court will generally tell you how much to deduct and where to send the money—although you might first have to tell the court how much the worker earns.
- **Child support orders.** When a judge orders a parent to pay child support, the judge will automatically issue a wage withholding order. This order

requires the employer to deduct the amount owed each month from the worker's paycheck, then send that money to the parent who has custody of the child.

- **Wage levy notices.** The Internal Revenue Service (IRS) has the right to take some portion of a worker's wages to satisfy his or her unpaid tax debt. In these situations, the employer will receive a wage levy notice from the IRS indicating the amount to be deducted (and sent to the government). Generally, state tax agencies have the same right.

Federal law prohibits employers from firing workers because their wages have been garnished to pay any one debt, no matter how many separate orders or lawsuits have been filed to collect that debt. However, a worker whose wages are garnished to pay off more than one debt can be terminated, under federal law. Some states don't allow termination of workers because their wages have been garnished for more than one debt, however. For information on state rules, see "State Laws on Wage Garnishments," at the end of this chapter.

Federal law limits how much can be deducted from a worker's paycheck for wage garnishments and child support orders. Generally, for wage garnishments an employer may deduct either 25% of the worker's actual earnings per pay period (after tax and required state and federal deductions) or the amount by which the worker's actual earnings exceed 30 times the minimum hourly wage, whichever is less. For child support or alimony orders, up to one-half of the worker's actual earnings may be taken if the worker is actually supporting a spouse or dependent child (other than the person for whom the money is being taken) and up to 60% if the worker is not. More may be taken from workers who are well behind in their support payments.

Wage garnishments can be tricky. If you have any questions about a wage garnishment or other withholding order, contact the authority that sent the order (for example, the IRS or a particular court). You might also consider asking a lawyer for advice.

Deductions to Pay a Debt to the Employer

If an employee owes the company money—for a salary advance, for example—the company is entitled (under federal law) to withhold money from the employee's paycheck to pay itself back. However, you cannot deduct so much that the employee's earnings for that pay period drop below the minimum wage. If an employee owes a substantial debt, the employer can avoid running afoul of this rule by deducting money in installments.

Some states prohibit employers from deducting money from their workers' paychecks or limit the circumstances under which they can do so. For more information on your state's law, contact your state labor department.

Deductions for Food and Lodging

Employers are allowed to deduct the reasonable cost of meals and housing provided to workers, even if the worker's pay, after these costs are deducted, falls below the minimum wage. However, these deductions are allowed only if *all* of the following are true:

- the company regularly provides room and board for workers
- the items were provided for the benefit of the employee
- the employee was told, before the arrangement began, that the company planned to take the deductions, and
- the employee voluntarily agreed, in writing, to accept less than the minimum wage in exchange for the food and lodging provided.

Some states place additional limits on deductions for food and lodging—for example, California allows employers to deduct only a specified amount for each meal provided. To learn more about your state's law, contact your state labor department

Other Deductions

Generally, an employer may not deduct money from its workers' paychecks to reimburse itself for other business expenses if doing so would cause the workers' pay to fall below the minimum wage. Examples of expenses subject to this rule include:

- uniforms
- tools used in the employee's work
- financial losses incurred in the ordinary course of business (for example, a shortfall in a cash register or a customer's failure to pay a bill)
- services the employee is required to purchase (such as a mandatory medical examination or a cleaning service), and
- damage to or theft of company property.

Some states, including California, prohibit employers from charging their workers for these types of business expenses—whether by wage withholding or any other method. Check with your state department of labor to find out what expenses (if any) can be charged back to workers.

Equal Pay

The Equal Pay Act (EPA), 29 U.S.C. § 206(d), prohibits employers from paying employees of one sex at a lower rate than employees of the opposite sex for doing equal work. The law was intended to combat what the Supreme Court called the "ancient but outmoded belief that a man, because of his role in society, should be paid more than a woman." *Corning Glass Works v. Brennan,* 417 U.S. 188, 195 (1974). Despite this gender-specific intent, however, the EPA protects both men and women from wage discrimination based on sex. (This section covers equal pay only. For more on gender discrimination, see "Gender" in Chapter 3.)

What Is Equal Work?

Male and female employees are entitled to equal pay even if their jobs are not absolutely identical. The law requires only that their jobs be "substantially" equal for the equal pay requirement to kick in. That is, the jobs must require equal skill, effort, and responsibility, and they must be performed under similar working conditions.

Job titles do not determine whether two jobs are substantially equal. For example, you may not offer to pay a male "administrative assistant" more than a female "secretary" if both do essentially the same tasks. Similarly, jobs that have the same official name may require different degrees of responsibility or effort, allowing men and women holding those jobs to be paid at different rates. For example, one court allowed a college to pay the male coach of its men's basketball team more than the female coach of its women's basketball team. The court decided that coaching the men's team carried with it more responsibilities, because the men's team had to bring in higher revenues.

What Is Equal Pay?

The EPA doesn't just apply to wages. It also applies to benefits, such as insurance coverage, pensions, and use of a company car, and other forms of compensation, like vacation time, profit sharing, and bonuses. In other words, you must also provide equal fringe benefits to workers of both sexes.

Managers can get into trouble here: If you make certain benefits or perks available to only some of your reports, you must make sure that those benefits are not being doled out along gender lines. If men and women doing the same work don't receive the same benefits, that could be an EPA violation; even if they aren't doing equal work, providing benefits based on an employee's gender could constitute sex discrimination.

However, this doesn't mean that men and women must receive identical paychecks. The EPA requires workers to be paid at the same rate, not the same amount. If workers are paid on commission or by the piece, for example, they must be paid according to the same formula (for example, 10% of the company's gross profit on each sale or $1 per piece). But it's okay if one worker earns more than another because he or she was more productive—for instance, because the worker made more sales or turned out more work in a given pay period than other workers doing the same job.

Financial incentives for good performance work the same way. You can't offer only salesmen the opportunity to earn a bonus for high sales volume while denying the same opportunity to saleswomen. But if you offer the bonus to your entire sales team and only men make enough sales to qualify, it's legal to pay the bonus only to those men.

Exceptions to the EPA

There are four exceptions to the EPA. Workers of one sex may be paid more for doing equal work if the **difference** is based on one of the four following factors:

- **Seniority.** Workers who have been with the company for a long time may be paid more than workers with shorter tenure, even if this results in workers of one sex making more than workers of the other.
- **Merit.** For example, if you give performance-based raises, you may give a higher raise to workers whose performance is better, regardless of gender.
- **Quantity or quality of production.** An employer may pay by the piece, for example, or pay higher rates for better quality work, as long as both men and women have the opportunity to earn this higher rate.
- **Any factor other than sex.** This "catchall" exception is intended to encompass the myriad reasons why one worker might be paid more than another—as long as they are unrelated to the worker's gender. For example, if you must pay a shift premium to entice workers to cover the night shift, that would not violate the EPA. Nor would offering a worker a higher starting rate based on his or her salary at a previous job.

For a discussion of gender discrimination as a whole, beyond the issue of equal pay, see "Gender, Pregnancy, and Sexual Harassment," in Chapter 3.

Record Keeping Requirements

Under the Fair Labor Standards Act, employers must keep records on wages, hours, deductions, and pay dates for all of their employees. These records must be kept for three years, even after a worker leaves the company.

Although employers must create administrative systems that properly preserve these records, the good news is that you are not required to keep them in any particular form, use a time clock, or require workers to fill in time cards.

What Records Must Be Kept?

Generally, an employer must keep records showing all of the following for each employee:

- name, address, occupation, sex, and birth date (only if the worker is under the age of 19)
- hour and day when the workweek begins
- total hours worked in each workday and workweek
- total daily or weekly regular earnings
- the worker's regular hourly pay rate in any week when the worker works overtime

- total overtime pay for each workweek
- any deductions from or additions to pay for each pay period
- total wages paid each pay period, and
- date of the payment and the pay period covered for each payment.

Employers may be required to keep additional information for certain workers, including employees who work at home, employees who receive tips, employees who live at the worksite, or employees who earn the youth minimum wage.

State law may require employers to keep additional records. To find out, contact your state labor department. (Contact information is available in the appendix.)

Penalties for Failure to Keep Records

If an employer doesn't keep records as required, an individual employee or the U.S. Department of Labor could sue the company just for inadequate record keeping. However, these claims usually come up only in the context of a larger lawsuit—for failing to pay overtime or taking improper deductions from workers' paychecks, for example.

The real danger of failing to keep adequate records is that your company will be unable to prove that it complied with wage and hour laws if the government or an employee challenges its practices. For example, if the Department of Labor decides to audit your company, you won't have any proof that you are complying with the law. This might encourage the government to dig deeper into your company's employment practices, something you probably want to avoid.

In addition, if an employer is unlucky enough to wind up on the wrong end of an employee lawsuit, it won't have records to prove the employee was paid properly. And once workers offer some evidence that they worked any hours for which they were not paid, the burden shifts to the company to prove its workers wrong—or at least to show that they are overstating their unpaid hours. A company that hasn't kept records won't be able to meet this burden.

Legal Dos and Don'ts: Compensation

Do:

- Require approval for overtime. If your reports work overtime—even without your knowledge or permission—the company will have to pay them for it. Cut down on surprises by requiring employees to get your approval in advance. And discipline employee who continue to work unauthorized overtime.
- Conduct an annual job classification audit. Once a year, review the job titles, classifications, and actual responsibilities of the employees reporting to you. Make sure employees who are classified as exempt from wage and hour laws meet the legal requirements.
- Keep proper records. Companies must keep certain payroll records for three years. Failing to keep required records is not only against the law; it will also hinder your company's ability to defend itself if employees sue for unpaid wages.

Don't:

- **Give comp time.** It's illegal for private employers to use comp time, but some managers have an informal practice of allowing it anyway. Even if your employees would rather take comp time than be paid overtime, don't fall into this habit without getting the facts.
- **Pay more attention to job titles than job duties.** When it comes to eligibility for overtime and compliance with equal pay and other wage discrimination laws, job titles don't matter—it's what employees actually do on the job that determines your company's obligations.
- **Dock an exempt employee's pay.** Find another way to discipline exempt employees for poor performance or minor misconduct. If you reduce an exempt employee's salary for these reasons, you risk making that employee—and all other employees who work for you in the same job classification—eligible for overtime.

Test Your Knowledge

Questions

1. When setting pay for a position, you should build a spreadsheet to calculate the value of the job based on the average pay internally (at your company) and at similar jobs externally (at other companies). ☐ True ☐ False

2. You don't have to pay tipped employees a regular wage as long as they earn at least the minimum wage in tips. ☐ True ☐ False

3. Only employees who are paid by the hour are entitled to earn overtime. ☐ True ☐ False

4. An employee who is entitled to earn overtime must be paid for every hour spent traveling for business. ☐ True ☐ False

5. Employees who must stay at the worksite while waiting to be called for work are entitled to be paid for that time. ☐ True ☐ False

6. If my company allows one worker to work on a flexible schedule, it must allow all employees to do so. ☐ True ☐ False

7. You can never pay an exempt employee less than his or her full salary. ☐ True ☐ False

8. You do not have to honor a wage garnishment order unless the employee gives you permission to withhold the money from his or her paycheck. ☐ True ☐ False

9. All men and women who hold the same position must receive the same pay. ☐ True ☐ False

10. Once an employee quits or is fired, you can recycle that employee's pay records. ☐ True ☐ False

Answers

1. False. To set pay for a particular position, you should go through a multi-step process to determine your company's top line; what is reasonable and competitive given the specifics of the position, internal equity, and external market data; and the job candidate's bottom line. You should then negotiate a compensation package that, hopefully, falls between these top and bottom line numbers and is reasonable to the job candidate. Setting pay is as much an art as it is a science: While averages will give you guidelines for setting pay, do not use them as absolute.

2. False. Tipped employees must be paid at least $2.13 an hour under federal law—or more, if their tips combined with this wage don't add up to at least the minimum hourly wage. State laws often require employers to pay more—and some don't allow a tip credit at all.

3. False. The right to earn overtime is not determined by how the employee is paid, but by the employee's job duties. Some exempt employees are paid by the hour; some nonexempt employees earn a salary.

4. It depends on the length of the trip and when the travel takes place. An employee who takes a one-day trip is entitled to pay for all hours spent traveling, less the time it usually takes the employee to commute. An employee who takes a longer business trip is entitled to be paid only for travel that falls during the employee's regularly scheduled hours of work.

5. True. Employees who must be on-call at the worksite are entitled to be paid for that time.

6. False. Like any other employment benefit (for example, vacation accrual rates or year-end bonuses), you can allow only certain employees to work flexible schedules as long as you do not base who gets the benefit on an illegal reason, such as discrimination. Seniority, whether the job is suited to a flexible schedule, and accommodating a disabled worker, for example, are all legally valid reasons why you might allow one worker to work a flexible schedule but not another.

7. False. There are some circumstances when you can dock an exempt employee's salary—if the employee takes family and medical leave or violates an important safety rule, for example.

8. False. You must honor valid wage garnishment orders, no matter how the employee feels about it.

9. False. Men and women who hold the same position can receive different compensation if the differential is based on seniority, quantity or quality of work, merit, or any factor other than sex.

10. False. You must keep certain payroll records for three years after an employee leaves.

State Minimum Wage Laws for Tipped and Regular Employees

The chart below gives the basic state minimum wage laws. Depending on the occupation, the size of the employer's business, or the conditions of employment, the minimum wage may vary from the one listed here. Minimum wage rates in a number of states change from year to year; to be sure of your state's current minimum, contact your state department of labor or check its website, where most states have posted the minimum wage requirements. (See "Department of Labor" in the appendix, for contact information.) Also, some local governments have enacted ordinances that set a higher minimum wage—contact your city or county government for more information.

"Maximum Tip Credit" is the highest amount of tips that an employer can subtract from the employee's hourly wage. The employee's total wages minus the tip credit cannot be less than the state minimum wage. If an employee's tips exceed the maximum tip credit, the employee gets to keep the extra amount.

"Minimum Cash Wage" is the lowest hourly wage that an employer can pay a tipped employee.

State and Statute	Notes	Basic Minimum Hourly Rate (*=tied to federal rate)	Maximum Tip Credit	Minimum Cash Wage for Tipped Employee	Minimum Tips to Qualify as a Tipped Employee (monthly unless noted otherwise)
United States 29 U.S.C. § 206	This is the current federal minimum wage	$5.15	$3.02	$2.13	More than $30
Alabama	No minimum wage law				
Alaska Alaska Stat. § 23.10.065; Alaska Admin. Code Tit. 8, § 15.120		$7.15	No tip credit	$7.15	N/A
Arizona	No minimum wage law				
Arkansas Ark. Code Ann. §§ 11-4-210 to -213	Applies to employers with 4 or more employees	$5.15	50%	$2.575	Not specified
California Cal. Code Regs. tit. 8, § 11000		$6.75	No tip credit	$6.75	N/A
Colorado Colo. Rev. Stat. § 8-6-109; 7 Colo. Code Regs. § 1103-1	Minimum wage applies to these industries: retail and service, commercial support service, food and beverage, and health and medical	$5.15	$3.02	$2.13	More than $30

State Minimum Wage Laws for Tipped and Regular Employees (continued)

State and Statute	Notes	Basic Minimum Hourly Rate (*=tied to federal rate)	Maximum Tip Credit	Minimum Cash Wage for Tipped Employee	Minimum Tips to Qualify as a Tipped Employee (monthly unless noted otherwise)
Connecticut *Conn. Gen. Stat. Ann. § 31-58(j)*		$7.10 or 0.05% more than FLSA minimum, if it is higher	29.3% waiters; 8.2% bartenders; $0.35 others	$5.02 waiters; $6.52 bartenders; $6.75 others	Not specified
Delaware *Del. Code Ann. tit. 19, § 902(a)*		$6.15 or FLSA rate if higher	$3.92	$2.23	More than $30
District of Columbia *D.C. Code Ann. §§ 32-1003 to -1004*		$6.60 $7 starting 1/1/06	$4.33	$2.27	Not specified
Florida *Fla. Const., Art X*		$6.15 effective May 05	$3.02	$3.13	More than $30
Georgia *Ga. Code Ann. § 34-4-3*	Applies to employers with 6 or more employees and more than $40,000 per year in sales	$5.15	Minimum wage does not apply to tipped employees	N/A	N/A
Hawaii *Haw. Rev. Stat. §§ 387-1 to 387-2*		$6.25	$0.25	$6.00	More than $20; employee's cash wage plus tips must be at least $.50 higher than the minimum wage
Idaho *Idaho Code § 44-1502*		$5.15	35%	$3.35	More than $30
Illinois *820 Ill. Comp. Stat. § 105/4; Ill. Admin. Code tit. 56, § 210.110*	Applies to employers with 4 or more employees	$6.50 $6 for employees under 18	$2.60	$3.90 $3.60 if under 18	At least $20
Indiana *Ind. Code Ann. § 22-2-2-4*	Applies to employers with 2 or more employees	$5.15	$3.02	$2.13	Not specified

State Minimum Wage Laws for Tipped and Regular Employees (continued)

State and Statute	Notes	Basic Minimum Hourly Rate (*=tied to federal rate)	Maximum Tip Credit	Minimum Cash Wage for Tipped Employee	Minimum Tips to Qualify as a Tipped Employee (monthly unless noted otherwise)
Iowa Iowa Code § 91D.1	Minimum wage does not apply to first 90 calendar days of employment	$5.15*	40%	$3.09	At least $30
Kansas Kan. Stat. Ann. § 44-1203	Applies to employers not covered by the FLSA	$2.65	40%	$1.59	More than $20
Kentucky Ky. Rev. Stat. Ann. § 337.275		$5.15*	$3.02	$2.13	More than $30
Louisiana	No minimum wage law				
Maine Me. Rev. Stat. Ann. tit. 26, §§ 663(8), 664		$6.35 $6.50 starting 10/01/05	50%	$3.18 $3.25 starting 10/01/05	More than $20
Maryland Md. Code Ann., [Lab. & Empl.] §§ 3-413, 3-419		$5.15*	$2.77	$2.38	More than $30
Massachusetts Mass. Gen. Laws ch. 151, § 1; Mass. Regs. Code tit. 455, §§ 2.02 & following		$6.75, or $0.10 above FLSA rate if it is higher	$4.12	$2.63	More than $20
Michigan Mich. Comp. Laws §§ 408.382 to 408.387a	Applies to employers with 2 or more employees. Excludes all employers subject to the FLSA, unless state minimum wage is higher than federal	$5.15	$2.50	$2.65	Not specified
Minnesota Minn. Stat. Ann. § 177.24	$4.90 for small employer (business with annual receipts of less than $500,000)	$5.15	No tip credit	$5.15	N/A

State Minimum Wage Laws for Tipped and Regular Employees (continued)

State and Statute	Notes	Basic Minimum Hourly Rate (*=tied to federal rate)	Maximum Tip Credit	Minimum Cash Wage for Tipped Employee	Minimum Tips to Qualify as a Tipped Employee (monthly unless noted otherwise)
Mississippi	No minimum wage law				
Missouri Mo. Rev. Stat. §§ 290.502, 290.512	Doesn't apply to retail or service business with gross annual sales of less than $500,000	$5.15*	Up to 50%	$2.575	Not specified
Montana Mont. Code Ann. §§ 39-3-404, 39-3-409; Mont. Admin. R. 24.16.1508 & following	$4.00 for businesses with gross annual sales of $110,000 or less	$5.15*	No tip credit	$5.15*	N/A
Nebraska Neb. Rev. Stat. § 48-1203	Applies to employers with 4 or more employees	$5.15	$3.02	$2.13	Not specified
Nevada Nev. Rev. Stat. Ann. §§ 608.160, 608.250	Voters approved $1 increase in 2004; will require another vote in 2006 to go into effect	$5.15*	No tip credit	$5.15	N/A
New Hampshire N.H. Rev. Stat. Ann. § 279:21		$5.15*	$2.57	$2.38 or 45% of minimum wage, if higher	More than $20
New Jersey N.J. Stat. Ann. § 34:11-56a4; N.J. Admin. Code tit. 12, §§ 56-3.1 & following, 56-14.4		$5.15*	Depends on occupation	Depends on occupation	Not specified
New Mexico N.M. Stat. Ann. § 50-4-22		$5.15*	50% minimum wage	$2.575	More than $30
New York N.Y. Lab. Law § 652; N.Y. Comp. Codes R. & Regs. tit. 12, § 137-1.4		$6.00 $6.75 starting 1/1/06 $7.15 starting 1/1/07	Depends on occupation	Depends on occupation	Depends on occupation

State Minimum Wage Laws for Tipped and Regular Employees (continued)

State and Statute	Notes	Basic Minimum Hourly Rate (*=tied to federal rate)	Maximum Tip Credit	Minimum Cash Wage for Tipped Employee	Minimum Tips to Qualify as a Tipped Employee (monthly unless noted otherwise)
North Carolina N.C. Gen. Stat. §§ 95-25.2(14), 95-25.3		$5.15*	$3.02	$2.13	More than $20
North Dakota N.D. Cent. Code § 34-06-03; N.D. Admin. Code R. 46-02-07-201(17) to -03		$5.15	33%	$3.45	More than $30
Ohio Ohio Rev. Code Ann. § 4111.02	$3.35 for employers with gross annual sales of $150,000 to $500,000; $2.80 for employers with gross annual sales of less than $150,000	$5.15	50%	$3.075; $2.01 for employers with sales under $500,000	More than $30
Oklahoma Okla. Stat. Ann. tit. 40, §§ 197.2, 197.4, 197.16	Applies to employers with 10 or more full-time employees OR gross annual sales over $100,000; $2.00 for all other employers who are not subject to the FLSA	$5.15*	50% for tips, food, and lodging combined	$2.58	Not specified
Oregon Or. Rev. Stat. §§ 653.025, 653.035(3)	Adjusted annually for inflation; posted at www.boli.state.or.us	$7.25	No tip credit	$7.25	N/A
Pennsylvania 43 Pa. Cons. Stat. Ann. §§ 333.104 & following; 34 Pa. Code § 231.1		$5.15*	$2.32	$2.83	More than $30
Rhode Island R.I. Gen. Laws §§ 28-12-3 & following		$6.75	$3.86	$2.89	Not specified

State Minimum Wage Laws for Tipped and Regular Employees (continued)

State and Statute	Notes	Basic Minimum Hourly Rate (*=tied to federal rate)	Maximum Tip Credit	Minimum Cash Wage for Tipped Employee	Minimum Tips to Qualify as a Tipped Employee (monthly unless noted otherwise)
South Carolina	No minimum wage law				
South Dakota *S.D. Codified Laws Ann. §§ 60-11-3 to -3.1*		$5.15	$3.02	$2.13	More than $35
Tennessee	No minimum wage law				
Texas *Tex. Lab. Code Ann. §§ 62.051 & following*	Applies to employers not covered by the FLSA	$5.15*	$3.02	$2.13	More than $20
Utah *Utah Code Ann. §§ 34-40-102 to -103; Utah Admin. R. 610-1*	Applies to employers not covered by the FLSA	$5.15*	$3.02	$2.13	More than $30
Vermont *Vt. Stat. Ann. tit. 21, § 384(a); Vt. Code R. 24 090 001 & following*	Applies to employers with 2 or more employees	$7.00	$3.35 for employees of hotels, motels, restaurants, and tourist places; no tip credit otherwise	$3.65	More than $30
Virginia *Va. Code Ann. §§ 40.1-28.9(D) to 28.10*	Applies to employers with 4 or more employees	$5.15*	Tips actually received	Minimum wage less tips actually received	Not specified
Washington *Wash. Rev. Code Ann. § 49.46.020; Wash. Admin. Code 296-126-022*	Adjusted annually for inflation; posted at www.lni.wa.gov	$7.35	No tip credit	$7.35	N/A
West Virginia *W.Va. Code §§ 21-5C-2, 21-5C-4*	Applies to employers with 6 or more employees at one location who are not covered by the FLSA	$5.15	20%	$4.12	Not specified

State and Statute	Notes	Basic Minimum Hourly Rate (*=tied to federal rate)	Maximum Tip Credit	Minimum Cash Wage for Tipped Employee	Minimum Tips to Qualify as a Tipped Employee (monthly unless noted otherwise)
State Minimum Wage Laws for Tipped and Regular Employees (continued)					
Wisconsin Wis. Admin. Code DWD 272.03		$5.15	$2.42	$2.33	Not specified
Wyoming Wyo. Stat. § 27-4-202		$5.15	$3.02	$2.13	More than $30
					Current as of February 2005

State Laws on Wage Garnishments

Alabama

Ala. Code §§ 30-3-70 to 30-3-71

State law protects: Child support garnishments only.

Employer's fee: $2 per payment.

Employer penalties: Contempt of court.

Alaska

Alaska Stat. § 25.27.062

State law protects: Child support garnishments only.

Employer's fee: $5 per payment.

Employer penalties: Fine of up to $1,000 if employer discharges, disciplines, or refuses to hire someone because of having child support withholding orders.

Arizona

Ariz. Rev. Stat. §§ 23-722.02, 25-505.01

State law protects: Child support garnishments only.

Employee protections that exceed federal law: Newly hired, rehired, or returning employees may be asked to disclose any child support wage assignment orders but may not be discriminated against, fired, or disciplined because of having them.

Employer penalties: Employer who refuses to hire, discharges, or disciplines employee because of having child support withholding orders is subject to contempt of court and fines. Employer who fails without good cause to comply with income withholding order may be liable for amounts not paid, reasonable attorney fees, and costs, and may be subject to contempt of court. Employee wrongfully refused employment, wrongfully discharged, or otherwise disciplined is entitled to recovery of damages suffered, reinstatement if appropriate, plus attorney fees and costs.

Arkansas

Ark. Code Ann. §§ 9-14-226 to 9-14-240, 9-14-515

State law protects: Child support garnishments and child's health care coverage only.

Employer's fee: $2.50 per payment.

Employer penalties: Contempt of court; fine of up to $50 per day.

California

Cal. Fam. Code §§ 5235, 5241; Lab. Code § 2929(b)

Employee protections that exceed federal law: Employee may not be fired or discriminated against for being threatened with a wage garnishment.

Employer's fee: $1.50 per payment.

Employer penalties: Liable for any amount of child support payments not withheld or not forwarded plus interest; liable for contempt of court (applies to child support withholding).

Colorado

Colo. Rev. Stat. §§ 13-54.5-110; 14-14-111.5(4), (16.7); 14-14-112(4); 26-13-121.5

Employer's fee: Up to $5 per month for child support garnishments.

Employer penalties: Liable to discharged employee for up to 6 weeks' wages, reinstatement, court costs, and attorney fees (applies to general wage garnishments, child support, and child national medical support order and health insurance withholding).

Connecticut

Conn. Gen. Stat. Ann. §§ 52-361a(j), 52-362(j)

Employee protections that exceed federal law: Employee may not be disciplined, suspended, or discharged for having wages garnished unless there are more than 7 within a calendar year.

State Laws on Wage Garnishments (continued)

Employer penalties, general wage garnishment: Liable to employee for all wages and benefits from time of discipline or discharge to reinstatement.

Employer penalties, child support withholding: Fine of up to $1,000 for discharging, refusing to employ, disciplining, or discriminating against an employee because of a withholding order.

Delaware

Del. Code Ann. tit. 10, §§ 3509, 9584; tit. 13, § 513(b)(10)

Employee protections that exceed federal law: Employer may not dismiss employee because employer was summoned to appear in court in a garnishment proceeding.

Employer penalties, child support withholding: For failing to comply with law or terminating employee, fine of up to $1,000 or up to 90 days' imprisonment, or both, for first offense; for each subsequent offense, fine of up to $5,000 or up to 1 year's imprisonment, or both. For refusing to employ because of a support withholding order, fine of up to $200 for each offense. Corporations are subject to criminal charges.

District of Columbia

D.C. Code Ann. §§ 16-584, 46-212(d), 46-219

Employer's fee: $2 for each child support payment.

Employer penalties, child support withholding: Employer who discharges, refuses to employ, takes disciplinary action against, or otherwise discriminates against employee is subject to a fine of up to $10,000, which employee may use to offset support obligations. Any adverse action employer takes within 90 days of receiving notice to withhold wages is presumed to be in violation of law.

Florida

Fla. Stat. Ann. §§ 61.12(2), 61.1301(2)(e)

State law protects: Child support and alimony garnishments only.

Employee protections that exceed federal law: Employer may not fire, refuse to hire, or discipline employee who has wages garnished for alimony or child support.

Employer's fee: $5 for first deduction, $2 for each subsequent deduction.

Employer penalties: Fine of up to $250 for first violation and up to $500 for each subsequent violation; employer may also be held in contempt of court.

Georgia

Ga. Code Ann. §§ 18-4-7, 19-11-20

Employer's fee: $25 for first child support deduction, $3 for each subsequent deduction (no fee specified for general wage garnishments).

Hawaii

Haw. Rev. Stat. §§ 378-2(5), 378-32(1), 571-52(b), 576E-16(5), 710-1077

Employee protections that exceed federal law: Employer may not fire, suspend, or discriminate against employee for having wages garnished or because employer was summoned as a garnishee in an action or proceeding where the employee is the debtor. Employer who refuses to hire or discharges an employee who has wages garnished for child support is guilty of unlawful discrimination.

Employer's fee: $2 for each deduction.

Employer penalties, child support withholding: Employer who discriminates against employee is guilty of criminal contempt of court.

State Laws on Wage Garnishments (continued)

Idaho

Idaho Code §§ 28-45-105, 32-1210(7), 32-1211

Employer's fee: $5 for each deduction.

Employer penalties, child support withholding: For discriminating against or firing employee, liable for double lost wages and other damages; may be fined up to $300 and ordered to hire or reinstate employee.

Illinois

735 Ill. Comp. Stat. §§ 5/12-818, 5/12-814; 740 ILCS § 170/10; 750 ILCS §§ 28/35, 28/50

Employee protections that exceed federal law: May not discharge or suspend employee for any indebtedness or for one wage garnishment.

Employer's fee: $12 or 2% of entire amount withheld, whichever is greater, for general wage garnishment; $5 per month for child support.

Employer penalties, general wage garnishment: Discharging or suspending employee is a class A misdemeanor, which carries a fine of up to $2,500 and imprisonment for up to one year.

Employer penalties, child support withholding: Liable for amount of wages not withheld or paid; if employer discriminated against employee, may be fined up to $200 and ordered to hire or reinstate employee.

Indiana

Ind. Code Ann. §§ 24-4.5-5-105 to 24-4.5-5-106

Employee protections that exceed federal law: Employer may not discharge employee for having wages garnished (no limit on number of garnishments).

Employer's fee: $12 or 3% of entire amount withheld, whichever is greater, for general wage garnishment, 50% paid by employee and 50% by creditor; $2 per deduction for child support.

Iowa

Iowa Code § 252D.17

Employer's fee: $2 for each child support deduction.

Employer penalties, child support withholding: Employer who fails to withhold or remit payment or who discriminates against employee is guilty of a misdemeanor.

Kansas

Kan. Stat. Ann. §§ 23-4,108(e),(j), 60-2311

Employer's fee: $5 per pay period or $10 per month for income withheld for child support, whichever is less.

Employer penalties, child support withholding: For not withholding and remitting payments, liable for 3 times the amount owed plus attorney fees; for discriminating against employee, subject to a fine of up to $500.

Kentucky

Ky. Rev. Stat. Ann. §§ 405.465, 405.991, 427.140

Employer's fee: $1 per payment for child support withholding.

Employer penalties, child support withholding: Fine of up to $500 or up to 1 year in the county jail, or both.

Louisiana

La. Rev. Stat. Ann. §§ 13:3921(B), 23:731

Employee protections that exceed federal law: Employee may not be fired for a wage garnishment unless there are 3 or more garnishments for unrelated debts in a 2-year period. However, employee may not be fired if garnishment resulted from an accident or illness that caused employee to miss 10 or more consecutive workdays.

Employer's fee: $3 per pay period for as long as garnishment is in effect.

State Laws on Wage Garnishments (continued)

Employer penalties, child support withholding: Employer who willfully fails to pay or willfully penalizes an employee is liable for wages not withheld or paid.

Maine

Me. Rev. Stat. Ann. tit. 9-A, § 5-106; tit. 14, § 3127-B; tit. 19-A, §§ 2306, 2652, 2662

Employee protections that exceed federal law: Employee may not be fired for having wages garnished (number of garnishments not specified).

Employer's fee: $1 per check issued to creditor for general wage garnishment; $2 per week for child support withholding payment.

Employer penalties, child support withholding: For failing to withhold or remit payments, fine of up to $100. For discharging, refusing to hire, or disciplining employee, fine of up to $5,000; liable for actual and punitive damages plus attorneys' fees and court costs.

Maryland

Md. Code Ann. [Com. Law] § 15-606; [Fam. Law] § 10-129

Employer's fee: $2 per child support withholding order.

Employer penalties, child support withholding: Employer who fails to withhold or to remit payments is liable for amount of wages not withheld or paid.

Massachusetts

Mass. Gen. Laws ch. 119A, § 12(f)

State law protects: Child support garnishments only.

Employee protections that exceed federal law: Employer may not discipline, suspend, discharge, or refuse to hire an employee because of having child support withholding orders.

Employer's fee: $1 per pay period.

Employer penalties, child support withholding: For discriminating against employee, liable for lost wages and benefits plus a fine of up to $1,000; for failing to comply with a withholding order, liable for amount not withheld or fine of up to $500, whichever is greater.

Michigan

Mich. Comp. Laws §§ 552.623, 600.4012, 600.4015

Employee protections that exceed federal law: Employer may not refuse to hire an employee because of a wage garnishment. May not discriminate against, discipline, or discharge employee who has had an occupational, recreational, or driver's license suspended under child support laws, unless license is legally required for employee's job.

Employer's fee: $6 per writ of garnishment.

Employer penalties, general wage garnishment: Must reinstate employee and pay back all lost wages and benefits.

Employer penalties, child support withholding: Guilty of a misdemeanor punishable by a fine of up to $500; must reinstate employee with back pay.

Minnesota

Minn. Stat. Ann. §§ 518.6111(Subd.5), 571.927

Employee protections that exceed federal law: Employer shall not discharge or otherwise discipline an employee as a result of an earnings garnishment (no number specified).

Employer's fee: $1 for each child support payment.

Employer penalties, general wage garnishment: Liable to employee for double wages lost.

Employer penalties, child support withholding: For failure to withhold or remit funds, liable for amount not paid plus interest from the time

State Laws on Wage Garnishments (continued)

payments were due; for violating employee protection laws, liable for double lost wages and subject to a fine of no less than $500.

Mississippi

Miss. Code Ann. § 93-11-111

State law protects: Child support garnishments only.

Employer's fee: $2 per payment inside Mississippi. If support payments administered by state agency, additional $15 per month (which employer then pays to the agency). The state agency was supposed to expire on July 1, 2005, but pending legislation would extend it. Contact the agency to verify the current fee.

Missouri

Mo. Rev. Stat. §§ 452.350, 454.505(3),(10), 525.030

Employer's fee: 2% or $8, whichever is greater, for general wage garnishment; up to $6 per month per payment for child support withholding.

Employer penalties, child support withholding: For failing to withhold or remit payments, employer is liable for support not withheld; may be fined up to $500 for not complying with a court order to correct or stop unlawful action. For illegal discharge or discipline of employee, liable to fine of up to $150, order to reinstate employee, and payment of back wages, costs, and attorneys' fees, plus support which should have been withheld during time employee was wrongfully discharged. (Discharge within 30 days of receipt of support order is presumed wrongful.)

Montana

Mont. Code Ann. §§ 39-2-302, 40-5-416(c), 40-5-422

Employee protections that exceed federal law: Employee may not be discharged or laid off because of wage garnishment (number not specified).

Employer's fee: $5 per month for child support payments.

Employer penalties, child support withholding: Subject to a fine of $150 to $500; must reinstate employee with back pay.

Nebraska

Neb. Rev. Stat. §§ 25-1558, 42-364.01, 42-364.12, 43-1725

Employee protections that exceed federal law: Employer may not fire, demote, discipline, or penalize employee because of any proceeding to collect child support.

Employer's fee: $2.50 per month for child support payments.

Employer penalties, child support withholding: For failing to remit payments, liable for entire amount owed plus interest, costs, and attorneys' fees; for violating employee rights, liable for damages plus interest, costs, and attorneys' fees. If support payments administered by the state, liable for a fine of up to $500.

Nevada

Nev. Rev. Stat. Ann. §§ 31.296, 31.298, 31A.090, 31A.120

Employee protections that exceed federal law: It is unlawful to discharge or discipline an employee because employer required to withhold earnings because of a garnishment (no number specified).

Employer's fee: $3 per pay period up to $12 per month for general wage garnishments; $3 per child support payment withheld.

Employer penalties, general wage garnishment: For willfully refusing to withhold payments or misrepresenting employee's income, must pay entire amount not withheld; may be liable to

State Laws on Wage Garnishments (continued)

employee for punitive damages of up to $1,000 per pay period.

Employer penalties, child support withholding: For violating employee rights, employer must reinstate employee and is liable for any payments not withheld plus a $1,000 fine; if employee wins in court, employer liable for costs and attorney's fees up to $2,500. For willfully refusing to withhold payments or misrepresenting employee's income, must pay entire amount not withheld; may be liable to person to whom support owed for punitive damages of up to $1,000 per pay period.

New Hampshire

N.H. Rev. Stat. Ann. §§ 161-H:5, 458-B:6

State law protects: Child support and child's medical support garnishments only.

Employer's fee: $1 per support payment.

Employer penalties, child support withholding: For violating employee rights, guilty of a misdemeanor with a fine of up to $1,000; for failing to withhold payments, guilty of a class B misdemeanor with a fine of up to $1,200, plus $100 fee per pay period to agency administering payments.

New Jersey

N.J. Stat. Ann. §§ 2A:17-56.11, 2A:17-56.12, 2C:40A-3

Employee protections that exceed federal law: Employer may take no disciplinary action against employee because of wage garnishment (no number specified).

Employer's fee: $1 per garnishment.

Employer penalties, general wage garnishment: For violating employee rights, guilty of a disorderly person offense; must rehire and compensate employee for damages.

Employer penalties, child support withholding:

For violating employee rights, employer liable to a fine and civil damages and must reinstate employee; if employee wins in court, liable for court costs, attorneys' fees, and lost income. For failing to withhold child support payments, liable for a fine or for amount not withheld. For failing to withhold payments under a medical support order, liable for children's medical expenses and any other amount that should have been withheld.

New Mexico

N.M. Stat. Ann. §§ 40-4A-8, 40-4A-11

State law protects: Child support garnishments only.

Employer's fee: $1 per payment.

Employer penalties, child support withholding: Employer who willfully fails to pay, liable to a fine for total amount not withheld. For discharging or taking action against employee, liable for reinstatement and damages; subject to action for contempt of court.

New York

N.Y. C.P.L.R. Law §§ 5241, 5252

Employee protections that exceed federal law: Current employee may not be fired, laid off, refused promotion, or disciplined and prospective employee may not be refused employment because of one or more current, past, or pending garnishments.

Employer penalties, general wage garnishment: Liable to employee for reinstatement and up to 6 weeks' lost wages, plus fine of up to $500 for first offense and up to $1,000 for each additional offense. May also be liable for civil contempt of court.

Employer penalties, child support withholding: Liable to employee for reinstatement and up to 6 weeks' lost wages, plus fine of up to $500 for

State Laws on Wage Garnishments (continued)

first offense and up to $1,000 for each additional offense.

North Carolina

N.C. Gen. Stat. §§ 110-136(c),(e), 110-136.8 to 110-136.14, 131E-49, 131E-50

Employee protections that exceed federal law: Employee may not be discharged or disciplined for having wages garnished to pay a public hospital debt.

Employer's fee: $1 per child support payment; $1 per payment to public hospital.

Employer penalties, child support withholding: Liable to employee for reinstatement and reasonable damages. Liable for a fine of $100 for first offense; $500 for second; and $1,000 for third (also applies to child medical support orders).

North Dakota

N.D. Cent. Code §§ 14-09-08.11, 14-09-09.3, 14-09-09.6, 32-09.1-18

Employee protections that exceed federal law: Employee may not be discharged because of wage garnishment (no number specified).

Employer's fee: $3 per month for child support.

Employer penalties, general wage garnishment: May be sued for reinstatement plus double lost wages. Employer's failure to deliver payments for 7 business days may result in late fees of $25 to $75 per business day. After 14 business days, penalties are actual damages or $200, whichever is greater, plus costs, interest, late fees, and attorneys' fees.

Employer penalties, child support withholding: May be punished for contempt of court, may have to reinstate employee with back pay; liable for damages plus court costs and attorneys' fees.

Ohio

Ohio Rev. Code Ann. §§ 2716.041(C)(4)(e), 2716.05, 3121.18, 3123.20, 3123.99

Employee protections that exceed federal law: Employee may not be discharged because of wage garnishments by a single creditor in a 12-month period.

Employer's fee: $3 per pay period that earnings withheld for general wage garnishment; $2 per support order or 1% of amount withheld, whichever is greater, for child support.

Employer penalties, child support withholding: For discharging employee, subject to fine of $50 to $200, and 10 to 30 days in jail.

Oklahoma

Okla. Stat. Ann. tit. 12, §§ 1171.3, 1190; tit. 14A, § 5-106; tit. 56, § 240.2

Employee protections that exceed federal law: Employee may not be discharged unless there are more than 2 garnishments in one year.

Employer's fee: $5 per payment (up to $10/month) for child support; $10 for each general wage garnishment.

Employer penalties, child support withholding: For discharging or disciplining employee, liable for wages and benefits lost from time of discharge or discipline to time of reinstatement or promotion. For failing to withhold or remit payments, liable for amount not withheld, plus fine of up to $200 for each payment not made.

Oregon

Or. Rev. Stat. §§ 23.185(9), 25.414(6), 25.424, 659A.885

Employer's fee: $5 per month for child support withholding.

Employer penalties, child support withholding: Liable for a fine of $250 for each willful failure to pay. For discharging, refusing to hire, or

State Laws on Wage Garnishments (continued)

discriminating or retaliating against employee, may be liable for reinstatement, back pay, compensatory damages or $200 (whichever is greater), punitive damages, costs, and attorney fees.

Pennsylvania

23 Pa. Cons. Stat. Ann. § 4348(j),(k),(l)

State law protects: Child support garnishments only.

Employer's fee: 2% of amount withheld per support payment.

Employer penalties, child support withholding: For discriminating against employee, liable for damages and subject to a fine of up to $1,000. For failing to withhold payment, may be jailed and fined for contempt of court.

Rhode Island

R.I. Gen. Laws §§ 10-5-8, 15-5-24(i), 15-5-26

State law protects: Child support garnishments only.

Employer's fee: $5 per general garnishment order; $2 per child support payment.

Employer penalties, child support withholding: For dismissing, demoting, or penalizing employee, liable for damages, interest, court costs, and attorneys' fees, and must reinstate employee with back pay; subject to a fine of up to $100.

South Carolina

S.C. Code Ann. §§ 20-7-1315(F),(I), 37-5-106

Employee protections that exceed federal law: Employee may not be discharged because of wage garnishment (no number specified).

Employer's fee: $3 per child support payment.

Employer penalties, child support withholding: For violating employee rights, liable to a fine of up to $500.

South Dakota

S.D. Codified Laws Ann. §§ 21-18-9, 25-7A-46, 25-7A-59

State law protects: Child support and children's health garnishments only.

Employer's fee: $15 for preparing a garnishment disclosure.

Tennessee

Tenn. Code Ann. §§ 36-5-501(i),(l), 40-35-111(e)(3)

State law protects: Child and spousal support garnishments only.

Employee protections that exceed federal law: Employee whose wages are ordered withheld for spousal support (alimony) may not be fired or disciplined.

Employer's fee: Up to 5% of amount withheld (no more than $5/month) for child support and spousal orders.

Employer penalties, child support withholding: Failure to comply with law is a class C misdemeanor, which carries a fine of up to $50 or up to 30 days' imprisonment, or both.

Texas

Tex. Civ. Prac. & Rem. Code Ann. § 63.006; Fam. Code §§ 8.204 to 8.209, 158.204, 158.209, 158.210

Employee protections that exceed federal law: Employee may not be fired, disciplined, or refused employment because of wage withholding orders for spousal support.

Employer's fee: Actual cost or up to $10 per month, whichever is less, for general wage garnishments under state or federal law; $10 per month for child support payments; $5 per month for spousal support payments.

Employer penalties, child support withholding: For violating employee rights, employer must reinstate employee with full benefits and

State Laws on Wage Garnishments (continued)

seniority and is liable for wages plus court costs and attorney fees. For knowingly failing to withhold or remit child or spousal support payments, $200 for each instance.

Utah

Utah Code Ann. §§ 62A-11-316, 62A-11-406, 62A-11-410, 70C-7-104; Utah R. Civ. Proc. Rule 64D

Employer's fee: $10 per month for child support orders.

Employer penalties, child support withholding: Liable to employee for damages; liable to state child support enforcement agency for amount of garnishment plus interest, costs, and attorneys' fees or for $1,000, whichever is greater.

Vermont

Vt. Stat. Ann. tit. 12, § 3172; tit. 15, §§ 787, 790

Employee protections that exceed federal law: If employee is discharged within 60 days of a garnishment order, presumed to be in violation of law (Vermont uses term "trustee process").

Employer's fee: $5 per month for child support withholding.

Employer penalties, general wage garnishment: Liable to discharged employee for reinstatement, back wages, and damages; if employee wins in court, also liable for costs and reasonable attorneys' fees.

Employer penalties, child support withholding: Liable to discharged employee for reinstatement, back wages, and damages; if employee wins in court, also liable for costs and reasonable attorney fees. Employers failing to forward payments may be subject to penalties of $100 to $1,000.

Virginia

Va. Code Ann. §§ 8.01-512.2 to 8.01-512.3, 20-79.3(6),(9), 34-29(f), 63.1-271

Employee protections that exceed federal law: Employee who voluntarily assigns earnings to settle a support debt may not be discharged.

Employer's fee: $10 for each general wage garnishment summons; $5 per child support withholding payment.

Employer penalties, child support withholding: Fine of up to $1,000 for violating employee rights.

Washington

Wash. Rev. Code Ann. §§ 6.27.170, 26.18.110, 74.20A.080, 74.20A.230, 74.20A.240

Employee protections that exceed federal law: Employee may not be discharged unless there are garnishments for 3 or more separate debts within a 12-month period. Employee may not be fired, disciplined, or refused employment because of wage withholding orders for spousal support.

Employer's fee: $10 for first payment, $1 for each successive payment for child or spousal support withholding; $15 for first payment, $1 for each successive payment for processing earnings assignment issued by department of social and health services.

Employer penalties, support withholding: Liable to employee for double lost wages, damages, costs, and attorney fees; must reinstate or hire employee. Liable to a civil fine up to $2,500 per violation (also applies to spousal support).

West Virginia

W. Va. Code §§ 46A-2-131, 46B-6-5, 48-14-406(c), 48-14-407, 48-14-418

Employee protections that exceed federal law: Employer may not take any form of reprisal against employee because of wage garnishment (no number specified).

State Laws on Wage Garnishments (continued)

Employer's fee: $1 per child support withholding order.

Employer penalties, child support withholding: Employer who violates employee's rights is guilty of a misdemeanor, punishable by a fine of $500 to $1,000.

Wisconsin

Wis. Stat. Ann. §§ 425.110, 767.265(3)(h),(6)(c), 812.43

Employee protections that exceed federal law: Employer may not charge a fee or take any adverse action because of a general wage garnishment (no number specified).

Employer's fee: $3 per child support payment.

Employer penalties, general wage garnishment: Employee may sue for reinstatement, back wages and benefits, restoration of seniority, and attorneys' fees.

Employer penalties, child support withholding: Liable to employee for reinstatement and back pay; plus fine of up to $500.

Wyoming

Wyo. Stat. §§ 1-15-509, 20-6-212(c), 20-6-218, 40-14-506

Employee protections that exceed federal law: Employee may not be discharged for having wages subject to continuing garnishment for any judgment (no limit on number).

Employer's fee: $5 per child support payment.

Employer penalties, general wage garnishment: Employee may sue for reinstatement, 30 days' lost wages, costs, and attorneys' fees.

Employer penalties, child support withholding: For violating employee rights, subject to fine of up to $200.

Current as of February 2005

3

Discrimination

....

Discrimination is a negative force in American culture, but it's particularly destructive when it occurs in the workplace, where an individual's livelihood is at stake. Discrimination undermines employee loyalty, destroys employee morale, and reduces productivity and work quality. It can also lead to costly and painful lawsuits and do irreparable harm to a company's reputation.

In addition to the obvious moral and ethical reasons to prevent discrimination, it makes good business sense for employers to keep discrimination out of the workplace. And the burdens of preventing and remedying discrimination fall heavily on managers; after all, you are the ones who represent the company to its employees, have an opportunity to see what's really going on in the workplace, and are responsible for important personnel decisions that could form the basis for a discrimination lawsuit.

This chapter provides an overview of the kinds of employment discrimination that federal and state laws prohibit, tips on how you can prevent discrimination and harassment in your workplace, and what to do if an employee complains of discrimination.

Frequently Asked Questions About Discrimination

■ **What types of discrimination are illegal in the workplace?**

If a characteristic is specifically listed in a federal or state antidiscrimination law, or even in a local ordinance, then it is illegal to discriminate against someone on the basis of that characteristic. Under federal law, employers may not discriminate on the basis of race, national origin, religion, sex, disability, age, or citizenship status. State and local laws may prohibit discrimination on the basis of additional characteristics, such as marital status or sexual orientation. (See "Antidiscrimination Laws," below, for more information.)

■ **Can we require employees to speak only English when customers are present?**

It depends on the reasons for the policy. If your company can show that the rule is necessary for business reasons and that the rule is not too restrictive, an English-only rule will probably pass legal muster. However, you must tell employees when they have to speak English and inform them of the consequences of breaking the rule. (See "Race and National Origin," below, for more information.)

Frequently Asked Questions About Discrimination (continued)

■ **Is it age discrimination to hire a younger applicant who knows a broad range of cutting-edge computer programs over an older applicant who barely understands word processing?**

No. You are not discriminating when you choose the most qualified candidate for a position. As long as the job requires the type of computer skills the younger applicant has, you're on safe ground. Age discrimination problems arise when you make assumptions based on age—for example, if you simply assumed that the older applicant didn't have up-to-date computer skills but he or she was actually a technology whiz, you could get into trouble. (For more information, see "Age," below.)

■ **Can I choose to reassign my pregnant employee to a job that requires less physical work or travel?**

Generally not. Unless your pregnant employee requests an accommodation or reassignment, you cannot force one upon her. As long as a pregnant employee can perform her job duties, to treat her differently based solely upon her pregnancy is to discriminate against her based on her sex—which is illegal. If the pregnant worker is having difficulty performing her job based on physical conditions due to her pregnancy, you should treat her the same way you treat all other temporarily disabled employees—such as a worker who had a heart attack or broke a leg. (For more information, see "Gender, Pregnancy, and Sexual Harassment," below.)

■ **What should I do if I notice racy posters and other sexual images in my team's workspace, but no one complains about it?**

You should report it, using the procedures laid out in your company's sexual harassment policy. If your company doesn't have a policy, bring it to the attention of higher management immediately. Employees may be offended by these images even if they haven't complained. And once you know about potential harassment, your company has an obligation to take action to stop it. (For more information, see "Gender, Pregnancy, and Sexual Harassment," below.)

■ **Our company has a largely gay clientele—can we give an edge in hiring to gay and lesbian applicants?**

As a legal matter, it depends on the laws of your city and state. Fifteen states, the District of Columbia, and many cities and counties prohibit discrimination in

Frequently Asked Questions About Discrimination (continued)

private workplaces on the basis of sexual orientation—and this applies equally to heterosexuals and homosexuals. Even if this type of discrimination isn't prohibited where you do business, however, discrimination is never a good idea. It can lead to other types of lawsuits, bad publicity, and more. And really, what should be important to your company is that employees understand the needs of its primarily gay customers—not whether the employees are gay themselves. (See "Sexual Orientation," below, for more information.)

Do we have to let a religious employee take his or her Sabbath day off?
It depends on how that would affect your company. Employers are required to accommodate their employees' religious practices, but only if accommodation doesn't cause hardship. If it's relatively easy to switch employee schedules around, you may be legally obligated to give this employee the day off. On the other hand, if no other employees are willing to work that day and employee schedules depend on seniority, this employee may not have the right to an accommodation. (See "Religion," below, for more information.)

If a disabled employee asks for a particular reasonable accommodation, do we have to provide it?
Not necessarily. Once an employee asks for an accommodation, the employer must brainstorm with the employee to figure out what kinds of accommodations might work. However, you don't have to provide exactly the accommodation the worker requests, nor do you have to provide an accommodation if it would cause your company undue hardship. (For information on accommodating disabilities, see "Disability," below.)

What is genetic discrimination?
Genetic discrimination occurs when an employer makes decisions based on an employee or applicant's genetic information—for example, whether the person carries a gene for certain types of inheritable diseases. Genetic discrimination is prohibited in many states. Although it isn't explicitly prohibited by federal law, the Americans With Disabilities Act prohibits employers from taking action based on an employee's disability or perceived disability, and many decisions based on genetic information fall into this category. (See "Genetics," below, for more information.)

Antidiscrimination Laws

Discrimination becomes a legal issue only when a state or federal law or local ordinance declares that a characteristic is "protected." Once that happens, an employer subject to the law cannot base employment decisions on that characteristic.

To know what forms of discrimination are prohibited, you must know a little about your federal, state, and local laws. Some of these laws apply only to businesses of a particular size (for example, five or more employees). In addition, each state's law is slightly different (for example, some states prohibit discrimination on the basis of sexual orientation, while others do not). To learn which characteristics are protected by your state antidiscrimination laws, see "State Laws Prohibiting Discrimination in Employment," at the end of this chapter.

Employer Duties Under Antidiscrimination Laws

In addition to not discriminating against its own employees, an employer must take steps to prevent discrimination. And when discrimination does occur, the company must stop it—and fast.

This means employers must:

- have policies that prohibit discrimination and tell employees what to do if they experience discrimination
- make sure its managers and supervisors don't discriminate

- make sure its policies and procedures don't have an unfair impact on a protected group of people (discussed in more detail below)
- investigate complaints of discrimination (see "Investigating Complaints" in Chapter 11), and
- take effective action against those who discriminate.

All of this may sound complicated, but it really isn't. If you and the company's other managers base all of your employment decisions on criteria related to the job, that's half the battle. And if someone does complain about discrimination, or if prejudicial behavior otherwise comes to your attention, follow your company's reporting policies—and don't retaliate or allow retaliation against the victim.

Federal Antidiscrimination Laws

The main federal laws that managers should be aware of are:

- Title VII of the Civil Rights Act ("Title VII")
- the Age Discrimination in Employment Act (ADEA)
- the Equal Pay Act (EPA)
- the Immigration and Reform and Control Act (IRCA), and
- the Americans With Disabilities Act (ADA).

We describe each of these laws below. Even if your company is so small that these federal laws don't apply, that's not a license to discriminate. Not only is it bad business, but it also might violate any state laws that cover smaller employers.

Although they each protect separate characteristics, federal antidiscrimination laws have a lot in common:

- **They prohibit retaliation.** All of the federal laws (and most state laws) prohibit employers from retaliating against applicants or employees who asserts their rights under the law. For example, an employer cannot fire someone for complaining about race discrimination. This is an area in which managers can really get into trouble, because they are often the ones who have to decide whether to separate, move, discipline, or otherwise take action that affects the employees involved. To learn more about this issue, see "Retaliation" in Chapter 11.

- **They cover the entire employment relationship.** The federal laws prohibit discrimination in all terms, conditions, and privileges of employment, including hiring, firing, compensation, benefits, job assignments, shift assignments, promotions, and discipline.

- **They prevent neutral practices that harm a protected group.** Each law prohibits employer practices that seem neutral but have a disproportionate or unfair impact on a protected group of people. A neutral practice that has an unfair impact on a certain group is legal

only if the employer has a valid business reason for using it. For example, a strength requirement for a job might be legal—even though it could exclude a disproportionately high number of women from that job—if an employer is using them to fill a job for which lifting a certain amount is a requirement, for example, a job in the logging industry. A strength requirement would not, however, be valid for a desk job.

- **Harassment is always a no-no.** In addition to prohibiting discrimination on the basis of the listed characteristics, all of the laws prohibit harassment based on those characteristics as well.

Title VII of the Civil Rights Act of 1964

Title VII of the Civil Rights Act of 1964 ("Title VII"), 42 U.S.C. §§ 2000e and following, prohibits employers from discriminating against applicants and employees on the basis of:

- race or color
- religion
- sex (including pregnancy and childbirth), and
- national origin (including membership in a Native American tribe).

A very narrow exception to Title VII allows an employer to discriminate on the basis of religion, sex, or national origin (but never on the basis of race) if a characteristic is intrinsic to the job—called a "bona fide occupational qualification" or "BFOQ" in legal lingo. For example, if you need to hire an actor to play the role of Hamlet's mother or you need to hire attendants for a women's restroom, you can discriminate against men in filling these positions. To rely on this exception, an employer must be able to show that no member of the group it discriminated against could perform the job—which is a very tough standard to meet.

Title VII applies to employers that fit into the following categories:

- private employers with 15 or more employees
- state governments and their political subdivisions and agencies
- the federal government
- employment agencies
- labor organizations, and
- joint labor-management committees and other training programs.

The Age Discrimination in Employment Act

The Age Discrimination in Employment Act (ADEA), 29 U.S.C. §§ 621-634, prohibits discrimination against employees who are age 40 or older. It does not protect people who are younger than 40 from being discriminated against on the basis of age. (Some state laws do, however.)

The ADEA applies to:

- private employers with 20 or more employees

- the federal government and its agencies
- interstate agencies
- employment agencies, and
- labor unions.

Although state government workers are protected by the ADEA, they do not have the right to sue their employers (the state for which they work) in court to enforce their rights. Only the Equal Employment Opportunity Commission (EEOC), the federal agency that interprets and enforces the ADEA, may sue a state to protect state employees from age discrimination.

To learn more about age discrimination, see "Age," below.

The Equal Pay Act

The Equal Pay Act (EPA), 29 U.S.C. § 206(d), requires that employers provide men and women with equal pay for equal work. For more about this law, see "Equal Pay" in Chapter 2.

The Immigration Reform and Control Act of 1986

The Immigration Reform and Control Act of 1986 (IRCA), 8 U.S.C. § 1324, prohibits employers from discriminating against applicants or employees on the basis of their citizenship or national origin. On the flip side, however, the IRCA also makes it illegal for employers to knowingly hire or employ people who are not legally authorized to work in the United States. Employers must keep records verifying that their employees are authorized to work in the United States.

The IRCA applies to employers with four or more employees. For more information, see "Race and National Origin," below.

The Americans With Disabilities Act

The Americans With Disabilities Act (ADA), 42 U.S.C. §§ 12101-12213, prohibits employers from discriminating against a person with a disability in any aspect of employment.

The ADA applies only to:

- private employers with 15 or more employees
- local governments and their agencies
- employment agencies, and
- labor unions.

The ADA does not apply to the federal government and its agencies or state governments and their agencies. To learn more about disability discrimination and the ADA, see "Disability," below. To learn more about how the ADA affects the hiring process, see "Applicants With Disabilities" in Chapter 1.

Which Federal Antidiscrimination Laws Apply to Your Company

Not every antidiscrimination law applies to every employer. Federal antidiscrimination laws apply to only private employers with more than a minimum number of employees— and this minimum number is different for each law.

Name of Law:	Discrimination Prohibited on the Basis of:	Applies to:
Title VII	Race, color, religion, sex, or national origin	Employers with 15 or more employees
Age Discrimination in Employment Act	Age (40 years old and over only)	Employers with 20 or more employees
Americans With Disabilities Act	Physical or mental disability	Employers with 15 or more employees
Equal Pay Act	Sex (wage discrimination only)	All employers
Immigration Reform and Control Act	Citizenship status, national origin	Employers with 4 or more employees

Race and National Origin

Employment discrimination on the basis or race or national origin still happens more often than anyone wants to believe. It exacts a very high price, both from its victims and from the companies where it occurs. Recent lawsuits prove the point: Large companies have paid millions of dollars to compensate victims of race and national origin discrimination and to pay for their own complicity in encouraging or allowing a discriminatory atmosphere to flourish in the workplace.

Race Discrimination

An employer commits race discrimination when it makes job decisions on the basis of race or when it adopts seemingly neutral job policies that disproportionately affect members of a particular race.

Federal and state laws forbid race discrimination in every aspect of the employment relationship, including hiring, firing, promotions, compensation, job training, or any other term or condition of employment. For example, an employer discriminates when it refuses to hire Latinos, promotes only white employees to supervisory positions, requires only African-American job applicants to take a drug test, or refuses to allow Asian-American employees to deal with customers.

An employer that discriminates on the basis of physical characteristics associated with a particular race—such as hair texture or color, skin color, or facial features—also commits race discrimination.

Even employment policies or criteria that seem to be neutral may be discriminatory if they have a disproportionate impact on members of a particular race. For example, a height requirement may screen out disproportionate numbers of Asian-American and Latino job applicants. Or an employment policy requiring men to be clean-shaven may discriminate against African-American men, who are more likely to suffer from Pseudofolliculitis barbae (a painful skin condition caused and exacerbated by shaving).

Rules or policies that have a disproportionate impact on people of a certain race will pass legal muster only if the employer can show that there is a legitimate and important work reason for the policy. For example, a height requirement might be legitimate if the company can show that an employee must be at least a certain height to operate a particular type of machinery.

National Origin Discrimination

An employer discriminates on the basis of national origin when it makes employment decisions based on a person's ancestry, birthplace, or culture, or on linguistic characteristics or surnames associated with a particular ethnic group. For example, an employer who refuses to hire anyone with a Hispanic-sounding last name discriminates, as does an employer who won't allow anyone with an accent to work with the public.

Language Rules

An employer may be able to prohibit on-duty employees from speaking any language other than English if it can show that the rule is necessary for business reasons. If your company has an English-only rule, you must tell employees when they have to speak English (for example, whenever customers are present) and the consequences of breaking the rule. And, if an employee challenges the English-only rule, the company will have to defend the rule's scope: A rule that forbids workers from ever speaking another language, even during breaks or when a customer who speaks that language is present, is probably too broad.

Accent Rules

Because an employee's accent is often associated with his or her national origin, employers must tread carefully when

Lessons From the Real World

A federal judge in Dallas ordered a Texas company to pay its Spanish-speaking workers $700,000 in damages for requiring them to speak only English on company premises. The judge said that the policy discriminated against the workers because language is part of one's national origin. Although the judge might have allowed the policy if the company could have come forward with a business justification, the company could not.

The company's policy was so broad that it prohibited workers from speaking Spanish during lunch, on breaks, when making personal telephone calls, and before and after work if they were in the building.

The rule even prevented a Spanish-speaking husband and wife from speaking Spanish to each other when they ate lunch together.

The company disciplined and terminated employees who violated the policy. Even employees who tried to follow the policy but occasionally slipped up and allowed a Spanish word or phrase to enter into the conversation were disciplined.

The only time employees were allowed to speak Spanish was when serving the company's Spanish-speaking customers.

Equal Employment Opportunity Commission v. Premier Operator Services, Inc., 113 F.Supp.2d 1066 (N.D. Texas 2000).

making employment decisions based on accent. An employer may decide not to hire or promote an employee to a position that requires clear oral communication in English if the employee's accent substantially affects his or her ability to communicate clearly. However, if the employee's accent does not impair his or her ability to be understood, you may not make job decisions on that basis—for example, a company cannot simply adopt a blanket rule that employees who speak accented English may not work in customer service positions.

Harassment Based on Race or National Origin Is Illegal

Harassment on the basis of race and national origin is also prohibited. Harassment is any conduct based on a person's race or national origin that creates an intimidating, hostile, or

---

Companies Pay the Price for Discrimination

In recent years, companies have been hit with huge verdicts—or have agreed to pay massive settlements—to employees who have been discriminated against or harassed on the basis of race or national origin. For example:

- In 2005, Consolidated Freightways Corporation of Delaware agreed to pay $2.75 million to settle a racial harassment lawsuit filed by the EEOC. Twelve African-American employees alleged that they were subjected to racial intimidation, threats, assault, racist graffiti, and property damage, among other things.
- In 2004, the Equal Employment Opportunity Commission (EEOC) announced a $50 million settlement of a race and sex discrimination

lawsuit against the clothing retail company Abercrombie & Fitch. Among the allegations was a claim that the clothier refused to hire female and nonwhite applicants because they did not fit the image or "look" the company was trying to project in the marketplace.

- In 2000, Coca-Cola settled a class action race discrimination lawsuit for $192.5 million. African-American employees said that Coke imposed a racial "glass ceiling" by discriminating against them in pay and promotions. Of the total settlement, $36 million was earmarked for monitoring the company's employment practices to make sure that the discrimination stopped.

offensive work environment or interferes with the person's work performance. Harassing conduct might include racial slurs, jokes about a particular ethnic group, comments or questions about a person's cultural habits, or physical acts of particular significance to a certain racial or ethnic group—for example, hanging or posting an offensive picture or object near an employee's workspace, like a swastika or racist graffiti.

Lessons From the Real World

Four employees at a steel plant in Stockton, California filed a lawsuit alleging that they were harassed because of their national origin and Muslim religion. The employees claimed that they were called names like "camel jockey" and "raghead," ridiculed during their daily prayers, and given undesirable job assignments.

The employees complained to the EEOC, which filed a lawsuit on their behalf. Rather than battling it out in court, the company decided to settle the claims for $1,110,000 and agreed to change its policies and conduct training to prevent discrimination.

"Pakistani-American Workers to Share $1.1 Million in Harassment Settlement With Stockton Steel," EEOC Press Release, March 19, 2003.

Age

There is an adage: "Hire a young doctor and an old lawyer." A young doctor, the theory holds, will have cutting-edge skills and knowledge of all the latest research and techniques; the old lawyer will have the experience and gravitas needed to convince a jury. If the adage resonates with you, you are not alone—stereotypes based on age fill our culture, from the irresponsible, beer-loving college student to the stale and slow, 60-something middle manager.

While the stereotypes may abound, it is illegal for your company to act on such age-based preconceptions when making employment decisions. A number of state and federal laws prohibit you from discriminating against employees and applicants because of their age. And, according to a recent report by Jury Verdict Research (www. juryverdictresearch.com), juries have reserved the highest damage awards in discrimination cases to employees complaining of age discrimination.

The Age Discrimination in Employment Act

The Age Discrimination in Employment Act (ADEA), 29 U.S.C. §§ 621-634, is the major federal law that addresses age discrimination. This law prohibits employers from discriminating against employees and applicants who are 40 years of age or older on the basis of their age. It does not, however, prohibit discrimination against people who are younger than 40. (Some state laws do; see the discussion below.) If you are a private employer with 20 or more employees, you must follow the ADEA.

The ADEA prohibits discrimination in all phases of the employment relationship, except benefits and early retirement, which are addressed by a different law. (See "Discrimination in Benefits and Early Retirement," below.) Not only does the ADEA prohibit you from discriminating against older workers in favor of those who are younger than 40, it also prohibits you from discriminating among older workers. For example, you can't hire a 43-year-old over a 53-year-old simply because of age.

State Laws

Many state laws also prohibit discrimination on the basis of age. Although some of these laws essentially mirror the federal law and only protect people older than 40, other laws are broader and protect workers of all ages.

State laws tend to cover employers with fewer than 20 employees, so you might have to comply with your state law even if your company isn't covered by the federal law. To find out more about the age discrimination law in your state, contact your state fair employment office. (See the appendix for contact information.)

Discrimination in Benefits and Early Retirement

The federal Older Workers Benefit Protection Act (OWBPA), 29 U.S.C. §§ 623 and following, makes it illegal to use an employee's age as a basis for discrimination in benefits and retirement. Like the ADEA, this Act only protects people who are at least 40 years old. Also like the ADEA, this Act applies to private employers with 20 or more employees, the federal government, and unions.

Under this law, a company cannot reduce health or life insurance benefits for older employees, nor can it stop their pensions from accruing if they work past their normal retirement age, which is usually set by the plan. In addition, the Act prohibits employers from forcing older employees to take a retirement earlier than the one specified in the plan. An early retirement plan is legal only if it gives the employee a choice between two options: keeping things as they are or choosing to retire under a plan that makes the employee better off. This choice must be a genuine one; the employee must be free to reject the offer. In addition, if either choice makes the employee worse off, the offer violates the Act.

Gender, Pregnancy, and Sexual Harassment

As with race or national origin discrimination, employment discrimination on the basis of sex continues to persist with surprising regularity today. Despite federal and state laws prohibiting discrimination on the basis of sex—which the law defines to include pregnancy and related conditions—employers still make the mistake of making decisions along gender lines or treating pregnant employees differently just because they are pregnant. Such mistakes can cost a company dearly in lawsuit judgments and settlements.

Gender and Pregnancy Discrimination

An employer commits sex discrimination when it makes job decisions on the basis of sex or pregnancy or when it adopts seemingly neutral job policies that disproportionately affect members of one gender.

Federal and state laws forbid sex discrimination in every aspect of the employment relationship, including hiring, firing, promotions, compensation, job training, or any other term or condition of employment. For example, an employer discriminates based on gender when it promotes only men to supervisory positions, hires only women to work in tipped service positions, denies only women the chance to participate in training opportunities, or reassigns pregnant employees to "dead-end" positions based on the assumption that they won't return to work after giving birth.

As with race discrimination, even employment policies or criteria that seem to be neutral may be discriminatory if they have a disproportionate impact on members of a particular gender. For example, a height or strength requirement may screen out disproportionate numbers of female job applicants. Again, such rules or policies will pass legal muster only if the employer can show that there is a legitimate and important work reason for the policy. For example, a strength requirement might be legitimate if the company can show that an employee must be able to lift a certain amount of weight in order to load and transport heavy goods.

When it comes to pregnancy, you can avoid sex discrimination by following two basic rules: (1) do not make any decisions about the employee based solely on the fact that she is pregnant, and (2) treat all pregnant employees the same way you would treat any other temporarily disabled employee—for example, a worker who suffered a heart attack or broke a leg. If your pregnant employee is able to perform her job duties, you may not reassign her or change any of her job duties or any other term or condition of her job simply because she is pregnant. If she is having trouble performing her job duties due to pregnancy-related conditions (for example, extreme nausea or medically required bed rest), under basic federal antidiscrimination law, you must treat her as you would any nonpregnant, temporarily disabled worker. For instance, if you offer light duty at full pay or paid time off for a worker who cannot perform his or her job duties because the worker injured his or her back, you must offer your pregnant employee the same type of accommodation on the same terms.

Beyond Title VII, however, your pregnant employee may have additional rights under the federal and/or state family and medical leave laws or under additional state laws that protect pregnant workers or require transfer or reasonable accommodation if the worker requests it. For more information, see "Family and Medical Leave," and "Pregnancy and Parental Leave" in Chapter 5 and contact your state labor and fair employment agencies. (Contact information is included in the appendix.)

Sexual Harassment

Sexual harassment is a form of sex discrimination. As with sex discrimination, Title VII is the main federal law that prohibits sexual harassment. (See "Antidiscrimination Laws," above.) In addition, each state has its own law prohibiting sexual harassment.

Sexual harassment is any unwelcome sexual advance or conduct on the job that creates an intimidating, hostile, or offensive working environment. Any conduct of a sexual nature that makes an employee uncomfortable has the potential to be sexual harassment. Sexual harassment can also include harassment that is not sexual in nature, but is based on one's gender— just as racial harassment would be based on one's race. This type of harassment typically takes place when women enter

workplaces have been traditionally male-dominated and are singled out and harassed because they are women.

Given such a broad definition, it is not surprising that sexual harassment comes in many forms. The following are all examples of sexual harassment:

- A supervisor implies to an employee that the employee must go on a date with him or her to receive a promotion. (In legal lingo, this is sometimes called "quid pro quo" harassment.)
- Employees regularly tell sexually explicit jokes within earshot of the office manager, who finds the jokes offensive.
- A cashier at a store pinches and fondles a coworker against the coworker's will.
- Several employees post sexually explicit jokes on an office intranet bulletin board.
- An employee sends emails to coworkers that contain sexually explicit language and jokes.
- A male sales clerk makes demeaning comments about female customers to his coworkers.
- A secretary's coworkers belittle her and refer to her by sexist or demeaning terms.
- The only woman on an otherwise all-male construction crew routinely has her work tools taken or broken by her male coworkers.

The harasser can be the victim's supervisor, manager, or coworker. The harasser can even be a nonemployee, if the person is on the premises with permission (for example, a customer or a vendor).

Anyone Can Be Sexually Harassed

Although it may sound counterintuitive, sexual harassment knows no gender: Men can sexually harass women, and women can sexually harass men.

However, harassment based on a person's sexual orientation is not illegal under federal law (although some states prohibit it—see "Sexual Orientation," below). A worker who is harassed for being gay or straight is not protected, but a worker who is harassed—even by a member of the same gender—because of his or her sex is. Sound confusing? That's because the courts are still trying to figure out how to handle same-sex harassment.

The bottom line is that you should try to prevent harassment in any form, regardless of where it falls on the legal spectrum. For information on how you can—and should—prevent sexual harassment in the workplace, see "Preventing Sexual Harassment" in Chapter 4.

Sexual Orientation

Traditionally, gay and lesbian employees have had little protection from discrimination and harassment in the workplace. Times are changing, however, and a growing number of employers must now provide these workers the same thing they must provide to members of other traditionally oppressed groups: a workplace free of discrimination and harassment.

Although no federal law prohibits private employers from discriminating on the basis of sexual orientation, a number of state and local laws do. Sixteen states prohibit sexual orientation discrimination in private employment: California, Connecticut, Hawaii, Illinois (as of January 1, 2006), Maine, Maryland, Massachusetts, Minnesota, Nevada, New Hampshire, New Jersey, New Mexico, New York, Rhode Island, Vermont, and Wisconsin. The District of Columbia and more than 100 cities and counties also prohibit sexual orientation discrimination in the workplace—from Albany, New York to Ypsilanti, Michigan. (In addition, seven states prohibit sexual orientation discrimination in public workplaces only: Colorado, Delaware, Indiana, Michigan, Montana, Pennsylvania, and Washington.)

To find out whether your state, county, or city has a law prohibiting discrimination on the basis of sexual orientation, contact your state labor department or your state fair employment office. (See the appendix for contact information.) You can also visit the Lambda Legal Defense and Education Fund website at www.lambdalegal.org. There, you will find a state-by-state (and city-by-city) list of antidiscrimination laws.

Even if there is no law in your state, city, or county prohibiting sexual orientation discrimination, that's not a license to discriminate. If a gay or lesbian employee feels unfairly treated and/or injured based on sexual orientation, that employee can still sue your company under a number of other legal theories. These include:

- intentional or negligent infliction of emotional distress
- assault
- battery
- invasion of privacy
- defamation
- interference with employment contract, and
- wrongful termination in violation of public policy.

Religion

The laws against religious discrimination present employers with a seeming contra-diction: They both prohibit employers from making decisions based on a person's religion and require employers to make decisions based on a person's religion.

This apparent contradiction comes from the fact that religion is more than just a characteristic: It is also a set of practices and beliefs. The law prohibits employers from discriminating based on the fact of someone's religion (for example, that an employee is Jewish, Catholic, Muslim, or Baptist), and it requires employers to make allowances for a person's religious practices and beliefs (for example, that an employee needs time after lunch to pray or that an employee needs Saturdays off to observe a Sabbath).

The first part is fairly simple. You can't refuse to hire someone or decide to promote someone or make any other employment decisions because of the person's religion. You must make those decisions for reasons that are not related to the employee's religion.

The second part is more complicated. You must work with employees to make it possible for them to practice their religious beliefs—within reason. This might mean not scheduling an employee to work on a Sabbath day, or relaxing a company dress code so that an employee can wear religious garments. The only time an employer does not have to accommodate an employee is when it would pose a hardship for the business. For instance, if changing an employee's schedule to accommodate a religious belief would wreak havoc on your company's seniority-based scheduling system and cause severe morale problems among other employees, you might not have to accommodate the worker.

As with many legal terms, it can be tough to figure out exactly what "accom-modation" and "hardship" mean in the practical context of your workplace. The following sections look at the meaning of these terms.

Accommodation

If an employee has a sincere religious belief that conflicts with an employment rule or requirement, the law requires you to accommodate the employee's beliefs—

to work with the employee to find a way around the conflict. This does not mean that you have to accept any accommodation that the employee suggests. If you don't like the employee's idea, you can suggest one of your own. In this way, the two of you should engage in a negotiation process that balances the employee's religious rights with your need for the job to get done.

Examples of reasonable accommodations include:

- flexible scheduling
- telecommuting
- splitting shifts, and
- transferring the employee to a different position.

Undue Hardship

You do not have to make an accommodation for an employee's religious beliefs that will cause your company an undue hardship. This means that you can deny an accommodation that would:

- cost too much money (anything more than a minor cost is too much in the eyes of the law)
- substantially harm the morale of other employees (in other words, more than mere grumbling), or
- substantially disrupt work routines.

Disability

As with the other topics covered in this chapter, federal and state laws prohibit discrimination at work on the basis of a worker's disability. The federal Americans With Disabilities Act (ADA), 42 U.S.C. §§ 12101-12213, and similar state laws both prohibit discrimination against people with disabilities and require employers to accommodate employees'—and applicants'—disabilities when possible.

Who Is Covered

The ADA and most state laws protect "qualified workers with disabilities." A qualified worker is a worker who can perform most basic and necessary job duties, with or without some form of accommodation from the employer.

A worker who falls into one of these three categories is considered disabled under the ADA:

- The worker has a physical or mental impairment that substantially limits a major life activity (such as the ability to walk, talk, see, hear, breathe, reason, work, or take care of oneself). Courts tend not to categorically characterize certain conditions as disabilities. Instead, they consider the effect of the particular condition on the particular employee.
- The worker has a record or history of impairment. In other words, you may not make employment decisions based on an employee's past disability.
- The employer regards the worker— even incorrectly—as having a disability. In other words, you can't treat workers less favorably because

you believe them to be disabled, even if you are wrong.

In addition, for an impairment to be a disability under the ADA, it must be long-term. Temporary impairments, such as pregnancy or broken bones, are not covered by the ADA (but they may be covered by other laws—for example, see "Gender and Pregnancy Discrimination," above).

Reasonable Accommodation

Accommodating a worker means providing assistance or making changes in the job or workplace that will enable the worker to do the job. For example, an employer might lower the height of a desktop to accommodate a worker in a wheelchair, provide TDD telephone equipment for a worker whose hearing is impaired, or provide a quiet, distraction-free workspace for a worker with Attention Deficit Disorder.

It is the employee's responsibility to inform you of the disability and request a reasonable accommodation—managers are not legally required to guess at what might help the employee do the job. However, once an employee reveals a disability, you must engage in what the law calls a "flexible interactive process"— essentially, a brainstorming dialogue with the worker to figure out what kinds of accommodations might be effective and practical. Your company does not have to provide the precise accommodation the worker requests, but you must work together to come up with a reasonable solution.

However, you don't have to provide an accommodation if it would cause your company "undue hardship." For instance, if the cost of an accommodation would eat up an entire year's profits (building a new wing on an office building, for example), it isn't required. Whether implementing an accommodation qualifies as undue hardship depends on a number of factors, including:

- the cost of the accommodation
- the size and financial resources of the business
- the structure of the business, and
- the effect the accommodation would have on the business.

Your company and the employee may have different opinions about what constitutes a reasonable accommodation and what would be an undue hardship. If you're unsure whether a disabled employee is entitled to a specific accommodation, you might want to get some legal help.

Alcohol and Drugs

Alcohol and drug use pose special problems under the ADA. Employees who use (or have used) alcohol or drugs may be disabled under the law. However, an employer can require these employees to meet the same work standards—including not drinking or using drugs on the job— as nondisabled employees. Here are some guidelines to follow when dealing with these tricky issues:

- **Alcoholism.** Alcoholism is a disability covered by the ADA. This means that an employer cannot fire or discipline a worker simply because he or she is an alcoholic. However, an employer can fire or discipline an alcoholic worker for failing to meet work-related performance and behavior standards imposed on all employees—even if the worker fails to meet these standards because of drinking.

- **Illegal drug use.** The ADA does not protect employees who currently use or are addicted to illegal drugs. These workers are not considered "disabled" within the meaning of the law and therefore don't have the right to be free from discrimination or to receive a reasonable accommodation. However, the ADA does cover workers who are no longer using drugs and have successfully completed (or are currently participating in) a supervised drug rehabilitation program.

- **Use of legal drugs.** If an employee is taking prescription medication or over-the-counter drugs to treat a disability, you may have to accommodate that employee's use of drugs and the side effects that the drugs have on the employee. However, you do not have to accommodate legal drug use if you cannot find a reasonable accommodation.

Genetics

As scientific advances yield ever more information about our genetic code, the legal system is grappling with how this information can and should be used. Should an employer or an insurance carrier be allowed to consider genetic information—including the likelihood, based on family history, medical tests, and genetic profiles, that a person will develop cancer or other diseases—in making decisions?

According to a survey conducted in 2001 by the American Management Association, some already do. More than 20% of major U.S. firms take family medical histories of employees and applicants—and more than 5% admitted to using this information when making employment decisions. Right now, no federal law prohibits private employers from discriminating on the basis of genetics—although legislation is proposed in Congress every year. However, some states prohibit genetic discrimination. And the Americans With Disabilities Act places some limits on the use of genetic testing in employment. (For more about the ADA, see "Disability," above, and "Applicants With Disabilities" in Chapter 1.)

State Laws

About half the states prohibit or limit the use of genetic tests. Some prohibit employers from requiring applicants to submit to such tests as a condition of employment. Some prohibit discrimination on the basis of genetic characteristics—in other words, an employer cannot fire, demote, or refuse to hire based on someone's genetic traits or predispositions. And some require employers to handle the results of any genetic test according to strict rules of confidentiality. A handful of states prohibit employers from discriminating on the basis of sickle cell trait.

To find out whether your state has a genetic testing law, see "State Laws Prohibiting Discrimination in Employment," at the end of this chapter.

Genetics and the ADA

The Americans With Disabilities Act (ADA) prohibits employment discrimination against workers with disabilities. (See "Disability," above, for more on the ADA.) Among other things, employers subject to the ADA may not discriminate against workers whom they perceive to be disabled. In other words, an employer who treats a worker as if he or she is disabled violates the ADA.

The U.S. Equal Employment Opportunity Commission (EEOC)—which enforces the ADA—has interpreted this provision to prohibit certain kinds of genetic discrimination. For example, suppose that a woman takes a genetic test that reveals that she carries a gene that puts her at greater risk of developing breast cancer. A potential employer who refuses to hire her based on these test results would be violating the ADA. Although the applicant is not actually impaired, the employer is treating her as if she is. Because few courts have considered this issue, it's not clear whether the EEOC's interpretation will govern in any given lawsuit.

Legal Dos and Don'ts: Discrimination

Do:

- **Use only job-related criteria when making decisions.** If you always have sound business reasons for your actions, employees are less likely to complain of discrimination—and much less likely to win any discrimination claims they might make.
- **Keep an open door.** The more comfortable employees are talking to you about problems and concerns, the more likely they are to come to you for help rather than running to a lawyer. Communication is the best way to nip problems in the bud.
- **Act out of enlightened self-interest.** Most managers want to keep their companies out of trouble. But if you need a little more incentive to refrain from harassing or discriminatory behavior, remember this: In some states, managers can be personally liable for harassment or discrimination they commit themselves.

Don't:

- **Hurt by helping**. Although it may seem like a good idea to move a victim out of a discriminatory or harassing environment, even well-intentioned actions taken against a victim might constitute retaliation. Solve these types of problems by moving the accused, not the accuser.
- **Drag your feet.** When you don't take immediate action to stop discrimination or harassment, you cost the company money. Allowing misconduct to continue causes morale and productivity to drop—and could set your company up to lose a million-dollar lawsuit.
- **Jump to conclusions.** Always report claims of discrimination and harassment. Managers get in trouble when they make assumptions—that they know what happened, that their employees wouldn't lie to them, or that "it could never happen here," for instance.

Test Your Knowledge

Questions

1. Only large companies need to worry about complying with antidiscrimination laws.
☐ True   ☐ False

2. Once a manager learns about discrimination, he or she should report it immediately, even if the employee is reluctant to come forward.
☐ True   ☐ False

3. It is illegal to consider an employee's accent when filling a position, even if the job requires extensive customer communication.
☐ True   ☐ False

4. It is discriminatory to hire or promote an employee based on age, even if all of the applicants are over the age of 40.
☐ True   ☐ False

5. If an employee complains about harassment, you should move that employee to another position until you can figure out what's really going on.
☐ True   ☐ False

6. Because no federal law prohibits discrimination based on sexual orientation, employers are free to discriminate against gay and lesbian applicants or employees.
☐ True   ☐ False

7. You are never allowed to take an employee's religion into account when making employment decisions.
☐ True   ☐ False

8. As a manager, you are responsible for asking your reports whether they are disabled and whether they need an accommodation to do their jobs.
☐ True   ☐ False

9. An employee can sue your company for disability discrimination even if he or she is not actually disabled.
☐ True   ☐ False

10. It's okay for employers to require applicants to submit to genetic testing, because these tests reveal which applicants are more likely to develop costly medical conditions, which could cause the employer's health insurance rates to go up.
☐ True   ☐ False

Answers

1. False. Some federal antidiscrimination laws apply to very small companies. And every state has an antidiscrimination law; some of these laws apply to every employer in the state, regardless of size.

2. True. Once you know about discrimination, the company is legally responsible to take steps to stop it—even if the employee who tells you about it doesn't want to come forward.

3. False. If an employee's accent is so pronounced that it seriously impairs the employee's ability to be understood, you may refuse to place that employee in a position that requires strong communication skills.

4. True. If you hire a 45-year-old applicant rather than a 65-year-old applicant because of age, that's discriminatory.

5. False. Moving the victim could lead to a claim that you retaliated against that employee for making a complaint.

6. False. Fifteen states, the District of Columbia, and many cities and counties prohibit discrimination on the basis of sexual orientation. And, even if it's not prohibited in your region, making decisions based on an employee's sexual orientation can lead to other kinds of legal trouble.

7. False. If a worker needs a reasonable accommodation to practice his or her religious beliefs, you are legally required to take the worker's needs into account in deciding whether you can offer an accommodation.

8. False. Employees are responsible for telling you that they are disabled and need an accommodation. Once they do so, you are legally obligated to work with the employee to try to come up with an accommodation that will work for the employee and the company.

9. True. If you make decisions based on your erroneous belief that an employee is disabled, or based on an employee's history of disability, that's disability discrimination.

10. False. Genetic discrimination is prohibited in many states. Even where it's not, it may violate the Americans With Disabilities Act.

State Laws Prohibiting Discrimination in Employment

State	Law applies to employers with	Private employers may not make employment decisions based on			
		Age (protected ages, if specified)	Ancestry or national origin	Disability	AIDS/HIV
Alabama *Ala. Code §§ 21-7-1, 25-1-20*	20 or more employees	✓ (40 and older)			
Alaska *Alaska Stat. §§ 18.80.220, 47.30.865*	One or more employees	✓ (40 and older)	✓	Physical and mental	✓
Arizona *Ariz. Rev. Stat. § 41-1461*	15 or more employees	✓ (40 and older)	✓	Physical	✓
Arkansas *Ark. Code Ann. §§ 16-12-101, 11-4-601, 11-5-403*	9 or more employees		✓	Physical and mental	
California *Cal. Gov't. Code §§ 12920, 12941; Cal. Lab. Code § 1101*	5 or more employees	✓ (40 and older)	✓	Physical and mental	✓
Colorado *Colo. Rev. Stat. §§ 24-34-301, 24-34-401, 27-10-115*	One or more employees	✓ (40 to 70)	✓	Physical, mental, and learning	✓
Connecticut *Conn. Gen. Stat. Ann. §§ 46a-51, 46a-60*	3 or more employees	✓ (40 and older)	✓	Present or past physical, mental, or learning	✓
Delaware *Del. Code Ann. tit. 19, § 710*	4 or more employees	✓ (40 to 70)	✓	Physical or mental	✓
District of Columbia *D.C. Code Ann. §§ 2-1401.01, 7-1703.03*	One or more employees	✓ (18 and older)	✓	Physical or mental	✓
Florida *Fla. Stat. Ann. §§ 760.01, 760.50, 448.075*	15 or more employees	✓	✓	"Handicap"	✓

[1] Employees covered by FLSA

Gender	Marital status	Pregnancy, childbirth, and related medical conditions	Race or color	Religion or creed	Sexual orientation	Genetic testing information	Additional protected categories
✓	✓ (Includes changes in status)	✓ Parenthood	✓	✓			• Mental illness
✓			✓	✓		✓	
✓		✓	✓	✓		✓[1]	
✓	✓	✓	✓	✓	✓	✓	• Gender identity • Medical condition • Political activities or affiliations
✓		✓	✓	✓			• Lawful conduct outside of work • Mental illness
✓	✓	✓	✓	✓	✓	✓	• Mental retardation
✓	✓	✓	✓	✓		✓	
✓	✓	✓ Parenthood	✓	✓	✓		• Enrollment in vocational, professional, or college education • Family duties • Perceived race • Personal appearance • Political affiliation • Smoker
✓	✓		✓	✓			• Family status • Sickle cell trait • Breastfeeding at work

	State Laws Prohibiting Discrimination in Employment (continued)				
State	Law applies to employers with	Private employers may not make employment decisions based on			
		Age (protected ages, if specified)	Ancestry or national origin	Disability	AIDS/ HIV
Georgia *Ga. Code Ann. §§ 34-6A-1, 34-1-23, 34-5-1*	15 or more employees (Disability) 10 or more employees (Gender)	✓ (40 to 70)		Physical or mental	
Hawaii *Haw. Rev. Stat. § 378-1*	One or more employees	✓	✓	Physical or mental	✓
Idaho *Idaho Code § 67-5909*	5 or more employees	✓ (40 and older)	✓	Physical or mental	
Illinois *775 Ill. Comp. Stat. §§ 5/1-101, 5/1-102, 5/2-101; Ill. Admin. Code tit. 56, § 5210.110*	15 or more employees	✓ (40 and older)	✓	Physical or mental	✓
Indiana *Ind. Code Ann. §§ 22-9-1-1, 22-9-2-1*	6 or more employees	✓ (40 to 70)	✓	Physical or mental (15 or more employees)	
Iowa *Iowa Code § 216.1*	4 or more employees	✓ (18 or older)	✓	Physical or mental	✓
Kansas *Kan. Stat. Ann. §§ 44-1001, 44-1111, 44-1125, 65-6002(e)*	4 or more employees	✓ (18 or older)	✓	Physical or mental	✓
Kentucky *Ky. Rev. Stat. Ann. §§ 344.040, 207.130, 342.197*	8 or more employees	✓ (40 or older)	✓	Physical	✓

[2] Wage discrimination only

Gender	Marital status	Pregnancy, childbirth, and related medical conditions	Race or color	Religion or creed	Sexual orientation	Genetic testing information	Additional protected categories
✓[2]							
✓	✓	✓ Breastfeeding	✓	✓	✓	✓	• Arrest and court record (unless there is a conviction directly related to job)
✓		✓	✓	✓			
✓	✓	✓	✓	✓	✓ (as of January 1, 2006)		• Arrest record • Expunged juvenile record • Citizen status • Military status • Unfavorable military discharge • Victim of domestic violence or sexual assault
✓			✓	✓			
✓		✓	✓	✓		✓	
✓			✓	✓		✓	• Military status
✓			✓	✓			• Smoker or nonsmoker

State Laws Prohibiting Discrimination in Employment (continued)

State	Law applies to employers with	Private employers may not make employment decisions based on			
		Age (protected ages, if specified)	Ancestry or national origin	Disability	AIDS/ HIV
Louisiana La. Rev. Stat. Ann. §§ 23:301 to 23:352	20 or more employees	✓ (40 or older)	✓	Physical or mental	
Maine Me. Rev. Stat. Ann. tit. 5, §§ 4551, 4552, 4571	One or more employees	✓	✓	Physical or mental	
Maryland Md. Code 1957 Art. 49B, § 15	15 or more employees	✓	✓	Physical or mental	
Massachusetts Mass. Gen. Laws ch. 151B, § 1	6 or more employees	✓ (40 or older)	✓	Physical or mental	✓
Michigan Mich. Comp. Laws §§ 37.1201, 37.2201, 37.1103	One or more employees	✓	✓	Physical or mental	✓
Minnesota Minn. Stat. Ann. §§ 363A.03, 363A.08, 181.974	One or more employees	✓ (18 or older)	✓	Physical or mental	✓
Mississippi Miss. Code Ann. §§ 33-1-15					
Missouri Mo. Rev. Stat. §§ 213.010, 191.665, 375.1306	6 or more employees	✓ (40 to 70)	✓	Physical or mental	✓
Montana Mont. Code Ann. §§ 49-2-101, 49-2-303	One or more employees	✓	✓	Physical or mental	

Gender	Marital status	Pregnancy, childbirth, and related medical conditions	Race or color	Religion or creed	Sexual orientation	Genetic testing information	Additional protected categories
✓		✓ (Applies to employers with 25 or more employees)	✓	✓		✓	• Sickle cell trait
✓		✓	✓	✓	✓	✓	• Past workers' compensation claim • Past whistleblowing
✓	✓	✓	✓	✓	✓	✓	
✓	✓		✓	✓	✓	✓	• Military service • Arrests
✓	✓	✓	✓	✓		✓	• Height or weight • Arrest record
✓	✓	✓	✓	✓	✓	✓	• Gender identity • Member of local commission • Perceived sexual orientation • Receiving public assistance
							• Military status (all employers) • No other protected categories unless employer receives public funding
✓		✓	✓	✓		✓	
✓	✓	✓	✓	✓			

State Laws Prohibiting Discrimination in Employment (continued)

State	Law applies to employers with	Private employers may not make employment decisions based on			
		Age (protected ages, if specified)	Ancestry or national origin	Disability	AIDS/ HIV
Nebraska Neb. Rev. Stat. §§ 48-1101, 48-1001, 20-168	15 or more employees	✓ (40 to 70) (Applies to employers with 25 or more employees)	✓	Physical or mental	✓
Nevada Nev. Rev. Stat. Ann. §§ 613.310 and following	15 or more employees	✓ (40 or older)	✓	Physical or mental	
New Hampshire N.H. Rev. Stat. Ann. §§ 354-A2 and following, 141-H:3	6 or more employees	✓	✓	Physical or mental	
New Jersey N.J. Stat. Ann. §§ 10:5-1 to 10:5-12; 34:6B-1	One or more employees	✓ (18 to 70)	✓	Past or present physical or mental	✓
New Mexico N.M. Stat. Ann. § 28-1-7	4 or more employees	✓ (40 or older) (Applies to employers with 20 or more employees)	✓	Physical or mental	
New York N.Y. Elec. Law § 296; N.Y. Lab. Law § 201-d	4 or more employees	✓ (18 and over)	✓	Physical or mental	✓
North Carolina N.C. Gen. Stat. §§ 143-422.2, 168A-1, 95-28.1, 130A-148	15 or more employees	✓	✓	Physical or mental	✓

[3] Employers with 15 or more employees.

Gender	Marital status	Pregnancy, childbirth, and related medical conditions	Race or color	Religion or creed	Sexual orientation	Genetic testing information	Additional protected categories
✓	✓	✓	✓	✓		✓	
✓		✓	✓	✓	✓	✓	• Lawful use of any product when not at work • Use of service animal
✓	✓	✓	✓	✓	✓	✓	
✓	✓ (Includes domestic partner)	✓	✓	✓	✓	✓	• Hereditary cellular or blood trait • Military service or status • Smoker or nonsmoker
✓	✓ (Applies to employers with 50 or more employees)	✓	✓	✓	✓[3]		• Gender identity (employers with 15 or more employees) • Serious medical condition
✓	✓	✓	✓	✓	✓	✓	• Lawful use of any product when not at work • Military status • Observance of Sabbath • Political activities
✓			✓	✓		✓	• Lawful use of any product when not at work • Military service • Sickle cell trait

State Laws Prohibiting Discrimination in Employment (continued)					
		Private employers may not make employment decisions based on			
State	**Law applies to employers with**	**Age (protected ages, if specified)**	**Ancestry or national origin**	**Disability**	**AIDS/ HIV**
North Dakota *N.D. Cent. Code §§ 14-02.4-01, 34-01-17*	One or more employees	✓ (40 or older)	✓	Physical or mental	
Ohio *Ohio Rev. Code Ann. §§ 4111.17, 4112.01*	4 or more employees	✓ (40 or older)	✓	Physical, mental, or learning	
Oklahoma *Okla. Stat. Ann. tit. 25, § 1301; tit. 36, § 3614.2; tit. 40, § 500; tit. 44, § 208*	15 or more employees	✓ (40 or older)	✓	Physical or mental	
Oregon *Or. Rev. Stat. §§ 659A.100 and following, 659A.303*	One or more employees	✓ (18 or older)	✓	Physical or mental (Applies to employers with 6 or more employees)	
Pennsylvania *43 Pa. Cons. Stat. Ann. § 953*	4 or more employees	✓ (40 to 70)	✓	Physical or mental	
Rhode Island *R.I. Gen. Laws §§ 28-6-17, 28-5-11, 2-28-10, 23-6-22, 23-20.7.1-1*	4 or more employees	✓ (40 or older)	✓	Physical or mental	✓
South Carolina *S.C. Code Ann. §§ 1-13-20 and following*	15 or more employees	✓ (40 or older)	✓	Physical or mental	
South Dakota *S.D. Codified Laws Ann. §§ 20-13-10, 60-12-15, 60-2-20, 62-1-17*	One or more employees		✓	Physical, mental, and learning	
Tennessee *Tenn. Code Ann. §§ 4-21-102, 4-21-401 and following, 8-50-103, 50-2-202*	8 or more employees	✓ (40 or older)	✓	Physical or mental	
Texas *Tex. Lab. Code Ann. §§ 21.002, 21.101, 21.401*	15 or more employees	✓ (40 or older)	✓	Physical or mental	

Gender	Marital status	Pregnancy, childbirth, and related medical conditions	Race or color	Religion or creed	Sexual orientation	Genetic testing information	Additional protected categories
✓	✓	✓	✓	✓			• Lawful conduct outside of work • Receiving public assistance
✓		✓	✓	✓			
✓			✓	✓		✓	• Military service • Smoker or nonsmoker
✓	✓	✓	✓	✓		✓	
✓		✓	✓	✓			• Familial status • GED rather than high school diploma
✓		✓	✓	✓	✓	✓	• Domestic abuse victim • Gender identity or expression
✓		✓	✓	✓			
✓			✓	✓		✓	• Preexisting injury
✓			✓	✓			• Refer to chart on Family and Medical Leave
✓		✓	✓	✓		✓	

State Laws Prohibiting Discrimination in Employment (continued)

State	Law applies to employers with	Private employers may not make employment decisions based on			
		Age (protected ages, if specified)	Ancestry or national origin	Disability	AIDS/ HIV
Utah *Utah Code Ann. § 34A-5-106*	15 or more employees	✓ (40 or older)	✓	Follows federal law	✓
Vermont *Vt. Stat. Ann. tit. 21, § 495; tit. 18, § 9333*	One or more employees	✓ (18 or older)	✓	Physical, mental, or learning	✓
Virginia *Va. Code Ann. §§ 2.2-3900, 40.1-28.6, 51.5-3*	Law applies to all employers	✓	✓	Physical or mental	
Washington *Wash. Rev. Code Ann. §§ 49.60.040, 49.60.172 and foll., 49.12.175, 49.44.090; Wash. Admin. Code 162-30-020*	8 or more employees	✓ (40 or older)	✓	Physical, mental, or sensory; use of a service animal	✓
West Virginia *W.Va. Code §§ 5-11-3, 5-11-9, 21-5B-1*	12 or more employees	✓ (40 or older)	✓	Physical or mental	✓
Wisconsin *Wis. Stat. Ann. §§ 111.32 and following*	One or more employees	✓ (40 or older)	✓	Physical or mental	✓
Wyoming *Wyo. Stat. §§ 27-9-105, 19-11-104*	2 or more employees	✓ (40 or older)	✓		

[4] Equal pay laws apply to employers with one or more employees

Gender	Marital status	Pregnancy, childbirth, and related medical conditions	Race or color	Religion or creed	Sexual orientation	Genetic testing information	Additional protected categories
✓		✓	✓	✓			
✓			✓	✓	✓	✓	• Place of birth
✓	✓	✓	✓	✓		✓	
✓	✓	✓	✓	✓		✓	• Hepatitis C infection • Member of state militia
✓[4]			✓	✓			• Smoking away from work
✓	✓	✓	✓	✓	✓	✓	• Arrest or conviction • Lawful use of any product when not at work • Military service or status
✓			✓	✓			• Military service or status • Smoking off duty

Current as of February 2005

4

Personnel Basics

Effective management starts with good personnel policies. Fair and sensible policies can help improve performance and productivity while discouraging misconduct. They can also help prevent lawsuits by employees or government agencies, or at least lay the groundwork for a solid defense. Here, you'll find information on:

- at-will employment
- employee handbooks
- sexual harassment policies
- communication skills
- performance evaluations

- personnel files, and
- policies to help employees balance work and family obligations.

Even if your job duties don't include creating policies, you'll want to be familiar with the information in this chapter. It will help you understand the legal framework within which you carry out your day-to-day supervisory responsibilities. And it will help you with basic management tasks, such as evaluating performance, communicating with employees, keeping personnel records, and more.

Frequently Asked Questions About Personnel Policies

■ What is at-will employment?

If employees work at will, the company has the right to fire them at any time, for any reason that is not illegal—and they have the right to quit at any time. In the United States, employees are presumed to work at will unless they have an employment contract that limits their employers' right to fire. (For more on at-will employment, including steps you can take to avoid changing an at-will employee's status inadvertently, see "At-Will Employment," below.)

■ Does every company need an employee handbook?

No law requires employers to have an employee handbook, but it's a good idea. A handbook tells employees about workplace rules in an efficient, uniform way. Employees will know what is expected of them and what they can expect of the company. And your company will be able to prove that all employees were aware of the rules if a worker later decides to sue. (For suggestions on what to include in an employee handbook, see "Employee Handbooks," below.)

■ Do we need a sexual harassment policy?

Absolutely. The Supreme Court has held that an effective antiharassment policy, which includes a procedure for making complaints, can provide a defense to certain types of sexual harassment lawsuits. And a good policy can prevent sexual harassment from happening in the first place, by letting workers know what kinds of behavior cross the line—and what action the company will take against a harasser. (To learn more, see "Preventing Sexual Harassment," below.)

■ **How can I improve my communication with my coworkers and employees?**

Here are a few principles you can follow to improve your communication at work: listen first; understand your audience; tailor your message appropriately (for your goals and your audience); deliver your message using the right medium (email is appropriate only for certain things); and speak and write clearly and concisely. (For an explanation of these principles, see "Communicating With Employees Effectively," below.)

■ **How do I avoid legal problems when giving employee performance evaluations?**

First, decide on the job requirements and performance goals you want each employee to meet. Create specific criteria that are directly related to the employee's success on the job. Write down the criteria you choose and let your employees know the basis for their evaluations—or, better yet, ask your employees to help you come up with appropriate performance goals. (For more on evaluating your workers, see "Performance Appraisal," below.)

■ **What documents should I keep in an employee's personnel file?**

Your company should have a personnel file for each employee. Keep every important job-related document in the file, including job applications, offer letters, employment contracts, benefits and salary information, government forms, performance evaluations, and memos about disciplinary actions. (For more on personnel files, including who has access to them, see "Creating and Maintaining Personnel Files," below.)

■ **What are some of the things I can do to make our workplace more family-friendly without costing the company a lot of money?**

There are many policies you can institute in the workplace that can help your employees balance the competing demands of work and family without significant cost to your company, including: flexible work schedules; telecommuting; job sharing or part-time work schedules; flexible spending accounts; and empoyee asistance programs that provide help finding child care, after-school care, or elder care. (For more on such policies, see "Family-Friendly Workplace Policies," below.)

Personnel Policies and the Law

There are surprisingly few legal requirements when it comes to personnel policies. For example, no law dictates what a company must put in its employee handbook—or even requires companies to have one in the first place. You aren't legally obligated to evaluate your employees, let alone use a particular form or follow a specified timetable. And although federal and state laws prohibit sexual harassment, employers don't have to adopt a certain type of antiharassment policy.

So why take the time and trouble to develop sound personnel policies? Because they keep the workplace running smoothly—and keep your company out of legal trouble. Written policies tell workers what the company expects of them and what they can expect in return. A fair evaluation process helps managers keep track of workers' performance, notice and reward those workers who are doing well, and warn and assist those workers who are getting off track. A good sexual harassment policy will help prevent misconduct in the first place—and encourage workers to bring problems to the company's attention so they can be resolved before they get out of control. And policies that help employees balance work and family obligations will decrease distractions and absenteeism, while increasing worker productivity and loyalty.

We can't emphasize the legal benefits of solid personnel policies enough. If your company is unfortunate enough to be sued by a former worker, good personnel policies will be a key piece in its defense. Performance evaluations can be used to show that a worker fired for poor performance was given notice and an opportunity to improve before being shown the door. Written policies can help show that a worker fired for misconduct knew the rules—and the consequences of violating them. And if your company maintains complete personnel files, it will have all the documents necessary to prove that, for example, a worker generated customer complaints, signed a noncompete agreement, or received written performance warnings.

State Law

Some states have laws that apply to various personnel issues. For example, many states give workers the right to see their personnel files (or, at least, certain documents in those files). (See "State Laws on Access to Personnel Records," at the end of this chapter, for information on your state's law.) In addition, many states have codified the principle of employment at will. This age-old legal doctrine is not written down in any federal statute, but virtually every state (except Montana) recognizes it—and many have incorporated it into their own statutes. Again, your state labor department should be able to tell you whether your state has such a law or any other laws that relate to your personnel policies.

At-Will Employment

Private employers in the United States start off with the law on their side when dealing with employees. Although workers have specified rights in some situations, employers generally have plenty of latitude to make the employment decisions they feel are right for their businesses. This latitude is protected by the legal doctrine of "employment at will," which means just about what it sounds like: At-will employees are free to quit at any time, for any reason, and employers are free to fire them at any time, for any reason—unless that reason is illegal. An illegal reason is one that is discriminatory (see Chapter 3) or retaliatory (see "Retaliation" in Chapter 11), violates a statute or public policy, or is in bad faith (see "Illegal Reasons for Firing Employees" in Chapter 12).

Companies that avoid these no-nos may fire an at-will employee for even the most whimsical or idiosyncratic reasons—for having annoying mannerisms, poor fashion sense, or lousy eating habits, for example. Employers are also free to change the terms of employment—job duties, compensation, or hours, for example—for any reason that isn't illegal. Workers can agree to these changes and continue working or reject the changes and quit. In other words, the employment relationship is voluntary. An employer cannot force its employees to stay forever, and employees cannot require their employers to keep them on indefinitely.

Montana is the only state that does not recognize the doctrine of employment at will. Employers in the Big Sky state must have "good cause" to fire an employee who has worked for the company for at least six months. (For more on what constitutes good cause, see Chapter 12.)

Legal Limitations on At-Will Employment

The doctrine of employment at will gives employers protection from wrongful termination claims. But this protection is limited in two ways:

- **Employment contract.** The doctrine doesn't apply to employees who have an employment contract, whether written, oral, or implied, that puts some limits on the company's right to fire them. For these employees, the language or nature of the contract usually spells out the terms of employment, including when and for what reasons the employees can be fired. (See "Firing Employees With Employment Contracts" in Chapter 12 for more information.)

- **State or federal laws.** Congress, state legislatures, and judges have carved out several exceptions to the doctrine of employment at will. Generally, as stated above, these exceptions prevent employers from taking any negative action against an employee (including disciplining, demoting, or firing) that is illegal—in bad faith, in violation of public policy, or for a discriminatory or retaliatory reason. (See "Illegal Reasons for Firing Employees" in Chapter 12 for more information.)

Practical Limitations on At-Will Employment

Although the law gives employers the right to fire or change the job of an at-will employee for any reason, no matter how frivolous, employers who lack a sensible basis for employment decisions take legal and practical risks. These risks include:

- **Productivity and morale problems.** If you fire or discipline a worker without a good reason, the rest of the workforce will be confused and uneasy. Employees who believe they might be fired or demoted even if they are doing a good job have less incentive to follow performance standards and other rules of the workplace.
- **Recruiting and hiring difficulties.** Once word gets out that an employer fires or disciplines employees without good reason, new employees will be harder to find. After all, why should an employee take a job where he or she could get fired at any time if another employer offers a little job security or at least a fair shake?
- **Lawsuits.** An employee who has been treated unfairly is more motivated to sue. And despite the

doctrine of employment at will, most jurors have been or are employees and will empathize with the fired worker. Juries find ways to punish an employer they perceive to be unfair, arbitrary, or callous. And even if the employee ultimately loses the lawsuit, the employer will spend precious time and money fighting it in court.

Because of this, many employers fire or demote workers only for legitimate business reasons—reasons that their other workers (and a judge or jury, if it comes to that) will understand. However, smart employers also hang on to their at-will rights, just in case. Even if your company generally fires only for cause, maintaining the right to fire at will can provide a valuable legal theory to fall back on if your company ever has to defend its actions in court.

Preserving Your At-Will Rights

If you want to keep your company's right to fire and discipline employees on its own terms, don't make promises or adopt policies that restrict that right—for example, don't state that employees will only be fired for certain reasons or that employees will have a job as long as they do good work. Despite your good intentions, a disgruntled former employee can use these statements as evidence of an employment contract that eliminates employment at will.

Here are some steps you can take to protect your company's right to fire and discipline employees at will:

- **State that employment is at will.** In written employment policies, including the employee handbook or personnel manual, state clearly that employment at your company is at will and explain what this means.

- **Ask employees to sign an at-will agreement.** Consider asking employees to sign a simple form or offer letter acknowledging that their employment is at will. A worker who has signed such a form will have a difficult time refuting it later.

- **Don't promise continued employment.** If you tell employees that their jobs are secure, that they will not be fired without good cause, or even that the company has never had to fire a worker, you risk creating an expectation that they will not be fired. Avoid these types of comments; they are particularly common when interviewing potential employees and giving performance reviews.

- **Train managers.** With few exceptions, the actions and statements of company managers will be legally attributable to your company. If your job includes training other managers, make sure they understand company policies and procedures, especially regarding discipline, performance reviews, and employment at will. If managers make any statements or take any actions contrary to these policies—like promising that workers won't be fired—the company may just lose its at-will rights.

- **Keep disciplinary options open.** If your company has a progressive discipline policy, make sure it includes clear language preserving the right to fire employees at will. If the policy lists offenses for which firing is appropriate, it should state that the list is not exhaustive and that the company reserves the right to fire for any reason.

- **Don't refer to employees as "permanent."** Many employers have an initial probationary or temporary period for new employees, during which the company is free to fire the worker. Workers who survive this period are called permanent employees, entitled to benefits and so forth. To some courts, this language implies that an employee who becomes permanent can be fired only for good cause. If your company uses a probation period and you are responsible for writing company policies, make clear that the company retains the right to fire at will once the probationary period is over.

Lessons From the Real World

Annunzio Ferraro worked as a security guard at the Hyatt hotel in Milwaukee. His job application form, which he signed, said that his employment could be terminated at any time. However, Hyatt's employment manual stated that employees would only be fired for just cause and outlined a progressive discipline policy under which employees would generally receive at least two prior warnings for similar offenses before getting fired. The manual allowed the company to fire an employee immediately for a "severe rule violation."

Ferraro was fired for physically assaulting a hotel guest. Amazingly, he then sued for wrongful termination, claiming that the hotel breached an implied employment contract by firing him without the two prior warnings promised in its disciplinary policy.

The Wisconsin Supreme Court agreed with Ferraro on one important issue: The court found that Hyatt's disciplinary policy created an implied contract promising that Ferraro would be fired only for just cause.

However, the court found that Ferraro's assault on a hotel guest constituted a "severe rule violation" and gave the hotel ample cause for termination—particularly since it was not Ferraro's first offense. Ferraro had previously hit an intoxicated guest, raised his voice in argument with a guest, and been accused of harassing the hotel's female employees—all in the space of less than a year. Faced with this less-than-stellar record, the court threw out a jury's verdict in Ferraro's favor, finding that no jury could reasonably believe Hyatt had breached Ferraro's implied employment contract.

Ferraro v. Koelsch et al., 368 N.W.2d 666 (Wis. 1985).

Employee Handbooks

Many companies—especially smaller businesses—get along fine without any written employment policies. But at some point, particularly as your company grows, it makes good business sense to create an employee handbook. Although compiling the policies will take some effort, your company will save time, headaches, and possibly legal fees in the long run.

The benefits of having an employee handbook are many. Every employee will receive the same, consistent information about workplace rules, benefit policies, company procedures, and other important issues. Employees will know what is expected of them and what they can expect from your company, particularly in the areas of performance, attendance, and discipline. The handbook can tell workers a bit about the history of the business and the company's structure and values. And the handbook will provide a measure of legal protection if an employee or former employee decides to sue.

What to Include in an Employee Handbook

Effective employee handbooks vary widely in size, style, and content. Some large corporations produce handbooks that come in multiple volumes and cover every possible aspect of the business. Smaller companies might have a more limited handbook that covers only the basics— and could probably fit into a pamphlet.

No matter which approach your company chooses, its handbook should incorporate the company's style and values. A handbook doesn't have to be written in legalese to be effective—in fact, the best policies are written in plain English. A handbook should communicate policies to workers in language they will understand.

Here are some topics to consider covering in a handbook. If you are assigned the responsibility for creating, updating, or troubleshooting your company's handbook, you can use this list as a starting point. For more detailed information and sample policies that you can modify, cut, and paste for use in your company, see "Create Your Own Employee Handbook," by Lisa Guerin and Amy DelPo (Nolo).

- **Information about the company.** If your company has an organizational chart, mission statement, or written history, you can include it here.
- **At-will statement.** If your company is an "at-will" employer, you should include a statement to that effect in the handbook. (See "At-Will Employment," above, for more information.)
- **Hiring rules.** Explain any rules or policies the company follows when hiring workers, including job posting, affirmative action or antidiscrimination policies, referral bonuses, and any testing required of new workers or applicants.
- **Pay.** Set out the rules on overtime, show up or on-call time, wage garnishments, and so on. If the company

has policies on expense reimbursements, pay advances, and raises, include them as well. And let workers know when they will be paid and according to what formula—for example, by commission or piece rate.

- **Hours.** Set the rules on rest breaks and meal breaks, attendance policies, schedules, flextime or other flexible scheduling arrangements, and time cards, if applicable. (For more information on compensation and hours, see Chapter 2.)

- **Leave.** If your company offers sick leave, vacation time, parental leave, pregnancy or disability leave, leave for civic duties, sabbaticals, bereavement leave, or other time off, explain those policies here. (You can find information on leave policies in Chapter 5.)

- **Performance.** If your company gives performance evaluations, explain the process here, including when evaluations are given. (See "Performance Appraisal," below, for more information.)

- **Benefits.** Explain the benefits available to employees, including health insurance, dental and vision coverage, life insurance, disability insurance, pensions or other retirement plans, profit sharing, and the like.

- **Discrimination and harassment.** Include a statement that discrimination and harassment violate company policies and will not be tolerated. State that immediate action will be taken against wrongdoers. (For more on discrimination and sexual harassment, see "Preventing Sexual Harassment," below, and Chapter 3.)

- **Complaints and investigations.** Describe how employees can report harassment or other misconduct. Tell employees how to make complaints, describe what steps the company will take to investigate, and state that retaliation will not be allowed against a worker who complains in good faith. Encourage them to report any concerns immediately. (For more on investigations, see "Investigating Complaints" in Chapter 11.)

- **Health and safety.** Detail any safety-related workplace rules (for example, that hard hats must be worn in certain areas) and any special health and safety issues that apply to your company. And encourage workers to bring health and safety concerns to management for resolution. (For more on health and safety issues, see Chapter 7.)

- **Violence.** State clearly that violence and threats of violence will be taken seriously. Explain how employees can report threats and violent incidents, and lay out your company's safety plan in case of violence. (For more on violence, see "Workplace Violence" in Chapter 11.)

- **Privacy.** If your company monitors workers' phone calls, voice mail, email messages, or Internet use, or if it conducts any workplace search or surveillance, let workers know. (For more about privacy issues in the workplace, see Chapter 6.)

- **Workplace conduct.** Include not only company standards of conduct (for example, no fighting or no conflicts of interest) but also policies on grooming or uniforms, bringing children (or pets) to work, and use of office equipment.

- **Discipline.** If your company has a progressive discipline policy, describe it here. You can also describe what infractions constitute grounds for termination, but be sure to keep management's options open. (See below.) (Disciplinary policies are covered in "Disciplining Workers" in Chapter 11.)

- **Firing.** Detail any layoff and termination policies—including provisions regarding severance, recall rights, and references. (Firing and layoffs are covered in Chapter 12.)

Don't Create Obligations That Will Haunt Your Company Later

Some courts—and employees—interpret the language in employee handbooks as contracts that create binding obligations on employers. If you include any unconditional promises in the employee handbook, there's a very real possibility that employees or former employees might try to enforce those promises in court. Here are some of the most common trouble spots:

- **Promises of continued employment.** Don't put language in the handbook that promises employees a job as long as they follow company rules. A court might interpret this as a contract of employment, guaranteeing that employees will not be fired without good cause. State in the handbook that your company reserves the right to terminate employees for reasons not stated in the handbook or for no reason at all. Even though the company may never have to rely on this language to provide a legal defense to a wrongful termination claim, at least employees will know where they stand. (See "At-Will Employment", above, for more details.)

- **Conduct not covered by the handbook.** Of course, no handbook can cover every possible workplace situation. It's best to make this clear to employees by saying so in the handbook. Otherwise, employees may argue that any action the company takes that goes beyond what's explicitly set forth in the handbook is unfair.

- **Progressive discipline.** Many employers follow some form of "progressive discipline" for performance problems or less serious forms of misconduct (attendance problems, difficulties getting along with coworkers, or missing deadlines, for example). Often, discipline starts with a verbal warning, followed by a written warning for a second offense, followed by a probationary period or suspension, then termination. Whatever system your company uses, don't obligate managers to follow a particular disciplinary pattern for every employee in every circumstance. It's better to leave the company's options open, to make sure it can fire workers, if necessary, without facing a legal challenge. (See "Disciplining Workers" in Chapter 11 for more information.)

- **Right to change the handbook.** You cannot be sure that the employment policies you come up with today will stand the test of time. Your company might later decide to change or get rid of a policy or to branch out into other endeavors that make additional policies necessary. Either way, the handbook should state that the company reserves the right to change the policies at any time, for any reason. This will give your company the necessary leeway to keep its policies in tune with its business.

Once you've created a comprehensive employee handbook, set aside time to review and update it regularly as company policies and procedures change. An outdated handbook doesn't do the company or its employees any good—and could create confusion or unwanted legal obligations. And a periodic handbook review will help you identify changes you want—or need—to make to company policies.

Preventing Sexual Harassment

Private employers have a responsibility to provide a workplace that is free of sexual harassment. This is a legal obligation, but it also makes good business sense. Companies that allow sexual harassment to flourish will pay a high price in terms of poor employee morale, low productivity, and lawsuits.

As a manager, you are on the front lines when it comes to avoiding, preventing, and reporting harassment. You also have the legal authority to act on behalf of your company, which means that your failure to act appropriately can get the company in a lot of trouble. If you harass employees yourself, your company will be legally responsible for your actions. And if employees report harassment to you or you otherwise become aware that harassment is taking place, your company will be on the hook—even if you choose to look the other way. That's why it's so important to learn what harassment is—and what you should do if it takes place.

Sexual Harassment Defined

Sexual harassment is any unwelcome sexual advance or conduct on the job that creates an intimidating, hostile, or offensive working environment. Any conduct of a sexual nature that makes an employee uncomfortable has the potential to be sexual harassment. Sexual harassment can also include harassment that is not sexual in nature but is based on one's gender. This type of harassment typically occurs when women enter workplaces that have been traditionally male-dominated—for example, a woman who joins an all-male construction crew and finds sexist graffiti on her locker, her car defaced, or that her male coworkers won't back her up as they do each other on dangerous work tasks. For examples of behavior that might qualify as sexual harassment, see "Gender, Pregnancy, and Sexual Harassment" in Chapter 3.

Strategies for Prevention

There are a number of steps that a company can take to reduce the risk of sexual harassment:

- **Adopt a clear sexual harassment policy.** In its employee handbook, your company should include a clear policy prohibiting sexual harassment. The policy should: define sexual harassment; state in no uncertain terms that sexual harassment will not be tolerated; warn that the company will discipline or fire any wrongdoers; set out a clear procedure for filing sexual harassment complaints; state that complaints will be investigated fully; and assert that the company will not tolerate retaliation again anyone who complains about harassment.
- **Train employees.** Once a year, your company should require employees to attend sexual harassment training. These sessions should teach employees what sexual harassment is, explain that employees have a right to a workplace free of sexual harassment, review the company's complaint procedure, and encourage employees to come forward with concerns.
- **Train supervisors and managers.** At least once a year, your company should train supervisors and managers in a separate session. (A few states, including California, now require such trainings, at least for certain employers.) The sessions should educate managers and supervisors about sexual harassment and explain how to deal with complaints.
- **Monitor your workplace.** You and other managers should walk the floor periodically. Talk to employees about the work environment. Ask for their input. Look around the workplace itself. Do you see any offensive posters or notes? Keep the lines of communication open.
- **Take all complaints seriously.** If someone complains about sexual harassment, immediately follow your company's reporting procedure. Prompt and thorough investigation can help your company defend against harassment lawsuits. If the complaint turns out to be valid, the company's response should be swift and effective. (For more information, see "Investigating Complaints" in Chapter 11.)

Lessons From the Real World

A male employee successfully sued his employer for sexual harassment because his coworkers made fun of him for not being "manly" enough.

Antonio Sanchez endured a lot of abuse for his less-than-macho ways. Coworkers referred to him as "she" and "her," told him that he walked and carried his tray "like a woman," made derisive comments because he did not have sex with a female friend, and taunted him for behaving like a woman.

Understandably, this barrage of verbal abuse upset and angered Sanchez. He complained to the general manager, an assistant manager, and the human resources director, but got no relief.

Eventually he sued, arguing that the abuse amounted to illegal sexual harassment. The court agreed. It said that Sanchez's coworkers abused him because he did not conform to their gender-based stereotypes. This was sexual harassment, plain and simple, and the employer had a legal obligation to stop the harassment once it knew about it.

Nichols v. Azteca Restaurant Enterprises, Inc., 264 F.3d 864 (9th Cir. 2001).

Communicating With Employees Effectively

More than any other aspect of successful management and leadership, good communication skills can have an enormously positive impact on your workforce. On the flip side, few things are as damaging to your workplace as poor communication. There are countless advantages to mastering good communication skills; effective communication enhances your ability to do any of the following:

- solve problems (and perhaps even anticipate them)
- supervise others successfully
- develop solid work relationships
- create a clear and compelling vision for your team (and your company)
- manage workflow between individuals and groups
- make well-informed decisions
- manage good performance, and
- eliminate poor performance.

Most of us believe that we know what we mean before we say something. Why, then, do so many people consistently misunderstand us and get what we say wrong? Good communication is multi-faceted. To communicate effectively, you need to get your point across in a way that whomever you're talking to can truly understand. Here are a few guiding principles to help you achieve that effectiveness:

- listen first
- understand your audience
- tailor your message appropriately (for your goals and your audience)

- deliver your message using the right medium, and
- speak and write well.

If you can accomplish all of these things, you will see immediate improvement in your own work, as well as the work of those you manage. You will have the power to influence your company, convince others of your ideas, and lead more effectively. And you will able to communicate about all of the improvement!

Listen

Listening to others is probably the most overlooked aspect of good communication in the workplace. In their haste to make their own points, direct others, provide input, or just get things done, many managers often issue declarative statements and pay little attention to the effect they have on the recipients of such statements. Your ability to really listen, to understand what someone else is saying, and to incorporate that information into whatever you are doing directly and positively impacts your skills and abilities as a manager. You should focus on listening, regardless of the size of your audience.

The easiest way to build your listening skills is in a one-on-one environment. As you go about communicating something to an employee or coworker, stop and ask if he or she is clear on what you are saying. As he or she answers, listen closely and then repeat the answer back to the speaker, paraphrasing. Then ask, "Am I understanding you correctly?" Too often,

managers ask questions and, as those questions are being answered, are already preparing their responses. By knowing that you will have to paraphrase the answer you hear back to the speaker, you can train yourself to really listen to what is being said.

Depending on your responsibilities as a manager, you may have to communicate with small and large groups in addition to individuals. Yet the importance of listening to your audience remains. How many times have you been sitting in a meeting, listening to a presentation, and noticed that your mind has wandered—perhaps sinking you into such boredom that you might even shut your eyes? If the speaker was paying close attention and listening to the cues of the audience, he or she would have known to either shorten the presentation or punch it up somehow to recapture the audience. When you are the speaker in such a situation, always stay alert to how your information is being received. Check in with your audience frequently for questions (you're really testing to see if they are still listening!) and shorten or modify your material if you see that you are losing people.

Understand Your Audience

Another common mistake in communication at work is failing to consider whom you are speaking to and how that listener best receives information. Do not assume that everyone absorbs information like you do: Although it may be more comfortable for you to fall back on what works best for you, chances are high that what works for you won't work for everyone.

In one-on-one communication, especially with employees you manage, simply ask the listener how he or she would prefer to hear things. Some employees may wish to receive a written email rather than a phone call or voicemail if you are providing directives or instructions. Others may wish to have a back-and-forth conversation. Some employees may require time to process or think about issues before they discuss them. For such folks, you'll want to set up meetings thoughtfully and provide an agenda in advance so that they know what you are expecting of them.

When it comes to providing criticism or negative feedback, you should be particularly sensitive to the needs of your individual employees. For instance, it is never appropriate to criticize someone's work in front of others or in a group setting. Some people need to be taken aside, have the issue pointed out to them, and then participate in deciding how to correct the issue. Others may want to be told what is wrong and how they could do it better, directly and forthrightly. By spending time with your team and learning how each of them hears things best, you will be much more effective in the long run.

In larger audiences, know whom you are talking to and what level of understanding they have of the material being presented. We have all heard the old adage that newspaper articles are written at the sixth-grade level, so that they are understood by all. While this guideline may work for the public as a whole, if you present a sixth-grade level presentation to the Board of Directors of your company, chances are you'll be searching for a new job soon. Your audience will greatly appreciate being engaged at the appropriate level of their knowledge and interests—and may tune out if you don't hit the mark.

Tailor Your Message Appropriately

As the logical next step to knowing your audience, once you have that knowledge, use it. There are many ways to tailor a message; knowing what you want to accomplish with it is key to getting the message across effectively. You should consider not only your audience, but also the goal of your communication—what you want it to accomplish.

Because of this, if you need to deliver the same information to a variety of different people on whom the information will have varying impacts, you may need to tailor your message differently depending on your goal for communicating with each group. For example, imagine that you are a manager in a small company that is about to be sold to a larger company and that you manage a very diverse group of employees—everyone from warehouse personnel to freelance writers. You know that the information will affect your reports differently, so you should prepare the appropriate communication for each group you will face. When delivering the news to the freelance writers, you might, for example, focus more on the future plans of the new company and how the work they are currently doing will be folded into those plans. For the warehouse staff, however, you might focus on their employment status in particular, letting them know what will likely happen to their positions.

The content and style of your communication should reflect both the audience with whom you are communicating and your goal with the communication— whether it be to inform, instruct, reassure, discipline, persuade, and so on.

Deliver Your Message Using the Right Medium

Another key to effective communications at work is to deliver your message using the right medium of communication— whether it be a conversation, an email, a meeting, a written memo, or the like.

While the advent of email has been a huge boon to efficiency and consistency, email can be very dangerous when used as a way to avoid difficult conversations or to vent frustrations. Email is appropriate for getting your simple questions answered quickly, making large group announcements, or documenting a conversation after the fact. But, unfortunately, email is often misused, allowing people who are uncomfortable with direct confrontation the means to raise difficult subjects while

avoiding the reactions they provoke. This can be terribly destructive to effective communication at work because it can feel inappropriate or even cruel to the recipient. Also, when you send an email, you have no way of knowing how the recipient is interpreting your communication, which can cause needless and sometimes harmful misunderstandings.

Given the obvious limitations of email, even if it is your preferred method of communicating with employees, you must consider all of the possible ways you can deliver information at work and choose the most appropriate and effective medium. Consider the following:

- **Email.** As mentioned above, email is a great tool to update people, pass along materials, make brief announcements, provide status reports, ask and answer simple questions, and the like. It is not appropriate for many kinds of communication.
- **Voice mail.** A bit more personal than email, voice mail allows you to convey meaning with your tone of voice. It is appropriate for leaving a short instruction or requesting an in-person conversation or meeting. Larger companies often use voice mail to send out a "blast message," or company announcement, to employees. This allows everyone to hear the same message but does not allow two-way communication.
- **One-on-one conversations.** These are in-person meetings or telephone

conversations if the person you are speaking to is at another location. Conversation is a terrific medium for reviewing any performance issues, getting updated on work in progress, setting goals, and discussing how your employee is doing overall. It also provides direct and immediate feedback—the key to strong two-way communication.

- **Small group meetings.** This medium is best for making group decisions, gathering input from multiple sources, educating or training people, brain-storming ideas, and so on. A small group meeting should still involve two-way communication, allowing discussions, questions, and feedback.

- **Large group meetings.** This medium is best for bringing a larger number of people up to speed on specific issues in the same way at the same time. The larger the group, the more difficult it will be to engage in two-way communication, collect feedback, or make decisions.

- **Informal gatherings or hallway conversations.** Take advantage of these devices to get to know your team (and their communication preferences) better outside the work environment. Be careful not to hand out or take on any action items during such communication, as assignments can be quickly forgotten.

The key point here is to match your medium or vehicle for communication with the message. Don't use a large group meeting to be critical of an employee, but do use it to celebrate someone's accomplishments. Don't use email to blow off steam if you're angry, but do use it to appropriately share information on a specific issue. And, most importantly, don't hide behind passive communication vehicles like email or voice mail when you really need to have a direct, courageous conversation with someone.

Speak and Write Well

Finally, put some time and care into your written and spoken communication. Be clear and concise. Use words correctly. Check for typos and misspellings, even in internal emails—and especially in external presentations, memos, or correspondence. Such carelessness in a business setting is distracting and looks unprofessional.

Beyond these negatives, there are many more positive reasons why you should put care and thought into all your communications in the workplace, including the following:

- You appear more professional and knowledgeable.
- You garner credibility and respect.
- You will convey your point without distraction.
- You can be much more compelling when making an argument.
- You can effectively model good communication practices for employees and coworkers.

Improving your communication skills will not only help you in your current workplace, but is also an investment in your own professional development. There are countless books and training courses available on how to write more clearly, improve your presentation skills, and the like. A few places for more information include the American Management Association, online at www.amanet.com, which provides training and seminars on communication skills; and the books *Harvard Business Review on Effective Communications,* by Ralph G. Nichols, et. al, and *The Articulate Executive: Orchestrating Effective Communication*, by Fernando Bartolome, both published by Harvard Business School Press.

Performance Appraisal

Managers who routinely review employee performance and conduct regular employee evaluations reap tremendous benefits. The evaluation process nips a lot of employment problems in the bud. Your reports will know what you expect of them; will receive feedback, praise, and criticism of their work; and will have notice of any shortfalls in their performance or conduct. You can recognize and reward good employees and identify and coach workers who are having trouble. And the communication involved in any good evaluation process ensures that you will stay in tune with the needs and concerns of the workers you supervise

Performance evaluations can also keep your company out of legal trouble.

They help you track and document employee problems. If you ever need to fire or discipline a worker, you will have written proof that you gave the employee notice and a chance to correct the problem—which will go a long way towards convincing a jury or judge that you acted fairly. This section provides an overview of the performance appraisal process; for more detailed information and forms you can use in your workplace, see *The Performance Appraisal Handbook,* by Amy DelPo (Nolo).

Create Job Requirements and Performance Goals

Before you can accurately evaluate an employee's performance, you need some way to measure that performance. For each employee in a particular position, you will need to come up with performance objectives—job requirements and performance goals.

Job requirements describe what you want a worker in a particular job to accomplish and how you want the job done. These requirements apply across the board, to every worker who holds the same position. For example, a job requirement for a salesperson might be to make $15,000 in sales per quarter; for a customer service representative, to answer each call cheerfully; for a delivery driver, to have a missed delivery rate of 5% or less. Make sure requirements are achievable and directly related to the employee's job. If other managers supervise some employees who hold the same position, work together to come up with requirements all of you will use.

Performance goals should be tailored to each employee; they will depend on the individual worker's strengths and weaknesses. For example, a goal for a graphic artist might be learning a new software design program; for an accounting professional, a goal might be to take the exam to become a Certified Public Accountant. Your workers can help you figure out what reasonable goals should be.

Once you have defined the requirements and goals for each position and worker, write them down and hand them out to your reports. This will let employees know what you expect and what they will have to achieve during the year to receive a positive evaluation.

Keep Track of Employee Performance

Throughout the year, track the performance of each employee. Keep a performance log for each worker, either on your computer or on paper. Note memorable incidents or projects involving that worker, whether good or bad. For example, you might note that a worker was absent without calling in, worked overtime to complete an important project, or participated in a community outreach program on behalf of the company.

If an employee does an especially wonderful job on a project or really fouls something up, consider giving immedi-

ate feedback. Orally or in writing, let the employee know that you noticed and appreciate the extra effort—or that you are concerned about the employee's performance. If you choose to give this kind of feedback orally, make a written note of the conversation for the employee's personnel file.

Conduct Performance Evaluations

At least once a year, formally evaluate the worker both by writing a performance evaluation and meeting with the worker to discuss the evaluation. First, gather and review all of the documents and records relating to the employee's performance, productivity, and behavior. Review your performance log for the employee and the employee's personnel file. You might also want to take a look at other company records relating to the worker, including sales records, call reports, productivity records, time cards, budget reports, and the like.

Once you have reviewed these records and gathered your thoughts about the employee's work, write the evaluation (or, if you will solicit input from other managers, ask each of them to complete an evaluation and compile them). Although a performance evaluation can take many forms, it should include:

- each requirement or goal you set for that worker and that job
- your conclusion as to whether the employee met the requirement or goal, and

4/22 THE MANAGER'S LEGAL HANDBOOK

- the reasons that support your conclusion.

Many companies use some kind of numerical scale or grading system to indicate how well the employee did on each goal or requirement. If yours is one of them, you should include these ratings in your evaluation. You should also leave space on the form for the employee's comments and your notes on your meeting with the employee.

When you have finished writing the evaluation, set up a meeting to discuss it with the employee. Remember, this is likely to be one of the most important meetings you have with that worker all year—be sure to schedule enough time to discuss each issue thoroughly. At the meeting, let the worker know what you think he or she did well and what he or she needs to improve. Using your evaluation as a guide, explain your conclusions about each requirement and goal. Listen carefully to the worker's comments—and ask the worker to write them down on the evaluation form. Take notes on the meeting and include those notes on the form.

Tips for Performance Appraisal

Giving evaluations can be difficult. A worker who is criticized might react defensively. And, sometimes, no one understands what merits a positive evaluation. If workers feel that you take it easy on some of them while coming down hard on others, resentment will build. Avoid problems by following these rules:

- **Be specific.** When you set requirements and goals for your workers, spell out exactly what they will have to do to achieve them. For example, don't say "work harder" or "improve quality." Instead, say "increase sales by 20 percent over last year" or "make three or fewer errors per day in data input." Similarly, when you evaluate a worker, give specific examples of what the employee did to achieve—or fall short of—the requirement or goal.
- **Give deadlines.** If you want to see improvement, give the worker a timeline for turning things around. If you expect something to be done by a certain date, say so.
- **Be realistic.** If you set unrealistic or impossible requirements and goals, everyone will be disheartened—and will have little incentive to do their best if they know they will still fall short. Don't make your requirements too easy to achieve, but do take into account the realities of your workplace.
- **Be honest.** If you avoid telling a worker of performance problems, the worker won't know which areas need improvement. Be sure to give the bad news, even if it is uncomfortable.
- **Be complete.** Write your evaluation so that an outsider reading it would be able to understand exactly what happened and why. Remember, the evaluation could potentially become evidence in a lawsuit, should the employee ever sue. If it does become

evidence, you will want the judge and jury to see why you rated the employee as you did.

- **Evaluate performance, not personality.** Focus on how well (or poorly) the worker did the job—not on the worker's personal characteristics or traits. Don't say, "You are angry and emotional." Instead, focus on the workplace conduct that is the problem—for example, "You have been insubordinate to your supervisor twice in the past six months. This behavior is unacceptable and must stop."

- **Listen to your employees.** The evaluation process will seem fairer to workers if they have an opportunity to express their concerns, too. Ask employees what they enjoy about their jobs and working at the company. Also ask about any concerns or problems each employee has. You'll gain valuable information, and the employee will feel like a real participant in the process. In rare cases, you might even learn something that could change your evaluation.

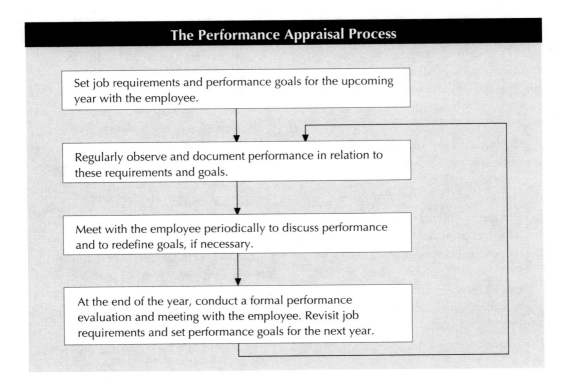

The Performance Appraisal Process

Set job requirements and performance goals for the upcoming year with the employee.

Regularly observe and document performance in relation to these requirements and goals.

Meet with the employee periodically to discuss performance and to redefine goals, if necessary.

At the end of the year, conduct a formal performance evaluation and meeting with the employee. Revisit job requirements and set performance goals for the next year.

Creating and Maintaining Personnel Files

Paperwork can be a bore, but setting up and maintaining personnel files will pay off in the long run. You will have all the important documents that relate to each employee in one place, where they'll be easily available when it's time to make decisions on promotions or layoffs, file tax returns, or comply with government audits. And if you have to fire a problem employee, careful documentation can protect your company from legal trouble.

What Goes in a Personnel File

Begin a personnel file for each of your employees on the date of hire. (If you are a manager or supervisor, talk to your human resources department about who should set up the personnel file—and whether you should have your own files on your reports or submit documents to the employee's main file.)

All important job-related documents should go in the file, including:

- the employee's job application and/ or resume
- letters of reference provided by or for the employee or notes from your conversations with references
- the offer letter
- IRS Form W-4 (the Employee's Withholding Allowance Certificate)
- forms relating to the employee's benefits

- forms providing next of kin and emergency contacts for the employee
- a signed acknowledgment that the employee received and read the employee handbook
- performance evaluations
- other documents relating to the employee's performance (such as written warnings, memos on disciplinary actions, recognition for good performance, and complaints or compliments from customers)
- records of attendance at, or completion of, training programs
- records of promotions, pay raises, and transfers
- any contract, written agreement, receipt, or other acknowledgment between the employee and the employer (such as a noncompete agreement, an employment contract, or an agreement relating to a company-provided car), and
- documents relating to the worker's departure from the company (such as reasons why the worker was fired or let go, unemployment documents, COBRA forms, and other benefit documents).

Although an employee's personnel file should contain every important job-related document, don't go overboard. In many states, employees have the right to view their personnel files (or at least certain items, such as contracts or other documents they have signed). In the worst-case scenario, that file may turn into evidence in a lawsuit brought by a disgruntled former employee. Indiscreet entries that do not directly relate to an employee's job performance and qualifications—like references to an employee's private life or political beliefs; unsubstantiated criticisms; or comments about an employee's race, sex, or religion—will come back to haunt your company. A good rule of thumb: Don't put anything in a personnel file that you would not want a jury to see.

What Does Not Go in a Personnel File

Although most employment-related documents should be kept in a worker's personnel file, there are a couple of exceptions to this rule. First, medical records should not go in a worker's personnel file. If a worker is disabled, the employer is legally required to keep all of the disabled worker's medical records in a separate file—and limit access only to a very few people. Although this rule only applies to disabled workers, it's good practice to segregate medical information into a separate file for all workers, disabled or not.

Second, Form I-9, the form you must complete for each employee verifying eligibility to work in this country, should be kept in a separate file. The U.S. Citizenship and Immigration Service (USCIS), the agency that replaced the INS, is entitled to inspect these forms (and often does). If you keep these forms in a worker's personnel file, the USCIS will

be looking at all those other documents as well. Not only does this compromise workers' privacy, but it also might open your company up to additional questions and investigation.

How to Maintain a Personnel File

Establish a time to periodically review each employee's personnel file, perhaps when you conduct the employee's evaluation. During this review, consider whether the documents in the file are accurate, up to date, and complete. Some questions to consider:

- Does the file reflect all of the employee's raises, promotions, and commendations?
- Does the file contain every written evaluation of the employee?
- Does the file show every warning or other disciplinary action taken against the employee?
- If company policy provides that written warnings or other records of discipline will be removed from an employee's file after a certain period, have they been removed?
- If the employee was on a performance improvement plan, a probationary or training period, or other temporary status, has it ended? Has the file been updated to reflect the employee's current status?
- If the employee handbook has been updated since the employee started work, does the file contain a receipt

or acknowledgment for the most recent version?

- Does the file contain current versions of every contract or other agreement between the company and the employee?

Once you get a regular filing system in place (for example, to make sure every new document a worker signs goes in the personnel file), these annual reviews should only take a few minutes.

Who May See Personnel Files

Generally, personnel files should be treated as private records belonging to the company and its employees. Obviously, not everyone in the company should be allowed to rummage through the performance evaluations, salaries, and job applications of employees. But, some employees may have a legitimate need to view the information in a personnel file. For example, you or another manager may need to review performance evaluations to decide whether to promote an employee, or the human resources manager may need to review an employee's salary information to decide what to pay a new hire in the same position.

Treat personnel files like any other private company records: Keep them confidential and store them in a locked cabinet. Allow only those with legitimate business reasons to have access to the files. For example, a reasonable policy might give only the human resources manager, the individual employee's

manager, and the employee him- or herself the right to see the employee's file. This will protect employees' privacy and limit opportunities for inappropriate documents to find their way into the files.

Employees' Rights to See Their Own Personnel Files

Most states give employees some right to view the contents of their own personnel files. This right may be limited, however. In some states, employers have to provide workers with copies of certain documents in their files. In others, the employee may only review the file in person, sometimes in the presence of a company representative. And in some states, the company can withhold certain documents that might compromise another person's privacy— letters of reference or investigation reports, for example. To find out your state's rules, see "State Laws on Access to Personnel Records," at the end of this chapter.

Even if your state does not expressly allow employees to inspect their personnel files, however, it's a sensible policy to allow them to do so, or at least to inform them about documents that are in their files. If you are planning to take action against an employee based on material in the personnel file—a complaint or documented performance problems, for example—let the employee know. That way, the employee will have a chance to explain or discuss the problem and an opportunity to improve. An employee who finds negative information in a file only after being fired is likely to believe, rightly or wrongly, that those documents were created after the fact.

Family-Friendly Workplace Policies

In addition to the personnel policies that you must adopt, an increasing number of companies today are choosing to adopt policies that help their employees to meet the competing demands of work and family.

Family-Friendly Policies Defined

For a variety of reasons, a growing number of companies today are adopting personnel policies that help their employees balance work and family obligations. Such policies are often referred to as "family-friendly policies," yet they do not benefit only employees with young children; in fact, employees with elderly parents or other relatives for whom they must care or employees who have their own health or personal needs that can interfere with work can benefit from such policies as well.

Adopting family-friendly policies can be an inexpensive, yet effective way to attract workers to your company these days, when the costs of employee benefits can be astronomical. You may not think of allowing workers more flexibility with their schedules or providing workers help to identify child or elder care services, for example, as traditional employment

benefits. Yet such policies can be valuable and inexpensive tools to attract the best workers, especially if your company may not be able to afford to pay for the most comprehensive health insurance plan for workers or to make large matching contributions to worker 401(k)s.

In addition, your company can reap cost savings by adopting policies that let employees deal with the family or other matters that often distract or interrupt their work. Family-friendly policies can increase loyalty, job satisfaction, and productivity, while reducing absenteeism, turnover, and the associated costs of finding and training new workers. Global consulting company Deloitte & Touche estimated that offering flexible work arrangements to 30,000 employees in the U.S. helped save $41.5 million in turnover and affiliated costs in 2003, while pharmaceutical company Merck & Co. estimated that it cost $38,000 to give an average employee a six-month parental leave with partial pay and benefits, but it cost $50,000 to replace the employee. (Elyane Robertson Demby, "Do Your Family-Friendly Programs Make Cents?," *HR Magazine*, January 2004, Vol. 49, No. 1.)

Below are some of the types of family-friendly policies that companies around the nation are implementing. (Note that these are just a handful of potential policies: The possibilities are limited only by the imaginations of your company's policymakers.)

- **Flexible work schedules.** This means allowing employees to work full time, yet outside of normal business hours—whether it be 7:00 a.m. to 3:00 p.m., 10 hours for four days a week, or a varying schedule each day. It can also mean the flexibility to leave work when necessary to take an elderly parent to a doctor's appointment or pick up a sick child early from school. For more on flextime, see "Flexible Work Schedules" in Chapter 2.

- **Telecommuting.** This refers to allowing employees to work offsite— for example, from home—for some or all of their workweek.
- **Job sharing.** This means allowing two employees to share one full-time job, with the position covered by one of them each day.
- **Flexible spending accounts.** These are accounts that allow employees to set aside pretax money from their income (like a 401(k)) which they can then use to reimburse their dependent care costs or medical expenses.
- **Employee assistance programs (EAPs) or work/life programs.** These are general terms for a host of supportive services that companies provide to their employees—for example, resource lists or other help finding child care, after-school care, or elder care providers
- **Caregiving services.** Some companies go as far as providing financial assistance for child care nearby,

providing onsite child care, or providing emergency caregiver services to be used when planned child or elder care falls through.
- **Allowing employees to donate sick or vacation time to each other.** Should one employee have an emergency situation, this allows others to help that employee out (while not requiring the company to provide any additional sick or vacation leave than it normally would have). For more on sick and vacation time, see "Vacation and Sick Leave" in Chapter 5.
- **Providing additional family and medical leave.** This means either providing more unpaid leave than what is required of the company by law or providing partial or total pay during an employee's otherwise unpaid leave. For more on family and medical leave, see Chapter 5.

Are Family-Friendly Policies Legal?

As with all employment benefits your company provides, any family-friendly policies your company decides to offer will be legally sound as long as the company offers and administers such policies fairly and consistently and free from illegal discrimination. Again, this does not mean that you have to provide every single worker with the same family-friendly benefits; it just means that you cannot decide who gets such benefits based on an impermissible reason, such as race, gender, national origin, religion, age, or disability. Your company may, for example, decide to provide paid family and medical leave only for top executives as part of an executive compensation package. Or you may decide who gets to work a flexible schedule based on seniority with the company. In addition, where appropriate, some of these policies may be used as reasonable accommodations for employees with disabilities—for example, allowing a worker to work flextime, to job share, or to telecommute. (See "Disability" in Chapter 3 for more or reasonable accommodations.)

Once you make such a policy, however, you cannot administer it discriminatorily— for example, allowing only mothers access to such benefits, but not fathers. One note of caution here: Some state and local laws may prohibit discrimination based on sexual orientation and/or marital status in addition to the characteristics protected by federal law, so be sure to follow any such laws that apply to your company when administering family-friendly policies. For more information on impermissible discrimination, see Chapter 3 and contact your state fair employment practices agency. (Contact information is in the Appendix.)

While some may complain that family-friendly policies favor workers who have children over those who don't or favor women over men, this is not necessarily true, so long as you make such policies available equally to all workers who may need them. For example, if you offer paid maternity leave, offer paid paternity leave, too. If you offer flexible work schedules to care for children after school, offer this benefit equally to mothers and fathers. If you allow job-sharing or part-time work for parents of young children, allow the same for workers who may need to care for an elderly parent or sick spouse. In short, be sure to make all of your family-friendly policies clear and consistent and to administer them fairly, without regard to race, gender, national origin, religion, age, disability, or any other characteristics protected by your state and local laws.

For more information on family-friendly workplace policies, consult any of the many organizations that focus on helping employees balance work and family, including the following:

- The Families and Work Institute (www.familiesandwork.org)
- The National Partnership for Women and Families (www.nationalpartnership.org)
- Workplace Flexibility 2010 (www.law.georgetown.edu/ workplace flexibility2010)
- Catalyst (www.catalyst.org)
- Winning Workplaces (www.winning workplaces.com), and
- Working Mother Magazine (www.workingmother.com), which publishes an annual list of the best 100 companies to work for based on their family-friendly policies.

Legal Dos and Don'ts: Personnel Basics

Do:

- **Keep your door open.** All good management practices and policies are based on communication between workers and managers. Keep your ear to the ground by having an open door policy that encourages your reports to come to you with concerns or ideas—and listening to what they have to say. You may be surprised at what you hear.

- **Blaze a paper trail.** Any time you evaluate, discipline, take a complaint from, or investigate an employee, write it down. Keeping a written record of an employee's performance and conduct is the best way to keep your company out of court. If you later have to fire that employee, your documents will make it much harder for him or her to find a lawyer willing to take the case.

- **Get help from your reports.** Your policies and practices will be most effective if workers believe they are reasonable and fair—and if they had a hand in their development. Encourage employees to help you develop performance requirements and goals, come up with training programs that would be helpful, or suggest ways you can help them do their jobs more effectively.

Don't:

- **Sugarcoat the truth.** Most of us dislike giving bad news or disappointing others. But when you are giving evaluations, you have to be honest. Employees will improve only if you tell them exactly what you expect and where they have fallen short.

- **Treat some workers better than others.** Discrimination claims start with inconsistency—when you treat some workers better (or worse) than others. By knowing your company's policies and applying them evenhandedly, you will avoid playing favorites or picking on scapegoats, practices sure to land your company in legal trouble.

- **Procrastinate.** Putting off important tasks is a bad habit for a variety of reasons, but managers who procrastinate can create lots of unnecessary problems. If you are always timely with your performance evaluations and personnel documents, you will be able to avoid claims that you created evidence after the fact to justify termination or other discipline.

Test Your Knowledge

Questions

1. All employees work at will unless they have a written employment contract stating otherwise. ☐ True ☐ False

2. Managers should always have a good reason for firing an employee, even if the employee works at will. ☐ True ☐ False

3. As long as company policies are written down in an employee handbook, managers are free to supervise employees and make decisions as they see fit. ☐ True ☐ False

4. You have no obligation to report or take action to stop sexual harassment unless the victim is willing to make a complaint in writing. ☐ True ☐ False

5. Sexual harassment training is not just a good idea; it may also be legally required. ☐ True ☐ False

6. Because it is so efficient, you should always communicate with employees you supervise via email. ☐ True ☐ False

7. You should give employees feedback throughout the year, not just at formal, year-end reviews. ☐ True ☐ False

8. I-9 forms should not be kept in employees' regular personnel files. ☐ True ☐ False

9. Employees are not entitled to see what's in their personnel files. ☐ True ☐ False

10. Family-friendly policies are discriminatory because they only benefit workers who have children. ☐ True ☐ False

Answers

1. False. If you make promises about continued employment to an employee, orally or in writing (for example, in an employee handbook), you risk creating an oral or implied contract that the employee will be fired only for good cause or other specified reasons.

2. True. Even if you have the legal right to fire at will, you don't gain anything by using it. Firing employees without a good reason leads to morale problems and employee lawsuits.

3. False. Written policies in an employee handbook are meaningless if managers don't follow those policies consistently.

4. False. Once a manager learns of harassment—whether through a complaint, personal observation, or any other means—the company is legally responsible to take action to stop it. Employees need not make a written complaint to put the company on notice.

5. True. Some states require companies to provide sexual harassment training.

6. False. Email is a great tool for certain types of communication—for example, to document a conversation after it occurs, update people with consistent information, pass along materials, make brief announcements, provide status reports, ask and answer simple questions, and the like. It is not, however, appropriate for many kinds of communication—for example, to provide feedback on an employee's performance or deliver bad news. Never use email as a way to avoid conversations that make you uncomfortable.

7. True. Ongoing feedback, both positive and negative, is an important part of a successful performance evaluation system.

8. True. I-9 forms should be kept in a separate file, so government auditors will be able to review them without rummaging through other employee personnel documents.

9. False. Most states give employees and former employees a right to see at least some of the documents in their personnel files.

10. False. Instituting policies that help workers balance the competing demands of work and family can benefit all workers, regardless of whether they have children or not. Such things as flexible work schedules, job-sharing, and flexible spending accounts can help workers to care for elderly parents or sick spouses or partners or to meet their own health or other needs. As long as such policies are written and applied consistently, fairly, and without regard to such protected characteristics as gender, race, national origin, age, and the like, they are legally sound.

State Laws on Access to Personnel Records

This chart deals with only those states that authorize access to personnel files. Generally, an employee is allowed to see evaluations, performance reviews, and other documents that determine a promotion, bonus, or raise; access usually does not include letters of reference, test results, or records of a criminal or workplace-violation investigation. Under other state laws, employees may have access to their medical records and records of exposure to hazardous substances; these laws are not included in this chart.

Alaska

Alaska Stat. § 23.10.430

Employers affected: All.

Employee access to records: Employee or former employee may view and copy personnel files.

Conditions for viewing records: Employee may view records during regular business hours under reasonable rules.

Copying records: Employee pays (if employer so requests).

California

Cal. Lab. Code §§ 1198.5; 432

Employers affected: All employers subject to wage and hour laws.

Employee access to records: Employee has right to inspect at reasonable intervals any personnel records relating to performance or to a grievance proceeding. Employee also has a right to a copy of any personnel document employee has signed.

Conditions for viewing records: Employee may view records at reasonable times, during break or nonwork hours. If records are kept offsite or employer does not make them available at the workplace, then employee must be allowed to view them at the storage location without loss of pay.

Connecticut

Conn. Gen. Stat. Ann. §§ 31-128a to 31-128h

Employers affected: All.

Employee access to records: Employee has right to inspect personnel files within a reasonable time after making a request, but not more than twice a year. Employer must keep files on former employees for at least one year after termination.

Written request required: Yes.

Conditions for viewing records: Employee may view records during regular business hours in a location at or near worksite. Employer may require that files be viewed on the premises and in the presence of employer's designated official.

Copying records: Employer must provide copies within a reasonable time after receiving employee's written request; request must identify the materials employee wants copied. Employer may charge a fee that is based on the cost of supplying documents.

Employee's right to insert rebuttal: Employee may insert a written statement explaining any disagreement with information in the personnel record. Rebuttal must be maintained as part of the file.

Delaware

Del. Code Ann. tit. 19, §§ 730 to 735

Employers affected: All.

Employee access to records: Current employee, employee who is laid off with reemployment rights, or employee on leave of absence may inspect personnel record; employee's agent is not entitled to have access to records. Unless there is reasonable cause, employer may limit access to once a year.

Written request required: Yes. Employer may require employee to file a form and indicate either the purpose of the review or what parts of

State Laws on Access to Personnel Records (continued)

the record employee wants to inspect.

Conditions for viewing records: Records may be viewed during employer's regular business hours. Employer may require that employees view files on their own time and may also require that files be viewed on the premises and in the presence of employer's designated official.

Copying records: Employer is not required to permit employee to copy records. Employee may take notes.

Employee's right to insert rebuttal: If employee disagrees with information in personnel file and cannot reach an agreement with employer to remove or correct it, employee may submit a written statement explaining her position. Rebuttal must be maintained as part of the personnel file.

Illinois

820 Ill. Comp. Stat. §§ 40/1 to 40/12

Employers affected: Businesses with 5 or more employees.

Employee access to records: Current employee, or former employee terminated within the past year, is permitted to inspect records twice a year at reasonable intervals, unless a collective bargaining agreement provides otherwise. An employee involved in a current grievance may designate a representative of the union or collective bargaining unit, or other agent, to inspect personnel records that may be relevant to resolving the grievance. Employer must make records available within 7 working days after employee makes request (if employer cannot meet deadline, may be allowed an additional 7 days).

Written request required: Yes. Employer may require use of a form.

Conditions for viewing records: Records may be viewed during employer's normal business hours at or near employee's worksite or, at employer's discretion, during nonworking hours at a different location. Employer may require that records be viewed on the premises.

Copying records: After reviewing records, employee may get a copy. Employer may charge only actual cost of duplication. If employee is unable to view files at worksite, employer, upon receipt of a written request, must mail employee a copy.

Employee's right to insert rebuttal: If employee disagrees with any information in the personnel file and cannot reach an agreement with employer to remove or correct it, employee may submit a written statement explaining his position. Rebuttal must remain in file with no additional comment by employer.

Iowa

Iowa Code § 91B.1

Employers affected: All employers with salaried employees or commissioned salespeople.

Employee access to records: Employee may have access to personnel file at time agreed upon by employer and employee.

Conditions for viewing records: Employer's representative may be present.

Copying records: Employer may charge copying fee for each page that is equivalent to a commercial copying service fee.

Maine

Me. Rev. Stat. Ann. tit. 26, § 631

Employers affected: All.

Employee access to records: Within 10 days of submitting request, employee, former employee, or authorized representative may view and copy personnel files.

Written request required: Yes.

State Laws on Access to Personnel Records (continued)

Conditions for viewing records: Employee may view records during normal business hours at the location where the files are kept, unless employer, at own discretion, arranges a time and place more convenient for employee. If files are in electronic or any other nonprint format, employer must provide equipment for viewing and copying.

Copying records: Employee entitled to one free copy of personnel file during each calendar year, including any material added to file during that year. Employee must pay for any additional copies.

Massachusetts

Mass. Gen. Laws ch. 149, § 52C

Employers affected: All. (Employers with 20 or more employees must maintain personnel records for 3 years after termination.)

Employee access to records: Employee or former employee must have opportunity to review personnel files within 5 business days of submitting request. (Law does not apply to tenured or tenure-track employees in private colleges and universities.)

Written request required: Yes.

Conditions for viewing records: Employee may view records at workplace during normal business hours.

Copying records: Employee must be given a copy of record within 5 business days of submitting a written request.

Employee's right to insert rebuttal: If employee disagrees with any information in personnel record and cannot reach an agreement with employer to remove or correct it, employee may submit a written statement explaining her position. Rebuttal becomes a part of the personnel file.

Michigan

Mich. Comp. Laws §§ 423.501 to 423.505

Employers affected: Employers with 4 or more employees.

Employee access to records: Current or former employee is entitled to review personnel records at reasonable intervals, generally not more than twice a year, unless a collective bargaining agreement provides otherwise.

Written request required: Yes. Request must describe the record employee wants to review.

Conditions for viewing records: Employee may view records during normal office hours either at or reasonably near the worksite. If these hours would require employee to take time off work, employer must provide another time and place that is more convenient for the employee.

Copying records: After reviewing files, employee may get a copy; employer may charge only actual cost of duplication. If employee is unable to view files at the worksite, employer, upon receipt of a written request, must mail employee a copy.

Employee's right to insert rebuttal: If employee disagrees with any information in personnel record and cannot reach an agreement with employer to remove or correct it, employee may submit a written statement explaining his position. Statement may be no longer than five 8½" by 11" pages.

Minnesota

Minn. Stat. Ann. §§ 181.960 to 181.966

Employers affected: All.

Employee access to records: Current employee may review files once per 6-month period; former employee may have access to records once only during the first year after termination. Employer must be given 7 days' advance request

State Laws on Access to Personnel Records (continued)

(14 days' if personnel records kept out of state). Employer may not retaliate against an employee who asserts rights under these laws.

Written request required: Yes.

Conditions for viewing records: Current employee may view records during employer's normal business hours at worksite or a nearby location; does not have to take place during employee's working hours. Employer or employer's representative may be present.

Copying records: Employer must provide copy free of charge. Current employee must first review record and then submit written request for copies. Former employee must submit written request; providing former employee with a copy fulfills employer's obligation to allow access to records.

Employee's right to insert rebuttal: If employee disputes specific information in the personnel record, and cannot reach an agreement with employer to remove or revise it, employee may submit a written statement identifying the disputed information and explaining her position. Statement may be no longer than 5 pages and must be kept with personnel record as long as it is maintained.

Nevada

Nev. Rev. Stat. Ann. § 613.075

Employers affected: All.

Employee access to records: An employee who has worked at least 60 days and a former employee, within 60 days of termination, must be given a reasonable opportunity to inspect personnel records.

Conditions for viewing records: Employee may view records during employer's normal business hours.

Copying records: Employer may charge only actual cost of providing access and copies.

Employee's right to insert rebuttal: Employee may submit a reasonable written explanation in direct response to any entry in personnel record. Statement must be of moderate length; employer may specify the format.

New Hampshire

N.H. Rev. Stat. Ann. § 275:56

Employers affected: All.

Employee access to records: Employer must provide employees a reasonable opportunity to inspect records.

Copying records: Employer may charge a fee related to actual cost of supplying copies.

Employee's right to insert rebuttal: If employee disagrees with any of the information in personnel record and cannot reach an agreement with the employer to remove or correct it, employee may submit a written statement of her version of the information along with evidence to support her position.

Oregon

Or. Rev. Stat. § 652.750

Employers affected: All.

Employee access to records: Employer must provide employees a reasonable opportunity to inspect personnel records used to determine qualifications for employment, promotion, or additional compensation, termination, or other disciplinary action. Employer must keep records for 60 days after termination of employee.

Conditions for viewing records: Employee may view records at worksite or place of work assignment.

Copying records: Employer must provide a certified copy of requested record to current or former employee (if request made within 60 days of termination). May charge only actual cost of providing copy.

State Laws on Access to Personnel Records (continued)

Pennsylvania

43 Pa. Cons. Stat. Ann. §§ 1321 to 1324

Employers affected: All.

Employee access to records: Employer must allow employee to inspect personnel record at reasonable times. (Employee's agent, or employee who is laid off with reemployment rights or on leave of absence, must also be given access.) Unless there is reasonable cause, employer may limit review to once a year by employee and once a year by employee's agent.

Written request required: At employer's discretion. Employer may require the use of a form as well as a written indication of the parts of the record employee wants to inspect or the purpose of the inspection. For employee's agent: Employee must provide signed authorization designating agent; must be for a specific date and indicate the reason for the inspection or the parts of the record the agent is authorized to inspect.

Conditions for viewing records: Employee may view records during normal business hours at the office where records are maintained, when there is enough time for employee to complete the review. Employer may require that employee or agent view records on their own time and may also require that inspection take place on the premises and in the presence of employer's designated official.

Copying records: Employer not obligated to permit copying. Employee may take notes.

Employee's right to insert rebuttal: The Bureau of Labor Standards, after a petition and hearing, may allow employee to place a counterstatement in the personnel file, if employee claims that the file contains an error.

Rhode Island

R.I. Gen. Laws § 28-6.4-1

Employers affected: All.

Employee access to records: Employer must permit employee to inspect personnel files when given at least 7 days' advance notice (excluding weekends and holidays). Employer may limit access to no more than 3 times a year.

Written request required: Yes.

Conditions for viewing records: Employee may view records at any reasonable time other than employee's work hours. Inspection must take place in presence of employer or employer's representative.

Copying records: Employee may not make copies or remove files from place of inspection. Employer may charge a fee reasonably related to cost of supplying copies.

Washington

Wash. Rev. Code Ann. §§ 49.12.240 to 49.12.260

Employers affected: All.

Employee access to records: Employee may have access to personnel records at least once a year within a reasonable time after making a request.

Employee's right to insert rebuttal: Employee may petition annually that employer review all information in employee's personnel file. If there is any irrelevant or incorrect information in the file, employer must remove it. If employee does not agree with employer's review, employee may request to have a statement of rebuttal or correction placed in file. Former employee has right of rebuttal for two years after termination.

Wisconsin

Wis. Stat. Ann. § 103.13

Employers affected: All employers who maintain personnel records.

State Laws on Access to Personnel Records (continued)

Employee access to records: Employee and former employee must be allowed to inspect personnel records within 7 working days of making request. Access is permitted twice per calendar year unless a collective bargaining agreement provides otherwise. Employee involved in a current grievance may designate a representative of the union or collective bargaining unit, or other agent, to inspect records that may be relevant to resolving the grievance.

Written request required: At employer's discretion.

Conditions for viewing records: Employee may view records during normal working hours at a location reasonably near worksite. If this would require employee to take time off work, employer may provide another reasonable time and place for review that is more convenient for the employee.

Copying records: Employee's right of inspection includes the right to make or receive copies. If employer provides copies, may charge only actual cost of reproduction.

Employee's right to insert rebuttal: If employee disagrees with any information in the personnel record and cannot come to an agreement with the employer to remove or correct it, employee may submit a written statement explaining his position. Employer must attach the statement to the disputed portion of the personnel record.

Current as of February 2005

5

Time Off

....

We all know that a little time off is a good thing. Workers get a chance to have fun and recharge their batteries when they can or deal with personal and family obligations when they have to. And your company benefits, too: A company is more productive if its employees (and managers!) are healthy, rested, and focused on their jobs.

Whether your company offers a generous leave program or only the minimum required by law, this chapter will give you an overview of the rules on:

- vacation time
- sick leave
- family and medical leave
- pregnancy and parental leave
- time off for jury duty
- voting leave
- leave for military service, and
- other types of legally required leave.

If you are responsible for setting company policy, this chapter will help you create sensible leave policies that stay well within the bounds of the law. If your job is to supervise employees, this information will help you figure out how to handle requests for leave, how to enforce your company's policies, and what kinds of requests should alert you to a potential legal problem for your company.

Frequently Asked Questions About Leave

■ Is my company legally required to offer paid vacation and sick leave?

No. Employers generally are not required by law to give their employees paid time off. However, most employers do offer some form of paid leave. A well-designed leave program can help a company attract high-quality employees—and improve office productivity and morale. (For more information on vacation and sick leave, see "Vacation and Sick Leave," below.)

■ Does my company have to provide family and medical leave?

It depends on how many employees work for your company. Under the federal Family and Medical Leave Act (FMLA), employers must allow employees to take up to 12 weeks of unpaid leave per year to care for a new child, care for a seriously ill family member, or deal with their own serious health condition. However, this law only applies if your company employs more than 50 people within a 75-mile radius. Even if a business is covered by the FMLA, only employees who have worked there for at least a year are eligible for leave. Some states have their own leave laws in addition to the FMLA, so be sure to find out about these, too. (For more on the requirements of the FMLA, see "Family and Medical Leave," below.)

■ **Can I fire a pregnant employee for poor attendance, even if the absences are pregnancy-related?**

It's illegal to fire an employee because she is pregnant. However, if you would fire any employee with poor attendance, you may legally fire your pregnant employee for that reason—as long as the absences for which you are firing her are not protected by the FMLA or a similar state law. (For more on pregnancy leave, see "Pregnancy and Parental Leave," below.)

■ **One of the employees I supervise just got called for jury duty. If she gets seated on a jury, can I replace her?**

No. Almost every state prohibits employers from firing or disciplining an employee for being called to jury duty and serving on a jury. However, most states do not require companies to pay employees for the time they spend on jury duty unless its own employment policies provide for such pay. (For more on employees and jury duty, see "Jury Duty and Voting," below.)

■ **Does my company have to pay employees for time spent voting?**

It depends on where your workplace is. Almost half of the states require employers to provide at least a few hours of paid leave so employees can vote, if the employee would not have enough time to vote without taking time off from work. Even if your company does business in a state that does not require paid leave for voting, you must not discipline any employee for taking time off to cast a ballot. (For more on leave to vote, see "Jury Duty and Voting," below.)

■ **Does my company have to give employees time off for National Guard training or other military service?**

Most likely. Federal law requires employers to reinstate workers who take up to five years of leave to serve in the Armed Forces. And in almost every state, employers must allow their employees to take leave for certain types of military service. In some states, only employees called for active duty are entitled to leave; other states require leave for training as well. (For more on leave for military duties, see "Military Leave," below.)

■ **Are employees entitled to take time off to attend a child's school conference?**

It depends on the laws of the state where your company does business. Many states require employers to let their employees take leave for a variety of reasons: to donate bone marrow, appear as a witness in court, or spend time at their child's school, for example. (For more on these requirements, see "Other Types of Leave," below.)

Vacation and Sick Leave

The law does not require employers to provide paid vacation or sick leave. (Although the state of California has a paid leave program, it is funded by employee contributions via payroll withholding, not by employers.)

A company could choose to offer no paid leave at all—although a policy like this will make it tough to attract (and retain) high-quality employees in a competitive market. If your company decides to adopt a policy that gives employees paid vacation or sick time, here are some things to keep in mind:

- **Apply the policy consistently to all employees.** Don't make individual decisions on who can take leave and for how long. Adopt a policy that applies to all workers in a particular position or job—or to everyone, period. And if your company already has a policy, apply it evenhandedly. If some employees are offered a more attractive leave package than others in the same position, you are opening your company up to claims of unfair treatment—and possible discrimination lawsuits.

- **Require employees to schedule leave in advance, if possible.** Sometimes, an employee cannot know ahead of time that he or she will need time off—for a sudden illness or family emergency, for example. In all other circumstances, however, you should ask your reports to schedule leave—

particularly vacations—at least a month in advance. This will help you meet your staffing needs, particularly during summers and holidays.

- **Adopt a sensible vacation accrual policy.** Many employees enjoy taking a longer vacation from time to time, and a policy that allows employees to save up a long stretch of vacation time—four weeks, say—for this purpose is reasonable. Your company may want to cap how much vacation time an employee can accrue or specify how much vacation an employee can take at one time, however. Otherwise, you may suddenly have several employees asking for months off at a time. And until those employees take their long vacation, they may suffer from job burn-out from years of work without time off.

- **Don't allow abuse of sick leave time.** Some employees treat sick leave as an extra allotment of vacation days. Crack down by requiring employees to call in each day they are ill, requiring a doctor's note for serious illnesses, and monitoring patterns of sick leave use. Do you have employees who only seem to call in sick on Mondays and Fridays? Do some employees claim illness at the end of every year, in an effort to take advantage of unused sick time? Counsel these employees about the proper use of sick leave, and discipline those who abuse the system.

- **Consider what you will pay when an employee quits or is fired.** If your company allows employees to accrue vacation days, it must decide whether to pay departing employees for unused leave. Some states, including California, require employers to pay for this accrued vacation time when employment ends. (See "State Laws That Control Final Paychecks," at the end of Chapter 12, for information on your state's rules.) Although employers are generally not required to pay out unused sick days, some do anyway, perhaps believing that this encourages employees not to misuse sick leave.

Family and Medical Leave

Working people often have a tough time balancing the demands of a job with personal and family needs. In response to this much-discussed problem, Congress passed the Family and Medical Leave Act (FMLA), 29 U.S.C. §§ 2601 and following. The FMLA requires certain employers to allow their employees up to 12 weeks of unpaid leave a year to care for a seriously ill family member, to deal with their own serious illness, or to take care of a newborn or newly adopted child. In most cases, the employer must reinstate an employee returning from leave to either the same position or to a position that is comparable in every important respect—including pay, benefits, and status.

When the FMLA Applies

An employer must comply with the FMLA if these three requirements are met:

- The company has 50 or more employees who work within a 75-mile radius. All employees on the payroll—including those who work part time and those on leave—count toward this total.
- The employee seeking leave has worked for the company for at least 12 months.
- The employee has worked at least 1,250 hours (about 25 hours a week) during the 12 months immediately preceding the leave.

When all three of these requirements are met, an employee is entitled to take FMLA leave only for specified reasons. Not every personal or family emergency qualifies for FMLA leave. The employee must be seeking leave for:

- **Birth, adoption, or foster care.** A new parent or foster parent may take FMLA leave within one year after the child is born or placed in the parent's home. A parent may go out on leave before the child arrives, if necessary for prenatal care or preparations for the child. If both parents work for the same employer, they may be entitled to less leave.
- **An employee's serious health condition.** The FMLA provides a specific definition of a "serious health condition." Generally, an employee who requires inpatient treatment,

has a chronic health problem, or is unable to perform normal activities for three days while under the treatment of a doctor has a serious health condition.

- **A family member's serious health condition.** An employee who needs to care for an ill family member is also entitled to leave. Under the FMLA, only parents, spouses, and children count as family members. Grandparents, same-sex partners, in-laws, and siblings are not included.

Reinstatement and Benefits

Under the FMLA, an eligible employee is entitled to take 12 weeks of unpaid leave in any 12-month period for the reasons listed above. When the employee's leave is over, the company must reinstate the employee to the same position the employee held prior to taking leave, or to a position that is comparable in every important respect, subject to these conditions:

- Employees have no greater right to reinstatement than they would have had if they had not taken leave. In other words, if an employee works in the accounting department and your company decides, while the employee is on leave, to cut the entire department and outsource your bookkeeping needs, the employee does not have a right to be reinstated just because he or she was on FMLA leave.
- Your company doesn't have to reinstate certain highly paid or high-level

employees. The FMLA recognizes how difficult it would be for many businesses to function without their top executives. The law allows an employer to refuse reinstatement if (1) the employee is among the highest-paid 10% of the salaried workers employed within 75 miles of the employee's workplace, and (2) taking back the employee would cause "substantial and grievous economic injury" to the company's business.

If your company has a group health plan for employees, it must also maintain insurance coverage for employees on FMLA leave. However, the company can choose to require the employee to reimburse it for the insurance premiums it paid for the employee if the employee chooses voluntarily not to return to work when the leave ends (but not if a serious health condition for which the employee took the leave continues or recurs or other circumstances beyond the employee's control prevent the return to work). Employers aren't required to continue any other employee benefits while an employee is on leave, nor must they allow a worker to accrue seniority, vacation leave, sick time, or other benefits while on leave. However, an employee who returns to work is entitled to benefits reinstatement as well—that is, the company must provide the same benefits that were available to the worker previously.

You cannot discipline a worker for taking FMLA leave. This means not only that you can't fire or demote a worker for going on leave, but also that you cannot count a worker's FMLA leave as an absence under a no-fault attendance policy. For example, if you give workers a disciplinary warning after ten absences in any year and fire workers after 15 absences, you may not count any days that a worker takes as FMLA leave as an "absence" under the policy. However, if a worker takes days off that are not covered by the FMLA, or takes more leave than the FLMA allows, you may count those days as absences under your policy.

Substituting Accrued Vacation Leave, Sick Leave, or PTO

Although FMLA leave is unpaid, employers must allow—and may sometimes require—employees to use their accrued paid leave in certain circumstances while on unpaid FMLA leave. An employee is always allowed to use accrued paid vacation leave, personal leave, or unspecified paid time off ("PTO") during unpaid FMLA leave. And, an employer may choose to require employees to do so.

An employee may also use accrued paid sick leave during unpaid FMLA leave, but only if the reason for the leave is covered by your company's sick leave policy or another state law. For example, your company doesn't have to allow an employee to substitute sick leave for FMLA leave to care for an ill family member unless your sick leave policy allows—or state law requires you to allow—employees

to take paid time off for this purpose. Likewise, an employer may only require an employee to use accrued paid sick leave during FMLA leave if the leave is for a reason otherwise covered by the employer's sick leave policy, such as the employee's own serious health condition.

If the employee does not choose to use and the company does not require the employee to use any accrued vacation, personal, or sick leave or PTO during an unpaid FMLA leave, the employee is entitled to any paid leave he or she has accrued in addition to the 12 weeks of FMLA leave.

Scheduling and Notice Requirements

An employee's 12-week absence can disrupt the workplace. Recognizing this, the FMLA requires employees to give 30 days' notice if the need for the leave is foreseeable. The most common "foreseeable" leave is leave the employee will take for the birth or adoption of a child or to care for a family member recovering from surgery or other planned medical treatment.

If the employee's need for leave is not foreseeable, the employee has to give whatever notice is possible and practical under the circumstances. For example, it might be impossible for an employee to give advance notice of a medical emergency such as a car accident or appendectomy.

In some circumstances, an employee may want to take the leave intermittently rather than all at once. If an employee requires physical therapy for a serious injury, for example, or needs to care for a spouse receiving periodic medical treatment, it might make more sense for the employee to take several hours off per week rather than all 12 weeks at once. This arrangement might also make more sense for your company, since you get to keep your employee's part-time services instead of planning for a protracted absence.

If it is medically necessary for an employee to take intermittent leave to care for a family member or for his or her own serious health condition, the employee has a right to do so. In other situations (for example, when an employee wants to take time off to care for a new child), you may, but are not required to, allow the employee to take leave on an intermittent schedule.

Medical Certification

Your company can choose to require an employee to provide proof that he or she (or the family member for whom he or she will be providing care) really suffers from a serious health condition. It may ask the employee for a certification from the treating doctor that provides certain details about the condition, including when it began, how likely it is to last, whether intermittent leave will be necessary, and so on. The U.S. Department of Labor has developed an optional form (Form WH-380) that you may ask employees to use when obtaining medical certification (available online at www.dol.gov). While you can use any form you like, you may not require the

employee to provide more information than what is requested on this form.

An employer can also ask for a second opinion from a doctor of its choice, as long as the company pays for it and the doctor it chooses is not regularly employed by your company. If the first and second certifications conflict, the company can require a third opinion from yet another doctor, selected by agreement between it and the worker. This third opinion will be binding on the company and the employee.

If your employee is absent for an extended period, the company may ask for a recertification periodically—generally, not more often than once every 30 days.

State Leave Laws

Over half the states now have their own family and medical leave laws in addition to the federal FMLA. If your company does business in one of these states, it will have to follow whichever law—federal or state—gives workers the most protection. For example, if your state has a family and medical leave law that gives workers the right to take more than 12 weeks off, your company will have to follow state law—even though the federal law doesn't require as much. And if state and federal law offer workers different benefits, your company has to follow both of them. For example, if your state law requires employers to offer family leave to allow parents to attend a child's school conference (a right that the federal law doesn't include), your company must let parents take that time in addition to their 12 weeks of federal FMLA leave.

To find out more about your state's laws on leave, see "State Family and Medical Leave Laws," at the end of this chapter.

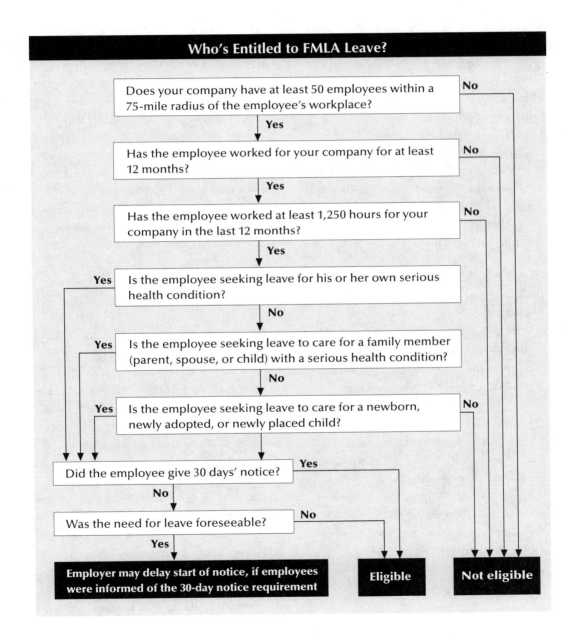

Who's Entitled to FMLA Leave?

Does your company have at least 50 employees within a 75-mile radius of the employee's workplace? — **No**

↓ **Yes**

Has the employee worked for your company for at least 12 months? — **No**

↓ **Yes**

Has the employee worked at least 1,250 hours for your company in the last 12 months? — **No**

↓ **Yes**

Yes ← Is the employee seeking leave for his or her own serious health condition?

↓ **No**

Yes ← Is the employee seeking leave to care for a family member (parent, spouse, or child) with a serious health condition?

↓ **No**

Yes ← Is the employee seeking leave to care for a newborn, newly adopted, or newly placed child? — **No**

Did the employee give 30 days' notice? — **Yes**

↓ **No**

Was the need for leave foreseeable? — **No**

↓ **Yes**

Employer may delay start of notice, if employees were informed of the 30-day notice requirement

Eligible

Not eligible

Lessons From the Real World

On September 26, 1995, Chem-Tronics fired Javier Mora for violating its attendance policy. Mr. Mora had taken a number of absences to care for his teenage son, Javier Jr., who suffered from AIDS and related infections. On these occasions, Mr. Mora cared for his son at home and took his son to necessary medical appointments.

The company claimed that Mr. Mora was not entitled to FMLA leave because his wife, Javier Jr.'s stepmother, should have handled Javier Jr.'s medical needs. Mr. Mora explained to company representatives that his wife was not his son's biological mother, that he was closer to his son, and that his son wanted him to provide care—all to no avail.

The company also argued that it didn't know that Javier Jr. suffered from a serious health condition covered by the FMLA. However, this argument was dramatically undercut by the company's own newsletter—in which an article appeared detailing Mr. Mora and his son's trip to the Superbowl, courtesy of the Make a Wish Foundation (a group that grants wishes to children who are terminally ill).

Mora v. Chem-Tronics, Inc., 16 F.Supp.2d 1192 (S.D. Cal. 1998).

Pregnancy and Parental Leave

Some employers assume that they must provide paid maternity leave to new mothers. Generally, however, this is not the case. You might be surprised to learn that in the United States (unlike most European countries), no law requires employers to provide paid maternity leave. However, your company may be required to offer unpaid parental leave or leave to pregnant employees who are temporarily unable to work. It will have to offer paid leave to pregnant employees who are temporarily unable to work only if it provides paid leave to workers who are temporarily disabled for other reasons. And it must provide benefits evenhandedly to avoid discrimination claims.

Unpaid Leave

The Family and Medical Leave Act (FMLA) requires employers who meet certain criteria to provide up to 12 weeks of unpaid leave to workers who need to care for a seriously ill family member, to care for a new child, or to recover from their own serious health condition. (See "Family and Medical Leave," above.)

FMLA leave can be used as pregnancy or parental leave in certain situations. Here are some of the rules that apply:

- Pregnant employees are entitled to use FMLA leave if complications from their pregnancy constitute a serious health condition. As a practical matter, if a woman's doctor determines that it is medically necessary for her to take time off from work, she will be able to use FMLA leave for that purpose.

- New parents may use FMLA leave as parental leave following the birth or adoption of a child or the placement of a foster child. This leave may be taken any time during the first year after the new child arrives. However, a worker is entitled to only 12 weeks of FMLA leave, total, in a single year. (Again, state law may provide additional leave.) So, if a worker has to take two weeks off for medical reasons during her pregnancy, she will have only ten weeks of FMLA leave remaining to use as parental leave (unless state law provides additional leave).

- If both parents work for your company (and are married to each other), they are entitled to a combined total of 12 weeks of parental leave. This rule does not apply to an employee who must take time off for her own serious health condition, however. So if an employee had a difficult birth and is unable to work for 12 weeks, her husband will still be entitled to a full 12 weeks of parental leave.

- Parental leave may be taken intermittently, but only with an employer's permission. For example, new parents may wish to work part time for a period or take some leave immediately following the birth and some leave later. As long as your company

agrees, you and the employee can work out a flexible leave arrangement under the FMLA.

Some states require employers to provide more than 12 weeks of leave, particularly if the leave is for "maternity disability"—the legal term for the period of time when women are actually unable to work because of pregnancy and childbirth. In a few of these states (including California), the maternity disability leave provided under state law is in addition to the leave provided by the FMLA or similar state statutes—in other words, the worker may take her full leave under state law and then take her full leave under the FMLA, as long as she qualifies for leave under the relevant statutes. To find out what your state requires, see "State Family and Medical Leave Laws," at the end of this chapter.

Paid Leave

Your company may be required to provide paid leave to pregnant employees and new parents, depending on its employment policies. Generally, if your company makes paid leave available to other workers in similar situations, it must make it available to pregnant employees and new parents. For example, if employees who are temporarily disabled (unable to work) for other medical reasons (such as a heart attack or stroke) typically receive paid time off, employees who are unable to work because of pregnancy must be given the same benefit.

Similarly, if your company provides personal or vacation leave to employees, new parents must be allowed to use this time off as parental leave, as long as they meet the other requirements of the policy (for example, providing adequate notice or scheduling the leave with a supervisor). Employers also have the right to require employees to use their accrued paid leave as FMLA leave—and most employers do. This allows companies to put an outer limit on employee absences. If your company doesn't require substitution, employees can take their total FMLA allotment—and then use their paid vacation or sick days to extend their time off.

Discrimination Claims

Federal and state laws prohibit discrimination on the basis of gender, including pregnancy. This means, of course, that you may not fire, demote, or take any other negative employment action against a worker because she is pregnant. Here are a few tips that will help you stay within the law when dealing with these issues:

- Employers cannot require a worker to take pregnancy or maternity leave. In the not-so-distant past, an employer could force a pregnant worker to stop working when she reached a certain stage of her pregnancy or was "showing." This is no longer legal. As long as she can get the job done, you must allow her to work—even up to the date she gives birth.

- Treat a pregnant employee who needs time off like any other temporarily disabled worker—an employee who suffers a back injury or has a mild heart attack, for example. Employers don't have to offer special benefits to pregnant workers, but these workers should get the same treatment as other workers who are temporarily unable to do their jobs because of disability or illness. Similarly, you may fire a pregnant employee who has excessive absences for pregnancy-related health problems (morning sickness, for example) if you would fire a nonpregnant employee for the same conduct. But make sure you are not penalizing a pregnant worker for absences taken under the FMLA or other state law. And make sure your state's law does not require you to provide a reasonable accommodation for your worker's pregnancy-related condition. (Check with your state's fair employment agency—the appendix contains contact information.)

- Offer parental leave, not maternity leave. And don't discourage new fathers from taking parental leave or penalize them for doing so. If your company offers any time off for a parent to spend with a newborn child, make it available to both fathers and mothers. If an employer offers a benefit that can only be used by women—like maternity leave—it might be accused of gender discrimination.

Jury Duty and Voting

Almost every state prohibits employers from firing or disciplining employees for jury service. A few states go further and make it illegal for employers to discourage or intimidate an employee from serving on a jury.

For most employers, the most important issue is whether they must pay an employee for time spent on jury duty. Generally, unless your company has promised otherwise in your employment policies or handbook, it does not have to pay employees for leave taken to serve on a jury. However, some states require at least some payment for this time off, including Alabama, Colorado, and Wisconsin. See "State Laws on Jury Duty," at the end of this chapter, for information on your state's rules.

Similarly, workers are entitled to time off work to cast their ballots. Almost every state prohibits employers from disciplining or firing an employee who takes time off work to vote. In many states, an employer must grant a certain number of hours of leave for employees to get to the voting booth—but only if the employee is unable, because of his or her work schedule or the distance the employee must travel to cast a ballot, to vote outside of work hours. In most of these states, an employer must pay the worker for

this time off. To find out what your state requires, see "State Laws on Taking Time Off to Vote," at the end of this chapter.

Military Leave

A federal law, the Uniformed Services Employment and Reemployment Rights Act of 1994 (USERRA), 38 U.S.C. §§ 4301 and following, prohibits discrimination against members of the United States military or those who serve in the military reserves. This law also requires employers to reinstate an employee who has taken time off to serve in the armed forces, if the employee meets these conditions:

- The employee must have given notice, before taking leave, that the leave was for military service.
- The employee must have spent no more than five years on leave for military service.
- The employee must have been released from military service under honorable conditions.
- The employee must report back or apply for reinstatement within specified time limits; these limits vary depending on the length of the employee's leave.

USERRA requires employers to reinstate workers to the same position they would have held had they been continuously employed throughout their leave, provided they are otherwise qualified for that job. This means that your company cannot simply return the worker to his old position; the worker is entitled to any promotions, increased pay, or additional job responsibilities that he or she would have gotten if not for taking leave—but only if the worker is qualified to do that job. If the worker is not qualified, your company must try to get him or her qualified. The worker is also entitled to the benefits and seniority that he or she would have earned if continuously employed. For purposes of benefits plans and leave policies, the time the worker spent on leave must be counted as time worked.

Returning members of the military receive one additional benefit: They cannot be fired without cause for up to one year after they are reinstated (the exact length of this protection depends on the length of the worker's military service). Thus, no matter what your company's employment policies say, these workers are no longer at-will employees for a limited period after they return. (For more on at-will policies and cause for firing, see "At-Will Employment" in Chapter 4.)

State Laws

Almost every state has a law prohibiting discrimination against those in the state's militia or National Guard. Most state laws also require employers to grant leave to employees for certain types of military service. Some states require leave only for those employees called to active duty; other states require leave for those called for training as well. Employers don't generally have to pay employees who

Lessons From the Real World

Charley Hill started working for Michelin North America in the early 1980s. In 1995, he became a member of the Naval Reserves of the United States, a position that required Hill to be absent from work for two weeks per year.

In 1998, Hill began working in the "Q-Laboratory" at Michelin. Although Hill wanted to keep working in the Q-Lab, his supervisor didn't think the lab could accommodate Hill's Navy Reserve schedule. Hill was required to transfer to another assignment, even though he wanted to stay in the Q-Lab.

Hill filed a lawsuit against Michelin, arguing that the company discriminated against him by making him transfer out of the Q-Lab. The court agreed, finding that the Q-Lab had better working conditions and a more regular work schedule, which made it superior to the job to which he was transferred. The court held that the Michelin's decision to transfer Hill because of his military service requirements effectively denied Hill the benefits of the Q-Lab job, in violation of the Uniformed Services Employment and Reemployment Rights Act.

Hill v. Michelin North America, Inc., Case No. 00-2202 (4th Cir., May 30, 2001).

take military leave, although some states provide paid leave for public employees.

When an employee takes military leave, your company must usually reemploy him or her without any loss of benefits or status or reduction in pay. These reemployment guarantees vary from state to state and sometimes contain additional conditions. To find out your state's rules, see "State Laws on Military Leave," at the end of this chapter.

Other Types of Leave

In addition to the kinds of leave covered above, many states require employers to provide leave for specified activities. Some of these entitlements are part of the state's family and medical leave law; others are standalone benefits. If your company does business in a state that has any such laws and meets the other coverage requirements (most often, that it have a certain minimum number of employees), it will have to provide the mandated leave.

Detail on every state law requiring employers to grant time off is beyond the scope of this book. For information on requirements imposed by your state, contact your state department of labor. (Contact information is in the appendix). Here are some common state leave requirements:

- **Time off to be an organ or blood marrow donor.** A handful of states require private employers to give employees time off to donate blood marrow or be an organ donor. Sometimes, this leave counts towards the employee's entitlement to state family and medical leave.
- **Use of sick leave to care for an ill family member.** Some states give employees the right to use accrued sick leave to care for a sick family member, even if the employer's own policies don't provide for it.
- **Time off relating to domestic violence.** In some states, an employee is entitled to take time off to handle issues caused by domestic violence—to get a restraining order, relocate, or seek medical care or counseling, for example.
- **Time off for court proceedings.** Many states give employees the right to take time off to appear as a witness in a court case.
- **Time off to serve as a volunteer firefighter or other emergency worker.** Some states require private employers to give workers time off to serve as a disaster relief worker, volunteer firefighter, emergency rescue worker, or Red Cross volunteer.
- **Time off for school activities.** In some states, parents are entitled to take a certain amount of leave each year to attend school functions, parent-teacher conferences, special education meetings, and the like.

Legal Dos and Don'ts: Leave

Do:

- **Help employees balance work and family.** Smart managers know that workers who can take time off occasionally to attend school conferences, care for a sick child, or take an elderly parent to the doctor will be more productive on the job. And companies that have a family-friendly reputation are better able to recruit—and retain—a high-quality workforce.
- **Be consistent.** Make sure you follow your company's policies faithfully when considering leave requests. If you play favorites, you could be setting your company up for a lawsuit.
- **Encourage employees to take accrued leave.** You don't want sick workers showing up, unable to work efficiently and infecting the rest of your team. Similarly, you don't want good employees to burn out because they never take a vacation.

Don't:

- **Allow abuse of leave.** Require sick employees to call in. Have your reports schedule vacation well in advance. And crack down on any employee who misuses leave. As long as you are evenhanded in applying these policies, they will go a long way towards keeping your workers in line.
- **Forget about fathers.** Although we've come a long way, many companies still offer maternity leave only—or discourage fathers from taking leave under seemingly neutral parental leave policies. These kinds of policies and practices can lead straight to the courthouse steps in a gender discrimination lawsuit.
- **Deny a leave request without checking the law.** If an employee asks to take time off for a particular reason, check with your human resources department—or your state labor department—to find out whether your state protects that type of leave. If you leap without looking, you may be violating the law.

Test Your Knowledge

Questions

1. All companies must give their employees some paid sick leave. ☐ True ☐ False

2. Employers are not allowed to cap the amount of vacation leave employees may accrue. ☐ True ☐ False

3. Only employees who work full time are entitled to take FMLA leave. ☐ True ☐ False

4. Employers may ask employees who take FMLA leave for their own serious health condition to provide a medical certification. ☐ True ☐ False

5. If both parents work for one company, each is entitled to a full 12 weeks of FMLA leave to care for their new baby. ☐ True ☐ False

6. Employers must allow employees to take intermittent FMLA leave to care for a new child. ☐ True ☐ False

7. Employers must pay employees for time spent on jury duty. ☐ True ☐ False

8. Employees who are reinstated after serving in the military cannot be fired without good cause for up to one year, even if they work for an at-will employer. ☐ True ☐ False

9. Employers must pay employees for time spent on military leave. ☐ True ☐ False

10. Your company may have a legal obligation to allow employees to take time off to serve as a witness in court. ☐ True ☐ False

Answers

1. False. Employers are not required to provide paid sick leave to their employees, although they may have to allow an employee with a serious health condition to take unpaid leave under the FMLA.

2. False. Some states prohibit employers from taking away accrued vacation time—by zeroing out an employee's balance at the end of the year, for example. But it is legal to put a limit on how much vacation time an employee may accrue in the first place.

3. False. An employee who has worked 1,250 hours for your company in the last twelve months and meets the other eligibility requirements is entitled to take FMLA leave. This works out to about 25 hours a week.

4. True. An employer may require an employee to provide a medical certification—proof that the employee (or the employee's family member) actually has a serious health condition.

5. False. If both parents work for one company, they are entitled to a combined 12 weeks of parental leave. However, you may have to give more time off if one parent needs leave for a serious health condition—for example, complications from a difficult childbirth.

6. False. Although employers are required to give intermittent leave if it is medically necessary for the employee's own or the employee's family member's serious health condition, intermittent leave is not required for parental leave. Employers may choose to provide it but do not have to.

7. It depends on the laws of your state. Most do not require employers to pay for this time, but some do.

8. True. Employees who are reinstated after taking military leave enjoy this special job protection for up to one year (the exact length of the protection depends on the length of the employee's military service).

9. False. Although many private employers choose to pay employees for at least some portion of their military service, this is not a legal requirement.

10. True. Some states give employees the right to take time off work to serve as a witness.

State Family and Medical Leave Laws

This chart covers the basic aspects of state family and medical leave laws. Federal FMLA applies to all covered employers in every state. However, an employer must follow the state or federal laws that provide the most protection for employees.

We don't address every aspect of the laws (such as notice requirements, medical certifications, or reinstatement rules). For more information, contact your state's department of labor and be sure to check its website, where most states have posted their family leave rules. (See "Departments of Labor," in the appendix for contact details.)

States that are not listed below do not have laws that apply to private employers or have laws that offer less protection than the FMLA.

California

Cal. Gov't. Code § 12945; Cal. Lab. Code §§ 230 and following; Cal. Unemp. Ins. §§ 3300 and following

Employers Covered: Employers with 5 or more employees must offer pregnancy leave; employers with 25 or more employees must offer leave for victims of domestic violence or sexual assault and school activity leave; employers with 50 or more employees must offer leave for domestic partners; employers whose employees contribute to state temporary disability insurance ("SDI") fund must allow employees to participate in state's paid family leave benefits program.

Eligible Employees: All employees for pregnancy leave, domestic violence, or school activity leave; employees eligible for leave under federal FMLA for domestic partners leave; employees who contribute to SDI fund for paid family leave benefits program.

Family Medical Leave: Up to 4 months for disability related to pregnancy (in addition to 12 weeks under state or federal FML if the employee is eligible). Up to 12 weeks of leave per year to care for seriously ill registered domestic partner. Employees who contribute to SDI fund may receive paid family leave benefits for up to 6 weeks of leave per year to care for a seriously ill family member (including a registered domestic partner) or bond with a new child. This leave is paid through employee contributions to the SDI fund; the employee will receive approximately 55% of regular earnings. Does not provide job protection unless the employee is otherwise covered by the state or federal FML.

School Activities: 40 hours per year.

Domestic Violence: Reasonable time for issues dealing with domestic violence or sexual assault, including health, counseling, and safety measures. Family member or domestic partner of a victim of a felony may take leave to attend judicial proceedings related to the crime.

Colorado

Colo. Rev. Stat. § 19-5-211, 24-34-402.7

Employers Covered: All employers who offer leave for birth of a child for adoption leave; employers with 50 or more employees for domestic violence leave.

Eligible Employees: All employees for adoption leave; employees with one year of service for domestic violence leave.

Family Medical Leave: Employee must be given same leave for adoption as allowed for childbirth (doesn't apply to stepparent adoption).

Domestic Violence: Up to 3 days leave to seek restraining order, obtain medical care or counseling, relocate, or seek legal assistance for victim of domestic violence, sexual assault, or stalking.

Connecticut

Conn. Gen. Stat. Ann. §§ 31-51kk to 31-51qq, 46a-51(10), 46a-60(7)

Employers Covered: Employers with 75 employees must offer childbirth, adoption,

State Family and Medical Leave Laws (continued)

and serious health condition leave; with 3 employees, must offer maternity disability.

Eligible Employees: Any employee with one year and at least 1,000 hours of service in last 12 months.

Family Medical Leave: 16 weeks per any 24-month period for childbirth, adoption, employee's serious health condition, care for family member with serious health condition, or bone marrow or organ donation. "Reasonable" amount of maternity disability leave. May also use up to 2 weeks accumulated sick leave.

Family Member: Includes parents-in-law.

District of Columbia

D.C. Code Ann. §§ 32-501 and following, 32-1202

Employers Covered: Employers with at least 20 employees.

Eligible Employees: Employees who have worked at company for at least one year and at least 1,000 hours during the previous 12 months.

Family Medical Leave: 16 weeks per any 24-month period for childbirth, adoption, pregnancy/maternity, employee's serious health condition, or care for family member with serious health condition.

School Activities: Up to 24 hours of leave per year.

Family Member: Includes anyone related by blood, custody, or marriage; anyone sharing employee's residence and with whom employee has a committed relationship (including a child for whom the employee assumes permanent parental responsibility).

Hawaii

Haw. Rev. Stat. §§ 398-1 to 398-11, 378-1, 378-71 to 378-74

Employers Covered: Employers with at least 100 employees must offer childbirth, adoption, and serious health condition leave; all employers must offer pregnancy leave and domestic

violence leave.

Eligible Employees: Employees with 6 months of service are eligible for childbirth, adoption, and serious health condition benefits; all employees are eligible for pregnancy and maternity leave.

Family Medical Leave: 4 weeks per calendar year for childbirth, adoption, or care for family member with serious health condition; "reasonable period" of pregnancy/maternity leave required by discrimination statute and case law; may include up to 10 days accrued leave or sick leave.

Family Member: Includes reciprocal beneficiary, parents-in-law, grandparents, grandparents-in-law, stepparents.

Domestic Violence: Employer with 50 or more employees must allow up to 30 days unpaid leave per year for employee who is a victim of domestic or sexual violence or if employee's minor child is a victim. Employer with 49 or fewer employees must allow up to 5 days leave.

Illinois

820 Ill. Comp. Stat. §§ 147/1 and following, 180/1 and following

Employers Covered: Employers with 50 or more employees.

Eligible Employees: Employees who have worked at least half-time for 6 months.

School Activities: 8 hours per year (no more than 4 hours per day); required only if employee has no paid leave available.

Domestic Violence: Up to 12 weeks unpaid leave per 12-month period for employee who is a victim of domestic violence or sexual assault or for employee with a family or household member who is a victim.

Iowa

Iowa Code § 216.6

Employers Covered: Employers with 4 or more employees.

State Family and Medical Leave Laws (continued)

Eligible Employees: All.

Family Medical Leave: Up to 8 weeks for disability due to pregnancy, childbirth, or legal abortion.

Kentucky

Ky. Rev. Stat. Ann. § 337.015

Employers Covered: All.

Eligible Employees: All.

Family Medical Leave: Up to 6 weeks for adoption of a child under 7 years old.

Louisiana

La. Rev. Stat. Ann. §§ 23:341 to 23:342, 23:1015 and following, 40:1299.124

Employers Covered: Employers with more than 25 employees must offer pregnancy/maternity leave; with at least 20 employees must comply with bone marrow donation provisions; all employers must offer leave for school activities.

Eligible Employees: All employees are eligible for pregnancy/maternity or school activities leave; employees who work 20 or more hours per week are eligible for leave to donate bone marrow.

Family Medical Leave: "Reasonable period of time" not to exceed four months for pregnancy/maternity leave, if necessary for pregnancy or related medical condition; up to 40 hours paid leave per year to donate bone marrow.

School Activities: 16 hours per year.

Maine

Me. Rev. Stat. Ann. tit. 26, §§ 843 and following

Employers Covered: All employers for domestic violence leave; employers with 15 or more employees at one location for family medical leave.

Eligible Employees: Employees with at least one year of service.

Family Medical Leave: 10 weeks in any two-year period for childbirth, adoption (for child 16 or younger), employee's serious health condition, or care for family member with serious health condition.

Domestic Violence: "Reasonable and necessary" leave for employee who is victim of domestic violence, sexual assault, or stalking, or whose parent, spouse, or child is a victim, to prepare for and attend court, for medical treatment, and for other necessary services.

Maryland

Md. Code Ann., [Lab. & Empl.] § 3-802

Employers Covered: Employers that allow workers to take leave for the birth of a child.

Eligible Employees: All employees.

Family Medical Leave: Employee must be given same leave for adoption as allowed for childbirth.

Massachusetts

Mass. Gen. Laws ch. 149, §§ 52D, 105D; ch. 151B, § 1(5)

Employers Covered: Employers with 6 or more employees must provide maternity and adoption leave; employers with 50 or more employees must offer leave for school activities.

Eligible Employees: Full-time female employees who have completed probationary period, or 3 months of service if no set probationary period, are eligible for maternity and adoption leave; employees who are eligible under FMLA are eligible for all other leave.

Family Medical Leave: 8 weeks total for childbirth/maternity or adoption of child younger than 18 (younger than 23 if disabled); additional 24 hours total per year (combined with school activities leave) to accompany minor child or relative age 60 or older to medical and dental appointments.

School Activities: 24 hours per year total (combined with medical care under "other").

State Family and Medical Leave Laws (continued)

Minnesota

Minn. Stat. Ann. §§ 181.940 and following

Employers Covered: Employers with at least 21 employees at one site must provide childbirth/maternity and adoption leave; with at least 20 employees must allow leave to donate bone marrow; all employers must provide leave for school activities.

Eligible Employees: Employees who have worked at least half-time for one year are eligible for maternity leave; at least 20 hours per week are eligible for leave to donate bone marrow; at least one year are eligible for school activities.

Family Medical Leave: 6 weeks for childbirth/maternity or adoption; up to 40 hours paid leave per year to donate bone marrow; parent can use accrued sick leave to care for sick or injured child.

School Activities: 16 hours in 12-month period; includes activities related to child care, pre-school, or special education.

Montana

Mont. Code Ann. §§ 49-2-310, 49-2-311

Employers Covered: All.

Eligible Employees: All.

Family Medical Leave: "Reasonable leave of absence" for pregnancy/maternity and childbirth.

Nebraska

Neb. Rev. Stat. § 48-234

Employers Covered: Employers that allow workers to take leave for the birth of a child.

Eligible Employees: All employees.

Family Medical Leave: Employee must be given same leave as allowed for childbirth to adopt a child under 9 years old or a special needs child under 19. Does not apply to stepparent or foster parent adoptions.

Nevada

Nev. Rev. Stat. Ann. §§ 392.490, 613.335

Employers Covered: All.

Eligible Employees: Parent, guardian, or custodian of a child.

Family Medical Leave: Same sick or disability leave policies that apply to other medical conditions must be extended to pregnancy, miscarriage, and childbirth.

School Activities: Employers may not fire or threaten to fire a parent, guardian, or custodian for attending a school conference or responding to a child's emergency.

New Hampshire

N.H. Rev. Stat. Ann. § 354-A:7(VI)

Employers Covered: Employers with at least 6 employees.

Eligible Employees: All.

Family Medical Leave: Temporary disability leave for childbirth or related medical condition.

New Jersey

N.J. Stat. Ann. §§ 34:11B-1 to 34B:16

Employers Covered: Employers with at least 50 employees.

Eligible Employees: Employees who have worked for at least one year and at least 1,000 hours in previous 12 months.

Family Medical Leave: 12 weeks (or 24 weeks reduced leave schedule) in any 24-month period for pregnancy/maternity, childbirth, adoption, or care for family member with serious health condition.

Family Member: Includes parents-in-law; child includes legal ward; parent includes someone with visitation rights.

New York

N.Y. Lab. Law §§ 201-c, 202-a

State Family and Medical Leave Laws (continued)

Employers Covered: Employers that allow workers to take leave for the birth of a child must allow adoption leave; employers with at least 20 employees at one site must allow leave to donate bone marrow.

Eligible Employees: All employees are eligible for adoption leave; employees who work at least 20 hours per week are eligible for leave to donate bone marrow.

Family Medical Leave: Employees must be given same leave as allowed for childbirth to adopt a child of preschool age or younger, or no older than 18 if disabled; up to 24 hours leave to donate bone marrow.

North Carolina

N.C. Gen. Stat. § 95-28.3

Employers Covered: All employers.

Eligible Employees: All employees.

School Activities: Parents and guardians of school-aged children must be given up to 4 hours of leave per year.

Domestic Violence: Employer may not discipline or fire an employee who takes "reasonable" leave to get a protective order.

Oregon

Or. Rev. Stat. §§ 659A.150 and following, 659A. 190 and following, 659A.312; Or. Admin. R. §§ 839-009-0200 and following

Employers Covered: Employers of 25 or more employees must provide childbirth, adoption, and serious health condition leave; all employers must allow leave to donate bone marrow.

Eligible Employees: Employees who have worked 25 or more hours per week for at least 180 days are eligible for childbirth, adoption, and serious health condition leave; employees who work an average of 20 or more hours per week are eligible for leave to donate bone marrow.

Family Medical Leave: 12 weeks per year for

pregnancy/maternity, adoption, or childbirth; additional 12 weeks per year for serious health condition, care for family member with serious health condition, or care for child who has an illness, injury, or condition that requires home care; up to 40 hours or amount of accrued paid leave (whichever is less) to donate bone marrow.

Family Member: Includes parents-in-law, same-sex domestic partner, and domestic partner's parent or child.

Rhode Island

R.I. Gen. Laws §§ 28-48-1 and following

Employers Covered: Employers with 50 or more employees.

Eligible Employees: Employees who have worked an average of 30 or more hours a week for at least 12 consecutive months.

Family Medical Leave: 13 weeks in any two calendar years for childbirth, adoption of child up to 16 years old, employee's serious health condition, or care for family member with serious health condition.

Family Member: Includes parents-in-law.

School Activities: Up to 10 hours a year.

South Carolina

S.C. Code Ann. § 44-43-80

Employers Covered: Employers with 20 or more workers at one site in South Carolina.

Eligible Employees: Employees who work an average of at least 20 hours per week.

Family Medical Leave: Up to 40 hours paid leave per year to donate bone marrow.

Tennessee

Tenn. Code Ann. § 4-21-408

Employers Covered: Employers with at least 100 employees.

Eligible Employees: All female employees who have worked 12 consecutive months.

State Family and Medical Leave Laws (continued)

Family Medical Leave: Up to 4 months of unpaid leave for pregnancy/maternity and childbirth (includes nursing); employee must give 3 months' notice unless a medical emergency requires the leave to begin sooner; these laws must be included in employee handbook.

Vermont

Vt. Stat. Ann. tit. 21, §§ 471 and following

Employers Covered: Employers with at least 10 employees must provide parental leave for childbirth and adoption; with at least 15 employees must provide family medical leave to care for a seriously ill family member or to take a family member to medical appointments.

Eligible Employees: Employees who have worked an average of 30 or more hours per week for at least one year.

Family Medical Leave: 12 weeks per year for childbirth, adoption of child age 16 or younger, employee's serious health condition, or care for family member with a serious health condition; combined with school activities leave, additional 4 hours of unpaid leave in a 30-day period (up to 24 hours per year) to take a family member to a medical, dental, or professional well-care appointment or respond to a family member's medical emergency.

School Activities: Combined with leave described above, 4 hours total unpaid leave in a 30-day period (but not more than 24 hours per year) to participate in child's school activities.

Family Member: Includes parents-in-law.

Washington

Wash. Rev. Code Ann. §§ 49.78.010 and following, 49.12.265 and following, 49.12.350 and following; Wash. Admin. Code 296-130-010 and following, 162-30-020

Employers Covered: All employers must allow employees to use available paid time off to care for sick family members; employers with 8 or more employees must provide pregnancy/childbirth leave; employers with 100 or more employees must provide maternity, adoption, and terminally ill child leave.

Eligible Employees: All employees are eligible for family care leave; employees who have worked at least 35 hours per week for the previous year are eligible for pregnancy/childbirth leave, maternity leave, and leave to care for a terminally ill child.

Family Medical Leave: In addition to any leave available under federal FMLA, employee may take leave for the period of time when she is sick or temporarily disabled due to pregnancy or childbirth; employers with 100 or more employees must allow up to 12 weeks during any 24-month period to care for a newborn or newly adopted child (under the age of 6) or to care for a terminally ill child under the age of 18; all employees can use any paid leave to care for a sick family member.

Family member: Includes parents-in-law, grandparents, and stepparents; in addition, may take 12 weeks during any 24-month period to care for a terminally ill child under 18.

Wisconsin

Wis. Stat. Ann. § 103.10

Employers Covered: Employers of 50 or more employees in at least six of the preceding 12 months.

Eligible Employees: Employees who have worked at least one year and 1,000 hours in the preceding 12 months.

Family Medical Leave: 6 weeks per 12-month period for pregnancy/maternity, childbirth, or adoption; additional 2 weeks per 12-month period to care for family member with a serious health condition.

Current as of February 2005

State Laws on Jury Duty

Alabama

Ala. Code §§ 12-16-8 to 12-16-8.1

Paid leave: Full-time employees are entitled to usual pay minus any fees received from the court.

Notice employee must give: Must show supervisor jury summons the next working day; must return to work the next scheduled hour after discharge from jury duty.

Employer penalty for firing or penalizing employee: Liable for actual and punitive damages.

Alaska

Alaska Stat. § 09.20.037

Unpaid leave: Yes.

Additional employee protections: Employee may not be threatened, coerced, or penalized.

Employer penalty for firing or penalizing employee: Liable for lost wages and damages; must reinstate employee.

Arizona

Ariz. Rev. Stat. § 21-236

Unpaid leave: Yes.

Additional employee protections: Employee may not lose vacation rights, seniority, or precedence. Employer may not require employee to use annual, sick, or vacation hours.

Employer penalty for firing or penalizing employee: Class 3 misdemeanor, punishable by a fine of up to $500 or up to 30 days' imprisonment.

Note: Employers with 5 or fewer employees: Court must postpone an employee's jury service if another employee is already serving as a juror.

Arkansas

Ark. Code Ann. § 16-31-106

Unpaid leave: Yes.

Additional employee protections: Absence may not affect sick leave and vacation rights.

Employer penalty for firing or penalizing employee: Class A misdemeanor, punishable by a fine of up to $1,000 or up to one year's imprisonment.

California

Cal. Lab. Code §§ 230, 230.1

Unpaid leave: Employee may use vacation, personal leave, or comp time.

Additional employee protections: Victims of crime, domestic violence, or sexual assault are protected against discharge, discrimination, or retaliation for attending a court proceeding or seeking judicial relief.

Notice employee must give: Reasonable notice.

Employer penalty for firing or penalizing employee: Employer must reinstate employee with back pay and lost wages and benefits. Willful violation is a misdemeanor.

Colorado

Colo. Rev. Stat. §§ 13-71-126, 13-71-133 to 13-71-134

Paid leave: All employees (including part-time and temporary who were scheduled to work for the 3 months preceding jury service): regular wages up to $50 per day for first 3 days of jury duty. Must pay within 30 days of jury service.

Additional employee protections: Employer may not make any demands on employee which will interfere with effective performance of jury duty.

Employer penalty for firing or penalizing employee: Class 2 misdemeanor, punishable by a fine of $250 to $1,000 or 3 to 12 months' imprisonment, or both. May be liable to employee for triple damages and attorneys' fees.

State Laws on Jury Duty (continued)

Connecticut

Conn. Gen. Stat. Ann. §§ 51-247 to 51-247c

Paid leave: Full-time employees: regular wages for the first 5 days of jury duty; after 5 days, state pays up to $50 per day.

Employer penalty for firing or penalizing employee: Criminal contempt: punishable by a fine of up to $500 or up to 30 days' imprisonment, or both. Liable for up to 10 weeks' lost wages for discharging employee.

Delaware

Del. Code Ann. tit. 10, § 4515

Unpaid leave: Yes.

Employer penalty for firing or penalizing employee: Criminal contempt: punishable by a fine of up to $500 or up to 6 months' imprisonment, or both. Liable to discharged employee for lost wages and attorneys' fees.

District of Columbia

D.C. Code Ann. §§ 11-1913, 15-718

Paid leave: Full-time employees: regular wages for the first 5 days of jury duty.

Employer penalty for firing or penalizing employee: Criminal contempt: punishable by a fine of up to $300 or up to 30 days' imprisonment, or both, for a first offense; up to $5,000 or up to 180 days' imprisonment, or both, for any subsequent offense. Liable to discharged employee for lost wages and attorneys' fees.

Florida

Fla. Stat. Ann. § 40.271

Unpaid leave: Yes.

Additional employee protections: Employee may not be threatened with dismissal.

Employer penalty for firing or penalizing employee: Threatening employee is contempt of court. May be liable to discharged employee for compensatory and punitive damages and attorneys' fees.

Georgia

Ga. Code Ann. § 34-1-3

Unpaid leave: Yes.

Additional employee protections: Employee may not be discharged, penalized, or threatened with discharge or penalty for responding to a subpoena or making a required court appearance.

Notice employee must give: Reasonable notice.

Employer penalty for firing or penalizing employee: Liable for actual damages and reasonable attorneys' fees.

Hawaii

Haw. Rev. Stat. § 612-25

Unpaid leave: Yes.

Employer penalty for firing or penalizing employee: Petty misdemeanor: punishable by a fine of up to $1,000 or up to 30 days' imprisonment. May be liable to discharged employee for up to 6 weeks' lost wages.

Idaho

Idaho Code § 2-218

Unpaid leave: Yes.

Employer penalty for firing or penalizing employee: Criminal contempt: punishable by a fine of up to $300. Liable to discharged employee for triple lost wages.

Illinois

705 Ill. Comp. Stat. § 310/10.1

Unpaid leave: Yes.

Additional employee protections: A regular night shift employee may not be required to work if serving on a jury during the day. May not lose any seniority or benefits.

State Laws on Jury Duty (continued)

Notice employee must give: Must give employer a copy of the summons within 10 days of issuance.

Employer penalty for firing or penalizing employee: Employer will be charged with civil or criminal contempt, or both; liable to employee for lost wages and benefits.

Indiana

Ind. Code Ann. § 35-44-3-10

Unpaid leave: Yes.

Additional employee protections: Employee may not be deprived of benefits or threatened with the loss of them.

Employer penalty for firing or penalizing employee: Class B misdemeanor: punishable by up to 180 days' imprisonment; may also be fined up to $1,000. Liable to discharged employee for lost wages and attorneys' fees.

Iowa

Iowa Code § 607A.45

Unpaid leave: Yes.

Employer penalty for firing or penalizing employee: Contempt of court. Liable to discharged employee for up to 6 weeks' lost wages and attorneys' fees.

Kansas

Kan. Stat. Ann. § 43-173

Unpaid leave: Yes.

Additional employee protections: Employee may not lose seniority or benefits. (Basic and additional protections apply to permanent employees only.)

Employer penalty for firing or penalizing employee: Liable for lost wages and benefits, damages, and attorneys' fees.

Kentucky

Ky. Rev. Stat. Ann. § 29A.160

Unpaid leave: Yes.

Employer penalty for firing or penalizing employee: Class B misdemeanor: punishable by up to 90 days' imprisonment or fine of up to $250, or both. Liable to discharged employee for lost wages and attorneys' fees. Must reinstate employee with full seniority and benefits.

Louisiana

La. Rev. Stat. Ann. § 23:965

Paid leave: Regular employee entitled to one day full compensation for jury service. May not lose any sick, vacation, or personal leave or other benefit.

Additional employee protections: Employer may not create any policy or rule that would discharge employee for jury service.

Notice employee must give: Reasonable notice.

Employer penalty for firing or penalizing employee: For each discharged employee: fine of $100 to $1,000; must reinstate employee with full benefits. For not granting paid leave: fine of $100 to $500; must pay full day's lost wages.

Maine

Me. Rev. Stat. Ann. tit. 14, § 1218

Unpaid leave: Yes.

Additional employee protections: Employee may not lose or be threatened with loss of health insurance coverage.

Employer penalty for firing or penalizing employee: Class E crime: punishable by up to 6 months in the county jail or a fine of up to $1,000. Liable for up to 6 weeks' lost wages, benefits, and attorneys' fees.

Maryland

Md. Code Ann., [Cts. & Jud. Proc.] § 8-105

Unpaid leave: Yes.

State Laws on Jury Duty (continued)

Massachusetts

Mass. Gen. Laws ch. 234A, §§ 48 and following

Paid leave: All employees (including part-time and temporary who were scheduled to work for the 3 months preceding jury service): regular wages for first 3 days of jury duty. If paid leave is an "extreme financial hardship" for employer, state will pay. After first 3 days state will pay $50 per day.

Michigan

Mich. Comp. Laws § 600.1348

Unpaid leave: Yes.

Additional employee protections: Employee may not be threatened or disciplined; may not be required to work in addition to jury service, if extra hours would mean working overtime or beyond normal quitting time.

Employer penalty for firing or penalizing employee: Misdemeanor, punishable by a fine of up to $500 or up to 90 days' imprisonment, or both. Employer may also be punished for contempt of court, with a fine of up to $250 or up to 30 days' imprisonment, or both.

Minnesota

Minn. Stat. Ann. § 593.50

Unpaid leave: Yes.

Employer penalty for firing or penalizing employee: Criminal contempt: punishable by a fine of up to $700 or up to 6 months' imprisonment, or both. Also liable to employee for up to 6 weeks' lost wages and attorneys' fees.

Mississippi

Miss. Code Ann. § 13-5-23

Unpaid leave: Yes.

Additional employee protections: Employer may not threaten or intimidate, persuade, or attempt to persuade employee to avoid jury service.

Employer penalty for firing or penalizing employee: If found guilty of interference with the administration of justice: at least one month in the county jail or up to 2 years in the state penitentiary, or a fine of up to $500, or both. May also be found guilty of contempt of court, punishable by a fine of up to $1,000 or up to 6 months' imprisonment, or both.

Missouri

Mo. Rev. Stat. § 494.460

Unpaid leave: Yes.

Additional employee protections: Employer may not take or threaten to take any adverse action.

Employer penalty for firing or penalizing employee: Employer may be liable for lost wages, damages, and attorneys' fees and ordered to reinstate employee.

Montana

Mont. Admin. R. 24.16.2520

Paid leave: No paid leave laws regarding private employers.

Nebraska

Neb. Rev. Stat. § 25-1640

Paid leave: Normal wages minus any compensation (other than expenses) from the court.

Additional employee protections: Employee may not lose pay, sick leave, or vacation or be penalized in any way; may not be required to work evening or night shift.

Notice employee must give: Reasonable notice.

Employer penalty for firing or penalizing employee: Class IV misdemeanor, punishable by a fine of $100 to $500.

Nevada

Nev. Rev. Stat. Ann. § 6.190

Unpaid leave: Yes.

State Laws on Jury Duty (continued)

Additional employee protections: Employer may not recommend or threaten termination; may not dissuade or attempt to dissuade employee from serving as a juror.

Notice employee must give: At least one day's notice.

Employer penalty for firing or penalizing employee: Terminating or threatening to terminate is a gross misdemeanor, punishable by a fine of up to $2,000 or up to one year's imprisonment, or both; in addition, employer may be liable for lost wages, damages equal to lost wages, and punitive damages to $50,000 and must reinstate employee. Dissuading or attempting to dissuade is a misdemeanor, punishable by a fine of up to $1,000 or up to 6 months in the county jail, or both.

New Hampshire

N.H. Rev. Stat. Ann. § 500-A:14

Unpaid leave: Yes.

Employer penalty for firing or penalizing employee: Employer may be found guilty of contempt of court; also liable to employee for lost wages and attorneys' fees and must reinstate employee.

New Jersey

N.J. Stat. Ann. § 2B:20-17

Unpaid leave: Yes.

Employer penalty for firing or penalizing employee: Employer may be found guilty of a disorderly persons offense, punishable by a fine of up to $1,000 or up to 6 months' imprisonment, or both. May also be liable to employee for economic damages and attorneys' fees and may be ordered to reinstate employee

New Mexico

N.M. Stat. Ann. §§ 38-5-18 to 38-5-19

Unpaid leave: Yes.

Employer penalty for firing or penalizing employee: Petty misdemeanor, punishable by a fine of up to $500 or up to 6 months in the county jail, or both.

New York

N.Y. Jud. Ct. Acts Law § 519

Unpaid leave: Yes.

Paid leave: Employers with more than 10 employees must pay first $40 of wages for the first 3 days of jury duty.

Notice employee must give: Must notify employer prior to beginning jury duty.

Employer penalty for firing or penalizing employee: May be found guilty of criminal contempt of court, punishable by a fine of up to $1,000 or up to 6 months in the county jail, or both.

North Carolina

N.C. Gen. Stat. § 9-32

Unpaid leave: Yes.

Additional employee protections: Employee may not be demoted.

Employer penalty for firing or penalizing employee: Liable to discharged employee for reasonable damages; must reinstate employee to former position.

North Dakota

N.D. Cent. Code § 27-09.1-17

Unpaid leave: Yes.

Additional employee protections: Employee may not be laid off, penalized, or coerced because of jury duty, responding to a summons or subpoena, serving as a witness, or testifying in court.

Employer penalty for firing or penalizing employee: Class B misdemeanor, punishable by a fine of up to $1,000 or up to 30 days'

State Laws on Jury Duty (continued)

imprisonment, or both. Liable to employee for up to 6 weeks' lost wages and attorneys' fees and must reinstate employee.

Ohio

Ohio Rev. Code Ann. § 2313.18

Unpaid leave: Yes.

Notice employee must give: Reasonable notice. Absence must be for actual jury service.

Employer penalty for firing or penalizing employee: May be found guilty of contempt of court, punishable by a fine of up to $250 or 30 days' imprisonment, or both, for first offense; a fine of up to $500 or 60 days' imprisonment, or both, for second offense; a fine of up to $1,000 or 90 days' imprisonment, or both, for third offense.

Oklahoma

Okla. Stat. Ann. tit. 38, §§ 34, 35

Unpaid leave: Yes.

Additional employee protections: Employee can't be required to use sick leave or vacation; may choose to take paid or unpaid leave.

Employer penalty for firing or penalizing employee: Misdemeanor, punishable by a fine of up to $5,000. Liable to discharged employee for actual and exemplary damages; actual damages include past and future lost wages, mental anguish, and costs of finding suitable employment.

Oregon

Or. Rev. Stat. § 10.090

Unpaid leave: Yes (or according to employer's policy).

Employer penalty for firing or penalizing employee: Employer must reinstate discharged employee with back pay.

Pennsylvania

42 Pa. Cons. Stat. Ann. § 4563; 18 Pa. Cons. Stat.

Ann. § 4957

Unpaid leave: Yes (applies to retail or service industry employers with 15 or more employees and to manufacturers with 40 or more employees).

Additional employee protections: Employee may not lose seniority or benefits. (Any employee who would not be eligible for unpaid leave will be automatically excused from jury duty.) Employee who must appear in court as a victim or witness, or as a family member of a victim or witness, must also be given unpaid leave.

Employer penalty for firing or penalizing employee: Liable to employee for lost benefits, wages, and attorneys' fees; must reinstate employee.

Rhode Island

R.I. Gen. Laws § 9-9-28

Unpaid leave: Yes.

Additional employee protections: Employee may not lose wage increases, promotions, length of service, or other benefit.

Employer penalty for firing or penalizing employee: Misdemeanor punishable by a fine of up to $1,000 or up to one year's imprisonment, or both.

South Carolina

S.C. Code Ann. § 41-1-70

Unpaid leave: Yes.

Additional employee protections: Employee may not be demoted.

Employer penalty for firing or penalizing employee: For discharging employee, liable for one year's salary; for demoting employee, liable for one year's difference between former and lower salary.

State Laws on Jury Duty (continued)

South Dakota

S.D. Codified Laws Ann. §§ 16-13-41.1, 16-13-41.2

Unpaid leave: Yes.

Additional employee protections: Employee may not lose job status, pay, or seniority.

Employer penalty for firing or penalizing employee: Class 2 misdemeanor, punishable by a fine of up to $200 or up to 30 days in the county jail, or both.

Tennessee

Tenn. Code Ann. § 22-4-108

Paid leave: Regular wages minus jury fees (does not apply to employers with fewer than 5 employees or to temporary employees who have worked less than 6 months).

Additional employee protections: Night shift employees are excused from shift work during and for the night before the first day of jury service.

Notice employee must give: Employee must show summons to supervisor the day after receiving it.

Employer penalty for firing or penalizing employee: Violating employee rights or any provisions of this law is a Class A misdemeanor, punishable by up to 11 months, 29 days' imprisonment or a fine up to $2,500, or both. Liable to employee for lost wages and benefits and must reinstate employee.

Texas

Tex. Civ. Prac. & Rem. Code Ann. §§ 122.001, 122.002

Unpaid leave: Yes.

Notice employee must give: Employee must notify employer of intent to return after completion of jury service.

Employer penalty for firing or penalizing employee: Liable to employee for not less than one year's nor more than 5 years' compensation and attorneys' fees. Must reinstate employee.

Utah

Utah Code Ann. § 78-46-21

Unpaid leave: Yes.

Additional employee protections: Employee may not be threatened or coerced and may not be requested or required to use annual or sick leave or vacation. Employer may not take any adverse employment action against employee.

Employer penalty for firing or penalizing employee: May be found guilty of criminal contempt, punishable by a fine of up to $500 or up to 6 months' imprisonment, or both. Liable to employee for up to 6 weeks' lost wages and attorneys' fees.

Vermont

Vt. Stat. Ann. tit. 21, § 499

Unpaid leave: Yes.

Additional employee protections: Employee may not be penalized or lose any benefit available to other employees; may not lose seniority, vacation credit, or any fringe benefits. Protections also apply to an employee appearing as a witness in court or testifying before a board, commission, or tribunal.

Employer penalty for firing or penalizing employee: Fine of up to $200.

Virginia

Va. Code Ann. § 18.2-465.1

Unpaid leave: Yes.

Additional employee protections: Employee may not be subject to any adverse personnel action and may not be forced to use sick leave or vacation. If employee has to attend any future hearings, the same protections apply. As of 7/1/05, employee need not work on day of jury service.

State Laws on Jury Duty (continued)

Notice employee must give: Reasonable notice.

Employer penalty for firing or penalizing employee: Class 3 misdemeanor, punishable by a fine of up to $500.

Washington

Wash. Rev. Code Ann. § 2.36.165

Unpaid leave: Yes.

Additional employee protections: Employee may not be threatened, coerced, harassed, or denied promotion.

Employer penalty for firing or penalizing employee: Intentional violation is a misdemeanor, punishable by a fine of up to $1,000 or up to 90 days' imprisonment, or both; also liable to employee for damages and attorneys' fees and must reinstate employee.

West Virginia

W.Va. Code § 52-3-1

Unpaid leave: Yes.

Additional employee protections: Employee may not be threatened or discriminated against; regular pay cannot be cut.

Employer penalty for firing or penalizing employee: May be found guilty of civil contempt, punishable by a fine of $100 to $500. Must reinstate employee. May be liable for back pay and for attorneys' fees.

Wisconsin

Wis. Stat. Ann. § 756.255

Unpaid leave: Yes.

Additional employee protections: Employee may not lose seniority or pay raises; may not be disciplined.

Employer penalty for firing or penalizing employee: Fine of up to $200. Must reinstate employee with back pay.

Wyoming

Wyo. Stat. § 1-11-401

Unpaid leave: Yes.

Additional employee protections: Employee may not be threatened, intimidated, or coerced.

Employer penalty for firing or penalizing employee: Liable to employee for up to $1,000 damages, costs, and attorneys' fees. Must reinstate employee with no loss of seniority.

Current as of February 2005

State Laws on Taking Time Off to Vote (continued)

Note: The states of Alabama, Connecticut, Delaware, District of Columbia, Florida, Idaho, Indiana, Louisiana, Maine, Michigan, Mississippi, Montana, New Hampshire, New Jersey, North Carolina, Oregon, Pennsylvania, Rhode Island, South Carolina, Vermont, and Virginia are not listed in this chart because they do not have laws or regulations on time off to vote that govern private employers. Check with your state department of labor if you need more information. (See the appendix for the contact list.)

Alaska

Alaska Stat. § 15.56.100

Time off work for voting: Not specified.

Time off not required if: Employee has 2 consecutive nonwork hours at beginning or end of shift when polls are open.

Time off is paid: Yes.

Arizona

Ariz. Rev. Stat. § 16-402

Time off work for voting: As much time as will add up to 3 hours when combined with nonwork time. Employer may decide when hours are taken.

Time off not required if: Employee has 3 consecutive nonwork hours at beginning or end of shift when polls are open.

Time off is paid: Yes.

Employee must request leave in advance: One day before election.

Arkansas

Ark. Code Ann. § 7-1-102

Time off work for voting: Employer must schedule work hours so employee has time to vote.

Time off is paid: No.

California

Cal. Elec. Code § 14000

Time off work for voting: Up to 2 hours at beginning or end of shift, whichever gives employee most time to vote and takes least time off work.

Time off not required if: Employee has sufficient time to vote during nonwork time.

Time off is paid: Yes (up to 2 hours).

Employee must request leave in advance: 2 working days before election.

Colorado

Colo. Rev. Stat. § 1-7-102

Time off work for voting: Up to 2 hours. Employer may decide when hours are taken, but employer must permit employee to take time at beginning or end of shift, if employee requests it.

Time off not required if: Employee has 3 nonwork hours when polls are open.

Time off is paid: Yes (up to 2 hours).

Employee must request leave in advance: Prior to election day.

Georgia

Ga. Code Ann. § 21-2-404

Time off work for voting: Up to 2 hours. Employer may decide when hours are taken.

Time off not required if: Employee has 2 nonwork hours at beginning or end of shift when polls are open.

Time off is paid: No.

Employee must request leave in advance: "Reasonable notice."

Hawaii

Haw. Rev. Stat. § 11-95

Time off work for voting: 2 consecutive hours excluding meal or rest breaks. Employer may not change employee's regular work schedule.

Time off not required if: Employee has 2 consecutive nonwork hours when polls are open.

Time off is paid: Yes.

Employee required to show proof of voting: Yes (voter's receipt). If employer verifies that employee did not vote, hours off may be deducted from pay.

State Laws on Taking Time Off to Vote (continued)

Illinois

10 Ill. Comp. Stat. §§ 5/7-42, 5/17-15

Time off work for voting: 2 hours. Employer may decide when hours are taken.

Time off is paid: No.

Employee must request leave in advance: One day in advance (for general or state election). Employer must give consent (for primary).

Iowa

Iowa Code § 49.109

Time off work for voting: As much time as will add up to 3 hours when combined with nonwork time. Employer may decide when hours are taken.

Time off not required if: Employee has 3 consecutive nonwork hours when polls are open.

Time off is paid: Yes.

Employee must request leave in advance: In writing "prior to the date of the election."

Kansas

Kan. Stat. Ann. § 25-418

Time off work for voting: Up to 2 hours or as much time as will add up to 2 hours when combined with nonwork time. Employer may decide when hours are taken, but it may not be during a regular meal break.

Time off not required if: Employee has 2 consecutive nonwork hours when polls are open.

Time off is paid: Yes.

Kentucky

Ky. Const. § 148; Ky. Rev. Stat. Ann. § 118.035

Time off work for voting: "Reasonable time," but not less than 4 hours. Employer may decide when hours are taken.

Time off is paid: No.

Employee must request leave in advance: One day before election.

Employee required to show proof of voting: No proof specified, but employee who takes time off and does not vote may be subject to disciplinary action.

Maryland

Md. Code Ann. [Elec. Law] § 10-315

Time off work for voting: 2 hours.

Time off not required if: Employee has 2 consecutive nonwork hours when polls are open.

Time off is paid: Yes.

Employee required to show proof of voting: Yes; also includes attempting to vote. Must use state board of elections form.

Massachusetts

Mass. Gen. Laws ch. 149, § 178

Time off work for voting: First 2 hours that polls are open. (Applies to workers in manufacturing, mechanical, or retail industries.)

Time off is paid: No.

Employee must request leave in advance: Must apply for leave of absence (no time specified).

Minnesota

Minn. Stat. Ann. § 204C.04

Time off work for voting: May be absent during the morning of election day.

Time off is paid: Yes.

Missouri

Mo. Rev. Stat. § 115.639

Time off work for voting: 3 hours. Employer may decide when hours are taken.

Time off not required if: Employee has 3 consecutive nonwork hours when polls are open.

Time off is paid: Yes (if employee votes).

Employee must request leave in advance: "Prior to the day of election."

Employee required to show proof of voting: None specified, but pay contingent on employee actually voting.

Nebraska

Neb. Rev. Stat. § 32-922

State Laws on Taking Time Off to Vote (continued)

Time off work for voting: As much time as will add up to 2 consecutive hours when combined with nonwork time. Employer may decide when hours are taken.

Time off not required if: Employee has 2 consecutive nonwork hours when polls are open.

Time off is paid: Yes

Employee must request leave in advance: Prior to or on election day.

Nevada
Nev. Rev. Stat. Ann. § 293.463

Time off work for voting: If it is impracticable to vote before or after work: Employee who works 2 miles or less from polling place may take 1 hour; 2 to 10 miles, 2 hours; more than 10 miles, 3 hours.

Time off not required if: Employee has sufficient nonwork time when polls are open.

Time off is paid: Yes.

Employee must request leave in advance: Prior to election day.

New Mexico
N.M. Stat. Ann. § 1-12-42

Time off work for voting: 2 hours. (Includes Indian nation, tribal, and pueblo elections.)

Time off not required if: Employee's workday begins more than 2 hours after polls open or ends more than 3 hours before polls close.

Time off is paid: Yes.

New York
N.Y. Elec. Law § 3-110

Time off work for voting: As many hours at beginning or end of shift as will give employee enough time to vote when combined with nonwork time. Employer may decide when hours are taken.

Time off not required if: Employee has 4 consecutive nonwork hours at beginning or end of shift when polls are open.

Time off is paid: Yes (up to 2 hours).

Employee must request leave in advance: Not more than 10 or less than 2 working days before election.

North Dakota
N.D. Cent. Code § 16.1-01-02.1

Time off work for voting: Employers are encouraged to give employees time off to vote when regular work schedule conflicts with times polls are open.

Time off is paid: No.

Ohio
Ohio Rev. Code Ann. § 3599.06

Time off work for voting: "Reasonable time."

Time off is paid: Yes.

Oklahoma
Okla. Stat. Ann. tit. 26, § 7-101

Time off work for voting: 2 hours, unless employee lives so far from polling place that more time is needed. Employer may decide when hours are taken or may change employee's schedule to give employee nonwork time to vote.

Time off not required if: Employee's workday begins at least 3 hours after polls open or ends at least 3 hours before polls close.

Time off is paid: Yes.

Employee must request leave in advance: One day before election.

Employee required to show proof of voting: Yes.

South Dakota
S.D. Codified Laws Ann. § 12-3-5

Time off work for voting: 2 consecutive hours. Employer may decide when hours are taken.

Time off not required if: Employee has 2 consecutive nonwork hours when polls are open.

Time off is paid: Yes.

State Laws on Taking Time Off to Vote (continued)

Tennessee

Tenn. Code Ann. § 2-1-106

Time off work for voting: "Reasonable time" up to 3 hours.

Time off not required if: Employee's workday begins at least 3 hours after polls open or ends at least 3 hours before polls close.

Time off is paid: Yes.

Employee must request leave in advance: Before noon on the day before the election.

Texas

Tex. Elec. Code Ann. § 276.004

Time off work for voting: Employer may not refuse to allow employee to take time off to vote, but no time limit specified.

Time off not required if: Employee has 2 consecutive nonwork hours when polls are open.

Time off is paid: Yes.

Utah

Utah Code Ann. § 20A-3-103

Time off work for voting: 2 hours at beginning or end of shift. Employer may decide when hours are taken.

Time off not required if: Employee has at least 3 nonwork hours when polls are open.

Time off is paid: Yes.

Employee must request leave in advance: "Before election day."

Washington

Wash. Rev. Code Ann. § 49.28.120

Time off work for voting: Employer must either arrange work schedule so employee has enough nonwork time (not including meal or rest breaks) to vote, or allow employee to take off work for a "reasonable time," up to 2 hours.

Time off not required if: Employee has 2 nonwork hours when polls are open or enough time

to get an absentee ballot.

Time off is paid: Yes.

West Virginia

W.Va. Code § 3-1-42

Time off work for voting: Up to 3 hours. (Employers in health, transportation, communication, production, and processing facilities may change employee's schedule so that time off doesn't impair essential operations but must allow employee sufficient and convenient time to vote.)

Time off not required if: Employee has at least 3 nonwork hours when polls are open.

Time off is paid: Yes (if employee votes).

Employee must request leave in advance: Written request at least 3 days before election.

Employee required to show proof of voting: None specified, but time off will be deducted from pay if employee does not vote.

Wisconsin

Wis. Stat. Ann. § 6.76

Time off work for voting: Up to 3 consecutive hours. Employer may decide when hours are taken.

Time off is paid: No.

Employee must request leave in advance: "Before election day."

Wyoming

Wyo. Stat. § 22-2-111

Time off work for voting: One hour, other than a meal break.

Time off not required if: Employee has at least 3 consecutive nonwork hours when polls are open.

Time off is paid: Yes (if employee votes).

Employee required to show proof of voting: None specified, but pay contingent on employee voting.

Current as of February 2005

State Laws on Military Leave

Alabama

Alabama Stat. §§ 31-12-1 and following

State national guard and militia members called to active duty for at least 30 consecutive days or for federally funded duty for homeland security have the same leave and reinstatement rights and benefits guaranteed under USERRA.

Alaska

Alaska Stat. § 26.05.075

Employees called to active service in the state militia are entitled to unlimited unpaid leave and reinstatement to their former or a comparable position, with the pay, seniority, and benefits the employee would have had if not absent for service.

Arizona

Ariz. Rev. Stat. §§ 26-167, 26-168

Members of state military forces or national guard members called up by state for training or duty have the same leave and reinstatement rights and benefits guaranteed under USERRA. Employer may not dissuade employees from enlisting in state or national military forces by threatening economic reprisal.

Arkansas

Ark. Code Ann. § 12-62-413

Employees called by the Governor to active duty in the Arkansas National Guard or the state militia have the same leave and reinstatement rights and benefits guaranteed under USERRA.

California

Cal. Mil. & Vet. Code §§ 394, 394.5, 395.06

Employees who are called into service in the state military or naval forces have the same leave and reinstatement rights and benefits guaranteed under USERRA. Employees in the U.S. armed forces, National Guard, or Naval Militia are entitled to 17 days unpaid leave per year for training or special exercises. Employer may not terminate employee or limit any benefits or seniority because a of temporary disability (up to 52 weeks).

Colorado

Colo. Rev. Stat. § 28-3-609

Permanent employees who are members of Colorado National Guard or U.S. armed forces reserves are entitled to 15 days unpaid leave per year for training and reinstatement to their former or a similar position with the same status, pay, and seniority.

Connecticut

Conn. Gen. Stat. Ann. § 27-33a

Employees who are active or reserve members of the state militia or National Guard are entitled to take leave to attend meetings or drills that take place during regular working hours, without loss or reduction of vacation or holiday benefits. Employer may not discriminate in terms of promotion or continued employment.

Florida

Fla. Stat. Ann. §§ 250.482, 627.6692(h) to (j)

Employees who are members of the Florida National Guard and are called into active duty by the governor may not be penalized for absence from work. Employees not covered by COBRA whose employment is terminated while on active duty are entitled to a new 18-month benefit period beginning when active duty or job ends, whichever is later.

Georgia

Ga. Code Ann. § 38-2-280

Members of U.S. armed forces or Georgia National Guard called into active federal or state service are entitled to unlimited unpaid leave for active service and up to 6 months leave in any 4-year period for service school or annual training.

State Laws on Military Leave (continued)

Employee is entitled to reinstatement with full benefits unless employer's circumstances have changed to make reinstatement impossible or unreasonable.

Hawaii

Haw. Rev. Stat. § 121-43

Employees serving in the state national guard have the same leave and reinstatement rights and benefits guaranteed under USERRA.

Idaho

Idaho Code §§ 46-224, 46-225, 46-407

Members of state national guard ordered to active duty by the Governor may take up to one year of unpaid leave and are entitled to reinstatement to former position. Returning employees may not be fired without cause for one year. Members of national guard and reserves may take up to 15 days leave per year for training; employee must give 90 days' notice of training dates.

Illinois

20 Ill. Comp. Stat. §§ 1805/30.1 to 1805/30.20; 330 Ill. Comp. State. § 60/4

Members of Illinois State Guard and members of U.S. uniformed services who are called into state active duty in the Illinois National Guard have the same leave and reinstatement rights and benefits guaranteed under USERRA.

Indiana

Ind. Code Ann. §§ 10-17-4-1 to 10-17-4-5

Members of U.S. armed services reserves may take up to 15 days unpaid (or paid at employer's discretion) leave per year for training. Leave does not affect vacation, sick leave, bonus, or promotion rights. Employee must be reinstated to former or a similar position with no loss of seniority or benefits.

Iowa

Iowa Code § 29A.43

Members of national guard, reserves, or state military called into temporary duty are entitled to reinstatement to former or a similar position. Leave does not affect vacation, sick leave, bonuses, or other benefits. Employee must give employer proof of satisfactory completion of duty and of employee's qualifications to perform the job's duties.

Kansas

Kan. Stat. Ann. §§ 48-517, 48-222

Members of state military forces called into active duty by the state have the same leave and reinstatement rights and benefits guaranteed under USERRA. In addition to unlimited leave for active duty, employees are entitled to 5 to 10 days leave each year to attend state national guard training camp.

Kentucky

Ky. Rev. Stat. Ann. § 38.238

Members of Kentucky National Guard are entitled to unlimited unpaid leave for training and reinstatement to former position with no loss of seniority or benefits. Employer may not in any way discriminate against employee or threaten to prevent employee from enlisting in the Kentucky national guard or active militia.

Louisiana

La. Rev. Stat. Ann. §§ 29:38, 29:38.1, 29:410

Employees called into active duty in any branch of the state military forces have the same leave and reinstatement rights and benefits guaranteed under USERRA.

Maine

Me. Rev. Stat. Ann. tit. 37-B, § 342(5)

Employer may not discriminate against employee

State Laws on Military Leave (continued)

for membership or service in state military forces.

Maryland

Md. Code Ann. [Public Safety] § 13-705

Members of the national guard and militia called to active duty or training by the Governor have the same leave and reinstatement rights and benefits guaranteed under USERRA.

Massachusetts

Mass. Gen. Laws ch. 149, §§ 52A to 52A 1/2

Employees who are members of U.S. armed forces reserves or the state armed forces may take up to 17 days per year for training. Leave does not affect vacation, sick leave, bonus, or promotion rights. Employee who is qualified must be reinstated to former or a similar position. Veterans who want to participate in a Veterans Day or Memorial Day exercise, parade, or service must be given leave.

Michigan

Mich. Comp. Laws §§ 32.271 to 32.274

Members of state or U.S. uniformed services called into active state or federal duty may take unpaid leave; employee may also take unpaid leave to take a physical, enlist, be inducted, or attend training. Returning employee must be reinstated to former position. Employer may not in any way discriminate against employee or threaten to prevent employee from enlisting in the state armed forces.

Minnesota

Minn. Stat. Ann. § 192.34

Employer may not discharge employee, interfere with military service, or dissuade employee from enlisting by threatening employee's job. Applies to employees who are members of the U.S., Minnesota, or any other state military or naval forces.

Mississippi

Miss. Code Ann. § 33-1-19

Members of U.S. uniformed services and Mississippi armed forces are entitled to unpaid leave for active state duty or state training duty. If still qualified to perform job duties, employee entitled to reinstatement to previous or similar position.

Missouri

Mo. Rev. Stat. §§ 41.730, 557.021, 558.011, 560.016

Employer may not discharge employee, interfere with employee's military service, or threaten to dissuade employee from enlisting; applies to members of the state-organized militia.

Montana

Mont. Code Ann. § 10-1-603

Members of the state organized militia called to active service during a state-declared disaster or emergency are entitled to unpaid leave for duration of service. Leave may not be deducted from sick leave, vacation, or other leave, although employee may voluntarily use that leave. Returning employee is entitled to reinstatement to same or similar position. Employer may not in any way discriminate against employee or dissuade employee from enlisting by threatening employee's job.

Nebraska

Neb. Rev. Stat. § 55-161

Employees who are members of the Nebraska National Guard and are called into active state duty have the same leave and reinstatement rights and benefits guaranteed under USERRA.

Nevada

Nev. Rev. Stat. Ann. §§ 412.139, 412.606, 683A.261

Employers may not discriminate against members of the Nevada National Guard and may not

State Laws on Military Leave (continued)

discharge any employee who is called into active service.

New Hampshire

N.H. Rev. Stat. Ann. §§ 110-B:65(II), 110-C:1

Members of the national guard or militia called to active duty have the same leave and reinstatement rights and benefits guaranteed under USERRA. Employer may not discriminate against employee because of connection or service with national guard; may not dissuade employee from enlisting by threatening job.

New Jersey

N.J. Stat. Ann. § 38:23C-20

An employee is entitled to take unpaid leave for active service in the U.S. or state military services. Upon return, employee must be reinstated to the same or a similar position, unless employer's circumstances have changed to make reinstatement impossible or unreasonable. Employee may not be fired without cause for one year after returning from service. Employee is also entitled to take up to 3 months leave for training or assemblies relating to military service.

New Mexico

N.M. Stat. Ann. §§ 28-15-1 to 28-15-3

Members of the state national guard or militia may take unpaid leave for service. Employee who is still qualified must be reinstated in former or similar position with no loss of status or seniority. Employee may not be fired without cause for one year after returning from service. Employer may not discriminate against or discharge employee because of membership in the national guard; may not prevent employee from performing military service.

New York

N.Y. Mil. Law § 317

Members of the state military forces called up by governor and members of U.S. uniformed services are entitled to unpaid leave for active service; reserve drills or annual training; service school; initial full-time or active duty training. Returning employee is entitled to reinstatement to previous position, or to one with the same seniority, status, and pay, unless the employer's circumstances have changed and reemployment is impossible or unreasonable.

North Carolina

N.C. Gen. Stat. §§ 127A-201 and following, 127B-14

Members of the North Carolina National Guard called to active duty by the governor are entitled to take unpaid leave. Returning employee must be restored to previous position or one of comparable seniority, status, and salary; if no longer qualified, employee must be placed in another position with appropriate seniority, status, and salary, unless the employer's circumstances now make reinstatement unreasonable. Employer may not deny employment, promotion, or any benefit because employee is a member of or enlists or serves in the state national guard; employer may not discharge employee called up for emergency military service.

Ohio

Ohio Rev. Code Ann. §§ 5903.01, 5903.02

Employees who are members of the Ohio militia or national guard called for active duty or training; members of the commissioned public health service corps; or any other uniformed service called up in time of war or emergency have the same leave and reinstatement rights and benefits guaranteed under USERRA.

Oklahoma

Okla. Stat. Ann. tit. 44, §§ 71, 208

State Laws on Military Leave (continued)

Employees called to state active duty in the Oklahoma National Guard have the same leave and reinstatement rights and benefits guaranteed under USERRA. Members of the national guard may take leave to attend state national guard training, drills, or ceremony. Employer may not fire employee or hinder or prevent employee from performing military service.

Oregon

Or. Rev. Stat. § 399.230

Members of state organized militia called into active duty by the governor may take unpaid leave for term of service. Returning employee is entitled to reinstatement with no loss of seniority or benefits including sick leave, vacation, or service credits under a pension plan.

Pennsylvania

51 Pa. Cons. Stat. Ann. §§ 7302, 7309

Employee who enlists or is drafted during a time of war or emergency called by the president or governor is entitled to unpaid military leave along with reservists called into active duty. Returning employee must be reinstated to same or similar position with same status, seniority, and pay. Employers may not discharge or discriminate against any employee because of membership or service in the military. Employees called to active duty are entitled to 30 days' health insurance continuation benefits at no cost.

Rhode Island

R.I. Gen. Laws §§ 30-11-2 to 30-11-6, 30-21-1

Members of state military forces and National Guard members on state active duty have the same leave and reinstatement rights and benefits guaranteed under USERRA. Employer may not discharge employee because of membership in the military, interfere with employee's military service, or dissuade employee from enlisting by threatening employee's job.

South Carolina

S.C. Code Ann. §§ 25-1-2310 to 25-1-2340

Members of the South Carolina National Guard and State Guard called to state duty by the governor are entitled to unpaid leave for service. Returning employee must be reinstated to previous position or one with same seniority, status, and salary; if no longer qualified, must be given another position, unless employer's circumstances make reinstatement unreasonable.

South Dakota

S.D. Codified Laws Ann. § 33-17-15.1

Members of the South Dakota National Guard ordered to active duty by the governor or president have the same leave and reinstatement rights and benefits guaranteed under USERRA.

Tennessee

Tenn. Code Ann. § 58-1-604

Employer may not refuse to hire or terminate an employee because of national guard membership or because employee is absent for a required drill or annual training.

Texas

Tex. Gov't. Code Ann. § 431.006

Members of the state military forces called to active duty or training are entitled to unpaid leave. Returning employee is entitled to reinstatement to the same position with no loss of time, efficiency rating, vacation, or benefits unless employer's circumstances have changed so that reemployment is impossible or unreasonable.

Utah

Utah Code Ann. § 39-1-36

Members of U.S. armed forces reserves who are called to active duty, active duty for training, inactive duty training, or state active duty may

State Laws on Military Leave (continued)

take up to 5 years of unpaid leave. Upon return, employee is entitled to reinstatement to previous employment with same seniority, status, pay, and vacation rights. Employer may not discriminate against an employee based on membership in armed forces reserves.

Vermont

Vt. Stat. Ann. tit. 21, § 491

Permanent employees who are members of an organized unit of the national guard or the ready reserves and are called to active state duty or training with the U.S. military are entitled to unpaid leave. Employee must give 30 days' notice for U.S. training and as much notice as is practical for state duty. If still qualified, returning employee must be reinstated to former position with the same status, pay, and seniority, including any seniority that accrued during the leave of absence. Employer may not discriminate against an employee who is a member or an applicant for membership in the state or federal national guard.

Virginia

Va. Code Ann. §§ 44-93.2 to 44-93.4

Members of the Virginia National Guard, Virginia State Defense Force, or naval militia called to active state duty by the governor are entitled to take unpaid leave and may not be required to use vacation or any other accrued leave (unless employee wishes). Returning employee must be reinstated to previous position or one with same seniority, status, and pay. If position no longer exists, then to a comparable position, unless employer's circumstances would make reemployment unreasonable.

Washington

Wash. Rev. Code Ann. §§ 73.16.032 to 73.16.035

Permanent employees who are Washington residents or employed within the state and who

volunteer or are called to serve in the uniformed services have the same leave and reinstatement rights and benefits guaranteed under USERRA.

West Virginia

W.Va. Code § 15-1F-8

Employees who are members of the organized militia in active state service have the same leave and reinstatement rights and benefits guaranteed under USERRA.

Wisconsin

Wis. Stat. Ann. § 45.50

Permanent employees who enlist, are inducted, or are called to serve in the uniformed services, or civilians requested to perform national defense work during an officially proclaimed emergency, may take up to 4 years leave for military service and/or training unless period of service is extended by law. Returning employee is entitled to reinstatement to previous position, or to one with the same seniority, benefits, and pay, unless the employee is no longer qualified or the employer's circumstances have changed and reemployment is impossible or unreasonable. Employee may not be fired without cause for one year after returning from service.

Wyoming

Wyo. Stat. §§ 19-11-101 to 19-11-123

Employees who are members of or who apply for membership in the uniformed services; employees who report for active duty, training, or a qualifying physical exam; or who are called to state duty by the governor, may take up to 4 years leave of absence. Employee may use vacation or any other accrued leave but is not required to do so. Returning employee is entitled to reemployment with the same seniority, rights, and benefits, plus any additional seniority and benefits that employee would have earned if there had been no absence, unless

State Laws on Military Leave (continued)

employer's circumstances have changed so that reemployment is impossible or unreasonable or would impose an undue hardship. Employee is entitled to complete any training program that would have been available to employee's former position during period of absence. Employee may not be terminated without cause for one year after returning to work.

Current as of February 2005

6

Privacy

As a manager, you may occasionally need (or want) to gather information about the employees you supervise. For example, you might want to monitor employee productivity by keeping track of Internet use, search the workspace of an employee suspected of theft, or ask applicants for a promotion to take a personality test.

However, you must balance your or your company's need (or desire) for this information with your employees' privacy rights. You certainly don't want to go so far overboard that your workers start thinking of your company as "Big Brother." And, of course, you should follow the basic legal rules that relate to employee privacy in order to steer clear of potential lawsuits.

This chapter covers some employment practices that might lead your company to run afoul of privacy protections— including testing, monitoring employee communications, and looking into an employee's off-duty conduct. We explain what you can—and what you cannot—do when it comes to gathering information about your employees.

Frequently Asked Questions About Workplace Privacy

■ **Can I require a worker to take a drug test?**
Generally, it isn't a good idea to require every worker to submit to a drug test. However, you can require drug testing for a particular employee if you reasonably suspect drug use (if the employee has glassy or red eyes, concentration problems, or other signs of impairment at work, for example). You may also test an applicant for drug use if you are filling a position that carries a high risk of injury or requires an employee to carry a weapon. (For more on drug testing of job applicants, see "Testing Applicants" in Chapter 1. For more on drug testing of current employees, see "Testing Current Employees," below.)

■ **Can I fire a worker whose personal beliefs clash with mine?**
Federal and state laws protect workers from discrimination on the basis of religious or political beliefs. However, if workers bring their beliefs into the workplace by, for example, attempting to convert other workers to their religion or publicizing their political beliefs during work time, you may put a stop to this. (For more information, see "Off-Duty Conduct," below. For information on religious discrimination, see "Religion" in Chapter 3.)

■ **Can my company read employees' email messages?**
Probably, although it might depend on your company's policies. If you have a policy of email privacy (if you tell your employees that their email will be

confidential or will not be read by the company, for example), then you should abide by that policy. Otherwise, you have the right to monitor employee email, as long as you have a legitimate business purpose for doing so. (For more information, see "Electronic Monitoring," below.)

■ **Can my company randomly search employees to discourage theft?**
Generally, you can perform a workplace search in order to serve important, work-related interests—as long as you don't unduly intrude on your workers' privacy rights. Random searches are less likely to pass legal muster than a search of a particular employee whom you reasonably suspect of theft. And, even if you have a reasonable suspicion, you must not search too invasively. (For more information, see "Workplace Searches," below.)

The Right to Privacy

Worker privacy is one of the more complex areas of law that employers have to navigate. The basic rule is fairly simple: An employer should stay out of its workers' personal lives, opinions, communications, and belongings. However, there are numerous exceptions to this basic rule—circumstances in which an employer can intrude even into these private areas, if there is a business-related reason to do so. We explain these guidelines in the discussions of specific topics that follow.

Privacy law is tricky, in part, because it comes from so many different legal sources. There is no one federal statute that lays out the content and limits of the right to privacy. Instead, privacy principles derive mainly from the "common law," a group of legal theories inherited from England when our nation was founded.

There are additional privacy protections in the U.S. Constitution, some state constitutions, various state and federal statutes, and court decisions by state and federal judges. Here's a brief roadmap through this complicated terrain of workplace privacy law.

Common Law

The term "common law" is what lawyers use to refer to legal rules that are not codified in a statute or constitution. Many of these rules originated in England and came to this country along with the colonists. As time passes and legal issues evolve, judges apply these ancient principles to more modern situations. In the sphere of privacy, for example, judges have had to stretch the time-honored right to be left alone to cover everything from people's homes to Internet chat rooms to celebrity weddings.

Most of the privacy rules that employers must follow come from the common law. But finding the common law can be tough. Because common law isn't codified, you have to read cases—written records of judicial decisions—to find out how judges have interpreted these rules. The good news is that these rules are fairly straightforward—and fairly uniform from state to state.

Constitutional Protections

The U.S. Constitution does not explicitly grant a right to privacy. Nonetheless, the U.S. Supreme Court has decided, in a series of decisions dealing primarily with sex and reproductive choice, that the Bill of Rights implies a right to privacy. However, private employers don't need to worry too much about exactly what this right entails: It applies mostly to the government. Private employers generally cannot be sued for violating the federal constitution.

However, some state constitutions also contain an explicit right to privacy—and some apply this right to private employers as well as state governments. If your company is faced with this kind of claim, courts will generally sort it out by weighing two competing concerns. On the one hand, the court will consider the employee's legitimate expectations of privacy—that is, whether the worker reasonably believed that the area intruded

on (a locker, email, or off-duty conduct, for example) was private, and the reasons for those beliefs. On the other hand, the court will look at the reasons for the intrusion—for example, whether the employer had a legitimate, job-related reason for searching or monitoring and whether the employer could have gathered the same information in a less intrusive way. The court will decide the case by weighing these competing concerns.

Federal Statutes

No single federal law lays out comprehensive rules on privacy. However, a few federal laws set down some privacy guidelines for employers. For example, the Fair Credit Reporting Act (discussed in more detail in "Background Checks" in Chapter 1) requires employers to get written consent from an employee or applicant before reviewing that person's credit report. The Employee Polygraph Protection Act generally prohibits employers from subjecting their workers to lie detector tests. (See "Testing Current Employees," below, for more information.) And the National Labor Relations Act prohibits employers from monitoring a worker's union activity, including off-the-job meetings. (See "Off-Duty Conduct," below, for more on this topic.)

State Statutes

Many states have laws outlawing particular privacy violations. For example, some states prohibit employers from considering an applicant's arrest records, require employers to notify workers when they listen in to a worker's telephone conversation, or prohibit employers from using particular surveillance techniques (such as a one-way mirror or video camera) in areas like restrooms and locker rooms. To find out more about your state's privacy laws, contact your state labor department.

Testing Current Employees

Workplace testing has become increasingly popular as employers screen their workers in an effort to figure out who would be the best candidate for promotion or who is responsible for a workplace problem. As long as a test is designed to predict a worker's actual ability to do the job (and is relatively noninvasive—for example, it doesn't require a worker to reveal personal information), it is probably legal. For example, an employer can generally require typing tests for clerical jobs or agility/strength tests for positions that require certain physical skills (but make sure that the test doesn't unfairly screen out disabled workers who could do the job with a reasonable accommodation—see "Applicants With Disabilities" in Chapter 1 for more information).

Generally, an employer should have a sound, work-related reason to require a current employee to submit to a test. But that might not be enough: If the test is too intrusive or delves too deeply into personal issues, it might invade the employee's right to privacy (and result in a lawsuit).

Unfortunately for employers, there are no hard-and-fast rules about whether a particular test is legal—courts generally decide these issues on a case-by-case basis, looking at all the facts and circumstances. For the most part, employers can stay out of trouble by using simple common sense. An employer who inquires into an employee's sex life, religious beliefs, or political affiliations probably crosses the line, while an employer who tests only for necessary job skills is probably on safe ground.

In addition to these general considerations, specific rules apply to the following types of tests.

Medical Examinations

Once an employee is on the job, an employer's right to conduct a medical examination is usually limited to so-called "fitness for duty" situations. If an employee has shown objective signs that he or she is physically or mentally unfit to perform the essential functions of the job—for example, by claiming that an injury prevents him or her from working—an employer may request that the employee's fitness for the job be evaluated by a medical examiner. Although the examiner can take a full history of the employee and conduct any tests necessary to evaluate the employee's fitness, the employer may not be entitled to all of this information.

Many states also impose strict limits on the information a doctor may disclose to an employer or an insurance company without the worker's consent.

The federal Americans With Disabilities Act (ADA) also requires certain privacy protections for the results of a medical examination. Data gathered in medical examinations must be kept in a separate file available only to those with a demonstrable need to know, such as supervisors who need information about the employee's work restrictions or reasonable accommodations and first aid and safety personnel (if the employee's disability might require emergency treatment or special evacuation procedures).

Drug Tests

Although an employer can generally require those applying for a job to submit to drug testing, an employer's right to test current employees is less clear. (For more on drug testing applicants, see "Testing Applicants" in Chapter 1 and "Drugs and Alcohol" in Chapter 7.) No federal law clearly authorizes drug testing of employees, except for certain workers in the defense and transportation industries. And many state laws limit the circumstances under which an employer may test and the types of tests an employer may conduct.

Because the law of drug testing is changing rapidly, and because state law varies widely in terms of what is allowed and prohibited, employers have to tread very carefully in this area. Before undertaking any drug testing, an employer should consult with a knowledgeable lawyer.

Employers are on safest ground if they have a strong, legitimate reason for testing workers. Your company is most likely to withstand a legal challenge if it limits testing to:

- workers whose jobs carry a high risk of injury to themselves or others (such as a pilot or a security guard who carries a gun)
- workers who have been involved in an accident that suggests the possibility of drug use (for example, a delivery person who causes a collision by driving erratically)
- workers who are currently in or have completed a rehabilitation program, and
- workers whom a manager or supervisor reasonably suspects are using drugs (based on obvious signs of impairment—for example, slurred speech or glassy eyes).

For information on your state's current rules, see the chart entitled "State Drug and Alcohol Testing Laws," at the end of Chapter 1.

Psychological Screening

Some employers use pencil and paper psychological tests to attempt to predict whether an employee will steal, fight, or engage in other negative conduct in the workplace. There are two problems with using such tests. First, mental health experts disagree about whether these tests can actually predict an employee's future conduct. Second, some of these tests include questions that are highly personal and invade the employee's privacy. For the most part, employers would be well-advised to steer clear of psychological tests absent some compelling justification—and some reason to believe that the test you use will yield relevant, accurate information about the employee.

Lie Detector Tests

A federal law, the Employee Polygraph Protection Act, 29 U.S.C. § 2001, prohibits all private employers from requiring workers to submit to lie detector tests, with a few exceptions. Employers who manufacture or distribute pharmaceuticals or provide certain security services may be allowed to require polygraphs. And an employer may require a worker accused of theft or embezzlement to take a polygraph, under certain circumstances.

Aside from these limited exceptions, however, a private employer may not require a current employee to take a lie detector test, use the results of any such test in making employment decisions, or discipline or fire any employee who refuses to take one. And, even if an exception applies, the employer must meet very strict technical requirements regarding the way the test is administered and interpreted, the employee's privacy rights, how the test results may be used, and more.

Lessons From the Real World

Marya Norman-Bloodsaw worked as an accounting administrator at the Lawrence Berkeley Laboratory (a research facility jointly operated by the State of California and the federal government). When she started work, Bloodsaw and other clerical and administrative employees were given a "general physical," including a blood test.

Employees were also offered the option of further "periodic health examinations" during their employment. But the Lab didn't just give workers a physical. It also tested them for syphilis, sickle cell trait, and pregnancy—without their consent or knowledge. When Bloodsaw found out, she and some of her coworkers filed a class-action complaint against the Lab, arguing that the Lab had violated their right to privacy.

The U.S. Court of Appeals for the Ninth Circuit agreed, saying, "[O]ne can think of few subject areas more personal and more likely to implicate privacy interests than that of one's health or genetic make-up."

The Lab agreed to settle the case, in December 1999, for $2.2 million.

Bloodsaw v. Lawrence Berkeley Laboratory, 35 F.3d 1260 (9th Cir. 1998); Dorothy Wertz, "Genetic Testing in the Workplace: The Lawrence Berkeley Labs Case," The Gene Letter (April 3, 2000); Matt Fleischer, "Protecting Genome Privacy Proves Hard," The National Law Journal (July 20, 2000).

Electronic Monitoring

Technology now makes it possible for employers to keep track of virtually all workplace communications by any employee—on the phone and in cyberspace. And many employers take advantage of these tracking devices: A survey of more than 700 companies by the Society for Human Resource Management found that almost three-quarters of the companies monitor their workers' use of the Internet and check employee email, and more than half review employee phone calls. According to a study by the American Management Association, businesses offering financial services—such as banks, brokerage houses, insurance firms, and real estate companies—are most likely to monitor their workers' communications.

Employers have a legitimate interest in keeping track of how their employees spend their work hours; after all, no one wants workers surfing X-rated websites, sending offensive email, or calling in bets on the ponies on the company's dime. And employers may want to take steps to make sure employees are not giving trade secrets to competitors, engaging in illegal conduct at work, or using company communications equipment to harass their coworkers.

Employers can monitor their employees' communications, within reasonable limits. But employers must make sure that their monitoring does not violate their workers' privacy rights. Employers must also decide, on a practical level, how much monitoring is necessary to serve their legitimate interests without making their employees feel like they are working under a microscope.

Generally, the law allows you to monitor an employee's communications in the workplace, with a few important exceptions as described in the sections that follow.

Phone Calls

Employers may monitor employee conversations with clients or customers for quality control. Some states require employers to inform the parties to the call—either by announcement or by signal (such as a beeping noise during the call)—that someone is listening in. However, federal law allows employers to monitor work calls unannounced.

An exception is made for personal calls. Under federal law, once an employer realizes that a call is personal, the employer must immediately stop monitoring the call. However, if your company has particular phones that are designated for business use only, and that restriction is publicized and strictly enforced, monitoring all calls on these phones is probably okay.

Voice Mail Messages

Although this question hasn't been settled yet, employers probably have the right to listen to their employees' voice mail, at least if the employer has a sound, work-related reason for monitoring. However, employees may have a legitimate gripe if they are led to believe their voice mail boxes are private, particularly if your company makes a statement to that effect in its policies.

Email Messages

Employers generally have the right to read employee email messages stored on the employer's system, unless company policy assures workers that their email messages will remain private. If the company takes steps to protect the privacy of email (by providing a system that allows messages to be designated "confidential" or creating private passwords known only to the employee, for example), a worker might have a stronger expectation of privacy in the messages covered by these rules. But most courts to consider the issue have decided in favor of employers, particularly if the company has a policy that restricts computer use to official business only. (Be aware, however, that such a policy might illegally prevent workers from discussing union issues during nonwork time—see "Shop Talk" in Chapter 8 for more information).

Internet Use

Employers are legally allowed to keep track of the Internet sites visited by their workers. Some employers install devices that block access to certain sites (sites with pornographic images, for example) or limit the time workers may spend on sites that are not designated as work-related.

Tips for Staying Within the Law

Employers currently have a lot of leeway in monitoring their employees' communications. However, the law in this field is evolving rapidly, as technological change and increasing concerns about privacy pressure legislators and courts to take action. If your company decides to monitor employee communications, consider these tips:

- **Adopt a clear policy.** Tell workers that they will be monitored and under what circumstances. If the company indicates that it will respect the privacy of personal phone calls or email messages, it will have to live up to that promise. The safest course is to ask employees to sign a consent form, as part of their first-day paperwork, acknowledging that they understand and agree to the company's monitoring policies.
- **Monitor only for legitimate reasons.** Your company will be on safest legal ground—and waste less time and money—if it monitors only for sound, business-related reasons. If, for example, you have a reasonable suspicion that a particular employee is using company email to send harassing messages to coworkers or surf the Web for hours at a time, that would qualify as a legitimate cause for monitoring. Equally sound reasons include keeping track of productivity or monitoring the quality of customer service.

- **Be reasonable.** Employees will not perform their best work if they are in constant fear of eavesdropping. Overzealous monitoring—or unnecessarily harsh policies about personal use of communications equipment—will only result in employee resentment and attrition. It is reasonable to prohibit workers from spending hours on the phone wooing a lover or catching up on gossip with an old friend. It is unreasonable to prohibit brief personal calls of the "I'll be home late" or "Where shall we meet tonight" variety.

- **Prevent electronic harassment.** Unfortunately, some employees see technological advances, particularly email, as just one more way to harass their coworkers. Recent lawsuits for sexual and racial harassment are filled with references to offensive emails—dirty jokes, racial slurs, or pornographic images—that were sent to coworkers, printed and left out for others to see, or opened in front of coworkers. Avoid these claims by adopting a strict policy against harassment and enforcing it—by monitoring, if you have good reason to believe a particular employee is breaking the rules.

Developing Rules for Email Use

If your job duties include creating company policies or reviewing the employee handbook, you should definitely include policies on the proper use of company computers, particularly email. Here's a checklist of questions to consider when you're designing your company's rules, followed by a sample policy:

- **Does your company allow employees to use its email system to send personal messages?** Most companies let employees send the occasional personal email, as long as things don't get out of hand. If your company wants to prohibit all personal messages, you might face la couple of problems— particularly, that the policy will be violated on occasion by most managers and employees. Also, such a policy could run afoul of rules that allow employees to discuss union issues outside of work hours. (See "Shop Talk" in Chapter 8 for more on these rules.)

- **Does your company plan to monitor email messages?** If so, the policy should say so. If you know how messages will be monitored (for example, if the company will use

Developing Rules for Email Use (continued)

monitoring software that copies every draft or searches for "red flag" keywords), briefly describe the system. Workers are less likely to break the rules if they think they might get caught.

- **Are your company's employees perfect?** Okay, that was a trick question. Even if your company chooses not to monitor regularly, the policy must reserve the company's right to monitor, just in case an employee is accused of using the email system to harass coworkers, steal trade secrets, or engage in other misconduct. Reserving your rights will ensure that the company can read messages if necessary, without creating any legal problems. You should also ask employees to sign a form acknowledging that they understand the company has the right to monitor email messages—

this type of signed consent is required in a couple of states.

- **Do your employees need some netiquette tips?** Many companies include some advice on using email, primarily to discourage employees from succumbing to the apparent informality of the medium. You might want to remind employees that email messages are professional communications, that they can be forwarded to unintended recipients, and/or that they should be written in ordinary sentence case—not in screaming capital letters.
- **How often will your company purge email messages?** Every company should periodically delete email messages that have not been archived or otherwise marked to be saved. The policy should explain how employees can save messages from the purge.

Lessons From the Real World

When Nissan hired Bonita Bourke to help car dealership personnel with its computer system, the company probably had no idea just how much Ms. Bourke planned to use that computer.

The first sign of trouble was during a training session. While demonstrating how dealership management could use email effectively, one of Ms. Bourke's coworkers pulled up a message at random to use as a teaching tool. Unfortunately for Ms. Bourke, it was a personal, sexual message she had sent to a dealership employee.

After the plaintiff's coworker reported the incident to management, the company reviewed the entire workgroup's email messages. It found a number of personal messages, including messages with sexual overtones, sent by Ms. Bourke.

After she was fired for poor performance, Ms. Bourke sued Nissan for violating her privacy rights, among other things. However, the court found that Ms. Bourke's privacy was not violated. Ms. Bourke had signed a form indicating her understanding that company policy restricted use of company computers to business purposes only. She also knew that email messages were, on occasion, read by someone other than the intended recipient. Therefore, the court found that, even though Ms. Bourke had a confidential password to use the computer, she could not have reasonably expected that her email messages were private.

Bourke v. Nissan Motor Corp., No. B068705 (California Court of Appeal, 2nd District, 1993) (unpublished decision). You can find this case through a link on Seattle University's website, at www.law. seattleu.edu/fachome/chonm/Cases/ bourke.html.

Sample Email Policy

An example of a company email policy is provided on the next two pages. This example is for illustrative purposes only; be sure any policy you adopt is appropriate for your workplace and consistent with your state's and federal law.

Company Email Policy

Our company provides employees with computer equipment, including an Internet connection and access to an electronic communications system, to enable them to perform their jobs successfully. This policy governs your use of the company's email system.

Use of the Email System

The email system is intended for official company business. Although you may use the email system for personal messages, you may do so during nonwork hours only. If you choose to send personal messages through the company's email system, you must exercise discretion as to the number and type of messages you send. Any employee who abuses this privilege may be subject to discipline.

Email Is Not Private

Email messages sent using company communications equipment are the property of the company. We reserve the right to access, monitor, read, and/or copy email messages at any time, for any reason. You should not expect that any email message you send using company equipment—including messages that you consider to be, or label as, personal—will be private.

Email Rules

All of our policies and rules of conduct apply to employee use of the email system. This means, for example, that you may not use the email system to send harassing or discriminatory messages, including messages with explicit sexual content or pornographic images; to send threatening messages; or to solicit others to purchase items for noncompany purposes.

We expect you to exercise discretion when using electronic communications equipment. When you send email using the company's system, you are representing the company. Make sure that your messages are professional and appropriate, in tone and content. Remember, although email may seem like a private conversation, email can be printed, saved, and forwarded to unintended recipients. You should not send any email that you wouldn't want your boss, your mother, or our company's competitors to read.

Deleting Email Messages

Because of the large number of email messages our company sends and receives, we discourage employees from storing large numbers of email messages. Please make a regular practice of deleting email messages once you have read and/or responded to them. If you need to save a particular message, you may print out a paper copy, archive the message, or save it on your hard drive or disk. The company will purge email messages that have not been archived after 90 days.

Violations

Any employee who violates this policy can be subject to discipline, up to and including termination.

Off-Duty Conduct

Today, employers have the technological means, and occasionally the inclination, to find out what workers are doing on their own time. However, there are legal limits to a company's right to monitor its employees' conduct off the job—and make decisions based on that conduct.

Privacy Law

Employees of government and public entities have a constitutional right to privacy that protects them from most employer monitoring of, or even questions about, their off-the-job conduct. For public employers, then, monitoring is largely off limits.

In the private sector, a number of laws prohibit employers from intruding into their employees' private lives. As noted, some state constitutions specifically contain a right to privacy, which prevents private employers from looking into their employees' off-duty activity. Some states also have laws prohibiting employers from taking any job-related action against a worker based on that worker's lawful conduct off the job, including smoking or other use of tobacco products.

Even in states that don't provide private workers with a constitutional or statutory right to privacy, it is generally illegal for an employer to intrude unreasonably into the "seclusion" of an employee. This means that physical areas in which an employee has a reasonable expectation of privacy (personal belongings, for instance) are off-limits to employers, unless there is a very good reason to intrude. And an employer is never allowed to physically enter an employee's home without consent (even when searching for allegedly stolen company property).

The same balancing approach applies to private information. Generally speaking, employers should not inquire about or otherwise obtain facts about employees' private lives. For example, an employer may not ask employees about their sexual practices.

Courts and legislatures have created some specific rules for certain types of private, off-duty activities, as described in the sections that follow.

Union Activity

Under the National Labor Relations Act (NLRA), 29 U.S.C. §§ 151 and following, it is illegal for an employer to monitor or conduct any surveillance of employee union activities, including off-the-job meetings or gatherings. This rule applies to any concerted activity (that is, activity undertaken by workers acting together, rather than individually), even if no union is involved, as long as employees are discussing their work conditions or terms of employment. An employer who sends a supervisor to eavesdrop on such meetings or plants a spy among employees engaged in this conduct violates the NLRA. (For more on this rule, see "Representation Elections and Organizing Campaigns" in Chapter 8.)

Drug Testing

Because drug testing has the potential to reveal an employee's use of drugs outside of work hours, it has been the subject of much privacy litigation. In general, drug testing is usually allowed of job applicants (as opposed to current employees), of employees who perform safety or security-sensitive work, or when an employee has given an employer some reason to believe that he or she is impaired by drugs at work. (See "Testing Current Employees," above, for more information about drug testing.)

Political and Religious Activities and Beliefs

An employee's off-the-job political and religious activities are generally off limits to the employer. Federal and state laws prohibit discrimination on the basis of religious or political affiliation. However, an employee who brings politics or religion to work, by proselytizing or attempting to convert others, for example, may be subject to discipline by the employer.

Moonlighting

Generally speaking, working more than one job is lawful. However, an employer

has the right to limit after-hours work that is in conflict with the employer's own business. For instance, going to work for the competition could provide grounds for discipline or discharge. As a general rule, the more senior the employee, the more likely a court will take a dim view of the employee moonlighting for a competitor.

Marital Status

Many states make it illegal for employers to discriminate on the basis of marital status. Employers in these states may not keep track of whether their employees are single, married, or divorced, except as may be necessary for providing certain benefits such as health insurance.

However, tricky issues can arise when, for example, one spouse applies for a position in which he or she would supervise the other, or an applicant's spouse works for your company's major competitor. To find out whether your state prohibits marital status discrimination, and how its law might apply to situations like these, contact your state fair employment practices agency. (You can find contact information in the appendix.)

Illegal Activities

May an employer take adverse employment action against an employee who has been arrested for driving under the influence or convicted of a crime? If an employer learns that a worker has engaged in illegal conduct outside of work, can the employer ask the worker about it? In many instances, the answer to these questions is "no," unless the off-duty illegality has some concrete impact on the employee's work or the employer's business interests. An employer would be entitled to look into the drunk driving arrest or conviction of a bus driver or the embezzlement conviction of a bank employee, for example.

Workplace Searches

It happens to even the best employers: a sudden rash of thefts, a worker threatening violence, or some other possible misconduct or illegal activity in the workplace. Your company's first step must be to investigate the situation. (See "Investigating Complaints" in Chapter 11.) As part of the investigation, you might even want to search a worker's desk or locker, install some kind of monitoring device (a video camera, for example), or ask to look inside an employee's purse or backpack. The following sections explain how you can get the information you need without violating workers' right to privacy.

Reasonable Expectations of Privacy

When judges evaluate whether a particular workplace search is legal, they usually try to balance two competing concerns. First, the law considers the employer's justification for performing

the search: An employer with a strong work-related reason for searching has the best chance of prevailing. For example, an employer who receives a complaint that an employee brought a gun to work and has threatened to use it has a strong justification for a locker search.

On the other hand, workers have reasonable expectations of privacy. A worker who legitimately expects, based on the employer's policies, past practice, and common sense, that the employer will not search certain areas has the strongest argument here. For example, a worker has a high expectation of privacy in an employee restroom or changing area, particularly if the employer has not warned workers that these areas might be monitored.

To decide if a workplace search is legal, a court considers the relative strengths of these two competing interests. The more steps employers take to diminish their workers' expectations of privacy and the stronger the employer's reason to search, the more likely a court is to find the search legal. Courts also have to consider whether a particular state or federal law prohibits the search.

Search Considerations

Privacy is a highly volatile area of law. Every year, workers bring lawsuits claiming that an employer invaded their privacy by conducting an improper search. The outcome of these cases depends on the judge's view of the worker's mis-conduct and the employer's methods for getting to the bottom of things. Because there are no legal guarantees in this area of law, most employers should talk to a lawyer before conducting any but the most routine searches. Here are a few considerations to keep in mind:

- **Search only if necessary.** In many companies, there will rarely be a need to search. Unless your employees routinely handle large amounts of money or valuable, easily hidden items (such as prescription drugs or jewelry), you may not need to search at all. If you do want to conduct a search, make sure you have a legitimate business reason (theft, for example).

- **If you plan to search, have a policy.** If you warn your employees in advance that certain areas (like desks or lockers) might be subject to search, employees will have lower expectations of privacy in those areas—and less reason to complain about a particular search.

- **Don't conduct random searches.** Courts tend to frown on employers who conduct random searches, even if the employer's policy puts em-ployees on notice of this possibility. These searches, particularly if con-ducted when the employer has no reason to suspect any wrongdoing, can get employers into trouble.

- **Never search an employee's body.** Some employers become so zealous that they want to conduct physical searches of their workers for contra-band or stolen items. This is always a bad idea. Workers have a very strong privacy interest in their own bodies. If your search reaches this level, consider calling the police in for help.

- **Restrooms and changing rooms are off limits.** Most workers legitimately expect that they will not be monitored while using the bathroom or changing their clothes. This expectation is highly reasonable. If you must monitor these areas, warn employees and monitor only to the extent necessary. For example, if you have received reports that some employees are selling illegal drugs in the restroom, you might install a camera or post a guard in the main part of the room, after notifying your workers. However, you would probably be going too far if you posted cameras in each stall. And some states prohibit any surveillance of these private areas.

- **Consider the worker's privacy expecta-tions.** Before you search, think about whether an average worker would consider a particular space private in your workplace. Do employees routinely lock their desk drawers? If so, they might have higher expectations of privacy. On the other hand, if no one has an assigned desk or if workers routinely use each other's desks, they shouldn't expect their desk drawers to be private.

- **Don't hold employees against their will.** Some employers detain workers in connection with a search—to keep the worker out of the area being searched, for example, or to exert a little pressure on the worker to consent to a search ("No one is leaving this room until you show me what's in your backpack!") This is a bad idea. Under a legal theory called "false imprisonment," an employee can sue an employer who leads the employee to believe that he or she is not free to leave. Although these claims often come up in the context of questioning (when employers refuse to let their employees leave the workplace until they have answered certain questions, for example), they also surface when searches are conducted.

Legal Dos and Don'ts: Workplace Privacy

Do:

6

Search, test, and monitor only if you really need to. Let's face it: Most smaller businesses will never have a strong need to dig into their employees' purses, psyches, or private lives. Absent a compelling reason to pry—such as a theft problem—your best course of action is to stay out of the spy business (and, hopefully, out of the courtroom).

- **Adopt clear written policies.** The more steps your company takes to diminish employee expectations of privacy, the better its legal position will be. What's more, telling employees that you reserve the right to monitor and search will help deter them from engaging in misconduct in the first place.

- **Get some legal advice if you need it.** The law of workplace privacy changes all the time—and your state may have some special requirements you should know about. Before installing surveillance cameras, adopting a search policy, or tailing employees off-site, talk to a lawyer.

Don't:

- **Detain employees physically.** If you prevent workers from leaving a room or building, or you lead them to believe they are not free to go, you are buying legal trouble for your company.

- **Use lie detector tests.** In most situations, it is illegal to require a worker to take a polygraph "test" or make any decisions based on the results of such a test. And even in the rare circumstances when polygraphs are allowed, employers must follow a number of technical rules to protect the worker's rights. The best rule of thumb for most employers: Just don't do it.

- **Become "Big Brother."** Too much monitoring will quickly lead to employee resentment. When you dig too deeply into workers' private lives, you risk alienating them. This type of resentment leads not only to lawsuits, but also to poor performance, plummeting morale, and retention problems.

Test Your Knowledge

Questions

1. The U.S. Constitution prohibits private employers from invading their employees' privacy. ☐ True ☐ False

2. Employers can require current employees to take lie detector tests as a condition of promotion. ☐ True ☐ False

3. Employers may never require employees to take a medical examination. ☐ True ☐ False

4. Employers can monitor employee phone calls. ☐ True ☐ False

5. Employers are not allowed to read employee email messages if those messages are marked "private" or "confidential." ☐ True ☐ False

6. Even though it's sneaky, it isn't illegal for an employer to send a manager to eavesdrop on an off-site employee meeting to discuss forming a union. ☐ True ☐ False

7. An employer may not make employment decisions based on an employee's political beliefs. ☐ True ☐ False

8. Employers are legally entitled to search anyone who enters or leaves company property. ☐ True ☐ False

9. If an employee won't answer legitimate questions about employee theft or other misconduct, the employer is legally entitled to detain the employee until he or she starts talking. ☐ True ☐ False

10. A company's email policy should always reserve the employer's right to read email messages, even if the company has no current plans to do so. ☐ True ☐ False

Answers

1. False. Although the U.S. Constitution does offer privacy protections, they restrain only actions taken by government entities, not private employers.

2. False. With a few very limited exceptions, employers may not require employees to take polygraph tests.

3. False. There are circumstances in which an employer may require an employee to take a "fitness for duty" exam, to prove that the employee is able to work following an illness or injury.

4. True, as long as the employer has made its intentions known. Also, in some states, the employer may be legally required to inform both parties to the call that it is being monitored.

5. False, as long as the employer has warned employees that email messages are not private.

6. False. Employers may not send spies or otherwise monitor employee discussions on union issues.

7. True. An employee's political beliefs are not a legitimate basis for employment decisions. However, employees may be disciplined if they bring their political beliefs into the workplace in a disruptive manner.

8. False. Even if an employer adopts a strict search policy, its employees may have a legitimate claim for invasion of privacy if they are routinely subjected to a physical search every time they leave the worksite.

9. False. Detaining an employee against his or her will is called "false imprisonment," and it is illegal.

10. True. A company should always reserve the right to monitor, just in case it faces a situation in which it must read employee email.

7

Health and Safety

Most employers want to maintain a healthy and safe work environment for their employees. Not only is it the moral and humane thing to do, but it is also good for business. Employees are happier and more productive in a safe, secure work environment. And the company will save money—with fewer workers' compensation claims and lower rates of absenteeism—by keeping employees and their work environment as healthy and safe as possible.

In addition to these practical concerns, your company also has a legal obligation to provide a safe workplace. Federal and state governments have passed laws designed to ensure healthy and safe work environments. These laws impose safety standards and posting, reporting, and record-keeping requirements on all employers. Your company will face investigations, fines, and—in serious cases—closure if it ignores these important laws.

In this chapter, we provide an overview of health and safety laws. We also look at workers' compensation statutes, drug and alcohol issues, and smoking.

Frequently Asked Questions About Health and Safety

■ **What kinds of penalties are imposed on companies that violate health and safety laws?**

Penalties range from minimal to major fines. The exact penalty depends on a number of factors, including the employer's record of violations, the severity of the violation, and whether the employer acted in good faith. (See "Health and Safety Laws," below, for more information about penalties.)

■ **Can an employee who is injured at work sue us for damages?**

Usually, an employee who suffers a work-related injury is limited to the benefits provided by workers' compensation; that is, the employee may not sue the employer for the injuries. If the employer willfully or recklessly caused the injury, however (for example, if the company knew about the hazardous condition that caused the worker's accident but didn't do anything about it), then the employee may be able to bypass the workers' compensation system and sue the company for damages. (See "Workers' Compensation," below, for more information.)

■ **Can we fire—or refuse to hire—employees who smoke?**

It depends on the laws of your state. Many states prohibit employers from discriminating against workers or applicants just because they smoke; in other states, however, companies are free to make hiring and firing decisions on this basis. (See "Smoking," below, for more information.)

■ **Can we fire an employee for being an alcoholic?**

No. You cannot fire or discipline an employee merely for being an alcoholic. You can, however, fire an employee for drinking at work or appearing at work under the influence of alcohol. You can also fire or discipline an employee for not meeting the conduct and performance standards that apply to all workers. (For more information about this issue, see "Drugs and Alcohol," below, as well as "Disability" in Chapter 3.)

Health and Safety Laws

All companies, regardless of size or industry, must comply with federal and state health and safety laws.

The Occupational Health and Safety Act

The major federal health and safety law is the Occupational Health and Safety Act (OSH Act), 29 U.S.C. §§ 651 to 678. The OSH Act requires employers to provide a workplace that is free of "recognized hazards" that are likely to cause serious harm or death to employees. As you can imagine, the term "recognized hazards" encompasses a wide range of things, from sharp objects to dangerous chemicals to radiation.

Employers must also conduct safety training sessions to educate employees about the materials and equipment they will be using, any workplace hazards (especially chemicals), and the steps the company is taking to control those hazards.

In addition, employers must comply with some administrative requirements. For instance, companies must post a notice informing employees of health and safety regulations, report employee deaths and hospitalizations, and maintain records of:

- employee injuries and illnesses
- employee exposure to hazardous chemicals and substances, and
- employee safety training.

There are thousands of pages of federal regulations interpreting this law and defining employer duties and obligations. That's the bad news. The good news is that you do not have to wade through all this paper to learn about the law. The U.S. Occupational Health and Safety Administration (OSHA), the federal agency that enforces the law, publishes lots of information designed especially for small businesses and employers. You can find this information on the agency's website, www.osha.gov.

Also, each state has an OSHA-funded agency that offers free on-site consultations. If you ask for a consultation, an expert will walk through your worksite with you, pointing out risks and hazards and providing practical advice on how to correct problems and comply with the law. You can ask for this consultation without fear that your company will be fined for any violations or hazards that the expert sees. You'll find a list of OSHA consultation agencies organized by state on the OSHA website, at www.osha.gov/dcsp/small business/consult_directory.html.

Companies that disregard their health and safety obligations run the risk of being investigated and perhaps fined by OSHA inspectors. Fines depend on a variety of factors. Generally, employers that knowingly and intentionally violate the law, fail to correct a problem that OSHA warned them about, and put their employees at risk of serious injury or death are going to face the largest penalties. Depending on these factors, fines range from minimal all the way up to $70,000. If OSHA identifies a hazard that your company fails to eliminate, it can impose a fine of up to $7,000 for each day that the hazard goes uncorrected.

If your company has ten or fewer employees and does business in an industry with a low injury rate, it is exempt

from random inspections by OSHA. If not, OSHA can inspect the workplace at any time without advance notice. And it can issue citations and impose penalties based on what it finds.

In addition to fines and citations, your company could face lawsuits from an injured employee—or from the family of a deceased employee—if the employee was hurt or killed because the company intentionally violated a workplace safety law.

State Laws

In addition to the federal health and safety law, you must comply with the laws of your state. State laws regulating workplace health and safety can include occupational health and safety laws (usually similar to the federal law described above), workers' compensation laws, drug testing laws, substance abuse laws, and smoking laws, among others.

To find out about your state health and safety laws, contact your state labor department and state OSHA agency. You'll find contact information for both in the appendix.

(For more information about workers' compensation laws, see "Workers' Compensation," below. For more information about smoking laws, see "Smoking," below.)

Employee Rights

Federal and state laws give employees the right to complain about hazards in the workplace and legal violations. They also give employees the right to refuse to do something that endangers their safety or the safety of others.

This means that you can't discipline or take any other negative action against an employee who exercises a right under these laws. If you do, you might face additional fines—or even a lawsuit.

Lessons From the Real World

The U.S. Occupational Health and Safety Administration (OSHA) sent investigators to Party City Corporation after employees complained of unsafe conditions. When investigators looked around the workplace, they found a whole host of problems, including:

- locked fire exits
- obstructed fire exits
- no training in the use of fire extinguishers
- no handrails on stairs
- no exit signs, and
- dangerously stacked boxes.

Even though no employees had been injured or harmed by the violations, OSHA imposed a hefty $111,150 fine because the potential for harm was so high. The possibility that employees might be unable to escape a fire or other emergency was unacceptable to the agency.

Workers' Compensation

Through the workers' compensation system, employers purchase insurance that provides benefits to employees who suffer work-related injuries and illnesses. The system strikes a compromise between employers and employees. Employees get benefits regardless of who was at fault: themselves, their employer, a customer, or a coworker. In return, the employer gets protection from lawsuits by injured employees seeking damages for pain and suffering or mental anguish.

Workers' compensation systems are governed by state, not federal, law. Although each state's system differs slightly in the details, the structure and operation of the overall system is the same from state to state. (The main differences are the rates paid to disabled employees and the procedural rules.) To find out the details of your state's law, contact your state department of industrial relations or workers' compensation. You can also find a state-by-state description of these laws at the U.S. Department of Labor's website, at www.dol.gov. From the home page, click "By Audience: Employers," then "Workers' Compensation," then "State Workers' Compensation Laws."

Coverage

An employee's injury or illness must be work-related to be covered by workers' compensation law. It does not, however, have to occur in the workplace. As long as it's job-related, it's covered. For example, employees are covered if they are injured while traveling on business, doing a work-related errand, or even attending a required business-related social function.

Workers' compensation covers injuries ranging from sudden accidents, such as falling off a scaffolding, to illnesses, such as those that result from exposure to workplace chemicals or radiation. Many workers receive compensation for repetitive stress injuries, including carpal tunnel syndrome and back problems. Workers may also receive compensation for illnesses and diseases that are the gradual result of work conditions—for example, heart conditions, lung disease, and stress-related digestive problems.

Of course, not all problems that occur in the workplace are covered. Generally, workers' compensation will not cover injuries that are caused by an employee who is intoxicated or using illegal drugs. Coverage may also be denied in situations involving:

- self-inflicted injuries (including those caused by a person who starts a fight)
- injuries a worker suffers while committing a serious crime
- injuries an employee suffers off the job, and
- injuries an employee suffers when engaged in conduct that violates company policy.

Similarly, employers aren't protected from all employee lawsuits related to injuries. If the employee is injured because of some intentional or reckless action by the company, that employee can bypass the workers' compensation system to sue you in court for a full range of damages, including punitive damages, pain and suffering, and mental anguish.

Benefits

The workers' compensation system provides replacement income, pays for medical expenses, and sometimes pays for vocational rehabilitation benefits—that is, on-the-job training, education, or job placement assistance.

An employee who is temporarily unable to work will usually receive two-thirds of his or her average wage up to a fixed ceiling. An employee who becomes permanently unable to do the work he or she was doing prior to the injury, or unable to work at all, may be eligible for long-term or lump-sum benefits. The system also pays death benefits to surviving dependents of workers who are fatally injured in a work-related incident.

Smoking

Smoking used to be as accepted a workplace activity as drinking coffee, but not any more. Concerns about the impact of secondhand smoke and the comfort of nonsmokers have prompted most states to enact laws—commonly called clean indoor air laws—that severely restrict smoking in the workplace.

Lessons From the Real World

The Exxon Corporation recently got a lesson in the limits of workers' compensation laws. Usually, these laws protect companies from lawsuits filed by employees who are injured on the job. As this case illustrates, however, the law only goes so far.

For several weeks, four workers welded sheets of steel to the inside of a huge tower at an Exxon plant in Louisiana. Exxon did not give the welders safety equipment such as masks or air-supplied respirators; it did not give the welders safety instructions on the equipment they were using; and it did not ventilate the tower with clear air. As a result, the welders breathed carcinogenic smoke and fibers while they worked.

After just a few days of work, the welders complained of physical problems, such as nosebleeds, blurry vision, night sweats, and vomiting blood. Still, day after day, the company sent them back to work in the tower without any safety equipment or training. This went on for a period of several weeks until the welders quit.

As it turned out, the manufacturer of the equipment the welders were using had given the company a safety manual that warned of severe physical problems and that suggested safety precautions. Not only did Exxon not pass the warnings on to the welders, it also failed to take a single one of the safety precautions suggested by the manufacturer.

The welders sued for punitive damages. The company argued that the welders had no right to go to court, because they were limited to the benefits that they could get from the workers' compensation system.

The court disagreed, concluding that the company's actions—or inactions—amounted to intentional conduct and holding that "[w]hen an employer repeatedly sends employees back to work without safety equipment or without remedial measures being taken, and the employees are inevitably injured each time they are sent back to work, then the employer can be considered to have committed an intentional act." And when an employer intentionally harms an employee, the employer cannot hide behind the workers' compensation laws. *Abney v. Exxon Corporation*, 755 So. 2d 283 (La. App. 1 Cir. 1999).

Some states prohibit smoking in all enclosed private workplaces. Other state laws prohibit smoking except in designated areas, prohibit smoking in private workplaces if the employer has more than a minimum number of employees, or prohibit smoking in certain kinds of workplaces, such as hospitals and restaurants.

In addition to these state laws, many city and counties have also enacted ordinances against smoking in the workplace.

Many employers choose to ban smoking in their workplaces, even if no state law requires them to do so. Smokers generally have higher-than-average health care costs and higher absenteeism rates than nonsmokers. In addition, nonsmokers complain about the quality of the air and about the smoking breaks that their smoking colleagues take. (For more about this issue, see "Off-Duty Conduct" in Chapter 6.)

However, many states prohibit employers from discriminating against smokers. This means that employers can limit an employee's on-site smoking but may not make job decisions based on an employee's or applicant's decision to smoke outside of work.

To check your state's rules on smoking, see "State Laws on Smoking in the Workplace," at the end of this chapter.

To learn whether your city or county has an ordinance that prohibits or restricts smoking in the workplace, contact your local government offices.

Drugs and Alcohol

Employees who abuse alcohol and drugs (including illegal drugs, prescription drugs, and over-the-counter drugs)—either on their own time or at work—can pose significant and wide-ranging problems for their employers, managers, and coworkers. These problems can include diminished job performance, lowered productivity, absenteeism, tardiness, high turnover, and increased medical and workers' compensation bills. Employees who abuse drugs and alcohol can also make a workplace more volatile and more dangerous, and they can expose employers to legal liability.

Alcohol Use at Work

Your company's employee handbook (or its verbally announced workplace policies) should make clear to employees that drinking on the job is not allowed. If you catch an employee actually using alcohol at work, you can deal with it through your company's standard disciplinary procedures. Depending on the circumstances and on your company's policies, the punishment can range from an oral reminder to immediate termination.

The consequences should depend in part on whether the employee has endangered the health and safety of others. For example, an employee who drinks a beer while operating a forklift might deserve more severe discipline than a secretary who drinks a glass of wine while sitting at a desk.

Off-Hours, Off-Site Use of Alcohol

Many people use alcohol when not at work. Most employers aren't concerned about an employee's occasional drink—or even the occasional overindulgence—as long as it doesn't affect the employee's work performance. But when off-site, off-hours drinking begins to take its toll on the worker's ability to do the job, employers may have reason to take action.

Handling a worker with a drinking problem is tricky business. As discussed in Chapter 3, the federal Americans With Disabilities Act (ADA) and many state disability rights laws protect alcoholics from workplace discrimination. (See "Disability" in Chapter 3 for more about the ADA.) The ADA doesn't allow employers to make an employment decision based solely on the fact that a person abuses alcohol. An employer can, however, make a decision—including a decision to discipline or terminate—based on the employee's inability to meet the same performance and productivity standards that it imposes on all employees.

Legal Drug Use

Many employees properly use prescribed or over-the-counter drugs, such as sleeping aids, cold medicine, or painkillers. Most employers sensibly believe that this is none of their business, as long as the drugs don't impair the employee's job performance.

Things get trickier, however, if legitimate drug use affects an employee's ability to do the job safely and well. For example, medications that cause drowsiness might make it downright dangerous for a worker to do a job that requires driving or operating machinery. Medication may also impair judgment and abilities, which could impair a worker's ability to meet job requirements.

If an employee's performance is affected by the proper use of prescription or over-the-counter drugs, state and federal disability laws may limit an employer's options. Depending on how the drug use affects the employee, and whether the employee suffers from a disability within the meaning of these laws, your company may have to accommodate the employee's use of the drugs. (See "Disability" in Chapter 3 for more information about disability rights laws and your duty to accommodate an employee's legal drug use.)

Illegal Drug Use and Possession

If an employee is under the influence of illegal drugs at work, disability rights laws do not limit your company's options. You may deal with that employee through your company's standard disciplinary procedures. If the employee has not created a safety threat and does not hold a highly sensitive position, a written reprimand might be appropriate for a first offense.

However, if the employee endangers the physical safety of others—for example, by driving the company van after smoking marijuana at home—something more drastic is called for. If the employee has a drug problem, one option is to suspend the worker until he or she successfully completes a treatment program. Some employers, however, opt for a zero-tolerance policy under these circumstances and immediately suspend and then terminate the employee.

Because using, selling, or possessing illegal drugs is a crime, most employers immediately suspend and then terminate employees who engage in this type of behavior at work.

Drug Testing Current Employees

Drug testing is a dicey legal issue for employers—and one that should be approached with extreme caution. Drug tests are highly intrusive, yet they can also be invaluable tools for preventing drug-related accidents and safety problems.

The law of drug testing is changing rapidly as more courts rule on employee lawsuits claiming that a particular drug test violated their right to privacy. Because drug testing is so intrusive, a worker who convinces a jury that a test was illegal (in violation of either your state's drug testing laws or your state's privacy laws) could cost your company a lot of money—and ruin its reputation as a fair

employer. Before performing any drug test or adopting a drug test policy, you must get some legal advice. If you decide to proceed with legal assistance, here are some guidelines to consider.

Whom to test. Avoid testing every employee for drugs, and avoid random drug testing. Unless all of your company's workers perform dangerous jobs, these sorts of tests cast too wide a net. A drug test is most likely to withstand legal scrutiny if you have a particular reason to suspect an employee of illegal drug use, or if the employee's job carries a high risk of injury.

When to test. Your company will be on the safest legal ground if your primary motive is to ensure the safety of workers, customers, and members of the general public. Employers are most likely to withstand a legal challenge if they limit testing to:

- employees whose jobs carry a high risk of injury to themselves or others (such as a forklift operator or pilot) or involve security (a security guard who carries a gun, for example)
- workers who have been involved in accidents (for instance, a delivery driver who inexplicably ran a red light and hit a pedestrian)
- employees who are currently in or have completed a drug rehabilitation program, and
- workers whom a manager or supervisor reasonably suspects are illegally using drugs.

How to test. Even if you have strong reasons for testing, you company can still get into legal trouble over the way the test is administered and interpreted. To be safe, employers should:

- use a test lab that is certified by the U.S. Department of Health and Human Services or an equivalent state agency
- consult with a lawyer in developing testing policy and procedures
- use a testing format that respects the privacy and dignity of each employee
- have a written policy in place about drug use in the workplace (including a discussion of the disciplinary steps the company will take and under what circumstances) and testing procedures (including when the test will be given, how the test will be administered, and what substances— at what levels—the test will detect)
- require employees to read the drug and alcohol policy and testing policy and sign an acknowledgment that they have done so
- for every drug test administered, document why it was necessary and how the test was performed
- keep the test results confidential, and
- be consistent in how the company deals with workers who test positive.

Employers cannot force workers to take a drug test against their will. However, an employee who refuses to take a drug test can be fired for that reason, as long as the employer had a solid basis for asking the employee to submit to the drug test in the first place.

Legal Dos and Don'ts: Health and Safety

Do:

- **Help employees stop smoking.** While many states prohibit employers from discriminating against smokers, nothing prevents your company from sponsoring programs to help employees kick the habit. It's generally easier for smokers to quit within the context of a supportive program than on their own—and your company will reap rewards like lower absenteeism and health care costs.

- **Consider rehab leave.** Workers with substance abuse problems cost a company plenty in lost productivity, higher health care costs, and missed work. Encourage these employees to clean up their acts by offering some paid leave to enter a rehabilitation program. You will more than earn that money back if the worker successfully rehabilitates and returns to work more productive—and more dedicated to the company.

- **Seek professional help for health and safety concerns.** Many experts offer free workplace consultations, so it makes sense to get an expert to come to your workplace and point out health and safety concerns, free of charge. This could save you a bundle in workers' compensation claims, fines, and health care costs.

Don't:

- **Disregard employee complaints.** If an employee expresses concern about a workplace hazard or other safety issue, take it seriously. If you don't, the employee might take his or her complaint to a federal or state agency. More seriously, workers might be injured or worse if the employee's fears were valid.

- **Ignore OSHA's advice.** If a federal or state inspector tells your company to make changes, do it. These agencies do not like to be ignored and won't hesitate to impose fines on employers that buck the system. Disregarding these recommendations also leaves a company more vulnerable to lawsuits from employees, customers, and vendors.

- **Go without workers' compensation coverage.** If you think your company is so safe that it doesn't need workers' compensation coverage, think again. Most states require all but the smallest employers to purchase coverage. Even smaller employers would be wise to get a policy—otherwise, one workplace accident could wipe out all of the company's profit.

Test Your Knowledge

Questions

1. Small companies don't have to worry about complying with OSHA. ☐ True ☐ False

2. Employees can be fired for complaining about a health or safety issue. ☐ True ☐ False

3. If an injury is covered by workers' compensation, the injured employee cannot sue the employer for damages. ☐ True ☐ False

4. An injury must occur at the workplace to be covered by workers' compensation. ☐ True ☐ False

5. An employee who is injured while committing a crime is not entitled to workers' compensation. ☐ True ☐ False

6. All employers must create a designated smoking area for employees who wish to smoke. ☐ True ☐ False

7. Employees who take breaks to smoke outside must stand at least a certain distance away from the workplace. ☐ True ☐ False

8. It is illegal to fire an employee for using alcohol at work, because that might be a sign of alcoholism, which is a disability. ☐ True ☐ False

9. Employers can fire an employee whose use of prescription or over-the-counter drugs interferes with his or her ability to do the job. ☐ True ☐ False

10. Drug testing current employees is illegal. ☐ True ☐ False

Answers

1. False. Although small employers (those with fewer than ten employees) and employers in industries with a low injury rate are exempt from some OSHA requirements, other OSHA obligations—including the obligation to maintain a safe workplace and report serious injuries and deaths to the government—apply to all employers, regardless of size.

2. False. Retaliating against employees who complain of workplace safety or health violations is illegal.

3. True. An employee whose injury is covered by workers' compensation is entitled to the benefits that system provides but may not sue the employer for damages relating to the injury.

4. False. An injury need not take place at the worksite—it must only be work-related. If an employee is injured at an off-site work event (such as at a company meeting or required social event or while driving a delivery route, for example), that injury is covered by workers' compensation.

5. True. An employee who is injured while committing a crime is not entitled to workers' compensation benefits. This is one of the exceptions to the generally broad coverage workers' compensation provides.

6. False. Employers are generally free to prohibit smoking throughout a workplace, if they wish to do so. Many states impose requirements on employers who choose to allow smoking (for example, that smoking areas be designated and separately ventilated).

7. It depends on local laws. Some cities have enacted laws that prohibit smoking within a certain distance of the entrance, exit, and/or ventilation openings of certain buildings (for example, those that are open to the public). Check with your local government on this issue.

8. False. Although the Americans With Disabilities Act prevents employers from firing an employee simply because he or she is an alcoholic, employers are free to discipline employees who use alcohol at work.

9. It depends on whether the employee has a disability. The Americans With Disabilities Act requires employers to make reasonable accommodations for employees with disabilities. One such change might involve making minor

alterations to an employee's job responsibilities to accommodate the effects of drugs necessitated by the employee's disability.

10. It depends on the laws of your state and the circumstances in which the test is administered. Most states allow some drug testing of current employees, depending on the situation.

State Laws on Smoking in the Workplace

Note: The states of Alabama, Arizona, Arkansas, Georgia, Kansas, Michigan, New Mexico, Ohio, and Texas are not included in this chart because they do not have laws governing smoking in private workplaces. Different rules may apply to workplaces that are also public spaces, such as restaurants, bars, hotels, or casinos—we don't cover those rules here. Check with your state department of labor (see the appendix for contact details) or with your state or local health department if you need more information.

Alabama

Ala. Code § 22-15A-4

Workplaces where laws apply: Enclosed places of employment with 5 or more employees.

Where smoking prohibited: Employer may prohibit smoking in all or part of workplace. Individual employee may designate his or her own work area as a nonsmoking area. No smoking in common work areas unless majority of workers in that area agree to designate it as a smoking area.

Where smoking permitted: Majority of workers in an area may decide to designate common work area as smoking area, unless employer prohibits.

Accommodations for nonsmokers: Employers must provide signs to post if an employee designates his or her own work area as nonsmoking.

Employer smoking policy: Written policy must meet minimum requirements and be communicated to all employees.

Alaska

Alaska Stat. §§ 18.35.300 and following

Workplaces where laws apply: Any private place of business that posts signs regulating smoking; restaurants serving more than 50.

Where smoking prohibited: Throughout workplace except in designated smoking area. Employer may designate entire site nonsmoking.

Where smoking permitted: Designated smoking area.

Smoking area requirements: Ventilated or separated to protect nonsmokers from active by-products of smoke.

Accommodations for nonsmokers: Reasonable accommodations to protect the health of non-smokers.

California

Cal. Lab. Code § 6404.5

Workplaces where laws apply: Workplaces with more than 5 employees.

Exceptions: Designated lobby areas; meeting and banquet rooms when food is not being served; warehouses over 100,000 sq. ft. with fewer than 20 employees; truck cabs if no nonsmoking employees are present.

Where smoking prohibited: Employer may not knowingly or intentionally permit smoking in any enclosed workplace; must take reasonable steps to prevent nonemployees from smoking. May designate entire site nonsmoking.

Where smoking permitted: Breakrooms designated for smokers.

Smoking area requirements: Breakroom must be in a nonwork area. No employee may be required to enter room as part of job (does not apply to custodial work when room is unoccupied). Air must be exhausted directly outside with a fan and cannot recirculate to other areas of the building.

Accommodations for nonsmokers: If there is a breakroom for smokers, must be enough breakrooms for all nonsmokers.

Accommodations for smokers: None required. However, employers with 5 or fewer employees may permit smoking if:

State Laws on Smoking in the Workplace (continued)

- all the employees agree
- no minors are allowed in the smoking area, and
- no employee is required to enter smoking area.

Colorado

Colo. Rev. Stat. §§ 25-14-103, 24-34-402.5

Workplaces where laws apply: Any enclosed indoor workplace.

Exceptions: Offices occupied exclusively by smokers even if visited by nonsmokers. Restaurants.

Accommodations for nonsmokers: Employers encouraged to create physically separate nonsmoking work areas; must make effort to provide separate nonsmoking areas in employee lounges and cafeterias.

Protection from discrimination: Employee may not be fired for lawful conduct off site during nonwork hours.

Connecticut

Conn. Gen. Stat. Ann. §§ 31-40q, 31-40s

Workplaces where laws apply: Enclosed facilities.

Where smoking prohibited: Employer may prohibit smoking throughout the workplace.

Smoking area requirements: Employers with fewer than 5 employees: Existing physical barriers and ventilation systems. Employers with 5 or more employees: Air must be exhausted directly outside with a fan and cannot recirculate to other areas of the building; room must be in a nonwork area where no employee is required to enter.

Accommodations for nonsmokers: Employers with fewer than 5 employees: Employer must provide one or more clearly designated work areas for nonsmoking employees. Employers with 5 or more employees: If there are smoking

rooms, employer must provide sufficient nonsmoking break rooms.

Protection from discrimination: Employer may not require employee to refrain from smoking as a condition of employment.

Delaware

Del. Code Ann. tit. 16, §§ 2902 to 2908

Workplaces where laws apply: Indoor areas.

Exceptions: Restaurants serving 50 or fewer.

Where smoking prohibited: Any place designated a smoke-free work area.

Smoking area requirements: Walls or other physical barriers that separate area.

Accommodations for nonsmokers: Employer must provide nonsmoking work area for every employee who requests one; must provide sufficient nonsmoking areas in lounges, lunchrooms, and cafeterias.

Accommodations for smokers: Employer may provide a smoking work area.

Protection from discrimination: Employer may not discriminate or retaliate against employee who files a complaint or testifies in a proceeding about workplace smoking laws.

Employer penalties and liabilities: $1,000 to $5,000 penalty for each discrimination violation.

Employer smoking policy: Must adopt and implement a written policy that outlines accommodations for nonsmokers and smokers.

District of Columbia

D.C. Code Ann. §§ 7-1701 & following, 7-1703.03

Workplaces where laws apply: Any private employer.

Where smoking prohibited: Throughout the workplace except for designated smoking area.

Where smoking permitted: Designated smoking area.

State Laws on Smoking in the Workplace (continued)

Smoking area requirements: Physical barrier or separate room.

Accommodations for smokers: Employer required to provide smoking area.

Protection from discrimination: Employee may not be fired or discriminated against in hiring, wages, benefits, or terms of employment because of being a smoker.

Employer smoking policy: Must have written policy that designates a smoking area; must notify each employee orally and post policy within 3 weeks after adopting it.

Florida

Fla. Stat. Ann. §§ 386.201 to 386.209

Workplaces where laws apply: All enclosed indoor workplaces (more than 50% covered and surrounded by physical barriers).

Exceptions: Private residences and standalone bars.

Where smoking prohibited: Smoking is prohibited throughout the workplace.

Employer smoking policy: Employer must develop and enforce a policy prohibiting smoking in the workplace. May post "No Smoking" signs to increase awareness.

Hawaii

Haw. Rev. Stat. §§ 328K-11 and following

Workplaces where laws apply: Any private business that receives state grants or subsidies.

Where smoking prohibited: Employer decides based on preferences of nonsmokers and smokers. If decision does not satisfy all employees, workers will vote to prohibit or permit smoking in their work area.

Where smoking permitted: Employer decides based on preferences of smokers and nonsmokers. If decision does not satisfy all employees, workers will vote to permit or prohibit smoking in their work area.

Smoking area requirements: Existing ventilation and partitions. No expenditures or structural changes required.

Accommodations for nonsmokers: If nonsmoker complains about smoke, employer must attempt reasonable accommodation between nonsmokers' and smokers' needs. If nonsmokers are not satisfied, a simple majority may appeal to the state director of health for a determination.

Accommodations for smokers: Employer must attempt reasonable accommodation between smokers' and nonsmokers' needs.

Employer smoking policy: Implement and maintain written policy that outlines accommodations for smokers and nonsmokers, procedures for voting and appeal. If employees vote to decide smoking and nonsmoking areas, policy must be announced and posted within 2 weeks after vote.

Idaho

Idaho Code §§ 39-5501 and following

Workplaces where laws apply: Enclosed indoor area used by the general public, including restaurants that seat 30 or more, retail stores, and grocery stores.

Exceptions: Bowling alleys, bars.

Where smoking prohibited: Everywhere except designated smoking area.

Where smoking permitted: Employer or proprietor designates.

Accommodations for nonsmokers: "Good faith effort" to minimize effect of smoke on nonsmoking areas.

Illinois

410 Ill. Comp. Stat. §§ 80/3 and following; 820 Ill. Comp. Stat. § 55/5

Workplaces where laws apply: Any enclosed indoor workplace.

State Laws on Smoking in the Workplace (continued)

Exceptions: Offices occupied exclusively by smokers, even if visited by nonsmokers. Factories, warehouses, and other workplaces not visited by the public.

Where smoking prohibited: Entire workplace except for designated smoking area.

Where smoking permitted: Designated smoking area only.

Smoking area requirements: Existing ventilation systems and physical barriers to minimize smoke in nonsmoking areas.

Protection from discrimination: Employee may not be discriminated against for asserting rights under the clean indoor air laws. May not be refused a job, fired, or discriminated against in terms of compensation or benefits because of using lawful products outside of work. Different insurance rates or coverage for smokers are not discriminatory if:

- difference is based on cost to employer, and
- employees are given a notice of carriers' rates.

Indiana

Ind. Code Ann. §§ 22-5-4-1 and following

Protection from discrimination: Employer may not require prospective employee to refrain from using tobacco products outside of work in order to be hired or discriminate against employee who uses them in terms of wages, benefits, or conditions of employment.

Iowa

Iowa Code §§ 142B.1, 142B.2

Workplaces where laws apply: Enclosed indoor area at least 250 sq. ft.; restaurants serving more than 50 people.

Exceptions: Offices occupied exclusively by smokers, even if visited by nonsmokers. Factories, warehouses, and other workplaces not visited by the public.

Where smoking prohibited: Entire workplace except for designated smoking area.

Where smoking permitted: Designated smoking area only (may not be entire workplace).

Smoking area requirements: Existing physical barriers and ventilation systems to minimize toxic effect of smoke.

Accommodations for nonsmokers: Employee cafeteria in warehouse or factory must have nonsmoking area.

Kentucky

Ky. Rev. Stat. Ann. § 344.040(3)

Protection from discrimination: As long as employee complies with workplace smoking policy, employer may not:

- discharge employee or discriminate in terms of wages, benefits, or conditions of employment because of being a smoker or nonsmoker
- require employee to refrain from using tobacco products outside of work as a condition of employment.

Louisiana

La. Rev. Stat. Ann. §§ 40:1300.21 and following, 23:966

Workplaces where laws apply: Office workplaces of employers with more than 25 employees.

Exceptions: Offices occupied exclusively by smokers, even if visited by nonsmokers.

Where smoking prohibited: Employer designates.

Where smoking permitted: Employer designates.

Smoking area requirements: Existing ventilation systems and partitions; no expenditures or structural changes required.

Accommodations for nonsmokers: Law protects the right of nonsmoking workers to breathe

State Laws on Smoking in the Workplace (continued)

smoke-free air in the workplace. If nonsmoker complains about smoke, employer must attempt reasonable accommodation between nonsmokers' and smokers' needs.

Accommodations for smokers: Law does not deny workers the right to smoke. Employer must attempt reasonable accommodation between smokers' and nonsmokers' needs.

Protection from discrimination: Employer may not:

- require prospective employee to refrain from using tobacco products outside of work as a condition of employment
- discriminate against smokers or nonsmokers regarding termination, layoffs, wages, benefits, or other terms of employment.

Employer smoking policy: Implement and maintain written policy that outlines smoking area requirements and procedures for accommodation and complaint. Must be announced and posted within 3 months of being adopted.

Maine

Me. Rev. Stat. Ann. tit. 22, §§ 1580-A and following; tit. 26, § 597

Workplaces where laws apply: Structurally enclosed business facilities.

Exceptions: Workplaces where employer and all employees have agreed upon a smoking policy.

Where smoking prohibited: Employer may prohibit throughout entire workplace.

Where smoking permitted: Designated smoking area.

Protection from discrimination: Employer may not discriminate or retaliate against employee for assisting with enforcement of workplace smoking laws. As long as employee follows workplace smoking policy employer may not:

- discriminate in wages, benefits, or terms

of employment because of use of tobacco products outside of work

- require employee to refrain from tobacco use as a condition of employment.

Employer penalties and liabilities: Failure to post or supervise implementation of policy, $100 fine.

Employer smoking policy: Written policy concerning smoking and nonsmoking rules. State bureau of health will assist employees and employers with creating policy.

Maryland

Md. Regs. Code 09.12.23.01 and following

Workplaces where laws apply: Indoor work areas. Employee lounges, restrooms, and cafeterias; work vehicle when occupied by more than one employee; conference or meeting room.

Where smoking prohibited: Entire workplace except for designated smoking area.

Where smoking permitted: Designated smoking area. Employer not required to provide one.

Smoking area requirements: May not be in location where any employee required to work (maintenance and cleaning to take place when no one is smoking in area). Must have:

- solid walls and closable door
- ventilation system that exhausts air outdoors
- no air recirculating to nonsmoking areas, and
- negative air pressure to prevent smoke migration.

Massachusetts

Mass. Gen. Laws ch. 270, § 22

Workplaces where laws apply: Any enclosed workspace.

Exceptions: Membership associations; guest rooms designated as smoking rooms; tobacco stores; smoking bars; part of nursing homes occupied by permanent residents; facilities

State Laws on Smoking in the Workplace (continued)

doing scientific research about tobacco; religious services involving tobacco; facilities used for tobacco quality control; and private residences, except when used as a child care or health care facility

Where smoking is prohibited: Where employees work in an enclosed workspace.

Employer penalties and liabilities: $100 to $300 per day; possible loss of license.

Minnesota

Minn. Stat. Ann. §§ 144.411 and following, 181.938

Workplaces where laws apply: Enclosed indoor workplace.

Exceptions: Offices occupied exclusively by smokers, even if visited by nonsmokers. Factories, warehouses, and other workplaces not visited by the public; however, state commissioner of health will restrict smoking if smoke pollution affects nonsmokers.

Where smoking prohibited: Entire workplace except for designated smoking area.

Where smoking permitted: Designated smoking area (may not be entire workplace).

Smoking area requirements: Existing barriers and ventilation systems to minimize toxic effects of smoke.

Protection from discrimination: Employer may not refuse to hire, discipline, or discharge an employee for using lawful products off site during nonwork hours; employer may restrict nonwork use if it is a genuine job requirement. It is not discrimination to have an insurance plan with different premiums and coverage for smokers if difference reflects actual cost to employer.

Mississippi

Miss. Code Ann. § 71-7-33

Protection from discrimination: Employer

may not make it a condition of employment for prospective or current employee to abstain from smoking during nonwork hours, as long as employee complies with laws or policies that regulate workplace smoking.

Missouri

Mo. Rev. Stat. §§ 191.765 and following, 90.145

Workplaces where laws apply: Enclosed indoor workplaces.

Where smoking prohibited: Entire workplace except for designated smoking area.

Where smoking permitted: Designated smoking area (may not be more than 30% of workplace).

Smoking area requirements: Existing physical barriers and ventilation systems that isolate area.

Protection from discrimination: Employer may not refuse to hire, discharge, or in any way discriminate against employee for lawful use of tobacco off site during nonwork hours, unless use interferes with employee's or coworkers' performance or employer's business operations.

Montana

Mont. Code Ann. §§ 50-40-104, 39-2-313

Workplaces where laws apply: Enclosed rooms where more than one person works.

Where smoking prohibited: Employer designates; may designate entire workplace as a nonsmoking area.

Where smoking permitted: Employer designates; may designate entire workplace as a smoking area.

Protection from discrimination: Employer may not discharge, refuse to hire, or discriminate against employee in regard to compensation, promotion, benefits, or terms of employment because of lawful tobacco use off site during nonwork hours. Use that affects job performance or other workers' safety or conflicts with a genuine job requirement is not protected. It is not dis-

State Laws on Smoking in the Workplace (continued)

crimination to have different insurance rates or coverage for smokers if:

- difference is based on cost to employer, and
- employees are given a written statement of carriers' rates.

Nebraska

Neb. Rev. Stat. §§ 71-5702 to 71-5709

Workplaces where laws apply: Any enclosed indoor workplace.

Exceptions: Offices occupied exclusively by smokers, even if visited by nonsmokers. Factories, warehouses, and other workplaces not visited by the public; however, state health department will restrict smoking if smoke pollution affects nonsmokers.

Where smoking prohibited: Entire workplace except in designated smoking area.

Where smoking permitted: Designated smoking area (may not be entire workplace).

Smoking area requirements: Existing barriers and ventilation systems to minimize toxic effects of smoke.

Employer smoking policy: Employer must make reasonable effort to prevent smoking and minimize secondhand smoke.

Nevada

Nev. Rev. Stat. Ann. § 613.333

Protection from discrimination: Employer may not fail or refuse to hire, discharge, or discriminate in terms of compensation, benefits, or conditions of employment because of employee's lawful use of any product off site during nonwork hours, unless use adversely affects job performance or the safety of other employees.

Employer penalties and liabilities: For discrimination, employee may sue for:

- lost wages and benefits
- reinstatement without loss of position, seniority, or benefits
- an offer of employment, and
- damages equal to lost wages and benefits.

New Hampshire

N.H. Rev. Stat. Ann. §§ 155:64 to 155.77, 275:37-a

Workplaces where laws apply: Enclosed workplaces where 4 or more people work.

Exceptions: Restaurants that seat fewer than 50.

Where smoking prohibited: Throughout the workplace except for designated smoking area. If smoking area cannot be effectively segregated, smoking will be totally prohibited. Employer may declare entire workplace nonsmoking.

Where smoking permitted: Designated smoking area.

Smoking area requirements: Effectively segregated so that smoke does not cause harm or enter nonsmoking area. It must:

- be located as close as possible to exhaust vents
- have 200 sq. ft. minimum contiguous workspace
- have (1) a continuous, physical barrier at least 56 in. high, or (2) a buffer zone space at least 4 ft. wide separating area from nonsmoking area.

Accommodations for nonsmokers: Special consideration for employees with medically proven conditions adversely affected by smoke, as documented by an occupational physician.

Protection from discrimination: Employer may not require employee or applicant to refrain from using tobacco products outside of work as a condition of employment, as long as employee complies with workplace smoking policy. Employer may not retaliate or discriminate against any employee who exercises rights under smoking laws; however, laws do not give employee right to refuse to perform normal duties, even if duties require entering a smoking area.

State Laws on Smoking in the Workplace (continued)

Employer penalties and liabilities: For discrimination, misdemeanor with a fine of up to $1,000 and up to 1 year in prison.

Employer smoking policy: Written policy outlining either smoking prohibition or areas where smoking permitted. Policy must be handed out or posted; employees must receive policy orientation. If there is a designated smoking area, must be written training procedures for:
- enforcing smoking policy
- handling complaints and violations, and
- accommodating employees with medical conditions.

New Jersey

N.J. Stat. Ann. §§ 26:3D-23 and following, 34:6B-1

Workplaces where laws apply: Enclosed workspaces with 50 or more employees.

Where smoking prohibited: Entire workplace except for designated smoking area. Employer may designate entire workplace nonsmoking.

Where smoking permitted: Designated smoking area.

Protection from discrimination: Employer may not discharge or discriminate in terms of hiring, compensation, benefits, or conditions of employment because employee does or does not smoke, unless smoking or not smoking relates to work and job responsibilities.

Employer smoking policy: Written policy and procedures to protect employees from harmful effects of tobacco smoke; must include designated nonsmoking areas and may include smoking areas. Employees must be given copy upon request.

New York

N.Y. Pub. Health Law §§ 1399-n and following; N.Y. Lab. Law § 201-d(2b),(6)

Workplaces where laws apply: Indoor workspaces.

Where smoking prohibited: Smoking is prohibited throughout the workplace, in copy machine and common equipment areas, and in company vehicles.

Protection from discrimination: Employee may not be discharged, refused employment, or discriminated against in terms of compensation or benefits because of lawful use of products off site during nonwork hours when not using employer's equipment or property. It is not discrimination to offer insurance with different rates or coverage for smokers if:
- difference is based on cost to employer, and
- employees are given a written statement of carriers' rates.

Employer penalties and liabilities: For discrimination, employee may sue for relief and damages. For violation of smoking prohibition, employers may be subject to a fine of $1,000 or $2,000.

Employer smoking policy: Must post "No Smoking" signs; must make good faith effort to ensure that employees do not smoke.

North Carolina

N.C. Gen. Stat. § 95-28.2

Workplaces where laws apply: Discrimination laws apply to employers with 3 or more employees.

Protection from discrimination: Employer may not discharge, refuse to hire, or discriminate in regard to compensation, benefits, or terms of employment because of employee's use of lawful products off site during nonwork hours. Use that affects employee's job performance or other workers' safety or conflicts with a genuine job requirement is not protected. It is not discrimination to offer insurance with different rates or coverage for smokers if:
- difference is based on cost to employer

State Laws on Smoking in the Workplace (continued)

- employees are given written notice of carriers' rates, and
- employer makes equal contribution for all employees.

Employer penalties and liabilities: For discrimination, employee may sue for lost wages and benefits, reinstatement, or offer of employment. Employer liable for costs and attorney fees.

North Dakota

N.D. Cent. Code § 14-02.4-03

Protection from discrimination: Employer may not refuse to hire, discharge, or discriminate with regard to training, apprenticeship, tenure, promotion, compensation, benefits, or conditions of employment because of employee's lawful activity off site during nonwork hours, unless it is in direct conflict with employer's essential business-related interests.

Oklahoma

Okla. Stat. Ann. tit. 40, §§ 500 to 503

Protection from discrimination: Employer may not:

- discharge or disadvantage employee in terms of compensation, benefits, or conditions of employment because of being a nonsmoker or smoking during nonwork hours, or
- require that employee abstain from using tobacco products during nonwork hours as a condition of employment.

Employer may restrict nonwork smoking if it relates to a genuine occupational requirement.

Employer penalties and liabilities: Employee may sue for lost wages and benefits. Employer may be liable for costs and attorney fees.

Oregon

Or. Rev. Stat. §§ 433.835 to 433.875, 659A.315

Workplaces where laws apply: All enclosed areas used by employees.

Where smoking prohibited: Entire workplace unless there are employee lounges designated for smoking.

Where smoking permitted: Employee lounges designated for smoking.

Smoking area requirements:

- Lounge must be inaccessible to minors.
- Lounge must be in a nonwork area.
- Air must be exhausted directly to the outside with a fan.
- Air may not recirculate to other areas of building.
- No employee may be required to enter lounge as part of job (does not apply to custodial work when lounge is unoccupied).

Accommodations for nonsmokers: If there is a lounge for smokers, must be enough lounges for nonsmokers.

Protection from discrimination: Employer may not require that employee refrain from lawful use of tobacco products during nonwork hours as a condition of employment, unless there is a genuine occupational requirement.

Employer penalties and liabilities: For discrimination, employee may sue for employment or reinstatement; may be awarded damages.

Pennsylvania

35 Pa. Cons. Stat. Ann. § 1230.1

Workplaces where laws apply: Enclosed indoor workplaces.

Exceptions: Factories, warehouses, and other workplaces not visited by the public.

Where smoking prohibited: Employer designates.

Where smoking permitted: Employer designates.

Employer smoking policy: Must have policy that regulates smoking. Must post and provide copy to any employee upon request.

State Laws on Smoking in the Workplace (continued)

Rhode Island

R.I. Gen. Laws §§ 23-20.10-1 and following

Workplaces where laws apply: Smoking shall be prohibited in all enclosed facilities within places of employment. Required signs must be posted.

Exceptions: Certain businesses are exempt from the law: private homes, unless licensed for child care or adult care; hotel or motel rooms designated as smoking rooms; tobacco stores and smoking bars; designated parts of assisted living facilities and nursing homes; certain facilities with Class C or D liquor licenses (until Oct. 1, 2006); licensed gaming facilities.

Where smoking permitted: Employer may designate outdoor area.

Smoking area requirements: Must be physically separate from enclosed workspace, to prevent smoke from getting into the workplace.

Protection from discrimination: Employers cannot prohibit the use of tobacco outside of work and cannot discriminate in compensation, terms, or benefits for tobacco use outside of work.

Employer penalties and liabilities: For violating restrictions on workplace smoking, penalties of $250 to $1,000 per day. For discrimination against smoker, treble damages, costs, and injunctive relief.

South Carolina

S.C. Code Ann. § 41-1-85

Protection from discrimination: Employer may not take personnel actions, including hiring, discharge, demotion, or promotion, based on use of tobacco outside the workplace.

South Dakota

S.D. Codified Laws Ann. §§ 22-36-2 and following, 60-4-11

Workplaces where laws apply: Any enclosed indoor work area; employee cafeterias, lounges, and restrooms; conference and classrooms; hallways.

Where smoking prohibited: It is a petty offense to smoke in the workplace.

Protection from discrimination: Employer may not discharge employee because of using tobacco products off site during nonwork hours, unless not smoking is a genuine occupational requirement. It is not discrimination to have insurance policies with different rates or coverage for smokers.

Employer penalties and liabilities: For discrimination, employee may sue for lost wages and benefits.

Tennessee

Tenn. Code Ann. § 50-1-304(e)

Protection from discrimination: Employee may not be fired for use of a lawful product during nonwork hours as long as employee observes workplace policy when at work.

Utah

Utah Code Ann. § 26-38-5

Workplaces where laws apply: Private workplaces.

Where smoking prohibited: Entire workplace except for designated smoking area. Employer may prohibit smoking entirely.

Where smoking permitted: Restricted to designated enclosed smoking area.

Smoking area requirements: Must be enclosed or may be unenclosed, if layout prevents smoke from reaching nonsmokers' work areas and 3/4 of employees agree.

Employer smoking policy: Written policy that either prohibits smoking entirely or restricts to designated areas (need not be written if there are fewer than 10 full-time employees).

State Laws on Smoking in the Workplace (continued)

Vermont

Vt. Stat. Ann. tit. 18, §§ 1421 and following

Workplaces where laws apply: Enclosed structures not usually open to the public.

Where smoking prohibited: Throughout workplace except for designated smoking area. Employer may prohibit smoking entirely.

Where smoking permitted: Restricted to designated enclosed smoking area. Up to 30% of employee cafeteria and lounge areas may be designated.

Smoking area requirements: Must be area that nonsmokers are not required to visit on a regular basis. Must be enclosed or may be unenclosed, if layout prevents smoke from irritating nonsmokers and 3/4 of employees agree.

Protection from discrimination: Employer may not discharge, discipline, or otherwise discriminate against employee who assists in enforcement of workplace smoking laws.

Employer penalties and liabilities: For discrimination, employee may sue for reinstatement with back pay.

Employer smoking policy: Written policy that either prohibits smoking entirely or restricts it to designated areas (need be written only if employer has 10 or more employees working more than 15 hours a week).

Virginia

Va. Code Ann. § 15.2-2807

Workplaces where laws apply: No state laws regulate smoking in the workplace. However, if local ordinance permits, employer may:

- regulate smoking, if smoking and nonsmoking areas are designated by written agreement between employer and employees, or
- totally ban smoking, if a majority of the affected employees vote for it.

Washington

Wash. Admin. Code 296-800-240 and following

Workplaces where laws apply: Office environment: indoor or enclosed space used for clerical, administrative, or business work. Includes offices in manufacturing, food service, construction, and agricultural facilities.

Exceptions: Outdoor structures, gazebos, and lean-tos provided for smokers.

Where smoking prohibited: Employer must prohibit throughout workplace or restrict to designated enclosed smoking area. Smoking is also prohibited in employee cafeterias and lunchrooms, meeting rooms, rest rooms, halls, and stairways.

Where smoking permitted: Designated enclosed smoking area.

Smoking area requirements:

- may not be in common areas or places where nonsmokers work or visit
- no employee required to enter room when someone is smoking (cleaning and maintenance must take place when room is unoccupied)
- ventilation at rate of at least 60 cu. ft./min. per smoker
- negative air pressure to prevent smoke migration
- separate mechanical exhaust system to move air directly outside
- no air recirculating into nonsmoking areas
- if exhaust system not working, room use is prohibited until repaired.

Outdoor smoking areas may not be close to doorways, air intakes, or other openings that allow airflow into an office.

West Virginia

W.Va. Code § 21-3-19

Protection from discrimination: Employer

State Laws on Smoking in the Workplace (continued)

may not refuse to hire, discharge, or penalize an employee with respect to compensation, conditions of employment, or other benefits for using tobacco products off site during nonwork hours. It is not discrimination to have insurance policies with different rates or coverage for smokers if:
  • difference is based on cost to employer, and
  • employees are given a notice of carriers' rates.

Wisconsin

Wis. Stat. Ann. §§ 101.123, 111.31, 111.35

Workplaces where laws apply: Professional, clerical, or administrative services work offices.

Exceptions: Offices occupied exclusively by smokers, even if visited by nonsmokers. Manufacturing plants.

Where smoking prohibited: Throughout the workplace except in designated smoking area.

Where smoking permitted: Designated smoking area. Employer may not designate entire building a smoking area.

Smoking area requirements: Existing ventilation systems and physical barriers to minimize smoke in nonsmoking areas; no new construction required.

Accommodations for smokers: Employer must arrange seating to accommodate nonsmokers if they work adjacent to smoking areas.

Protection from discrimination: Employer may not discriminate against employee who uses or does not use lawful products off site during nonwork hours. Use that impairs employee's ability to perform job or conflicts with a genuine occupational requirement is not protected. It is not discrimination to have insurance policies with different coverage and rates for smokers and nonsmokers if:
  • difference is based on cost to employer, and
  • each employee is given a written statement of carriers' rates.

Wyoming

Wyo. Stat. § 27-9-105(a,iv)

Protection from discrimination: Employer may not make use or nonuse of tobacco products outside of work a condition of employment unless nonuse is a genuine occupational qualification. May not discriminate regarding compensation, benefits, or terms of employment because of use or nonuse of tobacco products outside of work. It is not discrimination to offer insurance policies with different rates and coverage for smokers and nonsmokers if:
  • difference reflects actual cost to employer, and
  • employees are given written notice of carriers' rates.

Current as of February 2005

8

Unions

···

Many companies—particularly small businesses—will never have to deal with a union. In fact, union membership has steadily decreased in recent years—from 20.1% of the workforce in 1983 (the first year the government compiled statistics) to 12.5% of workers in the year 2004. The type of work your company does will also dictate how much contact you have with unions, which are more common in certain industries than others. For instance, there are more union workers in government than in private industry, where union membership is concentrated heavily in the fields of transportation, utilities, manufacturing, and construction.

If there is a union (or more than one) in your workplace—or even if workers at your company are just interested in forming one—a special set of rules comes into play. Federal and state labor laws dictate how management (including you) must deal with unions, as well as what rules can be imposed on workers. In this chapter, we explain the laws relating to:

- elections and organizing campaigns
- union discussions and literature in the workplace
- union dues
- union shops
- collective bargaining
- company unions, and
- strikes.

Frequently Asked Questions About Unions

■ Can managers join a union?

No. Some workers are excluded from the National Labor Relations Act (NLRA)—the set of federal laws that governs union issues. These workers include agricultural workers, domestic servants, those employed by a parent or spouse, and independent contractors, as well as managers and supervisors. A manager or supervisor is someone who has the authority to hire, assign work, reward, fire, or take or recommend similar types of actions on the employer's behalf. (For more on these laws, including how they are enforced, see "The National Labor Relations Act," below.)

■ If a union says it represents workers at our company, do we have to recognize it?

An employer can recognize a union as the bargaining representative of its employees only if the union has the support of a majority of workers in the "bargaining unit"—a group of employees who do similar types of work and have common concerns about wages, hours, and working conditions. Even if the union can show that a majority of workers signed union authorization cards (statements indicating that the workers want a union to represent them), the employer can refuse to recognize the union. Then, the union will have to ask for a secret election to prove its support. (For more on bargaining units, authorization cards, and elections, see "Representation Elections and Organizing Campaigns," below.)

■ Are there limits on what managers and other company officials can say about the union?

During an election campaign—the period of time between when the union asks for an election and when the election is actually held—management representatives have to watch their mouths. Employers and managers may voice their opinions about the union but cannot punish union supporters, threaten employees who support the union, make promises to workers if they vote against the union, spy on union activities, or ask workers about the union in a coercive manner. (For more on what you can and can't do, see "Election Statements," below.)

■ Can the company ban workers from talking about the union on the job?

An employer may prohibit workers from talking about union matters on work time, but only if it prohibits them from talking about other nonwork issues as well. The company can also prohibit workers from holding union discussions in work areas, even during nonwork hours, but only if this rule applies across the board to all nonwork topics. But the company cannot prohibit workers from talking about the union while off the clock in nonwork areas—like a lunch room or locker area. (For more on union discussions and literature, see "Shop Talk," below.)

■ Can union workers strike whenever they want?

They can, but the strike might not be legal. There are two kinds of legal strikes: strikes to gain economic concessions from the employer and strikes to protest an employer's unfair labor practice. And even one of these two types of strikes might be illegal if it violates a no-strike provision in the collective bargaining agreement, or if the striking workers engage in serious misconduct. (For more on strikes—including when a company can replace striking workers—see "Strikes," below.)

The National Labor Relations Act

Several federal laws cover labor-management relations. Together, these laws comprise the National Labor Relations Act (NLRA), 29 USC §§ 151 and following, which establishes the rights and obligations of employers, unions, and individual workers in the workplace.

Many states also have labor laws that cover public employees—those who work for state or local governments and are not protected by the NLRA.

The Act Itself

The cornerstone of the NLRA is the Wagner Act, passed in 1935. The Wagner Act guarantees covered employees the right to join a union, to bargain collectively with their employer, and to be free from discrimination or retaliation for belonging to a union. It also prohibits certain employer "union-busting" tactics and establishes the procedures for union elections. And it created the National Labor Relations Board (NLRB), the federal government agency that interprets and enforces the law. (See "The Role of the NLRB," below.)

In 1947, Congress passed the second piece of the puzzle, the Labor-Management Relations Act (LMRA), better known as the Taft-Hartley Act. The primary purpose of the LMRA was to rein in the unions' power. The Act outlawed certain kinds of strikes, including the secondary boycott (a strike against a company that is not a party to a labor dispute, like a customer or client of the employer), sympathy strike (a strike by one union to show support for another), and jurisdictional strike (a strike by one of two or more unions competing to represent the same group of workers). The act also declares an individual's right not to join a union—and protects this right by prohibiting unions from using violence, threats, or fraud to coerce workers to become members.

Finally, Congress passed the Labor-Management Reporting and Disclosure Act (LMRDA), also known as the Landrum-Griffin Act, in 1959. The LMRDA regulates internal union affairs: how officers are elected, what information the union must provide to its members and the government, and the rights of union members vis-à-vis the union. The LMRDA also imposes additional restrictions on union workers' rights to strike and picket.

Coverage of the NLRA

Not all workers are covered by the NLRA. The NLRA specifically excludes certain types of workers, including:

- agricultural workers
- domestic servants
- persons employed by a parent or spouse
- independent contractors
- government workers, and
- managers and supervisors.

As for employers, the NLRA applies only to businesses that are engaged in "interstate commerce." The National Labor

Relations Board and the courts interpret the term "interstate commerce" very broadly. Most employees are covered—engaging in interstate commerce includes making phone calls to or from another state, sending mail out of state, or handling goods that have come from or will go to another state. However, the NLRB will generally step in to resolve labor disputes only if the company involved has reached a certain size, as measured by its volume of business or revenue. Thresholds vary depending on the industry. For example, the NLRB will get involved in a dispute involving a retail establishment that does $500,000 or more in annual business volume, while it will step in to a dispute at a private university only if the school has at least $1 million in gross annual revenue.

Legal Rights and Wrongs Under the NLRA

The NLRA protects the rights of individual employees to form or join a union and to bargain collectively with their employer. An employer who interferes with these rights commits an illegal "unfair labor practice." Unfair labor practices include:

- firing, demoting, or taking other negative action (or threatening any of these actions) against employees who join or vote for a union
- threatening to close down a company if the workers unionize
- giving or promising to give benefits to workers for refusing to support a union

- asking employees about their union activities in a coercive or intimidating way
- spying on union meetings
- creating a "company union" or favoring one union over another, and
- firing, refusing to rehire, or otherwise penalizing employees for participating in legally protected union activities, such as legal strikes or proceedings before the National Labor Relations Board.

A union can also commit unfair labor practices. For example, a union may not coerce workers to join or require workers to pay excessive union fees or dues. Unions are also prohibited from taking certain actions against or making certain demands on employers, including:

- "featherbedding" (receiving payment for work that is not performed)
- striking to force the employer to bargain with a union other than the union elected by the employer's workers, and
- striking or picketing against an employer who is not a party to a labor dispute—for example, a "secondary strike" against a customer of the employer intended to convince that customer to take its business elsewhere.

The Role of the NLRB

As noted above, the National Labor Relations Board (NLRB) administers and enforces the NLRA. The NLRB is run by five appointed board members who decide cases that come before the agency. The NLRB also has a general counsel (who investigates charges and issues complaints) as well as regional and field offices throughout the country.

The NLRB conducts representation elections—in which workers decide whether they want a particular union to represent them—and stops unfair labor practices. In either scenario, the NLRB gets involved only when a party to the dispute requests its help. For instance, if an employer refuses to acknowledge a union after a representation election, the NLRB will conduct a secret representation election if either party (usually, the union) requests it.

The Board itself functions as a sort of court to decide cases alleging unfair labor practices. Administrative law judges (decision makers hired by the federal government) decide these cases, which the losing party can appeal up to the five-member Board. The Board has the power to order unions and/or employers to do certain things—or stop doing certain things. At that point, the losing party must obey the Board's order or ask a federal Court of Appeals to overrule the Board.

Representation Elections and Organizing Campaigns

Efforts to unionize a workplace often begin with employee dissatisfaction. Workers might start talking about unionizing in response to an unpopular workplace rule, low wages, or a perception that the company doesn't care about their concerns.

An actual union—as opposed to a group of unhappy workers—might enter a workplace in a number of ways. A worker might contact an existing union and ask for information and help. A union might send an organizer out to the company to look into whether a union campaign is likely to succeed. Or the workers might decide to form their own union—not a typical scenario, but certainly possible. Regardless of how a union starts, its goal will be the same: to earn the right to represent workers in their dealings with the company.

Bargaining Units

A union may only represent workers who form an appropriate "bargaining unit." A bargaining unit is a group of employees who do similar types of work and have common concerns about wages, hours, and working conditions. A bargaining unit generally won't combine professional with nonprofessional employees, nor will it contain workers with significantly different job duties, skills, or working conditions. If the employer claims that a particular bargaining unit is inappropriate (a strategy employers often use to challenge a successful representation election), the NLRB will also consider what the workers themselves want.

A bargaining unit can include employees from several different facilities. For example, all the cashiers in a chain of retail stores might be included in a single bargaining unit. And a single workplace might contain more than one bargaining unit—in a grocery store, for example, the butchers might be represented by one union, the checkers by another, and the janitors by yet another.

Authorization and Election

In order to represent a bargaining unit in negotiations with the company, a union must have the support of a majority of the workers in the unit. The union usually demonstrates this support by asking workers to sign authorization cards—forms that workers fill in and sign to indicate that they want the union to represent them in bargaining with the employer.

If the union gets support from the majority of workers in the unit, it will probably ask the company to recognize the union voluntarily. If the company decides to do this (and it has good reason to believe that the union's majority support is genuine), the company and the union can immediately begin hammering out a collective bargaining agreement. (See "Collective Bargaining," below.)

But many companies choose not to recognize a union voluntarily. Perhaps the company doubts the signatures on the authorization cards are authentic or suspects that the union coerced workers into signing. Or maybe the company just wants to do whatever it can to keep a union out of its workplace for as long as possible. For whatever reason, the company may refuse to recognize the union. In that case, the union will probably file a petition with the NLRB, asking it to hold an election.

The NLRB will then conduct a secret election in the workplace to figure out whether workers really support the union. Before the election, the union and the employer can engage in a pro- or anti-union campaign (subject to the rules discussed in "Election Statements," below). If the union receives a majority of the votes cast, the NLRB will certify it as the bargaining representative of the unit. Note that the union only has to get a majority of those workers who vote, not a majority of all the workers in a unit. This means turnout in secret elections can play a major role in the outcome.

Challenging an Election

Usually, everyone accepts the outcome of a representation election and moves on to the negotiating table. However, either the company or the union may object to the election results in the week following the election. Usually, one side will claim that the other side unfairly influenced the outcome of the election. For example, if the union incites workers to violence or offers special privileges to workers who vote for the union, the NLRB might set aside a union victory. Similarly, if the company threatens to fire workers who vote for the union or promises to give benefits to workers who oppose the union, the NLRB might void the election results—and could even declare the union to have won by default.

The union or the employer can also challenge the conduct of the election itself. Just as in a government election, certain NLRA rules restrict what can be posted near the voting booth. And the NLRB generally prohibits both unions and employers from making campaign speeches to groups of employees on company time within 24 hours of the election.

Decertifying a Union

Even a union once championed by employees might lose support as time goes on. This can happen for many reasons—perhaps the union hasn't been able to negotiate successfully for the workers, has corrupt leadership, or imposes dues and fees the workers find oppressive. Employees who wish to challenge the union can file a petition for a decertification election with the NLRB. In such an election, workers will vote on whether they still want the union to represent them in negotiations with their employer. If a majority of workers voting oppose the union, the union no longer has the right to represent the workers.

Election Statements

Many employers are not eager to deal with unionized workers and want to defeat a union organizing campaign. However, there are limits to how far employers can go in fighting the union. Employers hold the power of the purse and the pink slip, not to mention the opportunity to make their workers a captive audience for any opinions they might want to express. Recognizing this, the NLRA prohibits employers from using this advantage to unfairly influence the outcome of an election.

The NLRB will set aside the results of an election if the employer engages in conduct that tends to interfere with the employees' right to freely choose—or reject—a union, without fear of reprisal. If the employer's actions confuse or incite fear in its workers, the election won't count. However, employers—like everyone else—have free speech rights. The trick is to differentiate between free speech and coercion.

What You Cannot Do

Any of the following activities constitute unfair labor practices and might cause the NLRB to overturn a decision against union representation:

- **Punishing union supporters.** You may not retaliate or discriminate against workers who support the union.
- **Making threats.** You cannot threaten to fire, demote, impose pay cuts on,

or otherwise take any negative job action against workers for supporting a union. And employers can't threaten to shut down or move the business if the union is successful.

- **Inducements.** You are not allowed to promise or give benefits to workers who oppose the union. And, once an organizing campaign has begun, the company may not increase workers' benefits—by giving a pay raise or health insurance coverage, for example—to discourage them from forming or joining the union.
- **Infiltration.** Conducting surveillance of union meetings or of employees who support the union is coercive, as is planting a spy in union gatherings to report back to management.
- **Interrogation.** You may not question workers about their union membership, union meetings, or their support for the union. Similarly, you should not ask employees to report workplace union activities to you or tell you how their coworkers feel about the union.
- **Gag rules.** You may not prohibit workers from discussing the union in work areas unless you prohibit all conversations that aren't related to work. (See "Shop Talk," below.)

What You Can Do

Once you rule out the spying, threats, and strong-arming, what's left? Quite a bit, obviously. Employers are free to express their opinions, present reasons why a union might not be in the workers' best interests, and give employees information about the union—as long as these actions aren't coercive and the information is accurate.

Here are some examples of employer statements and actions that courts and the NLRB have said are okay:

- **Voicing an opinion.** Employers can tell employees that they don't want a union in the workplace—and why.
- **Providing information.** Employers can publicize true information about the union—such as how much it charges members for dues, the rules it imposes on members, and how often it has gone on strike at other companies.
- **Explaining workplace changes.** Employers can inform workers of changes a union might bring to the workplace—for example, that workers might have to bring problems to a shop steward instead of to a supervisor.
- **Giving wage and benefit comparisons.** Employers can compare the benefits and wages they offer workers to the benefits and wages the union has been able to negotiate from other companies.

Shop Talk

The one location where all of a company's workers are certain to gather is the workplace. Recognizing this, workers who are in favor of a union often spread their views or pass out union material in the workplace, whether in the lunchroom or on the assembly line.

For various reasons, some employers try to keep union organizing out of the workplace, arguing that their facility is private company property and that management dictates what goes on within its walls. And certainly, employers want to minimize the amount of work time employees spend on nonwork activities.

The NLRB and the courts try to balance these competing concerns by creating some rules about what union-related activities are allowed in the workplace. Here are the basic rules that apply to employees (but note that these rules do not apply to nonemployees who work for the union):

- Companies may prohibit workers from talking about nonwork issues in work areas during work hours.
- Companies must allow workers to talk about union matters during nonwork hours in nonwork areas (like the company lunchroom). Union discussions may be prohibited in work areas during nonwork hours only if such a rule is necessary to maintain productivity or discipline and the rule applies to all nonwork topics.
- Companies may prohibit distribution of union literature (such as pamphlets and fact sheets) in work areas at all times—as long as the prohibition

applies to all nonwork literature, not just union literature.
- Companies cannot single out union communications for special rules. For example, an employer cannot forbid employees to distribute union materials in work areas but allow them to distribute other nonwork documents.
- Companies cannot prevent workers from wearing clothing bearing pro-union logos or symbols, such as a button or cap, unless that type of apparel creates a safety hazard.

Using Company Email

Email has added a modern twist to these rules—one that the courts and the NLRB are still trying to straighten out. As it now stands, an employer who allows workers to use the company's email system to send personal or nonbusiness messages must allow them to send messages about the union. And an employer who prohibits personal email at work may not enforce that policy selectively against employees who send union-related messages. In other words, the employer must enforce the policy for all personal messages.

A trickier issue—and one that is currently in dispute—is whether an employer can impose and enforce a ban on all personal messages. In the past, the NLRB indicated that such a rule would violate workers' rights to talk to each other about the union. Remember, under the basic rules described above, employees are allowed to talk about union issues on nonwork time—and a broad prohibition against all personal email could prevent employees from exercising these rights.

More recently, however, the NLRB—which tends to reconsider its position when a new president from a different political party has had a chance to appoint a few board members—has been looking at this issue again. For example, the NLRB has indicated that an employer may adopt an email policy that bans particular types of messages—such as mass mailings or chain letters—without running afoul of the law, as long as it has a legitimate business reason for the policy and applies it consistently (that is, not just to union-related messages). This question hasn't yet been resolved.

Union Shops and Union Dues

Workers have the right, under the NLRA, to refuse to join a union. However, some collective bargaining agreements require a company to employ only union workers to do certain jobs. One major reason unions want these contracts is to share the burden of the union's work. The union is required to represent everyone in the bargaining unit, regardless of their union membership. Requiring everyone who gets the benefit of the contract to be a union member solves the problem of so-called "free riders," workers who reap the windfall of the union's work but don't pay the price.

Generally, a company can't require a worker to become a full union member as a condition of employment, but the worker may have to pay at least some portion of union dues, depending on the basis of his or her objection to the union and the laws of the state where the employer is located.

Union Security Agreements and "Right to Work" Laws

The NLRA allows a union and an employer to enter into a contract called a "union security agreement." Although these contracts cannot require a worker to join a union, they can require workers to make certain "agency fee" payments to the union as a condition of getting or keeping a job. An employer that enters into one of these agreements will be required to fire a worker who doesn't make the payments called for in the contract.

However, the NLRA also allows states to prohibit these agreements—and many states have done so. In these states, workers who decide not to join the union cannot be required to pay any fees to the union—and cannot be fired or otherwise penalized for failing to do so. These statutes, called "right to work" laws, basically require that every unionized workplace be an "open shop"—one in which workers are free to choose whether or not to join or support the union. To find out whether your state has such a law, see "State Right to Work Laws," at the end of this chapter.

Dues Objectors

Workers who object to paying union dues either on religious grounds or because they don't support the union's political or other activities (usually those that are unrelated to representing the workers in the bargaining unit) are also entitled to alternative arrangements, even in states that allow union security agreements.

A worker who refuses to join a union or pay union dues for religious reasons may be exempt from paying dues or fees. However, these workers can be required to make a similar contribution to a nonlabor, nonreligious charity organization. And the union can require them to pay the reasonable cost of any grievances the union handles on their behalf.

In states that allow union security agreements, nonmember workers who object to the union's use of fees for political or other nonrepresentational activities are entitled to get that money back. However, they still have to pay their fair share of union money spent on representing the bargaining unit's workers—including the costs of collective bargaining, contract administration, and grievance processing. Some states require the union to get the permission of workers—whether they are members of the union or dues-paying nonmembers—before collecting any fees for activities not related to representing the workers.

Lessons From the Real World

The Washington Education Association (WEA), Washington state's largest teachers' union, was fined $400,000 for spending fees on political campaigns.

The WEA was allowed to collect union fees from those teachers who did not want to join the union but benefited from the union's representation. However, Washington law prohibited the union from using these nonmembers' fees for political purposes—unless the worker gave the union permission to do so.

For five years, the union combined the fees collected from nonmembers with member fees and other union funds and spent some of that money on political causes—without seeking permission from the nonmembers. The union claimed that this was simply an accounting error, but a state court judge disagreed. Finding that the union's actions were intentional, the judge ordered the union to pay a $400,000 fine—and to clean up its accounting system.

Paul Queary, "WEA Fined for Political Spending" (Associated Press) (August 7, 2001).

Collective Bargaining

"Collective bargaining" refers to the negotiation process between the union (on behalf of the bargaining unit it represents) and the company to work out an agreement that will govern the terms and conditions of the workers' employment. The agreement reached through this negotiating process is called a collective bargaining agreement (CBA).

The NLRA requires a duly elected union and an employer to meet and negotiate over wages, hours, and other employment terms, as well as to negotiate over issues that may arise under an existing CBA. The two sides don't have to reach an agreement, but they always have to bargain in good faith. Although neither side is required to make a particular concession, a party who refuses to bend on a single issue or to put any offer on the table might be acting in bad faith.

Employers Have to Supply Information

Employers have a clear bargaining advantage over the union in one important respect: Employers have access to more information. Although the union can poll its members to find out what they know, the employer is almost always better informed about a variety of issues, especially the company's financial picture.

To level the playing field a bit, the NLRB and the courts require employers to make certain types of information

available to the union during the collective bargaining process. For example, if an employer claims that financial problems prohibit it from granting a requested wage increase, the union has the right to request and review documents that support the company's claims. Similarly, employers may have to supply the union with current employee salary and benefit data so the union can base its demands on accurate information.

Mandatory Bargaining Issues

An employer doesn't have to bargain over every conceivable employment issue. However, employers must bargain with the union over issues that are central to the employment relationship, such as wages, hours, and layoff procedures. Employers must give the union advance notice of any proposed workplace changes that involve these issues—but only if the union requests it. An employer who refuses to bargain or takes unilateral action in one of these mandatory bargaining areas commits an unfair labor practice. At that point, the NLRB can step in to remedy the situation, but the union may also take certain actions against the employer—including a strike.

Given these dire consequences, you might think that there would be a clear list of mandatory bargaining topics included in labor laws. Unfortunately, that's not the case. Although there is general agreement that mandatory bargaining is required on some issues—including wages, hours, layoff procedures, production quotas, and other substantial work rules—many other issues fall into a gray area. It is on issues that fall into this gray area where employers often find themselves in trouble.

Part of the problem is that some subjects may or may not qualify as mandatory bargaining topics, depending on the reasons for the employer's action. For instance, if the employer decides to close a plant in order to avoid paying union wages, that might be a mandatory topic. But if the employer bases its decision on concerns unrelated to the union—for example, if the employer's customer base in the area has dried up or the employer can reap significant tax advantages by moving to another location—the employer might not have to bargain on the issue.

What constitutes a mandatory bargaining topic is an evolving area of law. Consult an experienced labor lawyer if your company is facing one of these gray area issues.

Acting Unilaterally Can Get Employers in Trouble

Before changing a workplace rule or policy that clearly requires bargaining (such as adjusting pay scales or revamping a seniority system), a company must ask the union to negotiate. Mandatory bargaining applies whether the changes will benefit or harm workers. In other words, a company cannot give an across-the-board pay raise or offer more generous paid leave on its own initiative without consulting with the union.

Sounds silly? Consider that some employers make positive changes on their own to convince workers that they don't need a union. And some employers might try to disguise a controversial change as a "benefit"—for example, by tying a wage increase to higher production rates.

Yet the process of bargaining on mandatory topics isn't as onerous as it sounds. In the real world, if the proposed change is beneficial, the union is likely to agree to it without a lengthy negotiating session. And by seeking the union's approval, the employer avoids a claim that it committed an unfair labor practice.

Company Unions and Employee Committees

Under the NLRA, employers may not establish, dominate, or interfere with any labor organization. This rule exists to outlaw sham unions—company groups that appear to represent employees but are really employer-controlled. The reason for this rule is simple: Fair collective bargaining requires genuine employee participation. If an employer negotiates with a union of its own creation, the employees' chair at the bargaining table is empty.

To figure out whether an employer unfairly controls a particular union, the courts and the NLRB look at all the circumstances—including whether the employer started the group, whether the employer played a role in the group's organization and function, whether

Lessons From the Real World

Workers at the Frontier Hotel & Casino in Las Vegas belonged to a union. When the collective bargaining agreement between the union and Frontier expired, the two sides were unable to negotiate a new agreement.

And then things got ugly. A member of Frontier's management started eavesdropping on conversations between workers and their union representative. When it didn't like what it heard, Frontier kicked the union representative out of the workplace. Then Frontier instituted 63 new work rules and stopped making contributions to the employees' pension fund.

The union filed a charge against Frontier with the NLRB. Both the NLRB and the Ninth Circuit Court of Appeals decided that Frontier's actions were illegal under the NLRA. The eavesdropping was an obvious no-no, but the court also decided that ejecting the union representative from the premises interfered with the workers' right to discuss union issues.

Further, the court decided that Frontier's decision to issue major changes in work rules—including a requirement that workers suspected of being drunk or high on illegal drugs had to agree to undergo a medical exam or risk immediate termination—violated its duty to bargain with the union before implementing a major change. Even though the first collective bargaining agreement had expired, Frontier was legally required to negotiate these issues, as well as its decision to stop paying into the pension fund, with the union before taking action. Its failure to do so—and its insistence on filing legal appeals on issues that were such clear losers—convinced the court to slap the company and its attorney with a hefty fine for wasting everyone's time.

NLRB v. Unbelievable, Inc., 71 F.3d 1434 (9th Cir. 1995).

management actually attends the group's meetings or otherwise tries to set its agenda, and what the group's purpose is.

Employee Committees May Cross the Line

Many companies have established "committees—informal groups of workers and management meet to resolve workplace problems. Common examples include committees on safety, policy review, or productivity. But even if these groups are not unions, they may still constitute employer-dominated labor organizations, which are illegal under the NLRA.

Whether these groups qualify as sham unions depends on their purpose and on the role both employees and management play in their activities. To constitute an illegal sham union, the group must deal with the employer on traditional union bargaining topics—wages, hours, or working conditions, for example. The group doesn't have to bargain formally with the employer; even a group that simply comes up with proposals for management to consider might be considered illegal, if those proposals involve bargaining issues.

To be illegal, management must also dominate or support the group. For example, if a group is established by the company, management chooses the employee representatives to the group, management employees sit in on the meetings, or management sets the committee's agenda, this group is probably dominated by the company.

Lessons From the Real World

Crown Cork & Seal, a company that manufactures aluminum cans, adopted an unusual decision-making structure at its Texas plant. Under the "Socio-Tech System," employees serve on one of four production teams. These teams have substantial authority to make and carry out workplace decisions, including decisions on safety, discipline, training, production, and more.

One level above the production teams are three more committees, which recommend changes in policies, terms and conditions of employment, safety procedures, and pay. These committees make their recommendations to the plant manager, who has always adopted them without question.

The NLRB found that these teams and committees were not illegal company unions because they did not "deal with" management—in effect, they *were* management. They had the power to make important decisions—to discipline employees, shut down the production line, or stop delivery of products—that are traditionally made by managers. Even though the plant manager had the right to disapprove some of these decisions, he never did so, instead letting the committees and teams effectively run the plant.

Crown Cork & Seal Company, Inc., 334 NLRB No. 92 (2001).

Tips for Nonunion Employers

If your workplace is not unionized, you might think that the rules in this chapter don't apply to you. In fact, some of these rules apply to all employers who are covered by the NLRA, regardless of whether their workers are represented by a union or not. The NLRA applies generally to any collective action workers take in an effort to change their working conditions or wages, whether or not a union is involved and whether or not workers are explicitly trying to form a union.

Here are some tips for nonunion companies:

- All of the rules described above about union discussions—that employers cannot prohibit such discussions in nonwork areas when employees are off duty, for example—apply to employee discussions of wages, benefits, hours, and other working conditions as well. And employers may not adopt a policy prohibiting workers from discussing their salaries with each other.

- All of the NLRA's prohibitions on retaliation, threats, coercion, and so on apply equally to nonunion employers. An employer may not, for example, fire employees for joining together to ask the company for a raise or a better benefit plan, plant a spy in an employee meeting where employees are discussing working conditions, or threaten to demote employees who are trying to convince other workers to protest a work rule.

- A nonunion employer may not create a company or "sham" union—an employee group that is dominated or supported by management and deals with the company on traditional bargaining issues (wages, working conditions, and so on). Even though such a group doesn't compete with an existing union, it is illegal under the NLRA.

Strikes

Strikes are, perhaps, the most common image that comes to mind when people think of the history of unions over the last century. But strikes are much less common than they were in the past. For a number of reasons—including "no-strike" clauses in contracts, employers' right to replace some striking workers, and a decline in union membership generally—many employers will never have to face a strike.

However, if your company's workforce does take to the streets, you need to know whether their actions are protected by law—and what steps the company can legally take to stay open for business.

Legal Strikes

The right to strike is protected by the NLRA, but not all strikes are legal. Whether a strike is lawful depends on the purpose of the strike, when the strike takes place, and the conduct of the strikers.

To qualify for protection under the NLRA, a strike must have a legal motive. Generally, a strike is legal if the workers are striking (1) for economic reasons or (2) to protest an unfair labor practice by the employer. In the first scenario, workers strike to try to get some economic concession from the employer, like higher wages, increased benefits, or better working conditions. In the second, workers strike because the employer has engaged in some practice that violates the NLRA, like refusing to bargain with the union or discriminating against union members.

However, even a strike that has a lawful purpose might be illegal if the workers strike in violation of a "no-strike" provision in the collective bargaining agreement. With a few limited exceptions, these strikes are not protected by the Act. And a strike to end or change a collective bargaining agreement might be illegal if the workers haven't complied with whatever conditions the agreement sets for such changes.

Finally, even a lawful strike may cross the line if the strikers engage in serious misconduct. Workers who are violent or threaten violence, who physically prevent others from entering or leaving the workplace, or who engage in a sit-down strike—a strike in which employees refuse to leave the workplace and refuse to work—are not legally protected.

Strike Replacements

Although the NLRA protects the right to strike, employers do not have to shut down their business for the duration of the walkout. Instead, employers are legally allowed to hire replacement workers (sometimes called "scabs" in union lingo) to take the place of strikers during the strike. Once the strike ends, the employer's obligation to rehire the striking workers depends on the reasons for the strike.

Workers who strike to protest an unfair labor practice cannot be fired or permanently replaced. When the strike is over, these strikers must be reinstated to their jobs, even if it means replacement workers have to be let go.

However, workers who strike for economic reasons don't enjoy the same right. Although they cannot be fired, they can be replaced. And if they are replaced permanently, they aren't entitled to their jobs back. Instead, if they are unable to find similar employment, employers are required only to call them back for job openings as they occur.

Legal Dos and Don'ts: Unions

Do:

- **Make employees happy.** If your company is intent on keeping a union out of the workplace, it should give workers what a union would get for them. This means providing competitive pay, good benefits, safe working conditions, some form of job protection, and a meaningful complaint process.
- **Review your company's employee handbook.** Work rules must allow employees to exercise their rights under the NLRA. Make sure, for example, that your company's dress code doesn't prohibit workers from wearing pro-union messages and that your email policy doesn't single out union talk.
- **Get some help if you plan to fight the union.** The rules about what employers can and can't do to defeat a union in a representation election are very nuanced. Sometimes, a single word or act can make the difference between a sustainable victory and an unfair labor practices charge. If your company is planning to get into it, get some help from an experienced labor lawyer.

Don't:

- **Prevent employees from discussing union issues.** Although your company can prohibit workers from discussing any nonwork issue in work areas, it cannot selectively enforce this policy to prohibit only union matters—and it cannot prohibit union discussions in nonwork areas when employees are off duty. And if you, as a representative of management, try to discourage workers from exercising this right, you could get the company in big trouble.
- **Bypass the union.** If your company has a union, it must bargain with the union before changing the terms and conditions of employment. This means no new policies on wages, hours, or working conditions without consulting the union.
- **Coerce workers during a union election.** As a manager, what you say and do will be attributed to the company. If you threaten to fire workers who vote for the union, promise benefits to workers who vote against the union, or otherwise put pressure on workers, the NLRB might find that you've unduly influenced the outcome of the election—and declare the union to have won by default.

Test Your Knowledge

Questions

1. Managers can join a union, as long as the union is made up of managers and employees who work in the same field. ☐ True ☐ False

2. Independent contractors may not join a union. ☐ True ☐ False

3. Employers should not make any statements about the union during a union election. ☐ True ☐ False

4. If employees try to organize a union and they are unsuccessful, the employer may discipline or fire them. ☐ True ☐ False

5. Employers can prohibit employees from talking about union issues anywhere on the employer's premises. ☐ True ☐ False

6. Closed shops—in which employers may hire only union members—are illegal. ☐ True ☐ False

7. Although employees can be required to join a union, they cannot be forced to pay union dues. ☐ True ☐ False

8. An employer may not decide, on its own, to offer more generous benefits; it must bargain on this issue with the union. ☐ True ☐ False

9. Companies may establish safety committees, made up of employees and managers, as long as those committees don't have the power to make decisions. ☐ True ☐ False

10. Once workers go out on strike, their jobs are not protected. ☐ True ☐ False

Answers

1. False. Managers may not join a union, period.

2. True. Independent contractors may not join a union, even if the union is comprised of employees who do similar types of work for the same hiring firm.

3. False. Although employers should not make threats, coerce, or interrogate workers during an election, they can give accurate information about the union and express their opinions about whether workers should unionize.

4. False. Employees who engage in "concerted activity" are protected from retaliation, even if they ultimately fail in their efforts.

5. False. Companies must allow workers to talk about union issues in nonwork areas—such as a lunch area, locker room, or break room—on nonwork time.

6. True. Employees cannot be required to join a union.

7. False. This is exactly backwards—employees cannot be required to join a union but can be required to pay at least some portion of union dues in states that have adopted "right to work" laws.

8. True. Even if the employer is trying to do something good for its workers, it must include the union in the decision. (If it's really a win for workers, chances are good that the union will agree to it.)

9. False. Even if the committee simply makes recommendations, it might be considered a company union if it deals with the company on traditional topics of union bargaining and is dominated by management. A committee that has the right to make important decisions might be legal, if it is acting in the place of management.

10. It depends on the reasons for the strike. Workers who strike over an unfair labor practice are entitled to get their jobs back when the strike is over.

State Right to Work Laws

Alabama .... Ala. Code §§ 25-7-30 to 25-7-35	Montana .... No right to work law.
Alaska .... No right to work law.	Nebraska .... Neb. Const. art XV, §§ 13 to 18; Neb. Rev. Stat. § 48-217
Arizona .... Ariz. Const. art. 25; Ariz. Rev. Stat. §§ 23-1301 to 23-1307	Nevada .... Nev. Rev. Stat. Ann. §§ 613.230 to 613.300
Arkansas .... Ark. Const. art. 34; Ark. Code Ann. §§ 11-3-301 to 11-3-304	New Hampshire ..... No right to work law.
California .... No right to work law.	New Jersey .... No right to work law.
Colorado .... No right to work law.	New Mexico .... No right to work law.
Connecticut .... No right to work law.	New York .... No right to work law.
Delaware .... No right to work law.	North Carolina ...... N.C. Gen. Stat. §§ 95-78 to 95-84
District of Columbia .... No right to work law.	North Dakota .... N.D. Cent. Code §§ 34-01-14 to 34-01-14.1
Florida .... Fla. Const. art. 1, § 6; Fla. Stat. Ann. § 447.17	Ohio .... No right to work law.
Georgia .... Ga. Code Ann. §§ 34-6-20 to 34-6-28	Oklahoma .... Okla. Const. Art. 23, § 1A
Hawaii .... No right to work law.	Oregon .... No right to work law.
Idaho .... Idaho Code §§ 44-2001 to 44-2009	Pennsylvania .... No right to work law.
Illinois .... No right to work law.	Rhode Island .... No right to work law.
Indiana .... No right to work law.	South Carolina ...... S.C. Code Ann. §§ 41-7-10 to 41-7-100
Iowa .... Iowa Code § 731.1	South Dakota .... S.D. Const. art. VI, § 2; S.D. Codified Law Ann. §§ 60-8-3 to 60-8-8
Kansas .... Kan. Const. art. 15 § 12; Kan Stat. Ann §§ 44-808(5), 44-831	Tennessee .... Tenn. Code Ann. §§ 50-1-201 to 50-1-204
Kentucky .... No right to work law.	Texas .... Tex. Lab. Code Ann. §§ 101.004, 101.052, 101.053, 101.111
Louisiana .... La. Rev. Stat. Ann. §§ 23:981 to 23:987 (all workers) and 23:881 to 23:889 (agricultural workers)	Utah .... Utah Code Ann. §§ 34-34-1 to 34-34-17
Maine .... No right to work law.	Vermont .... No right to work law.
Maryland .... No right to work law.	Virginia .... Va. Code Ann. §§ 40.1-59 to 40.1-69
Massachusetts .... No right to work law.	
Michigan .... No right to work law.	Washington .... No right to work law.
Minnesota .... No right to work law.	West Virginia .... No right to work law.
Mississippi .... Miss. Const. Art. 7, § 198-A; Miss. Code Ann. § 71-1-47	Wisconsin .... No right to work law.
Missouri .... No right to work law.	Wyoming .... Wyo. Stat. §§ 27-7-108 to 27-7-115

Current as of February 2005

9

Independent Contractors

ndependent contractors exist in virtually every type of workplace, large and small, blue collar and professional. The federal Bureau of Labor Statistics estimates that more than ten million people work as independent contractors in occupations ranging from farming to computer technology to upper-level management. Contractors go by any one of a number of names—consultants, freelancers, the self-employed, entrepreneurs, and business owners—but they all have two common traits: They are in business for themselves, and they don't rely on a single employer for their livelihood.

Hiring independent contractors can be a smart, cost-effective alternative to taking on employees. They can add a lot of flexibility and expertise to a company's workforce without the financial and legal burdens of hiring employees.

Using independent contractors does have some drawbacks, however. The biggest potential problem is that numerous federal and state government agencies keep a close watch on any employer who uses independent contractors. These agencies want to make sure employers aren't taking advantage of workers (and skipping out on their tax obligations) by calling them independent contractors when they should really be classified as employees. Companies that try to get the benefits of the arrangement without following the rules can end up in legal trouble.

In this chapter, you'll find:

- an overview of the issues that arise when companies hire independent contractors

- an examination of the various government definitions of independent contractor and employee, as well as advice on how to steer clear of legal trouble

- the benefits and drawbacks of this type of arrangement, and

- advice on creating a written independent contractor agreement.

Frequently Asked Questions About Independent Contractors

■ **What is an independent contractor?**

Independent contractors, also sometimes referred to as freelancers or consultants, are independent businesspeople who perform services for other people or businesses. In other words, they are people who do work for a company but are not its employees. Figuring out the difference between employees and independent contractors is not always easy, and the answer often depends on who is asking the question. (For more about this, see "Classifying Workers," below.)

What are the benefits of using independent contractors?

Because companies don't have to pay taxes and benefits (such as health insurance) for independent contractors, it can be less expensive to use them. In addition, using independent contractors gives a company flexibility and reduces its exposure to certain kinds of lawsuits. (For more about this issue, see "Benefits and Drawbacks of Using Independent Contractors," below.)

What are the drawbacks of using independent contractors?

A company does not have the same right to control independent contractors as it does with employees, nor can a company demand or expect the same type of loyalty from independent contractors. In addition, independent contactors can sue your company if they are injured while working for you, while employees cannot. (For more about this issue, see "Benefits and Drawbacks of Using Independent Contractors," below.)

Do we need to use any special paperwork to hire independent contractors?

Your company can greatly reduce the chances of a worker being reclassified as an employee by requiring the worker to fill out an independent contractor questionnaire, provide copies of business licenses, and sign a written independent contractor agreement. (For more information, see "Important Documents When Hiring Independent Contractors," below.)

Do we have to use a written agreement with independent contractors?

With a few exceptions, the law does not require companies to use a written agreement with independent contractors. Still, it's a good idea to write things down, for a number of reasons. (To learn more about this, see "Written Agreements With Independent Contractors," below.)

Who owns the rights to the intellectual property we hire an independent contractor to create for us?

Unless the work falls into one of nine categories defined by law, the intellectual property rights to any works an independent contractor created will belong to the independent contractor, not to your company. This is true even if you hired and paid the independent contractor specifically to create the product for your company. But you can use a written contract to ensure that the copyright belongs to your company. (For more information, see "Copyright Ownership," below.)

Classifying Workers

You may think that a worker's status as an independent contractor or an employee depends on what your company and the worker decide. As long as both parties agree on the terms of the relationship, that's all that matters, right?

Wrong. The federal and state governments care a lot about how a worker classified. Not surprisingly, the root of their concern is money. Your company will pay fewer taxes (including expensive payroll taxes such as Social Security and Medicare) for an independent contractor, and it will have fewer legal obligations to an independent contractor than to an employee. Thus, it's often in a company's interest to call a worker an independent contractor. (For more on this, see "Benefits and Drawbacks of Using Independent Contractors," below.) By contrast, it's in the government's interest to label the worker as an employee—the more employees there are in this world, the more money flows straight into government coffers through payroll withholding (and the fewer opportunities workers have to hide or underreport their income).

Unfortunately, there are as many tests to determine whether a worker qualifies as an independent contractor as there are government agencies that deal with workers—from your state unemployment office to the federal Internal Revenue Service. Figuring out how to treat a worker so that agencies classify the worker as an independent contractor can be a complicated undertaking.

Employers who don't learn the rules before they hire an independent contractor can get hopelessly confused—and get into trouble with one agency or another. To avoid problems such as audits, fines, and taxes, you should learn the rules of all of the following agencies before you hire a worker. (For more about fines and taxes, see "Benefits and Drawbacks of Using Independent Contractors," below.)

The Internal Revenue Service

The Internal Revenue Service (IRS) is probably the most important agency to satisfy when it comes to classifying a worker as an independent contractor. Under the IRS's test, workers are considered employees if the company they work for has the right to direct and control the way they work, including the details of when, where, and how the job is accomplished. In contrast, the IRS will consider workers independent contractors if the company they work for does not manage how they work, except to accept or reject their final results.

The IRS looks at a number of factors when determining whether a worker is an employee or an independent contractor. The agency is more likely to classify as an independent contractor a worker who:

- can earn a profit or suffer a loss from the activity
- furnishes the tools and materials needed to do the work

- is paid by the job
- works for more than one company at a time
- invests in equipment and facilities
- pays his or her own business and traveling expenses
- hires and pays assistants, and
- sets his or her own working hours.

On the other hand, the IRS is more likely to classify as an employee a worker who:

- can be fired at any time
- is paid by the hour
- receives instructions from the company
- receives training from the company
- works full time for the company
- receives employee benefits
- has the right to quit without incurring liability, and
- provides services that are an integral part of the company's day-to-day operations.

If the IRS would consider the worker an independent contractor, your company does not have to withhold federal payroll taxes for the worker, including Social Security taxes, federal disability taxes, and federal income taxes. If the IRS would consider the worker an employee, your company must withhold these on behalf of the worker. If you're not sure how to classify a worker, you can ask the IRS to determine the worker's status, but we don't recommend it. Not surprisingly, the IRS will usually decide that the worker is an employee (and your company will be stuck with that decision). If you're really confused, you're better off consulting with an experienced employment lawyer.

To find out more about the IRS independent contractor test, you can refer to the agency's website at www.irs.gov.

The U.S. Department of Labor

The U.S. Department of Labor also cares about how your company classifies workers: If a worker is an independent contractor, then the worker is not covered by the Fair Labor Standards Act (FLSA), the major federal law regarding wages and hours. This means, among other things, that the worker is not entitled to minimum wage or overtime.

Like the IRS, the Department of Labor has no single rule or test for determining whether someone is an independent contractor under the FLSA. However, the U.S. Supreme Court has said that the following factors are significant when determining whether a worker is an independent contractor under the FLSA:

- whether the worker's services are an integral part of your company's business (this points to employee status)
- the permanency of the relationship (the more permanent the relationship, the more likely it is that the worker is an employee)
- whether the worker has invested in facilities and equipment (if so, this points to independent contractor status)

- how much control your company has over the worker (the more control, the more likely it is that the worker is an employee)
- whether the worker has opportunities to make a profit or suffer a loss (as opposed to always earning a set amount of money no matter what happens, like an employee)
- whether the worker competes in the open market (if so, this points to independent contractor status), and
- the extent to which the worker operates a truly independent business (if so, this points to independent contractor status).

The U.S. Supreme Court has also said that the following things have no bearing on whether a worker is an independent contractor or an employee:

- where the worker performs the work
- the absence of a formal employment contract, and
- whether the worker is licensed by a state or local government.

For more information about the Department of Labor's test, refer to the Wage and Hour portion of the agency's website at www.dol.gov.

For more about wages and hours, see Chapter 2.

Your State Unemployment Compensation Board

If the worker meets your state unemployment compensation board's definition of independent contractor, your company doesn't need to pay unemployment insurance for the worker. If the worker does not meet this test, your company should provide unemployment coverage for the worker, even if the worker qualifies as an independent contractor under other tests (such as the IRS test).

To learn more about your state unemployment department's test, contact your state unemployment compensation board or your state department of labor. You can also try your local office of the Small Business Administration (SBA). For a list of local SBA offices, refer to the SBA's website, at www.sba.gov.

As a manager, it's a good idea to learn about your state's unemployment department test for independent contractor status *before* you hire an independent contractor. That way, you can create an independent contractor relationship from the beginning that satisfies the test—and averts possible problems later.

Your company could get into trouble if a worker whom you thought was an independent contractor decides to apply for unemployment compensation—a benefit that is reserved for employees. Should this happen, it will be your company's word against the worker's: You say the worker was an independent contractor, but the worker—eager for that unemployment check—claims to have been an employee. In such a situation, you'll have to be prepared to back up your assertion.

Your State Workers' Compensation Insurance Agency

As with unemployment insurance, only employees are entitled to receive workers' compensation. If a worker meets your state workers' compensation agency definition of independent contractor, your company does not have to pay for workers' compensation coverage for that worker. Otherwise, your company should pay for workers' compensation coverage, even if the worker qualifies as an independent contractor under other tests.

To find out more about the workers' compensation test in your state, contact your state department of industrial relations or workers' compensation or your state labor department. Your local office of the SBA might also have information on the subject. (For a list of SBA offices, refer to the SBA's website, at www.sba.gov.)

Again, you should find out what test your state's workers' compensation board uses before you hire an independent contractor. If an independent contractor is injured on the job and applies for workers' compensation—again, a benefit reserved for employees—your company might face an audit.

Your State Tax Department

If your state collects income tax, then you need to know your state tax department's rules regarding independent contractors. If the worker will qualify as an independent contractor under your state tax department's test, your company does not need to withhold state income taxes from the worker's compensation. Otherwise, you must withhold state income taxes (if your state imposes them), even if the worker qualifies as an independent contractor under other tests. Contact your state tax board for details. This is an especially important test to learn, because many independent contractor audits begin with a state tax agency: State tax agencies are often more aggressive about independent contractor audits than the IRS.

Your State Department of Labor

If your state department of labor would consider the worker an independent contractor, then your company does not have to pay the worker minimum wage or overtime according to your state wage and hour laws. (But federal wage and hour laws might apply—see above for more information.) Contact your state labor department for details. (See the appendix for contact information.)

Lessons From the Real Word

Bennett Harrington, who worked as a hunting guide for Gueydan Duck Club in Louisiana, was injured one day when his dog stepped on a client's loaded gun, causing it to go off. The shell ripped into Mr. Harrington's leg, seriously injuring him.

When Mr. Harrington applied for workers' compensation benefits, he was surprised to learn that the club owner had classified him as an independent contractor. This meant that Mr. Harrington could not get the benefits, which were for employees only.

The Louisiana Court of Appeal looked at the relationship between Mr. Harrington and the club and decided that Mr. Harrington had been misclassified. The court decided he was an employee and should get benefits. The court based its opinion on the amount of control the club had over Mr. Harrington. The court decided that the following facts, taken together, made Mr. Harrington an employee:

- The club had recruited Mr. Harrington to work as a guide.
- The club, not Mr. Harrington, set the price that the clients paid for the guided hunt.
- The clients paid the club, not Mr. Harrington.
- There was no formalized agreement between Mr. Harrington and the club, which meant that the club could choose not to use Mr. Harrington at any time, for any reason.
- The club assigned clients to Mr. Harrington.
- The club told Mr. Harrington which hunting blind to use.
- The club told Mr. Harrington how to act around the clients—to entertain them, to make them happy, and to ensure their safety.
- The club maintained facilities and land for its guides, including Mr. Harrington, to use.
- The club provided blinds and decoys for the hunts.
- The club provided cell phones and transportation to the guides.
- Mr. Harrington thought he was an employee.

Harrington v. Herbert, 2001 WL 541772 (La. App. 3 Cir. 2001).

Benefits and Drawbacks of Using Independent Contractors

Using independent contractors is a double-edged sword. For every benefit, there is an equally important drawback. In the end, your company will have to weigh all of the factors and decide what is best for the business when deciding what sort of worker to hire.

Benefits

Independent contractors require a much smaller cash outlay than do new employees. As a result, cash-strapped companies are often tempted to classify workers as independent contractors. Companies that hire independent contractors instead of employees reap these financial benefits:

- They do not have to pay a whole host of federal taxes for independent contractors, including Social Security and Medicare taxes.
- They do not have to withhold any state or federal income taxes from an independent contractor's paycheck.
- They do not have to pay workers' compensation insurance for independent contractors.
- They do not have to pay unemployment insurance for independent contactors.
- They do not have to provide employee benefits (such as health insurance, paid sick leave, paid holidays, and retirement benefits) to independent contractors.
- Unless the project requires otherwise, they do not have to provide facilities, equipment, or training to independent contractors.

These and other expenses associated with employees add about 20% to 30% to a company's payroll costs. Although independent contractors generally earn more per hour than employees for doing the same work, the company will still pay less overall because it won't have to pay these extra employee expenses and administrative costs.

In addition to the monetary benefits, independent contractors give companies the flexibility to add expertise to their workforce as needed. A company can hire independent contractors for specific tasks and take advantage of their specialized knowledge and experience without the cost and obligations of hiring full-time employees. This allows a company to run a lean operation, using employees for integral parts of the business and independent contractors for other projects as they arise.

Companies also have less exposure to lawsuits from independent contractors than from employees. Antidiscrimination laws and wrongful termination laws are all designed to protect employees, not independent contractors. In addition, employees have the right to unionize; independent contractors do not.

Companies that hire independent contractors also have less exposure to lawsuits from third parties. Although a company is liable to third parties for anything an employee does on the job, it is not liable for what an independent contractor does unless the company had some part in causing the injury or accident (for example, it gave the independent contractor poor directions or hired an independent contractor who wasn't qualified for the job).

Drawbacks

After reading about the financial and other benefits of hiring independent contractors, it might be tempting to convert your company's entire workforce to independent contractors. Not so fast: There are some definite drawbacks to using independent contractors instead of employees that you should consider.

The primary drawback of classifying any worker an independent contractor is the risk that one government agency or another will audit your company and reclassify the worker as an employee. According to *Business Wire* magazine, the government loses about $20 billion a year in taxes because more than half of the independent contractors in the country are really misclassified employees. The government—particularly the IRS—does not take these losses lightly, and it is happy to audit any company it suspects is misclassifying workers.

State agency audits are even more common, spurred by independent contractors who apply for unemployment benefits and workers' compensation— benefits exclusively reserved for employees. If a government agency decides that your company has misclassified a worker, your company will owe all of the back taxes associated with that worker, plus interest on those taxes and penalties. This could add up to quite a hefty sum. In addition, the worker might be entitled to overtime and back pay, as well as any unpaid unemployment or workers' compensation benefits.

Another drawback to classifying a worker as an independent contractor is that your company will not be able to control that worker as it could an employee (for instance, setting work hours or requiring a project to be done in a certain manner). Under all of the agency tests, control is a big factor. The more the hiring company controls (or has the right to control) the way the worker does the job, the more likely it is that one agency or another will classify that worker as an employee instead of an independent contractor. When your company hires an independent contractor, it must allow the worker to do the job as he or she wishes—or suffer the consequences.

Control isn't the only thing your company loses by using an independent contractor. It also loses continuity when independent contractors come and go for short-term projects. Each new independent

Lessons From the Real World

When Julianne Eisenberg sued the warehouse at which she worked for sexual harassment, the warehouse claimed that she was an independent contractor, not an employee, so she was not protected by workplace anti-discrimination laws. As proof of her status, the warehouse pointed out that it called her an independent contractor in tax documents and didn't pay her any employee benefits.

The warehouse's arguments did not convince the federal court that reviewed the case, however. Looking at the way the warehouse treated Ms. Eisenberg, the court said she was an employee, not an independent contractor. That meant the warehouse was on the hook for the sexual harassment that Ms. Eisenberg suffered.

What tipped the balance in Ms. Eisenberg's favor? The court noted the following facts:

- The warehouse gave Ms. Eisenberg, whose job was to load and unload trucks, orders on a daily basis.
- At the job site, someone from the warehouse would instruct the crew, of which Ms. Eisenberg was a member, on what objects to move and where.
- Ms. Eisenberg's job did not require any specialized skill. (Examples of jobs that require a specialized skill include computer programmers, architects, graphic artists, and photographers. A worker with specialized skills is more likely to be classified as an independent contractor than an unskilled laborer.)
- The warehouse supplied all of the necessary supplies and equipment for Ms. Eisenberg to do her job.
- Ms. Eisenberg performed her job almost exclusively in the warehouse or on its trucks.
- Ms. Eisenberg was not hired for a specific move or project. Instead, she worked on whatever move or project the warehouse had at the time.
- Ms. Eisenberg was paid on an hourly basis, not by project.
- Ms. Eisenberg's job was an integral part of the warehouse's business.

Eisenberg v. Advance Relocation & Storage, Inc., 237 F.3d 111 (2nd Cir. 2000).

contractor will have to become familiar with your business and the project, and you'll have to establish a working relationship with each new person you bring on. In contrast, employees know your company's inner workings and needs. They know your company's people and practices, which can improve the efficiency and consistency of your operations.

Your company also can't simply get rid of an independent contractor who isn't working out. Unlike an employee, who can usually be fired for any reason at any time (see "At-Will Employment" in Chapter 4 for more information), an independent contractor will be protected by the terms of the contract—and your company will have to honor that contract or risk a lawsuit. (For more about contracts, see "Written Agreements With Independent Contractors," below.)

If your company hires an independent contractor to create works that can be copyrighted, the company might not own the rights to the work unless the contractor signs a written agreement transferring copyright ownership in advance. This is not the case with employees; for the most part, your company owns copyrightable works created by its employees. (For more about this, see "Copyright Ownership," below.)

Although independent contractors cannot sue your company for violating antidiscrimination laws, they can sue for on-the-job injuries, if your company was at fault. Employees, on the other hand, cannot: They are limited to the benefits provided by the workers' compensation system. (See "Workers' Compensation" in Chapter 7 for more information.)

Important Documents When Hiring Independent Contractors

If your company hires an independent contractor, there are certain key steps you can—and should—take to reduce the chances of a government agency reclassifying the contractor as an employee. You can take these steps even before the independent contractor starts work. If you gather the documents described here, you will have already gone a long way toward establishing the worker's independent contractor status.

Independent Contractor Questionnaire

Ask prospective independent contractors to complete an independent contractor questionnaire. Design the questionnaire to elicit information that will help prove that the independent contractor is a separate business entity and not merely an employee in independent contractor's clothing. The questionnaire should ask the prospective hire about the following:

- whether the independent contractor has a fictitious business name

- how the independent contractor's business is structured (for example, sole proprietorship, partnership, corporation, or limited liability company)
- the independent contractor's business address and phone number
- the number of people, if any, the independent contractor employs
- any professional licenses the independent contractor holds
- any business licenses the independent contractor holds
- contact information for other companies for whom the person has worked as an independent contractor
- how the independent contractor markets his or her business (for example, in the Yellow Pages or other advertising)
- whether the independent contractor has an office separate from home
- a description of the business equipment and facilities the independent contractor owns
- whether the independent contractor has business cards, professional stationery, and invoice forms, and
- a list of all types of business insurance the independent contractor carries.

The answers to these questions will help you accurately assess whether the worker is an independent contractor. However, none of them is conclusive evidence of independent contractor status. Each answer is just one factor among many you should consider when deciding how to classify the worker.

Make sure that anyone you may hire as an independent contractor fills out this questionnaire instead of your company's standard employment application. A government agency can—and probably will—try to use the fact that the independent contractor filled out an "employment" application as evidence that the worker is actually an employee.

Business Documents

Once you've received a completed questionnaire and conducted the interview, the next step is to make sure the worker has enough documentation to establish that the worker is a separate business entity if the government decides to audit your company. Make copies of all these documents and file them along with the questionnaire described above.

The documents you should request include the following:

- copies of any business or professional licenses
- certificates showing that the independent contractor has insurance, including general liability insurance and workers' compensation insurance if the independent contractor has employees
- copies of the independent contractor's business card and stationery
- copies of any advertising that the independent contractor has done,

including advertising in the Yellow Pages

- a copy of the independent contractor's White Pages business listing, if there is one
- if the independent contractor is operating under a fictitious or assumed business name, a copy of the fictitious or assumed business name statement or application
- a copy of the invoice form that the independent contractor uses to bill for services
- if the independent contractor rents business space, a copy of the office lease
- if the independent contractor has employees, a document containing the independent contractor unemployment insurance number
- copies of IRS Form 1099-MISC other firms have issued to the independent contractor, and
- if the independent contractor is a sole proprietor and will agree to do so (this is a big if), copies of the independent contractor's tax returns for the previous two years showing that the independent contractor has filed a Schedule C, *Profit or Loss From a Business* (which will show that the independent contractor has been operating as an independent business).

Although the contractor may balk at showing you a few of these items—especially those that contain sensitive financial information—stress that you will keep everything confidential and that you only want these items to verify the contractor's status.

Written Agreements With Independent Contractors

For most types of projects, the law does not require companies to enter into a written contract with independent contractors. You can talk to the independent contractor, agree on the terms of the arrangement, and have an oral contract that any court will enforce.

As your mother no doubt told you, however, just because you can do something doesn't mean you should. Oral agreements invite costly misunderstandings because there's no clear written statement of what the independent contractor is to do, how much your company will pay, or what will happen if a dispute arises. These misunderstandings might be innocent—you and the independent contractor genuinely may have different memories about what was agreed to—or they may be purposeful. Either way, it'll be your word against the worker's, and there is no telling whom a judge or jury will believe. It's much safer to rely on a written document that clearly sets out the details of your relationship.

Even better, a written independent contractor agreement can also help establish a worker's independent contractor status by showing the IRS and other agencies that both your company and the worker intended to create a hiring firm/independent contractor relationship, not an employer/employee relationship. But don't expect the written agreement to be a magic bullet: A written agreement won't make much difference if your company treats the worker like an employee. (For more about classification rules, see "Classifying Workers," above.)

When writing the independent contractor agreement, remember the tests for classifying workers. Don't put anything in the agreement that would tend to show the worker is an employee rather than an independent contactor. For example, don't describe in the agreement the details of how the independent contractor is to accomplish the work; remember, if the hiring company controls the details of the work, that's a sign that the worker is really an employee.

A written independent contractor agreement should contain at least the following terms:

- a description of the services the independent contractor will perform
- a description of how much your company will pay the worker (usually either a fixed fee for a finished product or a sum based on unit of time—for example, by the hour or by the week)
- a description of how and when the worker will be paid
- an explanation of who will be responsible for expenses (true independent contractors are usually responsible for their own expenses, although this isn't true in every field)
- an explanation of who will provide materials, equipment, and office space (independent contractors usually provide these things, but not always)
- a statement that your company and the worker agree to an independent contractor relationship
- a statement that the independent contractor has all of the permits and licenses that the state requires for the work
- a statement that the independent contractor will pay all state and federal income taxes
- an acknowledgment that the independent contractor is not entitled to any of the benefits your company provides employees
- a statement that the independent contractor carries liability insurance
- a description of the term of the agreement (for example, one week, one season, or until the project is completed)
- a description of the circumstances under which your company or the independent contractor can terminate the agreement, and
- an explanation of how any disputes will be resolved.

Other terms you could include range from copyright ownership (see below) to naming who will be responsible for the independent contractor's employees.

Sometimes, You Have to Write It Down

While agreements between your company and the independent contractor can generally be oral (even though we don't recommend relying on oral understandings), many states' laws require certain kinds of contracts to be in writing to be enforceable. These laws, usually called a state's "Statute of Frauds," typically require that the following types of agreements be in writing:

- any contract that will last longer than a year
- contracts for the sale of goods (tangible property, such as a work of art or a car) worth $500 or more
- a promise to pay someone else's debt
- contracts involving the sale of real estate
- real estate leases that last for more than one year, or
- any transfer of copyright ownership.

If your company's agreement with the independent contractor meets any of these definitions (for instance, your relationship will last longer than a year, or the contractor is assigning or transferring copyright ownership to the company), then the agreement will probably need to be in writing to be enforceable.

Sample Independent Contractor Agreement

Below is an example of an agreement one company used to hire an independent contractor (referred to as the "Consultant"). This example is for illustrative purposes only; be sure any agreement you create is appropriate for your situation and consistent with your state's and federal law. For sample contracts language you can use to create your own agreements, see *Consultant & Independent Contractor Agreements*, by Stephen Fishman (Nolo).

Independent Contractor Agreement

This Agreement is made between FunWorks, Inc., ("Client"), with a principal place of business at Berkeley, California, and John Cunningham ("Consultant"), with a principal place of business at Berkeley, California.

1. Services to be Performed

Consultant agrees to perform the following consultant services on Client's behalf:

Create new design for Client's packaging and promotional materials.

2. Payment

In consideration for the services to be performed by Consultant, Client agrees to pay Consultant $10,000 according to the terms of payment set forth below.

3. Terms of Payment

Client shall pay according to the schedule of payments set forth in Exhibit A, attached to this Agreement.

4. Expenses

Consultant shall be responsible for all expenses incurred while performing services under this Agreement.

5. Materials

Consultant will furnish all materials, equipment, and supplies used to provide the services required by this Agreement.

6. Independent Contractor Status

Consultant is an independent contractor, and neither Consultant nor Consultant's employees or contract personnel are, or shall be deemed, Client's employees. In its capacity as an independent contractor, Consultant agrees and represents, and Client agrees, as follows:

- Consultant has the right to perform services for others during the term of this Agreement.

- Consultant has the sole right to control and direct the means, manner, and method by which the services required by this Agreement shall be performed.

- Consultant has the right to perform the services required by this Agreement at any place or location and at such times as Consultant may determine.

- Consultant has the right to hire assistants as subcontractors or to use employees to provide the services required by this Agreement.

- The services required by this Agreement shall be performed by Consultant, consultant's employees, or contract personnel, and Client shall not hire, supervise, or pay any assistants to help Consultant.

- Neither consultant nor Consultant's employees or contract personnel shall receive any training from Client in the professional skills necessary to perform the services required by this Agreement.

7. Business Permits, Certificates, and Licenses

Consultant has complied with all federal, state, and local laws requiring business permits, certificates, and licenses required to carry out the services to be performed under this Agreement.

8. State and Federal Taxes

Client will not:

- withhold FICA (Social Security and Medicare taxes) from Consultant's payments or make FICA payments on Consultant's behalf

- make state or federal unemployment compensation contributions on Consultant's behalf, or

- withhold state or federal income tax from Consultant's payments.

9. Fringe Benefits

Consultant understands that neither Consultant nor Consultant's employees or contract personnel are eligible to participate in any employee pension, health, vacation, pay, sick pay, or other fringe benefit plan of Client.

10. Workers' Compensation

Client shall not obtain workers' compensation insurance on behalf of Consultant or Consultant's employees. If Consultant hires employees to perform any work under this Agreement, Consultant will cover them with workers' compensation insurance and provide Client with a certificate of workers' compensation insurance before the employees begin work.

11. Term of Agreement

This agreement will become effective when signed by both parties and will terminate on the earlier of:

- the date Consultant completes the services required by this Agreement
- November 30, 200x, or
- the date a party terminates the Agreement as provided below.

12. Terminating the Agreement

Either party may terminate this agreement at any time by giving 30 days' written notice to the other party of the intent to terminate.

13. Exclusive Agreement

This is the entire agreement between Consultant and Client.

14. Intellectual Property Ownership

Consultant assigns to Client all patent, copyright, trademark, and trade secret rights in anything created or developed by Consultant for Client under this Agreement. Consultant shall help prepare any papers that Client considers necessary to secure any patents, copyrights, trademarks, or other proprietary rights at no charge to Client. However, Client shall reimburse Consultant for reasonable out-of-pocket expenses incurred.

Consultant must obtain written assurances from Consultant's employees and contract personnel that they agree with this assignment. Consultant agrees not to use any of the intellectual property mentioned above for the benefit of any other party without Client's prior written permission.

15. Resolving Disputes

If a dispute arises under this Agreement, the parties agree to first try to resolve the dispute with the help of a mutually agreed-upon mediator in Berkeley, California. Any costs and fees other than attorney fees associated with the mediation shall be shared equally by the parties. If the dispute is not resolved within 30 days after it is referred to the mediator, any party may take the matter to court.

16. Applicable Law

This Agreement will be governed by the laws of the state of California.

Signatures

Client: FunWorks, Inc.

By: _____

   Dylan Irons, President

Date: _____

Consultant: _____

   John Cunningham

Taxpayer ID#: _____

Date: _____

Copyright Ownership

When your company hires an independent contractor to create a work for the company—such as a computer program, written work, artwork, musical work, photograph, or multimedia work—you might wonder who will own the copyright to work. Generally, whoever owns the copyright to a work owns significant rights, including the right to use, license, or sell the work to someone else.

Although you might think that your company owns any work it pays a contractor to create, that isn't automatically the case. Copyright law contains a major trap for the unwary: Unless the work an independent contractor creates falls into one of nine "work for hire" categories described below, your company will *not* automatically own the copyright to the work. The independent contractor must "assign" the copyright to the company in writing. It's critical to obtain this assignment (transfer of copyright ownership) before an independent contractor starts work so that there is no disagreement later over who owns the copyright. You can include the copyright assignment in the written independent contractor agreement described above.

If the work was specially commissioned or ordered by the hiring company and falls into one of the nine categories described, it is considered a "work for hire" in legal parlance. The hiring company automatically owns the copyright to such works for hire; however, your company and the independent contractor must sign a written agreement stating that the work is made for hire. Again, you can include this statement in the independent contractor agreement described above.

Works for hire include:

1. a contribution to a collective work—for example, a work created by more than one author like a newspaper, magazine, anthology, or encyclopedia

2. a part of an audiovisual work—for example, a motion picture screenplay

3. a translation

4. supplementary works—for example, forewords, afterwords, supplemental pictorial illustrations, maps, charts, editorial notes, bibliographies, appendices, and indexes

5. a compilation—for example, an electronic database

6. an instructional text

7. a test

8. answer material for a test, and

9. an atlas.

Legal Dos and Don'ts: Independent Contractors

Do:

- **Say what you mean.** Never use the words "employment" or "employee" when referring to the independent contractor. Have the worker complete an independent contractor questionnaire (*not* an employment application) and be careful when naming or referring to any written agreement you create (do *not* call it an "employment contract").
- **Spread the work around.** The more consistently a worker works for your company, the more likely an agency is to view the worker as an employee who depends on your company for a living. If you can, don't use the same independent contractor every time.
- **Hire corporations.** If you have the choice, hire independent contractors who have incorporated or otherwise formally structured their business— as a limited liability company, S corporation, or C corporation. This will go a long way toward establishing that the worker has a separate business.

Don't:

- **Buck the trend.** When deciding whether a worker is an independent contractor, auditors will sometimes look at what how others in the same industry categorize those workers. If workers who do particular types of jobs are always characterized as employees, your company is more likely to attract an audit if it tries to call them contractors.
- **Rely on labels.** When it comes to classifying workers, it's what you do that matters, not what you say. If you treat an independent contractor like an employee (especially by trying to control every aspect of how the worker does the job), you'll find yourself paying fines and taxes—no matter what you call the worker.
- **Take the worker's word for it.** Don't just accept a worker's claim that he or she operates an independent business: Get proof. You never know when the worker might decide to argue that he or she was really an employee (for instance, to receive workers' compensation or unemployment benefits).

Test Your Knowledge

Questions

1. As long as your company calls a worker an independent contractor and doesn't withhold employment taxes, it won't have to worry about government audits. ☐ True ☐ False

2. A company has essentially the same obligations to independent contractors as it does to its employees, except that it doesn't have to withhold and pay taxes for contractors. ☐ True ☐ False

3. Independent contractors are not entitled to workers' compensation benefits if they are injured on the job. ☐ True ☐ False

4. It is generally more expensive to hire employees than it is to hire independent contractors. ☐ True ☐ False

5. Someone who works for more than one company at a time cannot be classified as your company's employee. ☐ True ☐ False

6. You can use your company's regular employment application with independent contractors. ☐ True ☐ False

7. Even very basic arrangements with independent contractors should be put in writing. ☐ True ☐ False

8. Your company shouldn't hire independent contractors unless they have incorporated their own businesses. ☐ True ☐ False

9. If your company hires someone to create a work of art, the company will automatically own the copyright to the work, regardless of whether the worker is an employee or an independent contractor. ☐ True ☐ False

10. Even if your company pays an independent contractor to create a work, the contractor might own the copyright. ☐ True ☐ False

Answers

1. False. What matters is how your company treats the worker. Not paying taxes or calling the worker an employee is a good start, but the real issues are whether the worker is truly operating an independent business and whether your company has the right to exercise a great degree of control over how the work gets done.

2. False. Employees are protected by laws that require overtime pay, prohibit discrimination, and provide benefits for on-the-job injuries. None of these protections extend to independent contractors.

3. True. Independent contractors are not covered by the workers' compensation system.

4. True. Although independent contractors typically command higher pay than employees, your company won't have to pay taxes; provide benefits, workspace, and training; or otherwise lay out so much overhead for independent contractors.

5. False. An employee might work two part-time jobs, for example. What matters is whether the worker has an independent business and whether your company controls how the worker does the job.

6. False. You shouldn't use an employment application with independent contractors, because a court or agency might see that as proof that you thought the worker was really an employee.

7. True. The best course of action is to always use a written agreement, spelling out the terms of the job.

8. False. Although it's safest to hire contractors who have formed corporations or LLCs, it's fine to hire an unincorporated contractor—as long as he or she is really running an independent business.

9. False. Although a company generally owns the copyright to works created by its employees, this is not the case with independent contractors.

10. True. Your company must have a written agreement with the contractor either stating that the work is a work for hire (if it falls into one of the nine categories explained above) or assigning the copyright to your company.

■

10

Trade Secrets

Often, workers never seem as precious to their employer as they do the moment they walk out the door—taking a vast amount of knowledge and a keen understanding of the employer's business with them, perhaps to the doorstep of a competitor.

Companies do not have to sit back and just watch this happen, however. You can help protect your company's most private and secret business information, while also protecting valuable employees and independent contractors. In this chapter, we look at how the law protects company trade secrets and what steps companies can take to stop them from leaking out.

Frequently Asked Questions About Trade Secrets

■ **What is a trade secret?**

The answer to this question will vary slightly depending on the state where your company does business. Generally speaking, a trade secret is a novel piece of information a business has that gives the business a competitive advantage. A trade secret can be anything from a formula to a marketing plan to a customer list to the recipe for Coca Cola (one of the most famous trade secrets in history). (For more information, see "The Law of Trade Secrets," below.)

■ **Can we prevent employees from revealing the company's trade secrets?**

Yes. You can take many steps to prevent current and former employees from revealing your company's trade secrets, including the most basic step of letting employees know about them on a need-to-know basis only. (To learn how, see "Protecting Trade Secrets," below.)

■ **What is a nondisclosure agreement?**

A nondisclosure agreement is a contract an employee or independent contractor signs promising to protect the confidentiality of secret information learned while working for your company. The company must give something of value in exchange, such as money, a promotion, or a raise. (For more information, see "Nondisclosure Agreements," below.)

■ **What is a noncompete agreement?**

A noncompete agreement is a contract an employee or independent contractor signs promising not to work for a direct competitor for a specified period of time after leaving your company. As it would for a nondisclosure agreement, the company must give something of value in exchange for the worker's promise. (For more information, see "Noncompete Agreements," below.)

■ **What is a nonsolicitation agreement?**
A nonsolicitation agreement is a contract an employee or independent contractor signs promising not to solicit your company's clients and customers after leaving your company. This type of agreement can also contain a promise not to solicit other employees to leave. Again, in exchange for signing the agreement, your company must provide the worker with something of value. (For more about this, see "Nonsolicitation Agreements," below.)

■ **Does it violate trade secret law to hire an employee from a competitor?**
You can hire employees who worked for a competitor, but you should always be careful when you do so, especially if the new hire signed a nondisclosure or noncompete agreement with the previous employer. (For more information, see "Hiring From Competitors," below.)

The Law of Trade Secrets

More often than not, what gives a business a competitive advantage over others is the specialized knowledge it has gained through ingenuity, innovation, or just plain old hard work. This specialized knowledge could be something as mundane as a list of customers who have a specific need for your company's services or as glamorous as the top secret formula for its best-selling product, from a cookie recipe to an industrial chemical.

Each state has a trade secret law designed to protect these confidential bits of specialized knowledge. Although each law differs in the details, the basic structure tends to be the same. In fact, the vast majority of states have adopted something called the Uniform Trade Secrets Act. You can find a list of states that have adopted some version of the Act, along with citations to each state's law, on Nolo's website, at www.nolo.com. (Click the tab for "patents, copyright & art," select "Trade Secrets," then select "Trade Secret Basics FAQ.")

There are many complicated definitions of trade secrets under the law, but generally, a trade secret is information that has the following characteristics:

- **Value.** The information has economic value to your company's business because you know it and competitors don't. (In other words, it's valuable because it is a secret.) Information that doesn't give your company a competitive edge is not a trade secret.
- **Secrecy.** The information is not generally known, nor is it easy to find out.

If a competitor could learn the same information easily without much work or ingenuity, it's probably not a trade secret. Similarly, if some competitors already know the information, then it is not a trade secret.

- **Effort.** Your company must take reasonable steps to keep the information as secret as possible. For example, if a company posts the information in a place where anyone, including employees, customers, and vendors, can see it, then it's probably not a trade secret. Similarly, it's not a trade secret if it's posted on the company's public website.

Examples of trade secrets include a formula for a sports drink, survey methods used by professional pollsters, a recipe, a new invention for which a patent application has not yet been filed, marketing strategies, manufacturing techniques, and computer algorithms.

Unlike other forms of intellectual property such as patents, copyrights, or trademarks, trade secrecy is basically a do-it-yourself form of protection. Companies don't register with the government to secure their trade secrets; it's the company's responsibility to keep the information confidential and make sure it fits the definition laid out above. Trade secret protection lasts for as long as the secret is kept confidential. Once a trade secret is made available to the public, trade secret protection ends—sometimes even if the secret was taken or disclosed without permission.

Rights of the Trade Secret Owner

A trade secret owner has the right to prevent the following groups of people from copying, using, and benefiting from its trade secrets, or disclosing them to others without permission:

- people who are automatically bound by a duty of confidentiality not to disclose or use trade secret information (for example, your company's employees)
- people who acquire a trade secret through improper means such as theft, industrial espionage, or bribery
- people who knowingly obtain trade secrets from people who have no right to disclose them (for example, a competitor who hires one of your company's employees and then intentionally tries to exploit that employee's knowledge of your company's trade secrets)
- people who learn about a trade secret by accident or mistake but have reason to know that the information is a protected trade secret (for example, a competitor who hires one of your company's employee's away but then accidentally learns information that turns out to be a trade secret), and
- people who sign nondisclosure agreements (also known as "confidentiality agreements") promising not to disclose trade secrets without authorization from the owner. (For more about these, see "Nondisclosure Agreements," below.)

Lessons From the Real World

Christopher Warman devised the perfect recipe for fudge and turned it into a successful business called Christopher M's Hand Poured Fudge, Inc.

Warman hired Clyde Hennon to work as his assistant in daily operations. In the course of his employment, Hennon learned all about Warman's fudge-making operations, from the details of Warman's secret fudge recipe to Warman's unique manufacturing process.

After a year of working at Christopher M's, Hennon struck out on his own, opening his own fudge-making operation called The Fudge Works, Inc. Warman sued, arguing that Hennon was illegally using trade secret information he had learned from Warman including, among other things, Warman's secret fudge recipe.

The court agreed with Warman and ordered Hennon to stop making fudge. The court decided that the fudge recipe was a trade secret based on the following facts:

- Warman developed the recipe after several years of trial and error from a recipe that he had purchased for $140,000.
- Certain aspects of the recipe were unique and were not commonly used in the industry.
- Warman took great care to protect the secrecy of the recipe. He kept only one written copy of the recipe that he stored off the premises; he compartmentalized the manufacturing process so that employees only knew the portion of the recipe relating to their specific tasks; and he revealed the entire recipe to only a handful of people.
- The recipe had a multimillion dollar value.

Christopher M's Hand Poured Fudge, Inc., v. Hennon and The Fudge Works, Inc., 699 A.2d 1272 (1997).

Each state imposes a duty of loyalty on current and former employees not to disclose a company's trade secrets, so they automatically come under the umbrella of trade secret laws. Your company does not have to ask its employees to sign a nondisclosure agreement to impose a duty on them to keep its secrets, but it's still a good idea to do so. (See "Nondisclosure Agreements," below, for some reasons why a company might want to take this extra step.)

Unlike current and former employees, however, the only way to impose liability on independent contractors, customers, or vendors for disclosing trade secrets is to have them sign a nondisclosure agreement. (For more about this, see "Nondisclosure Agreements," below.) Unless such people sign a nondisclosure agreement, they are free to disclose any trade secrets they learn while working for or with your company to others, because trade secret law does not impose a duty on them to keep quiet.

Finally, there is one group of people whom your company cannot prevent from using its trade secret information: people who discover the secret independently, without using illegal means or violating agreements or state laws. For example, it is not a violation of trade secret law to analyze (or "reverse engineer") any lawfully obtained product to determine its trade secret. Although it's highly unlikely, if someone managed to exactly reproduce Kentucky Fried Chicken's 11-herb-and-spice recipe by experimenting in the kitchen, Kentucky Fried Chicken could not sue that person for violating trade secret laws.

Protecting Trade Secrets

Employees and independent contractors pose a thorny dilemma for businesses with valuable trade secrets. After all, your company has to let some of these people in on its trade secrets—either because they need the information to do their jobs or because they helped develop the information in the first place. Yet these same people may leave your company and take that special knowledge with them—perhaps into business for themselves or to work for a competitor.

Simple preventative measures can reduce the risk that departing employees or independent contractors will take your company's trade secrets with them on their way out the door. We suggest a six-step approach:

- First, identify your company's trade secrets.
- Second, grant access to these trade secrets only on a need-to-know basis.
- Third, tell employees and independent contractors which pieces information the company considers confidential.
- Fourth, use nondisclosure agreements.
- Fifth, make sure the company keeps its own secrets.

- Sixth, conduct exit interviews with departing employees and independent contractors.

The following sections look at each of these steps in more detail.

Identify Trade Secrets

You can't protect something if you don't know it exists. The first step in protecting your company's trade secrets is to figure out what valuable information needs to be protected.

Periodically, take an "information inventory" and ask yourself and other managers and supervisors the following questions:

- What information does my company know that gives us an advantage?
- Do our competitors know this information?
- Is it information that they would want to know or find valuable?
- How did we gain the information? Was the process difficult? Time-consuming? Expensive? Unique?
- What kind of damage would our business suffer if competitors discovered this information?
- What do we know that we really don't want our competitors to know?

Because businesses are in an almost constant process of developing this inform-ation, you should probably conduct this sort of review once a year.

Limit Access

The fewer people who know your company's trade secrets, the better. Limiting access to trade secrets limits the number of potential loose lips. And departing employees or independent contractors can't reveal secrets that they don't know.

Of course, no companies can keep all of its employees and independent contractors in the dark about everything. But always carefully consider whether an individual actually needs to know a secret you or other managers are about to reveal. Once you give it some thought, you might realize that an individual needs to know only one piece of the puzzle; other times, you might realize that the individual needs only a summary of the information, not the details.

If an employee or independent contractor really needs to know a trade secret to work effectively, go ahead and reveal it. But before you do, make sure they know it's a trade secret, which they are obligated to keep under wraps (see below).

Alert Your Workers That the Information Is Secret

Once you've identified your company's trade secrets and the employees or contractors who need to know them, the next step is to inform them that they must keep the secrets confidential. After all, you can't expect them to keep information a secret if they don't know that they are supposed to.

Often, your company's internal security procedures will be enough to put people on notice about trade secrets. (See "Keep the Secret," below.) But you should review these security procedures periodically to make sure that they're still appropriate. For example, once a formula that's been in research and development hits the production line, your company will need to change its security procedures to include the production floor and any workers involved in the manufacturing process.

Use Nondisclosure Agreements

Because employees have an automatic duty to keep trade secrets confidential, telling them that something is confidential is technically sufficient: You do not have to ask them to sign a nondisclosure agreement to impose this legal duty on them. Still, nondisclosure agreements underscore the importance of confidentiality and clear up any ambiguity about what information your company considers a trade secret. They can also be helpful if your company ever has to haul that employee into court for revealing the trade secret, whether the employee is still working for your company or not.

Independent contractors do not have an automatic duty to protect your company's confidential information, so you should make a practice of presenting a nondisclosure agreement to every independent contractor who will learn any trade secrets before you share those secrets. When you disclose confidential information to independent contractors, tell them that the information is confidential and remind them of their obligations under any nondisclosure agreement. (For more about this type of contract, see "Nondisclosure Agreements," below.)

Keep the Secret

As explained above, information can't qualify as a trade secret if your company doesn't take steps to protect it and keep it confidential. And once information loses its trade secret status, your company loses the right to prevent employees and others from disclosing it to competitors. The security measures you take to protect a trade secret can make or break your company's rights to the exclusive use of the information.

Security measures include the following:
- labeling all documents that contain trade secret information "Confidential" (which you can do using a "Confidential" ink stamp, available for a few dollars at most stationery stores)
- keeping a log of all confidential documents and the people who have access to them
- keeping a list of all trade secrets and the people who know them
- keeping all documents and evidence of trade secrets in a locked cabinet or locked room

- requiring employees to sign out confidential documents and materials and return them when they're done
- using a paper shredder to destroy any discarded documents that contain trade secret information
- password-protecting any computer files that contain proprietary information
- requiring all visitors to sign in, wear badges, and be accompanied by an employee at all times
- locking all exterior doors
- using nondisclosure agreements with employees, independent contractors, vendors, and customers
- using noncompete and nonsolicitation agreements with key employees and independent contractors, and
- periodically providing employees who have access to confidential information with a list identifying which pieces of information your company views as confidential.

Although it's rare that a business will want to use all of these security measures, using at least some of them will go a long way toward maintaining the confidentiality of its trade secrets. Moreover, if someone does pilfer your company's trade secrets, implementing these procedures will show a judge that the company has taken reasonable steps to keep the information a secret.

Conduct Exit Interviews

When an employee or independent contractor stops working for your company—for whatever reason—you must take extra care to ensure that the individual does not turn around and disclose the company's trade secrets to competitors.

An effective way to do this is to conduct an exit interview. Identify all of the trade secret information that the employee has learned and remind him or her of the obligation to keep the information confidential. If possible, present the worker with a topical list of all trade secrets so that there is no doubt about what the company expects. If the person leaving has any documents that are confidential, retrieve them at the interview.

If the individual signed a nondisclosure or noncompete agreement, review that at the interview and reiterate that your company will enforce it, if necessary.

Finally, once employees or independent contractors are gone, make sure they no longer have access to the company's computer files and physical premises, by retrieving keys and changing passwords.

Checklist: Trade Secret Protection Program

Once you identify your company's trade secrets, how can you keep them confidential? Here are some tips, adapted from *Nondisclosure Agreements,* by Richard Stim and Stephen Fishman (Nolo):

☐ Require anyone who will have access to your company's trade secrets to sign a nondisclosure agreement ahead of time.

☐ Maintain the physical security of your company's trade secrets by, for example, keeping them in a locked room, file cabinet, or desk drawer.

☐ Increase computer security to prevent unauthorized access to the system. For example, you might want to use secret passwords, firewalls, and access procedures; keep trade secrets in coded or encrypted form; and/or consider using a separate computer system, without Internet or network access, for your company's most sensitive information.

☐ Stamp or label your company's trade secrets "confidential."

☐ Don't write down trade secrets—tell others what they need to know orally.

☐ Limit employee access to trade secrets by, for example, having them sign confidential materials in and out and creating project logs to keep track of which employees have access to which confidential information.

☐ Restrict photocopying. Many trade secrets are lost through unauthorized photocopying—and a good way to limit this is by requiring employees to use key cards and passwords every time they use a company copy machine.

☐ Shred documents. Whenever anyone at your company disposes of a document that includes confidential information, it should be shredded—not left in a dumpster or garbage can for the world to see.

☐ Screen employee presentations. Companies can inadvertently lose trade secret protection if an employee reveals or refers to them in a speech or presentation at a trade show, convention, or professional conference.

Nondisclosure Agreements

A nondisclosure agreement—also called an NDA or a confidentiality agreement—is a contract in which the parties promise to protect the confidentiality of secret information that they learn during employment or another type of business transaction. A company can use a nondisclosure agreement to protect any type of trade secret or confidential information. For example, a nondisclosure agreement can prohibit someone from disclosing a secret invention design, an idea for a new website, or confidential financial information about your company.

If your company has entered into a nondisclosure agreement with someone who then uses or discloses its trade secrets without permission, your company can ask a court to stop the violator from making any further disclosures and sue for damages.

There are five important elements in a nondisclosure agreement:
- definition of confidential information
- exclusions from confidential information
- obligations of receiving party
- time periods, and
- miscellaneous provisions.

This section looks at each of these elements in more detail.

Definition of confidential information. Every nondisclosure agreement provides a general description of the types or categories of confidential information or trade secrets that the agreement covers.

The purpose is to establish the boundaries or subject matter of the disclosure, without actually disclosing the secrets.

Exclusions from confidential information. Every nondisclosure agreement excludes some information from protection. The party that receives the trade secret has no obligation to protect the excluded information. Typical areas of excluded information include:
- information that is already generally known outside of the business at the time the nondisclosure agreement is signed
- information that becomes known outside of the business through no fault of the employee or independent contractor
- information the employee or independent contractor knew prior to working for your company, and
- information the employee or independent contractor learns independently.

Obligations of the receiving party. The employee or independent contractor generally must keep the information in confidence and limit its use. Under most state laws, he or she can neither reveal the information nor assist others in acquiring it improperly or revealing it.

Time periods. Most nondisclosure agreements provide that the employee or independent contractor cannot disclose confidential information both during and after employment with your company.

Miscellaneous provisions. Miscellaneous standard terms are usually included at the end of the agreement. They include such matters as which state's law will apply if the agreement is breached, whether the parties will use arbitration to settle disagreements over the contract, and whether attorneys' fees will be awarded to the party who wins.

As noted above, even if an employee already has a legal duty to keep your company's secrets confidential under your state's trade secrets law, it's still a good idea to ask an employee to sign a nondisclosure agreement. A nondisclosure agreement:

- shows a judge that your company take its responsibility to protect its trade secrets seriously
- defines exactly what information the employee must keep secret, and
- can specify the jurisdiction in which disputes will be resolved, the state's law that will apply, and any dispute resolution method the parties agree on.

Nondisclosure agreements are even more important for independent contractors, customers, and vendors, because none of these people have a duty to keep your company's secrets confidential without an agreement.

Noncompete Agreements

Sometimes, an employee or independent contractor is so integral to your company's business or so thoroughly immersed in its

trade secrets that his or her departure—particularly to work for a competitor—would cause your company a great deal of harm. In such a situation, a nondisclosure agreement probably will not be sufficient to protect your company. Instead, you should ask, or require, the worker to sign a noncompete agreement. A noncompete agreement takes nondisclosure one step further by prohibiting the worker from performing services for a direct competitor—or by prohibiting the worker from competing against you in his or her own business—for a specified period of time after leaving the company.

You do not need to ask every worker to sign a noncompete agreement. Indeed, you should reserve this type of contract for the most valuable and key members of the workforce. So how do you determine which workers fall into this category? Consider the following questions:

- Is the worker so valuable and, if he or she is an employee, has the company spent so much money training the employee, that losing him or her to a competitor would damage your company's business?
- Does the worker have access to a great deal of important information that you don't want revealed to a competitor?
- If that individual were to work for a competitor, is it practically inevitable that he or she would use your company's trade secrets in the new job?

Noncompete agreements are not enforceable against employees in California, Montana, North Dakota, Oklahoma, and, in certain circumstances, Alabama, Colorado, and Texas. If your company does business in one of these states, it will have a difficult time using noncompete agreements to protect its business. However, you can use nonsolicitation agreements and nondisclosure agreements to protect trade secrets, client lists, and employees when a worker leaves. (For more about these types of contracts, see "Nondisclosure Agreements," above, and "Nonsolicitation Agreements," below.)

Make the Agreement Legal

While noncompete agreements may be an effective way to protect your company's trade secrets, the legal system also puts a high value on a person's right to earn a living. This means that a court will balance your company's interest in protecting itself against an individual's interest in being able to work where he or she wants to work. If the agreement isn't reasonable or necessary, your company will have a hard time convincing a court to enforce it.

If your company follows the guidelines set out in this section, its agreements should pass legal muster.

Have a good business reason. First and foremost, your company must have a good business reason for asking an employee

to sign a noncompete agreement. In other words, you can't simply use the agreement to punish someone for leaving the company. The typical business reason is to protect trade secrets or a customer base that a company has worked long and hard to develop. By being selective about which workers are asked to sign noncompete agreements, your company can increase its chances of success, because judges are much more likely to enforce noncompete agreements against workers who truly possess inside information.

Provide a benefit. Next, your company must provide a benefit to the worker in exchange for the promise not to compete. Making a job offer contingent on signing a noncompete agreement probably satisfies this requirement, because the worker is receiving a benefit (a job) in exchange for the promise. It's more difficult to provide an existing worker with a benefit, but usually coupling the agreement with a promotion or a raise will do the trick.

Be reasonable. A noncompete agreement must also be "reasonable." This means that the agreement can't:

- last too long
- cover too wide a geographic area, or
- prohibit a former worker from engaging in too many types of businesses.

Generally, the biggest issue with noncompete agreements is how long the noncompete agreement lasts. In most states, there's no set rule, and noncompete agreements ranging from six months to two years are generally considered "reasonable," while anything longer than that will receive closer scrutiny. Other states, such as Florida, Louisiana, and South Dakota, place statutory limits on how long a noncompete agreement can last. Check your state's law to make sure any agreement you create complies with your state's legal restrictions.

Lessons From the Real World

Anita Walia worked as an Account Manager in the San Francisco office of Aetna U.S. Healthcare. Aetna decided, in 1997, to start requiring its employees to sign noncompete agreements. When Walia was asked to sign the agreement, which would have prohibited her from working for any health care organization in the state of California for six months after leaving Aetna, she did some research on the Internet and learned that noncompete agreements are generally illegal in California.

Walia spoke to four Aetna managers, starting with her supervisor, about her concerns. She offered to sign the nondisclosure and confidentiality provisions of the agreement if the noncompete were removed. She had a lawyer write to Aetna's president, explaining that the noncompete portion was illegal in California. Her efforts were unsuccessful, however, and Aetna eventually fired her for refusing to sign the agreement.

Walia sued, claiming that she was illegally terminated. A jury agreed, and awarded her more than $1.2 million— most of it for punitive damages. Aetna's failure to take a closer look at California law, even after Walia and her attorney told the company that its agreement was illegal, led the jury to believe that the company needed a wake-up call.

Walia v. Aetna, Inc., 93 Cal.App.4th 1213 (2001).

Nonsolicitation Agreements

It's inevitable: If your company is a service or sales business, workers will develop good relationships with the company's best clients and customers. Similarly, employees often develop close working relationships with each other. But when an employee or independent contractor leaves, your company will probably want to stop him or her from using those relationships to solicit its clients' business and steal away other valuable workers. With just a little advance planning, you can prevent both of these things from happening by using a nonsolicitation agreement.

A nonsolicitation agreement is exactly what it sounds like: an agreement in which the worker promises not to solicit your company's clients and customers, for his or her own benefit or for the benefit of a competitor, after leaving your company. A nonsolicitation agreement can also contain a promise by the worker not to solicit other employees to leave when he or she quits or moves on.

Often, a nonsolicitation agreement is part of a larger employment agreement, noncompete agreement, or nondisclosure agreement. But it doesn't need to be. For example, if your company isn't concerned about a former employee competing against it but just wants to prevent him or her from stealing its customers and clients, a nonsolicitation agreement alone will do the trick.

Nonsolicitation agreements are effective tools for protecting your company's clients and customers. And if your company is located in a state such as California, which doesn't enforce noncompete agreements against employees, nonsolicitation agreements may be one of the only ways to discourage employees from going to work for a competitor or opening a competing business.

Of course, there are some limits on nonsolicitation agreements. Courts sometimes won't enforce a nonsolicitation agreement that makes it too difficult for an employee to earn a living or unfairly limits a competitor's ability to hire workers or solicit customers through legitimate means. Generally, courts will balance your company's and the employee's circumstances to judge whether a nonsolicitation agreement is fair.

As with most things in law, the key to drafting an effective nonsolicitation agreement is to be reasonable. A judge who thinks the agreement is overreaching may refuse to enforce it at all. For instance, if your company is worried about an employee stealing only a specific client or clients, it's best to limit the nonsolicitation agreement to those clients instead of creating a blanket prohibition on soliciting any customers. Similarly, if there are a few specific employees you're afraid the departing employee will try to take, list them, too. Remember, the more reasonable the agreement, the easier it will be to enforce (if it comes to that).

Just like noncompete agreements, nonsolicitation agreements must comply with some basic legal requirements before a judge will agree to enforce them.

Your company must have a valid business reason. A judge who reviews a nonsolicitation agreement will want to see a valid business reason for putting restraints on a former employee. (As tempting as it might be, a company can't keep a former employee from soliciting its customers and employees just because it wants to.) This valid business reason can include:

- protecting a valuable customer list
- protecting trade secrets and other confidential information, or
- protecting the business from the mass departure of valuable employees with specialized skills, knowledge, and access to trade secrets.

Your company's customer list has to be worth protecting. If the average person could figure out who your company's customers or clients are just by looking in the Yellow Pages, a judge probably won't enforce a nonsolicitation agreement against a former employee who tries to get the company's business. Unless your company has spent a lot of time, energy, and money establishing its client database (and it contains information that isn't readily available to the general public), the list may not merit protection.

Employees and customers can leave voluntarily. Nonsolicitation agreements generally don't (and can't) prevent a client, customer, or employee from moving to a competitor voluntarily. There isn't much a company can do to stop its other employees from leaving to join the former employee at a new company, as long as the departing employee hasn't improperly solicited them (and as long as the departing employees aren't subject to noncompete agreements). And if customers want to take their business to a competitor, a nonsolicitation agreement probably isn't going to be much help, unless the departing employee has improperly pressured them or used your company's information (for example, the prices the company has charged the customer in the past) to get their business.

Hiring From Competitors

Although your company may be most concerned about protecting its own business, trade secret laws are a two-way street: Competitors are just as intent on preventing your company from taking what belongs to them. If your company oversteps the bounds of trade secret laws—even unwittingly—it might end up in a heap of trouble.

Sometimes, what makes a prospective employee most desirable is also what makes him or her a risky hire. Although no law could require a person to erase his or her memory, a new employee who uses a former employer's trade secrets while working for your company poses a serious lawsuit risk.

Some potential trade secret violations are obvious—for instance, explicitly asking a new employee to reveal trade secrets, violate a confidentiality agreement, or violate a nonsolicitation agreement. Always tread very carefully if you want to hire someone who is bound by a noncompete agreement—you might want some help from a good employment law attorney. Even if your company wins, fights between competitors over employees bound by noncompete agreements can be expensive and downright nasty.

Although it's less obvious, it's just as important not to create a situation in which the employee will be likely to, or even tempted to, reveal trade secrets. Even if no one at your company specifically asks for the information, the company could be liable for a trade secret law violation if an employee reveals a former employer's trade secrets and your company created a fertile environment for the deed. For example, if you hire someone who you know has knowledge of a competitor's trade secrets, and put that employee in a job where it's likely he or she will use that trade secret information to your advantage, your company could be held liable in a trade secret misappropriation or unfair trade practices lawsuit, even if no one directly asked the employee to use the competitor's trade secrets.

To avoid winding up on the losing end of a trade secret lawsuit, consider the following:

- **Honor noncompete agreements.** If you really want to hire someone who's bound by a noncompete agreement, be honest about it. Talk to the former employer and negotiate some sort of arrangement. Sometimes, companies will allow a new employer to buy out an employee's noncompete, or they will agree to release an employee from a noncompete if your company promises to impose certain security measures.
- **Get promises from the new hire.** Before hiring employees, verify that they will not be bringing trade secrets and will not need to use a former employer's trade secrets in order to do their jobs well.
- **Do your own research.** Don't trust the employee's opinion about who owns what. Many employees don't understand intellectual property laws and think that anything they create belongs to them. This isn't always so. Many people also don't take agreements they signed seriously, but your company should. Ask to review any agreement the new hire signed with a former employer, even if the employee assures you it's "nothing serious" or it doesn't apply to the new job.
- **Manage the situation.** Don't put an employee in a job where use of a former employer's trade secrets is inevitable.

Legal Dos and Don'ts: Trade Secrets

Do:

- **Keep your own secrets.** Treat your company's trade secrets like the valuable commodity they are by keeping them in a secure location (such as a locked file cabinet) and revealing them only if and when necessary. If your company doesn't treat its trade secrets in a confidential way, it will be tough to convince a court to help you stop others from revealing them.
- **Keep track of who knows what.** Carefully label everything your company considers a trade secret, and implement procedures to track which employees have access to them. For example, you might require employees to use a sign-in sheet to access confidential information or keep a roster of all employees who have access to the company's customer lists.
- **Use nondisclosure agreements.** From employees to independent contractors to customers to vendors, using confidentiality agreements gives your company a triple dose of protection. The agreements let these people know what information you consider secret, bind people to not to reveal those secrets, and provide proof that your company actively safeguarded its trade secrets.

Don't:

- **Dip into your competitor's pool.** No matter how tempting it is, your company shouldn't hire a competitor's employee in order to get at the competitor's trade secrets. Company executives who engage in this type of sneaky behavior risk a lawsuit, fines, and possible jail time.
- **Cry "wolf."** If you classify every company document as a trade secret, employees won't know what's really worthy of protection. Courts won't know, either, and your company might actually get less protection for its real trade secrets as a result.
- **Overreach in trying to restrict your employees.** Do some research (and perhaps talk to a lawyer) before implementing a noncompete, nondisclosure, or nonsolicitation agreement. Companies that go too far in their efforts to prohibit employees from taking away business, other employees, or information can find themselves in court.

Test Your Knowledge

Questions

1. Your company must get a patent to make sure its trade secrets are protected from unauthorized use by others. ☐ True ☐ False

2. Independent contractors have a duty not to reveal their clients' trade secrets, even if they never sign a nondisclosure agreement. ☐ True ☐ False

3. All of a company's internal documents should be marked "Confidential," just to be safe. ☐ True ☐ False

4. A company can lose its trade secret protection if it reveals the secret information on its website or in publicly available documents. ☐ True ☐ False

5. Companies can use nondisclosure agreements to prohibit nonemployees with whom it works—such as vendors or customers—from revealing trade secrets. ☐ True ☐ False

6. All companies should ask every employee to sign a noncompete agreement. ☐ True ☐ False

7. Companies should give employees something in exchange for signing a noncompete or nonsolicitation agreement. ☐ True ☐ False

8. A company can use a nonsolicitation agreement to prevent customers from taking their business to a competitor. ☐ True ☐ False

9. As long as no one at your company asks a new hire to reveal a former employer's trade secrets, your company cannot be sued for trade secret theft. ☐ True ☐ False

10. It's best not to ask an applicant whether he or she is subject to a noncompete agreement, because that protects your company from legal problems. ☐ True ☐ False

Answers

1. False. Trade secret protection is do-it-yourself; you don't have to file anything with the government.

2. False. Although employees have an automatic duty not to reveal their employer's trade secrets, independent contractors do not—which is why they should be required to sign a nondisclosure agreement if they will work with the company's trade secrets.

3. False. You should only designate truly secret information as "Confidential," so employees know what they are obligated to protect and courts will know that your company didn't unreasonably restrict employees.

4. True. If your company reveals its own trade secrets, it cannot expect a court to prevent others from revealing them.

5. True. Your company can enter into nondisclosure agreements with customers, vendors, other businesses with which it's considering joint ventures, and others who are not employees.

6. False. Noncompete agreements are illegal in some states, and others prohibit employers from using them unless they are necessary. If you ask every employee to sign a noncompete agreement, your company will have a tough time convincing a court that it really had to go to such lengths to protect its business.

7. True. Your company should give something of value to employees whom it asks to sign a noncompete or nonsolicitation agreement, in order to make sure that a court treats it as a legally binding contract.

8. False. Your customers are free to take their business wherever they wish. A nonsolicitation agreement prohibits a former employee from actively going after their business but doesn't limit your customers in any way.

9. False. Your company can also get in trouble if it puts an employee in a work situation where disclosure of the former employer's trade secrets is virtually inevitable.

10. False. If your company hires an employee who is bound by a noncompete agreement with a previous employer, the previous employer might ask you to fire the employee or otherwise honor the agreement. If your company fails to comply, it could risk facing a lawsuit.

11

Handling Workplace Problems

No manager likes dealing with workplace problems. Misconduct, harassment, interpersonal problems, violent outbursts—all are issues most of us would rather avoid if at all possible. But, as a manager, you must get involved. If you ignore such issues, you risk even more serious problems for you and your company—ranging from poor performance and bad morale to workplace injuries, violence, and lawsuits.

In this chapter, we provide some information about, and techniques for handling, common workplace problems. We cover:

- creating and enforcing discipline policies
- tips on handling a workplace investigation
- retaliation
- violence in the workplace, and
- a company's responsibility for employees' misconduct or criminal acts.

Frequently Asked Questions About Handling Workplace Problems

■ **How can I safely discipline problem employees?**

Make sure your company has a clear written disciplinary policy that sets out the consequences of failing to meet its performance standards. Apply the policy fairly and consistently to all employees. And avoid claims of discrimination or favoritism by imposing similar discipline for similar offenses. (To learn more about creating and using a disciplinary policy, see "Disciplining Workers," below.)

■ **What should I do if an employee complains of harassment or other misconduct?**

The most important thing to do is to take the complaint seriously, no matter how frivolous it seems. Make sure not to take any negative action against an employee who complains—that could be considered illegal retaliation. Report the complaint immediately, in accordance with company policy. If you are responsible for handling the complaint, investigate thoroughly. Once you get to the bottom of things, take action to remedy the situation, if necessary. (For more on handling workplace complaints, see "Investigating Complaints," below.)

■ **How can my company prevent violence in the workplace?**

There's no way to guarantee that violence will never occur in your company, but there are steps you can take to minimize the risk. For example, screen applicants to make sure that they have no criminal convictions for violent conduct. Make sure your company has both a zero-tolerance policy for threats or violence and a strict no-weapons policy. You can also learn and train other managers about the warning signs of violence. Most importantly, treat workers—even those workers whom you must discipline or fire—with dignity and respect. (For more, see "Workplace Violence," below.)

■ **Can I fire or discipline an employee for complaining about discrimination or another workplace problem?**

No. Most antidiscrimination laws forbid retaliation against employees who assert certain rights, such as complaining about discrimination, reporting unsafe working conditions, or making a workers' compensation claim. Both firing and discipline constitute retaliation. (To learn more about what retaliation is and how to avoid it, see "Retaliation," below.)

■ **Is the company responsible if one of our workers injures a customer?**

Yes and no. If the worker is doing his or her job when the injury happens, your company is probably legally responsible. The company might also be liable for criminal acts a worker commits against a customer, client, or coworker if the company knew, or should have known, that the worker was dangerous and failed to prevent it. (For more, see "Liability for an Employee's Bad Acts," below.)

Disciplining Workers

Most managers don't like to discipline employees. It's unpleasant to give criticism, even when an employee desperately needs it. But an effective, carefully administered disciplinary policy is an invaluable workplace tool.

Advantages of a Good Disciplinary Policy

A clear and effective disciplinary policy offers many benefits, including the following:

- **Clear guidelines for employee behavior.** A straightforward, easy-to-understand disciplinary policy will tell employees what the company expects of them and what conduct will not be tolerated. Enforcing the policy uniformly will show employees that you take these rules seriously and administer them fairly.

- **Employee morale.** The employee you discipline is not likely to enjoy a morale boost, but the rest of your employees will. Just like siblings, other employees do not like to see a coworker "getting away with it." And if a problem employee is allowed to misbehave without suffering any consequences, others in the workforce will assume that they can get away with slacking off or misbehaving, creating an even larger problem.

- **Protection against employee lawsuits.** If your company informs employees of the consequences of poor behavior and enforces its policy fairly, it can buy itself some insurance in future disputes. It will be more difficult for an employee to argue wrongful termination if the company can show that employees knew what types of conduct would result in discipline and that this particular employee violated a clearly defined workplace rule.

Writing a Disciplinary Policy

The trick to writing an effective disciplinary policy is to give employees clear notice of the consequences of poor behavior without locking the company into following one course of action in every situation. For example, even though your company may generally follow a policy of progressive discipline (for instance, a first offense is met with a verbal warning, a second offense with a written warning, and so on), you want to reserve the right to immediately fire an employee who crosses the line.

More importantly, you should avoid even a hint of a promise that employees will not be fired unless they engage in specified misconduct. You may find that employees dream up bad acts you never considered or that your company has to fire employees for reasons entirely unrelated to their performance or behavior (an economic downturn or plant closing, for example).

Breaking the Bad News

Once an employee violates a company rule, you will have to dispense the discipline promised in your company's disciplinary policy. Here are some guidelines for doing so:

- **Don't procrastinate.** Set up a meeting with the employee right away. The sooner you let the employee know there's a problem, the sooner he or she will have an opportunity to improve.

- **Keep it private.** Meet one on one with the employee to discuss the problem.

Make sure to meet in a private place, out of the earshot of coworkers or others to avoid embarrassing the employee.

- **Be honest.** The purpose of this meeting is to notify the employee of his or her poor behavior or performance so that the employee can improve. You must tell the employee precisely what the problem is, what steps he or she must take to correct it, and the consequences of failing to do so.
- **Be respectful.** Even bad news should be delivered with respect. Let the employee know that you want to see improvement and that you will help if you can. Set aside enough time for the meeting so that the employee will have an opportunity to respond. Make sure to listen to the employee's concerns; it may be that a performance problem is the result of a misunderstanding or could be easily corrected if you work together.
- **Write it down.** Document every disciplinary meeting, action, or discussion you have with an employee and place that record in the employee's personnel file. In the case of a written warning, give the employee a copy of the warning and ask him or her to sign it to acknowledge receipt. These records help the company show that you informed the employee of the problem if the employee decides to file a lawsuit later.

- **Follow up.** If you tell an employee that you must see improvement by a certain date, make sure to follow up. Check with the employee periodically to make sure that things are going smoothly and improving. If the problem persists, get ready to take the next step in your disciplinary policy. (For more on safely firing employees, see Chapter 12.)

Investigating Complaints

Most managers are anxious when faced with complaints of workplace misconduct, such as violence or harassment. And with good reason: Such complaints can lead to workplace tension, government investigations, and even costly legal battles. If the company mishandles the complaint, even unintentionally, it may unwittingly put itself out of business.

However, a company that takes complaints seriously and follows a careful strategy for dealing with them can reduce the likelihood of a lawsuit and even improve employee relations in the process.

This section provides some basic rules to follow if you receive a complaint of workplace misconduct. (For an in-depth discussion of how to conduct an investigation of harassment or other misconduct at work, see *Workplace Investigations*, by Lisa Guerin (Nolo).)

- **Promptly report any complaints you receive.** If your company has established procedures for making or reporting complaints, follow them to the letter. As a manager, you are considered a representative of the company. Once you know about a complaint, the company is considered to be on notice—and it will be responsible for taking action to resolve the issue. This means that you must report complaints to the appropriate person or department, right away.

- **Keep an open mind.** Many managers have a hard time believing that harassment, violent behavior, or other misconduct could be happening right under their noses. As a result, they often fail to take complaints seriously, assuming that the complaint could not possibly be true. Unfortunately, ignoring a complaint is a surefire way to land your company in court.

- **Treat the complainer with respect and compassion.** Employees often find it extremely difficult to come forward, particularly if the complaint involves harassment. They feel vulnerable and afraid, which can have an impact on the quality of their work—and lead them to seek outside assistance from a lawyer. When an employee comes to you with concerns, be understanding. An employee who feels that you are taking the complaint seriously is less likely to take the complaint to a government agency or to court.

- **Don't retaliate against the complainer.** It is against the law to punish someone for complaining about discrimination, harassment, illegal conduct, or unsafe working conditions. The most obvious forms of retaliation are termination, discipline, demotion, pay cuts, or threats to do any of these things. More subtle forms of retaliation may include changing the shift hours or work area of the accuser, changing the accuser's job responsibilities, or isolating the accuser by leaving him or her out of meetings and other office functions. (To learn more about retaliation, see "Retaliation," below.)

- **Follow established procedures.** If your company has an employee handbook or other documented policies relating to discrimination, harassment, or other workplace misconduct, follow those policies. Don't open the company up to claims of unfair treatment by bending the rules for a favorite employee.

- **Interview the people involved.** If you are responsible for investigating the complaint, start by talking to the person who complained. Find out exactly what the employee's concerns are. Get the details: who said or did what, when, where, and who else was there. Take notes of your interviews. Then talk to any employees who are being accused of misconduct. Get details from them as well. Be sure to interview any witnesses who may have seen or heard any problematic conduct.

- **Look for corroboration or contradiction.** Many workplace complaints, especially those of harassment, come down to one person's word against another's. Often, the accuser and the accused offer different versions of incidents, leaving you with no way of knowing who's telling the truth. If you conduct the investigation, you may have to turn to other sources for clues. For example, schedules, time cards, and other attendance records (for trainings, meetings, and so on) may help you determine whether everyone was where they claimed to be. Witnesses—including coworkers, vendors, customers, or friends—may have seen all or part of an incident. And in some cases, documents will prove one side right. After all, it's hard to argue with a sexually provocative email or a written threat to harm a coworker.

- **Keep it confidential.** Complaints can polarize a workplace. Workers will likely side with either the complaining employee or the accused employee, and the rumor mill will start working overtime. Worse, if too many details about the complaint are leaked, you may be accused of damaging the reputation of the alleged victim

or alleged wrongdoer—and get yourself (and the company) slapped with a defamation lawsuit. Avoid these problems by insisting on confidentiality and practicing it in your investigation.

- **Write it all down.** Take notes during your interviews, if you conduct the investigation. Before the interview is over, go back through your notes with the interviewee to make sure you got it right. Keep a log of your investigation. Write down the steps you take to get at the truth, including the dates and places of interviews you conduct. Keep track of any documents you review. Document any action taken against the accused or the reasons for deciding not to take action. This written record will protect the company later if the employee claims that you ignored the complaint or conducted a one-sided investigation.

- **Cooperate with government agencies.** If the employee makes a complaint with a government agency—such as the federal Equal Employment Opportunity Commission (EEOC) or Office of Safety and Health Administration (OSHA)—the agency may investigate. It will probably ask your company to provide certain documents, give its side of the story, and explain any efforts it made to deal with the complaint. Be cautious but cooperative. Try to provide the agency with the materials it requests, but remember that the agency is gathering evidence that could be used against the company later. This is a good time to consider hiring a lawyer.

- **Consider hiring an experienced investigator.** Many law firms and private consulting agencies will investigate workplace complaints for a fee. You might consider bringing in outside help if more than one employee complains; the accused is a high-ranking official in your business (like the president or CEO); the accuser has publicized the complaint, either in the workplace or in the media; the accusations are extreme (allegations of rape or assault, for example); or you feel too personally involved to make a fair, objective decision.

- **Take appropriate action against the wrongdoer(s).** If you are responsible

for disciplinary decisions, you'll have to decide how to handle the complaint. Once you have gathered all the information available, sit down and decide what you think really happened. If you conclude that some form of misconduct occurred, figure out how to discipline the wrongdoer(s) appropriately. Termination may be warranted for violence, extreme misconduct, or egregious harassment, such as threats, stalking, or repeated and unwanted physical contact. Lesser discipline, such as a warning or counseling, might be in order if the misconduct arises out of a misunderstanding (a blundered attempt to ask a coworker on a date, for example). Once you have decided on an appropriate action, take it quickly, document it, and notify the accuser.

Checklist: Ten Steps to an Effective Workplace Investigation

If you are tapped to conduct a workplace investigation, these tips will help you get the job done right. (For more information on investigating workplace issues, including detailed instructions on looking into harassment, discrimination, violence, and theft, see *Workplace Investigations*, by Lisa Guerin (Nolo).)

1. **Decide whether to investigate.** Before you put on your detective's hat, take some time to decide whether you really need to investigate. In a few situations—for example, if all employees agree on what happened or the problem appears to be minor—you may reasonably decide that a full-blown investigation is unnecessary. Usually, however, it's best to err on the side of conducting an investigation. If the problem is more serious than it seemed, failing to investigate can lead to legal trouble—and continuing workplace problems. And sometimes, you just can't tell how widespread or substantial a problem is until you do a little poking around.

2. **Take immediate action, if necessary.** You might have to act right away—even before you begin your investigation—if a situation is volatile or could otherwise cause immediate harm to your company. If an employee is accused of sexually assaulting a coworker, stealing valuable trade secrets, or bringing a weapon to work, you'll probably want to suspend the accused employee temporarily, with pay, while you look into the matter. But be careful not to prejudge the situation or lead the accused employee to believe that you've already made up your mind.

3. **Choose an investigator.** You'll want an investigator who is experienced and/or trained in investigation techniques, is impartial and perceived as impartial by the employees involved, and is capable of acting—and, if necessary, testifying in court—professionally about the situation. If your company has someone who meets this job description on the payroll (perhaps you!) you're in luck. If not, you can look into hiring an outside investigator.

4. **Plan the investigation.** Take some time up front to organize your thoughts. Gather any information you already have about the problem, including an employee complaint, a supervisor's report, written warnings, or materials

Checklist: Ten Steps to an Effective Workplace Investigation (continued)

that are part of the problem (such as X-rated emails or threatening letters). Using this information as your guide, think about what you'll need to find out to decide what happened. Whom will you interview and what will you ask? Are there additional documents that employees or supervisors might have? Is there anyone who witnessed important events—or should have?

5. **Conduct interviews.** The goal of every investigation is to gather information, and the most basic way to do that is by asking people questions. Most investigations involve at least two interviews: one of the employee accused of wrongdoing and another of the employee who complained or was the victim. Sometimes, you will also want to interview witnesses—others who may have seen or heard something important. When you interview people, try to elicit as much information as possible by asking open-ended questions.

6. **Gather documents and other evidence.** Almost every investigation will rely to some extent on documents: personnel files, email messages, company policies, correspondence, and so on. And some investigations will require you to gather other types of evidence, such as drugs, a weapon, photographs, or stolen items.

7. **Evaluate the evidence.** The most challenging part of many investigations—especially if witnesses disagree or contradict each other—is figuring out what actually happened. There are some proven methods of deciding where the truth lies—methods all of us use in our everyday lives to get to the bottom of things. You'll want to consider, for example, whose story makes the most sense, whose demeanor was more convincing, and who (if anyone) has a motive to deceive you. And in some situations, you may just have to throw up your hands and acknowledge that you don't have enough information to decide what really happened.

8. **Take action.** Once you decide what happened, you'll have to figure out what to do about it. If you conclude that serious wrongdoing occurred, you will have to take disciplinary action quickly to make sure your company isn't held liable for that employee's behavior and to protect your

Checklist: Ten Steps to an Effective Workplace Investigation (continued)

company and other workers from harm. In deciding how to handle these situations, you should consider a number of factors, including how serious the actions were and how your company has handled similar problems in the past.

9. **Document the investigation.** Once your investigation is complete, you should write an investigation report that explains what you did and why. This will not only give the company some protection from lawsuits relating to the investigation, but will also provide a written record in case of future misconduct by the same employee(s). Among other things, your report should explain how and when the problem came to the company's attention, what interviews you conducted, what evidence you considered, what conclusions you reached, and what you did about the problem.

10. **Follow up.** The last step is to follow up with the employees to make sure that you've solved the problem that led to the investigation. Has the misconduct stopped? Has the wrongdoer met any requirements imposed as a result of the investigation—for example, to complete a training course on sexual harassment? If the investigation revealed any systemic workplace problems (such as widespread confusion about company policy or lack of training on issues like workplace diversity or proper techniques for dealing with customers), some training might be in order.

Retaliation

When an employee exercises a legal right—such as complaining about discrimination, harassment, or unsafe working conditions—you must treat that employee with care. Don't take any action that might be viewed by the employee as punishment or retaliation for complaining. It is usually illegal to retaliate against an employee for complaining about these issues, and retaliation is often in the eye of the beholder.

All employers, managers, supervisors, and human resources professionals should become familiar with the law of retaliation, because retaliation claims are becoming more and more common, especially with respect to complaints about discrimination and harassment. And they are also becoming more costly: Juries seem especially offended by retaliation and tend to slam retaliating employers with high damage awards. Even if the original complaint turns out to be unfounded, the employee can still win a retaliation claim by showing that something negative happened because of the complaint.

Retaliation Defined

An employer retaliates when it punishes a worker for reporting or complaining of discrimination, harassment, or even unsafe working conditions. Any negative job action, such as demotion, discipline, firing, salary reduction, negative evaluation, change in job assignment, or change in shift assignment, can constitute retaliation.

Retaliation can also include hostile behavior or attitudes toward an employee who complained.

Good Intentions Can Still Be Retaliatory

Retaliation obviously includes any action intended to harm the employee for complaining. However, it can also include actions that managers take with the best of intentions—if those actions have a negative impact on the employee.

For example:

- A female employee complains that her supervisor is sexually harassing her. In response, you change the employee from the day shift to the night shift so that she doesn't have to work with the supervisor anymore. Even though you didn't intend to hurt the employee, this action could be retaliatory if the employee preferred the day shift.

- An African-American employee complains that the store in which he works is racially hostile toward him because his coworkers tell racial jokes and refer to him with racially derogatory names. In response, you transfer the employee to another store. This action could be retaliatory if the new store is farther from the employee's home or is less desirable in some other way.

In both of the above examples, the manager made the mistake of focusing on the complaining employee rather than focusing on the problem. When someone complains or exercises a legal right, the employer's job is to fix the problem—not avoid it by removing the complaining employee from the situation. By focusing on the complaining employee, the manager took actions that could be viewed as retaliatory.

With discrimination and harassment, you won't need to separate workers every time someone makes a complaint. Unless the complaining worker and the accused worker share an office, work closely together, or have a reporting relationship, you can simply tell each to stay away from the other until you (or someone else assigned to investigate) get to the bottom of things. However, if the complaint is serious and the employees involved work together, your best bet is to separate them by moving the accused worker. Even if the investigation later shows that the complaint was unfounded, the accused worker will have a hard time showing that your action was unreasonable, given the circumstances.

Strategies to Prevent Retaliation

As soon as an employee complains about discrimination, harassment, or unsafe working conditions, retaliation becomes a possibility. You can reduce your chances of being accused of retaliation by taking the following precautionary steps:

- **Establish a policy against retaliation.** Your company should have in place a clear policy against retaliation. It should spell out exactly what retaliation is, and it should make perfectly clear that retaliation will not be tolerated. It should also tell employees what steps to take if they feel they are being retaliated against.

- **Communicate with the complaining employee.** Explain that the company is taking the complaint seriously. Tell the employee that you want to hear about anything that the employee considers hostile or negative. Refer the employee to your company's antiretaliation policy and explain what retaliation is.

- **Keep complaints confidential.** The fewer people who know about a complaint, the smaller the chances are that someone will retaliate against the complainer. Of course, if you investigate the employee's complaint, you will have to tell some people about it. Make sure that you only tell the people who absolutely need to know. And when you tell them, explain what retaliation is and tell them that it is prohibited. Take immediate disciplinary action against any employee who retaliates against a complaining employee.

- **Document, document, document.** Take notes of everything you do to prevent retaliation. Send the complaining employee a letter confirming what you have said about retaliation.

Actions That Are Not Retaliatory

An adverse action is retaliatory only if it is done *because* the employee complained. The company is free to take adverse actions against an employee for other reasons, even if that employee has complained. For example, the following actions would not qualify as retaliation:

- If the employee performs poorly, you can give the employee a negative evaluation.
- If the employee is habitually late for work, you can discipline the employee for tardiness.
- If the employee brings a gun to work, you can fire the employee.

The problem is that some employees who have complained may claim that an adverse action is retaliation—even if your decision had nothing to do with the employee's complaint.

If you must take an adverse action against an employee who has complained, be prepared to show that you had valid reasons, unrelated to the complaint, for taking the action. Your reasons will be most persuasive if they are supported by documentation—like performance evaluations and disciplinary warnings—showing that the employee's performance problems predated the complaint.

(For more information on employees who report workplace health and safety issues, see Chapter 7. For more information on illegal reasons to fire employees, see Chapter 12.)

Workplace Violence

Unless you've been hiding under a rock, you've heard horror stories about violence in the workplace. A disgruntled worker, an employee's former lover, or an enraged customer or client bursts through the door, shooting first and asking questions later.

Workplace violence is a major problem in the United States: Government studies estimate that there are about two million assaults and violent threats made against workers each year. And such violence costs businesses more than $36 billion each year, according to the Workplace Violence Research Institute.

So what can you do to prevent violence in the workplace? More than you might think. You can't guarantee your company will never face a violent incident, but you can take steps to reduce its risk. And your company can adopt a policy and a safety plan to improve its chances of avoiding trouble.

Workplace Violence Defined

Workplace violence can take many forms and come from several different sources. Perhaps the most familiar source of violence is the infamous "disgruntled employee"—the former or current worker who returns to the workplace to avenge a perceived injustice or settle a score. But violence might also be committed by an angry customer or client or by a stranger intent on robbing a business or assaulting

Lessons From the Real World

Rena Weeks walked into the lion's den in July of 1991, when she started working as a secretary to Martin Greenstein, a partner in the law firm of Baker & McKenzie. Greenstein treated Weeks boorishly right from the start, reaching into her breast pocket, grabbing her rear end, asking her about "the wildest thing she'd ever done," and pulling her shoulders back so he could see "which breast is bigger."

Weeks complained almost immediately. The firm transferred her to another position, but she still felt uncomfortable. Shortly thereafter, Weeks' performance was questioned, and she left the firm. Weeks' complaint was not investigated.

Sound like the wrong way to handle a complaint? The jury sure didn't like it—especially when they heard that Greenstein had been accused by at least seven other women of sexual harassment and the firm had never done a thing about it. There was no documentation in Greenstein's file, he was never disciplined, and no investigation was ever conducted. What's worse, many of the women who complained were transferred or fired.

Perhaps the final blow to the law firm's defense was the fact that Greenstein himself was finally fired, in the midst of the lawsuit—but not for sexual harassment. He was fired immediately when the firm learned that he had been improperly dating documents. Apparently that was an offense that merited firing, but propositioning and fondling a long line of female subordinates was not. The law firm was ordered to pay Weeks almost $4 million, not including attorney fees.

Weeks v. Baker & McKenzie, 63 Cal. App.4th 1128 (1998).

its workers. And domestic violence can spill into the workplace.

You should treat any conduct that is menacing or assaulting as violence under your company's policies. This includes threats, actual assaults, unwelcome physical contact, destruction of property, stalking, and intimidation.

Warning Signs

There is no "profile" of a perpetrator of workplace violence; like any other crime, just about anyone can commit workplace violence. But experts agree that an employee who commits a violent act often exhibits certain signs of trouble. All managers should keep an eye out for clues that intervention might be necessary. They include:

- an unexplained rise in absences
- angry outbursts at coworkers and customers
- verbal abuse or threats toward coworkers
- strained workplace relationships
- overreaction or resistance to even minor changes in the workplace
- lack of attention to one's own appearance, including hygiene
- comments about firearms or weapons
- signs of paranoia ("everyone's out to get me") or withdrawal, and
- substance abuse problems.

Clearly, not every worker who displays some of these traits poses a threat. There are numerous reasonable explanations for

absences (a sick child, for example) or a decline in personal appearance (perhaps the end of a personal relationship that has nothing to do with the workplace). But a worker who demonstrates a number of these indicators—especially if the behavior appears to be intensifying—may be dangerous and need some help.

Preventing and Addressing Violence

In addition to watching for danger signs, there are a few other things you can do to reduce the incidence of violence in the workplace:

- **Screen applicants before hiring.** Check for past criminal convictions (if your state allows it), restraining orders, or a history of difficulties with coworkers. (See "Background Checks" in Chapter 1 for more information.) This is important to protect other workers, but also to protect the company's bottom line. An employer who doesn't properly investigate a potentially violent employee could face a lawsuit from a coworker or customer who is injured or harmed when the employee becomes violent.
- **Conduct evaluations and use your company's progressive discipline policy.** Experts say that employees are more likely to become violent if they believe they have been treated unfairly, taken by surprise, or sandbagged. Prevent these reactions

by giving employees fair warning and a chance to improve on minor problems.

- **Treat workers with respect.** Always treat workers decently, especially when you have to discipline or fire them. Depriving a worker of dignity—by disparaging the person in front of coworkers or calling the employee names—can trigger violent behavior.

- **Adopt a zero-tolerance policy toward workplace violence.** Create a company policy that states that violence of any kind—as defined above—will not be tolerated. Violence should be grounds for immediate termination.

- **Never allow weapons in the workplace.** Unless employees have a compelling need to be armed (for example, they work as security guards), don't allow weapons in the workplace, and immediately discipline any employee who violates this rule.

- **Consider an employee assistance program.** Workplace violence often begins off-site—with a failing marriage, a substance abuse problem, or money troubles. Help employees manage these problems with an employee assistance program (EAP) before they result in workplace violence. An EAP might include counseling, rehabilitation services, or anger management classes. For information on offering an EAP to employees, contact your company's insurance carrier—many

offer EAP services as part of an overall mental health benefit.

- **Take threats seriously.** Investigate every incident of violence. Don't assume a worker "didn't mean it" or was just "blowing off steam." While you may think an incident was misperceived or exaggerated, you should make that decision only after looking into all the facts. If a threat seems serious, increase security and tell the police.

- **Develop a safety plan.** Instruct employees on what to do if violence starts. Plan escape routes and know where first aid supplies are. And have the telephone numbers of local police or building security handy—preferably on speed dial.

- **Require reporting.** Your company should require all employees to report any incident of violence that they witness. Stress that employees who report incidents of violence will be assured confidentiality to encourage reporting.

- **Train managers.** If you are responsible for company training, make sure other managers know the warning signs for violence, the safety plan, and the requirements of your company's reporting policy.

Domestic Violence in the Workplace

An employee's domestic violence issues can make their way into the workplace—

and because the perpetrator is usually not a company employee, this presents unique prevention concerns. Among the strategies a company can adopt to address this problem are:

- increasing security whenever you become aware that an employee is a victim of domestic violence

- encouraging employees who are victims of domestic violence to report any potential problems or developments (if the employee's violent partner made a threat or is getting out of jail, for example)

- making sure that the security staff in the office or building are aware of any outstanding restraining orders or threats against your employees—and know what the abuser looks like

- getting a restraining order (or helping the employee get one) that prohibits the abuser from entering the workplace; a handful of states allow employers to apply for such orders directly (for more information, go to the website of the NOW Legal Defense and Education Fund, at www.nowldef.org, and select "Violence Against Women" and then "Working Women and Violence") and

- moving a victim of violence so she is not easily located by her abuser (for example, to a different floor or wing), which will protect her and buy your company some time to defuse a potentially violent encounter.

Liability for an Employee's Bad Acts

Under a handful of legal theories, courts have held employers liable (that is, have allowed them to be sued) for injuries their employees have inflicted on others— whether the injured person is a coworker, a customer, or a complete stranger. Here, we explain those theories—and a few steps you can take to keep your company out of this kind of trouble.

Employer Liability for Actions Within the Scope of Employment

Under a legal doctrine sometimes referred to in legal jargon as "respondeat superior," an employer is legally responsible for the actions of its employees. However, there's a big exception to this rule: An employer is liable only if the employee acted within the course and scope of the employment. In other words, if the employee was doing his or her job, carrying out company business, or acting on the employer's behalf, the employer will generally be liable.

The purpose of this rule is fairly simple: to hold employers responsible for the costs of doing business—including the cost of employee carelessness and misconduct. If the injury the employee caused is simply one of the risks of the business, the employer will be liable. But if the employee acted independently or purely out of personal motives, the employer might not be liable. Here are a couple of examples to illustrate the difference:

- A restaurant promises delivery in 30 minutes "or your next order is free." If a delivery person hits a pedestrian while trying frantically to beat the deadline, the company may be liable to the pedestrian.
- A technology services company gives its sales staff company cars to make sales calls. After work hours, a sales person hits a pedestrian while using the car to do personal errands. Most

likely, the company cannot be sued for the incident.

If your company is sued under this legal theory, the employee's victim generally won't have to show that the company should have known the employee might cause harm, or even that the company did anything demonstrably wrong. If the employee caused the harm while acting within the scope of employment, your company will have to answer to the victim.

Lessons From the Real World

Charles Smith was the superintendent of Amtrak's Rail Weld and Cropping Plant in New Haven, Connecticut. On March 20, 1981, Smith reprimanded one of the employees he supervised, Joseph Leonetti, for sitting in a restaurant eating breakfast when he should have been at work.

A few hours later, Leonetti came into Smith's office and shot Smith twice with a shotgun. Smith's kneecap was shattered, he was hospitalized for months, and he suffered a heart attack and a stroke related to the shooting.

Smith sued Amtrak, arguing that the company put him in harm's way by ignoring previous incidents involving Leonetti, who was never reported or disciplined for some prior violent

behavior. Smith argued that Amtrak's failure to take these earlier incidents seriously led to his injury.

Amtrak contended that Smith would have been injured regardless of what it did. Amtrak pointed out that when Smith reprimanded Leonetti, he immediately responded violently. Therefore, the company argued, if Leonetti had been disciplined for his earlier misconduct, those disciplinary measures would have resulted in violence as well.

But the jury didn't buy it. They found that Amtrak's failure to take action after the earlier incidents led to the shooting and awarded Smith $3.5 million in damages.

Smith v. National Railroad Passenger Corporation, 856 F.2d 467 (2d Cir. 1988).

Employer Carelessness in Hiring and Retaining Employees

Under two different legal theories, known as "negligent hiring" and "negligent retention," someone who is injured by an employee can sue the employer for failing to take reasonable care in selecting its workers. These legal theories apply even to actions workers take that are outside the scope of employment—in fact, they often are used to hold an employer responsible for a worker's violent criminal acts on the job, such as rape, murder, or robbery. However, an employer is responsible under these theories only if it acted carelessly—that is, if it knew or should have known that an applicant or employee was unfit for the job, yet did nothing about it.

Here are a few situations in which employers have had to pay up:

- A pizza company hired a delivery driver without looking into his criminal past—which included a sexual assault conviction and an arrest for stalking a woman he met while delivering pizza for another company. After he raped a customer, he was sent to jail for 25 years—and the pizza franchise was liable to his victim for negligent hiring.
- A car rental company hired a man who later raped a coworker. Had the company verified his resume claims, it would have discovered that he was in prison for robbery during the years he claimed to be in high school and

college. The company was liable to the coworker.

- A furniture company hired a delivery man without requiring him to fill out an application or performing a background check. The employee assaulted a female customer in her home with a knife. The company was liable to the customer for negligent hiring.

Many states have allowed claims for negligent hiring and retention. Although these lawsuits have not yet appeared in every state, the clear legal trend is to allow injured third parties to sue employers for hiring or keeping on a dangerous worker. So what can you do to keep your company out of trouble? Here are a few tips:

- **Perform background checks.** Run a routine background check before you hire an applicant. Verify information on resumes, look for criminal convictions (but only to the extent legally allowed in your state—see "Background Checks" in Chapter 1 for more information), and check driving records. These simple steps will weed out many dangerous workers—and help show that your company was not careless in its hiring practices.
- **Use special care in hiring workers who will have a lot of public contact.** A company is more likely to be found responsible for a worker's actions if the job involves working with the public. Workers who go to

a customer's home (those who make deliveries, perform home repairs, or manage apartment buildings, for example), workers who deal with children or the elderly, and workers whose jobs give them access to weapons (like security guards) all require more careful screening.

- **Root out problem employees immediately.** Under the theory of negligent retention, your company can be responsible for keeping a worker on after it learns (or should have been aware) that the worker posed a potential danger. If an employee has made violent threats against customers, brought an unauthorized weapon to work, or racked up a few moving violations, for example, take immediate action.

Lessons From the Real World

Minimed Inc. hired a pest control company to rid its facility of fleas. The company sprayed pesticide overnight. Some employees who reported to work the next day felt nauseated and ill from the fumes—including Irma Hernandez, who felt sick and left work at noon. Her supervisor asked whether she felt well enough to drive home, and she said she did.

Ms. Hernandez rear-ended a car stopped at a red light on her way home. She told officers that she felt dizzy and light-headed immediately before the crash. The person Ms. Hernandez hit, Barbara Bussard, sued Minimed for her injuries, claiming that Ms. Hernandez was acting within the scope of her employment when she drove home.

The court agreed and held Minimed responsible for the accident. Although an employer is ordinarily not legally liable for any actions an employee might take while commuting to and from work, the court found that Ms. Hernandez was exposed to pesticide at work, within the scope of her employment. The court decided that it was fair to attribute the injuries to Minimed's actions because they were a foreseeable result of the pesticide exposure, even though they occurred after Ms. Hernandez left work.

Bussard v. Minimed, Inc., 105 Cal. App.4th 798 (Cal.App. 2nd District, 2003).

Legal Dos and Don'ts: Handling Workplace Problems

Do:

- **Consider zero-tolerance policies.** Some workplace misconduct is so serious that firing is called for. If, after an investigation, you conclude that a worker has made serious threats of violence, committed egregious harassment, or brandished a weapon, show that worker the door.

- **Make the punishment fit the crime.** Just as some types of misconduct are clearly firing offenses, others just as clearly are not. A progressive discipline policy that differentiates between serious and minor problems will help employees know what is expected of them—and help you weed out the real troublemakers while getting your minor miscreants to shape up.

- **Get help on the tough issues.** If you are faced with a potentially violent employee and you don't know what to do, a workplace violence consultant can help. A professional investigator can help you get to the bottom of a workplace dispute, if you feel like you are in over your head. You can find these professionals in the phone book or over the Internet.

Don't:

- **Drag your feet.** Once you discover or learn about an employment problem—whether it's a performance issue, harassing conduct, or threats of violence—take action right away. It's only human to put off unpleasant confrontations, but procrastinating will only compound the problem.

- **Minimize threats and outbursts.** None of us wants to believe that someone we know could become violent. But if you assume that a worker who threatens or rages is only "blowing off steam," you could be putting others in danger. Take all threats and violent acts seriously.

- **Blame the messenger.** Though it might not seem like it, a worker who complains of a workplace problem is doing you a favor. You then have a chance to investigate and act quickly to nip the problem in the bud. Take action against the problem, not against the worker who brought it to your attention.

Test Your Knowledge

Questions

1. Your company's progressive discipline policy should try to anticipate every conceivable type of employee misconduct, so employees will know what discipline will be imposed. ☐ True ☐ False

2. Employees can use a poorly written progressive discipline policy as part of a lawsuit against your company. ☐ True ☐ False

3. If an employee complains that she was sexually harassed, but the alleged harasser denies it, there's nothing the company can do. ☐ True ☐ False

4. You don't have to investigate every workplace incident or complaint. ☐ True ☐ False

5. If an employee complains that another employee is harassing him or her, it's best to move the complaining employee to another work area until you figure out what really happened. ☐ True ☐ False

6. Keeping complaints confidential can help you avoid claims of retaliation. ☐ True ☐ False

7. There's very little a company can do to reduce its risk of a violent workplace incident. ☐ True ☐ False

8. Employers in some states can get a restraining order, prohibiting someone who has committed domestic violence against one of their employees from coming on the worksite. ☐ True ☐ False

9. A company can be sued for damage caused by an employee only for incidents that take place on the worksite, during work hours. ☐ True ☐ False

10. A company can be legally liable for an employee's criminal behavior. ☐ True ☐ False

Answers

1. False. You couldn't possibly list every possible employee offense, and you shouldn't try to. The best progressive discipline policies reserve the company's right to decide how to handle incidents on a case-by-case basis.

2. True. If the policy appears to lock the company into a particular course of action, and the company departs from it, then the worker might have a legal claim for breach of contract.

3. False. The investigator can talk to any witnesses, examine relevant documents (such as emails between the workers), and consider each employee's demeanor, motives, and consistency.

4. True. Although it's best to err on the side of investigating, there may be situations in which the alleged wrongdoing is extremely minor or the employees involved agree about what happened. In these cases, you may be able to skip the investigation.

5. False. If you move the employee who complained, the company could be accused of retaliation. If you must separate workers temporarily, it's a better idea to move the accused employee.

6. True. A negative employment action qualifies as retaliation only if it is done because an employee complained. The fewer people who know about a complaint, the fewer people who are in a position to commit illegal retaliation.

7. False. Although there are no guarantees, treating employees with respect, and giving them fair warning of misconduct and performance problems through evaluations and progressive discipline, can help avert trouble.

8. True. Traditionally, only a victim of abuse could get this type of order, but the laws of some states allow employers to get them to protect an employee, as well.

9. False. A company can be held liable for any harm an employee causes within the course and scope of the employment, whether on site or off, during work hours or not. But if the employee acted independently or purely out of personal motives, the employer probably won't be liable.

10. True. A company can be held liable for criminal acts a worker commits against a customer, client, or coworker if the company knew, or should have known, that the worker was dangerous and failed to prevent potential crimes—for example, by conducting a background check (as allowed by state law) or screening before hiring a delivery- or repairperson who will enter customers' homes.

12

Firing and Layoffs

Letting workers go—whether you're firing a single worker or conducting a large layoff—is one of the toughest tasks you'll face as a manager. And because of the emotional stakes involved, it's also the task most likely to land your company in legal trouble. When you terminate a worker, some amount of his or her dignity, self-esteem, and livelihood is on the line; it's understandable that a poorly handled termination or layoff might lead a disgruntled employee to the courthouse door.

Firing and layoffs are two distinct but closely related concepts. "Firing" means letting a worker go—for any reason. A "layoff" is an employment termination based on economics, usually involving more than one worker. For example, if a business decides to cancel a product line or downsize its staff to save money, workers would be laid off as a result.

Because firing and layoffs pose considerable risks to your company, it pays to consider the decision carefully. In this chapter, we will explain some of the legal rules that govern firing and layoffs, discuss some factors you should consider in deciding whether to fire, and give you advice about how to break the news without driving the worker to a lawyer's office. We cover:

- legal and illegal reasons for firing
- special rules for employees with contracts
- deciding whether to fire or lay off workers
- deciding whom to lay off, and
- how to lay off or fire workers.

Frequently Asked Questions About Firing and Layoffs

■ **Can at-will workers be fired for any reason?**

No. A company cannot fire an at-will worker for illegal reasons—such as to discriminate, retaliate, or get rid of a whistleblower. However, as long as your reason is not illegal, you don't need a business-related reason to let an at-will worker go. For example, you can fire an at-will worker simply because you don't get along with him or her. (See "Illegal Reasons for Firing Employees," below, for more information.)

■ **Does a written employment contract limit our right to fire?**

If an employee has a written contract, the terms of the contract will dictate the circumstances under which the worker can be fired. (See "Firing Workers With Employment Contracts," below, for more on written agreements.)

■ **How can I protect our company from lawsuits when firing workers?**

Make sure you always have a legitimate, business-related reason—known in the legal world as "good cause"—to fire. (While this is not required to fire an at-will worker, it is always a good idea.) And make sure you have documented evidence that the worker didn't meet company standards, in the form of performance reviews, disciplinary warnings, and so on. Consistency is also important. (For more tips on troubleshooting a firing decision, see "Making the Decision to Fire," below.)

■ **Does it really matter how we fire workers?**

In a word, yes. Surveys have shown that the manner in which a worker is fired plays a very important role in determining whether that worker decides to file a wrongful termination lawsuit. (For more information on how to break the bad news, see "How to Fire," below.)

■ **What should we consider before laying workers off?**

Think carefully about whether the company really needs to lay workers off—would other, less-drastic alternatives, like pay cuts or a hiring freeze, do the trick? Make sure your company has valid, business-related reasons for the layoff. Also consider whether your company's right to lay off workers might be limited by personnel policies, employment contracts, or a collective bargaining agreement. (For more on deciding whether to lay workers off, see "Before Conducting a Layoff," below.)

■ **How should we choose the workers who will be laid off?**

The safest legal bet is to use objective criteria—factors that can be measured and compared, such as seniority, productivity, or sales figures. If you want to use some subjective measures—like quality of work, skills, or teamwork—make sure to apply them consistently in evaluating workers. And make sure your list doesn't include a disproportionately large number of workers in a protected class. (For more on deciding who to lay off, see "Making the Cut," below.)

■ **How should we tell workers that they are being laid off?**

Resist the temptation to just get it over with by laying workers off in a group, in an email, or in a rush. Meet with each worker, explain the decision, and take the time to answer the worker's questions about what will happen next. If at all possible, offer a severance package that will help ease the blow. (See "Conducting a Layoff," below, for more information.)

Illegal Reasons for Firing Employees

If your company employs workers at will, you don't need good cause to fire them—you can let them go for any reason or for no reason at all. (See "At-Will Employment" in Chapter 4.) However, you can't fire them for an illegal reason. Here, we list some of the most common illegal reasons for firing an employee. (If you want to end your company's relationship with an independent contractor, see Chapter 9.)

Discrimination

Federal law makes it illegal for most employers to fire an employee because of the employee's race, gender, national origin, disability, religion, or age (if the person is at least 40 years old). Federal law also prohibits most employers from firing a worker because she is pregnant, has recently given birth, or has a pregnancy-related medical condition.

Most states also have antidiscrimination laws that include all of the characteristics listed in the federal law—and then some. Many state laws impose additional limits (for example, prohibiting discrimination on the basis of sexual orientation or marital status). Some also include a wider range of employers—for example, cover employers of fewer employees than federal law. For more information on antidiscrimination laws, see Chapter 3.

Retaliation

It is illegal for employers to fire employees for asserting their rights under the state and federal antidiscrimination laws described above. You cannot fire an employee for complaining of discrimination or harassment, filing a lawsuit or a charge with a government agency alleging discrimination or harassment, or testifying on behalf of a coworker who was discriminated against or harassed. (For more, see "Retaliation" in Chapter 11.)

Refusal to Submit to a Lie Detector Test

A federal law, the Employee Polygraph Protection Act, prohibits most employers from firing employees for refusing to take a lie detector test. Many state laws contain a similar prohibition. (See "Testing Current Employees" in Chapter 6 for more.)

Alien Status

Under the federal Immigration Reform and Control Act (IRCA), an employer cannot fire an employee based on lack of citizenship. As long as the employee is legally eligible to work in the United States, the employer cannot discriminate against the worker based on alien or legal resident status.

Complaining About OSHA Violations

The federal Occupational Safety and Health Act (OSH Act) makes it illegal for employers to fire employees for complaining about unsafe work conditions.

Violations of Public Policy

Most states prohibit employers from firing an employee in violation of public policy—that is, for reasons that most people would find morally or ethically wrong. Of course, morals and ethics are relative things, so the range of prohibited reasons for firing varies from state to state. Some state and federal laws explicitly prohibit employers from firing workers for taking advantage of certain rights, like taking family medical leave or supporting a union. In some states, a worker can successfully argue that he or she was fired in violation of public policy even if no statute spells out exactly what the employer can and cannot do. For example, even if no state law prohibits employers

Lessons From the Real World

Kaaren Yarborough worked as a manager in the recruiting department of People-Soft, Inc., a software maker in California. Because PeopleSoft has significant contracts with the Department ofDefense and other federal agencies, it was required to comply with federal guidelines relating to the recruiting and hiring of women and minority workers.

In 1995, Ms. Yarborough saw reports that management sent to the Office of Federal Contract Compliance, a government agency that monitors companies with government contracts. According to Ms. Yarborough's lawyer, these reports falsely claimed that the company had a significantly higher percentage of female and minority workers than it actually did. Although the company claimed that 60% of its workforce was female and 21.7% were racial minorities, the true figures were 45% and 13%, respectively.

Ms. Yarborough reported these problems but was fired two days before she was scheduled to meet with auditors from the federal agency. Although PeopleSoft claimed it fired Ms. Yarborough for poor performance, the Alameda County jury that heard the case thought otherwise. The jury awarded Ms. Yarborough $5.45 million in damages on August 16, 2001.

John Roemer, "Wrongful Termination Suit Brings $5.45M," *The Daily Journal*, August 17, 2001; "PeopleSoft Whistle-blower Awarded $5.4 Million," Reuters, August 16, 2001.

from firing a worker who refuses to falsify corporate filings, many courts would allow such a worker to sue for violation of public policy.

Although the laws and rules vary from state to state, most states agree that firing an employee for any of the following reasons would violate public policy:

- refusing to commit an illegal act (like falsifying insurance claims or submitting false tax returns)
- being a whistleblower—that is, for complaining about illegal workplace conduct (such as your failure to pay the minimum wage or your submission of false reports to government officials), and
- exercising a legal right (such as voting or filing a workers' compensation claim).

To find out more about the law regarding public policy in your state, contact your state labor department or your state fair employment office. (You'll find contact information in the appendix.)

Firing Employees With Employment Contracts

If an employee has an employment contract—whether written or oral, express or implied—that contract may limit your ability to fire the employee. Usually, if an employment contract exists (which is not always easy to figure out), the company must treat the employee fairly and fire him or her only for "good cause."

Is There a Contract?

Before you fire someone, you have to determine whether your company has an employment contract with that worker. This might be as simple as looking in the employee's personnel file for a document labeled "employment contract," but often it's not that easy.

Employers sometimes create employment contracts without meaning to—or even knowing they are doing so. These types of contracts—called implied contracts because they are not written down, but instead are inferred from your actions and statements—are every bit as binding as signed, written contracts.

Employers create implied contracts when they promise the employee something, usually job security. You might inadvertently make these promises in all sorts of circumstances, such as during a casual conversation with an employee or as part of a discussion in an employee handbook. No matter how the promise is made, if the promise has enough weight and the employee has relied on that promise (usually by staying at the job), a court might decide the promise is a contract—and bind your company to it.

Figuring out whether the company has unintentionally created one of these types of contracts can be a tricky business. However, past court decisions do provide some guidance. Courts have found implied contracts in the following circumstances:

- While trying to convince a prospective employee to take a job, an employer promises the employee that he or she will be fired only if he or she does not do the job well.

- An employee manual states that once new workers successfully make it through a 90-day probation period, they become "permanent" employees.
- During an evaluation, a supervisor gives an employee a glowing review and tells the employee he or she has a long future at the company unless he or she really messes up. (See "At-Will Employment" in Chapter 4 for more on creating implied contracts.)

Don't let the specter of implied contracts worry you too much, however. The vast majority of employees in this country are working without a contract—written or implied. If you are dealing with an employee who has only been with your company for a short time (say, a year or two) and you are sure no one ever promised the employee job security, chances are good that the employee does not have an implied contract. This means the employee is at will and you can fire the employee for any reason that isn't illegal. (See "Illegal Reasons for Firing Employees," above).

Remember, too, that a contract doesn't mean you can never fire a worker—it just limits the circumstances under which the worker can be terminated. For workers with implied contracts, this generally means that you must have good cause—such as poor performance or violation of important workplace rules—to fire the employee.

For workers with written contracts, you must abide by whatever limits the contract places on the company's right to fire.

Firing Employees With Written Contracts

If your company has a formal written contract with an employee, it will usually list the reasons for which the employee can be fired. If you want to terminate that employee, you must follow what the contract says. Often, contracts will simply state that an employee can only be terminated for good cause. Sometimes, however, the contract will be more detailed. For example, some contracts say that a worker can be fired only for gross misconduct, for committing a crime, or in connection with a sale of the company. Either way, you must follow the contract terms or risk a lawsuit.

Good Cause

As explained above, many written employment contracts—and almost all implied contracts—allow employers to terminate the employee only for good cause. What exactly constitutes good cause varies from state to state, but generally it means what it says: You must have a legitimate reason for firing the employee. In general, the termination must be based on reasons related to business needs and goals. Firing an employee because you don't like the fact that she has an illegitimate child, for example, isn't good cause. Firing an employee because he harasses female coworkers is.

Other examples of good cause include the following:

- poor job performance
- low productivity
- refusal to follow instructions
- habitual tardiness
- excessive absences from work
- possession of a weapon at work
- threats of violence
- violating company rules
- stealing or other criminal activity
- dishonesty
- endangering health and safety
- revealing company trade secrets
- harassing coworkers
- disrupting the work environment
- conviction of a felony or a crime involving "moral turpitude"
- preventing coworkers from doing their jobs, and
- insubordination.

Good Faith and Fair Dealing

If your company has a contract with an employee, then it has an obligation to be fair and honest in its dealings with that employee. Although this rule might seem to override your company's ability to terminate contracted employees, it really doesn't. To breach this obligation, employers have to engage in very egregious conduct, such as:

- firing employees to prevent them from collecting sales commissions

- firing employees just before their retirement benefits vest, and
- fabricating evidence of poor performance to fire workers when the real motivation is to replace them with employees who will work for lower pay.

Making the Decision to Fire

Most employers start thinking about firing a worker in one of two situations. In the first, a worker commits a single act of serious misconduct that's dangerous or potentially harmful to the business—for example, threatens or commits violence, steals from the company, violates major safety rules, or reveals important company information to a competitor. These problems require a quick and careful response.

More commonly, a "problem" employee has persistent performance or conduct problems (despite managerial efforts to counsel and correct). An employee who is repeatedly absent or tardy, is insubordinate, or simply can't seem to meet reasonable performance and productivity goals falls into this category. Though not as urgent, these problems can also threaten your company's well-being. Left unchecked, they will eventually erode the morale and discipline of other workers—and the productivity of the business.

No matter what your reasons are, consider all the angles before you take action. Remember, firing is the one decision you will make as a manager that is most likely to land your company in court. Stay out of legal trouble by making sure you give the worker a fair shake before showing him or her the door. We provide some suggestions below.

Questions to Ask Yourself Before Firing

If you're contemplating firing an employee, ask yourself these important questions:

- **Do we have a legitimate reason?** Make sure you have good cause—that is, a solid, business-related reason—to fire the worker. (While this is not required for at-will employees, it is always a good idea.) In either of the two scenarios described above, you probably will have good cause. But don't use that reason as an excuse to fire a worker for an illegal motive—for example, because the worker complained about unsafe working conditions or asked for a reasonable accommodation for a disability. (See "Illegal Reasons for Firing Employees," above, for more information.)

- **Should we investigate first?** If the incident has already been investigated or if the accused worker admits committing the misconduct in question, you can skip this step. But if the situation is not so clear-cut, you have to figure out what happened. Take the time to investigate—even

when the employee is caught "in the act." There is always the possibility, no matter how slim, that things are not what they appear to be. And the worker might have an explanation or reason for the misconduct that is not immediately apparent. (See "Investigating Complaints" in Chapter 11 for more information on performing an investigation).

- **Does the worker's personnel file support the reasons for firing?** Always review the employee's personnel file before firing. If you are considering firing for persistent problems (poor performance or attendance, for example), make sure the file documents these problems—in evaluations and disciplinary warnings. And make sure the file does not contradict your reason for firing—an employee fired for poor performance should not be able to point to merit increases and glowing performance reviews. If you are firing for a single serious offense, the worker's file might not mention any problems— and that's okay.

- **Have we followed company policy?** If your company has written work rules or disciplinary policies, make sure they have been followed to the letter. Was the worker notified that the conduct could result in termination? Did the worker receive any promised warnings and opportunities to improve? Also check to see if company policies put any limitations on your right to fire. If employees work at will, this shouldn't be a problem.

- **Does the worker have a contract?** If the worker has a written employment contract, you can fire only for the reasons stated in the contract. If the worker doesn't have a written contract, consider whether any company representative made any promises or statements that the worker would be fired only for certain reasons. Have employees been told that they would only be fired for serious misconduct? If promises like these have been made, make sure you have honored them. (See "Firing Employees With Employment Contracts," above, for more information.)

- **Would firing this worker be consistent with the way the company has handled similar problems?** Think about how your company has dealt with other employees who have committed similar offenses. Have they always been fired? Or have some of them been given a second chance? If your company isn't consistent with discipline, it may be at risk for a claim of discrimination or unfair treatment.

- **Is this worker likely to sue?** Although it's always hard to predict what another person will do, you should take some time to consider whether this worker seems likely to sue. Has he or she threatened to sue, thrown

legal terms around with ease, or talked about hiring a lawyer? Does the employee have a history of butting heads with people—such as neighbors or previous employers—and running to the courthouse? Will the employee have difficulty finding another job? Does the employee consistently see him- or herself as the victim? Has your company treated the employee unfairly? If your answer to any of these questions is "yes," your company might be at higher risk for a lawsuit, so handle the termination very carefully.

- **Is there an alternative to firing?** Would less extreme discipline be effective? Do you think it's likely that the employee will be able and willing to improve? If so, you might want to give the employee a probationary period to fix things instead of firing immediately. Just make sure you don't play favorites or bend the rules without a good reason. You especially might want to consider an alternative to termination if the worker's problems are due to difficulties outside of work, increased responsibilities that the employee can't handle, or trouble working with a particular supervisor—or if your company has made some managerial missteps with the worker.

- **Is the firing decision impartial and fair?** Make sure your decision makes sense—and that it can be defended if necessary. Get a second opinion from a colleague. This will help ensure that your decision is legitimate, reasonable, and well supported. A secondary review should make sure that the decision is based on objective, work-related concerns and has not been influenced by favoritism, discrimination, or other subjective factors.

- **Should we talk to a lawyer?** If it's a close call, or if the company has made some management mistakes, consider talking to a lawyer before firing. For example, getting legal help is probably a good idea if firing would dramatically change workplace demographics, if the worker recently complained of discrimination or harassment, if the worker has an employment contract that strictly limits your company's right to fire, if the worker is due to vest pension or other benefits soon, or if the worker denies the acts for which you are firing.

Once you have run through these questions and are satisfied with the answers, the only thing left to do is to document your decision. Write an internal memorandum to the worker's file explaining why you have decided to fire the worker. It doesn't have to be a novel—a concise statement of your reasons for firing is enough. Describe any misconduct the worker has committed and, if the worker has had ongoing performance or other problems, the dates and details of any prior evaluations or warnings and any efforts the company has made to try to help the worker improve.

How to Fire

The 15 minutes or so you spend telling an employee that you are terminating his or her employment may be the most important in your company's relationship with that worker. And they will certainly be the most unpleasant—surveys have shown that managers dread this aspect of their jobs more than any other.

Although you might be tempted to rush the process—a hurried review of the employee's personnel file, a quick meeting with other managers to make sure they're on board with the decision—this isn't the best approach. While you might want to get the task off your plate as soon as possible, the time you spend planning this meeting (such as deciding who will break the news, where it will be held, and what will be said) will pay off in the long run. Prior planning helps ensure that you will treat the employee with respect, provide all necessary information, and avoid doing or saying anything unnecessarily cruel or provocative—all of which will make the meeting a bit easier and help you avoid future legal trouble.

Who Should Break the News

The person who actually fires the employee should be someone with whom the worker has a positive, or at least a neutral, relationship. Don't assign someone who has clashed frequently with the worker or who is emotionally involved in the decision to fire the employee. This means the employee's supervisor might be the wrong person for the job. If you have a human resources manager, that person might be a good choice.

Where and When to Hold the Meeting

There are many different theories about when an employee should be fired. Some say it's best to fire a worker early in the week, to give him or her the chance to immediately begin her job search and hook up with outplacement services while businesses are still open. Others advise waiting until Friday, reasoning that this will give the worker a chance to exit quietly and use the weekend to let the news sink in. Unless you fear violence from a fired worker (in which case, you should break the news at the end of the day on Friday, when few other workers are around), you should do whatever feels right.

Whichever day you choose, make sure to tell the worker early in the day. This will give him or her the chance to pack, tie up loose ends, and say goodbye to coworkers.

Above all, respect the worker's privacy. Hold the meeting in a private, quiet place away from prying eyes. An open cubicle is a lousy spot for a termination meeting, as is a conference room that coworkers can see into, a lunchroom, or any other common area. If possible, avoid holding the meeting in a location that will require the worker to make a long, sad march past coworkers after the meeting is over. The best place to break the news is probably the worker's own office, if it is private. This will allow you to end the meeting when you wish (by getting up and leaving) and will give the fired worker a chance to process the news privately before having to face coworkers in the hall.

What to Say

At the meeting, be firm but kind. Don't joke around or make pleasant small talk with the employee to put off the inevitable—it will ring hollow or, worse, seem cruel once the real purpose of the meeting becomes apparent.

Start the meeting by telling the employee that his or her employment is being terminated and why. Long explanations or justifications will only draw the worker into an argument or an effort to change your mind, so skip them. It can be tough to strike the right tone in giving this information: If you're too direct, you risk seeming cold. But if you sugarcoat it, the worker won't understand why he or she is being fired and might use your sympathetic words against you later to show that the termination wasn't justified. It's a difficult line to walk; the best you can do is to try for an honest, professional tone.

Once the deed is done, explain what will happen next and discuss tying up loose ends. Give the worker his or her final paycheck and any accrued vacation pay. (To find out your state's requirements for final paychecks, see "State Laws That Control Final Paychecks," at the end of this chapter.) Explain the worker's severance package, if you will offer one. Let the worker know whether you will continue to pay for benefits for any period of time, or of the right to continued health insurance coverage under COBRA. Explain your company's reference policy. (See "References" in Chapter 13.) This is also a good time to review any confidentiality or noncompete agreements the worker has signed, to make sure those obligations are clear. (See Chapter 10 for more information on these agreements.)

Finally, try to end the meeting on a positive note. Shake hands, wish the worker good luck, and give him or her the name of someone at the company to contact with any questions.

Company Property

Figuring out when and how to collect company property and block the employee's access to the building and computer system is a matter of judgment and tact. If you trust the employee and don't fear violence or sabotage, don't treat the employee like a criminal, especially at a time when he or she is apt to be feeling pretty low. Unless you fear violence or sabotage, you shouldn't march the worker off the premises. Give the worker time to digest the termination before you swoop in for the company credit card and cell phone.

If you do fear violence, theft, or sabotage—or if the employee held a highly sensitive position in your company (such as managing your computer system)— act quickly to block the employee's access to the computer system, confidential files, trade secrets, and the building. If you can arrange it, the best time to have access blocked is while you are in the termination meeting with the employee. If you choose this route, explain the steps you have taken during the meeting. Offer to help the employee retrieve any personal information that might be located on your computer network or in his or her email account. Tell the employee what kinds of reply email messages and voice mail messages will be established to explain his or her absence, and implement them right away.

Documenting the Meeting

As soon after the meeting is over as possible, write down what happened. Note what you said and how the employee responded. Also keep a record of any issues left up in the air—for example, if the employee wants to negotiate a different severance package or continue to use the company car for a few weeks.

Checklist: Things to Do Before the Termination Meeting

☐ Cut a final paycheck for the employee that includes all unused accrued vacation time (if required by company policy or your state's law). Also include earned commissions.

☐ Issue any outstanding expense reimbursements.

☐ Tell the payroll or accounting staff to drop the employee from the payroll.

☐ Determine who else needs to know about the termination and inform them.

☐ Choose someone (if not you) to conduct the termination meeting.

☐ Choose someone to be the employee's contact after the meeting.

☐ Make sure that the person who conducts the meeting is familiar with the employee's personnel file and benefits status.

☐ Plan an exit interview, if you choose to conduct one.

☐ Decide whether the employee will be offered a severance package.

☐ If the employee had access to confidential information, take steps to make sure that the employee understands his or her obligations to keep that information secret.

☐ Create an action plan for handing off the employee's current projects.

☐ Decide how the company will handle calls from prospective employers seeking a reference for the employee.

☐ Decide what you will tell coworkers about the termination.

☐ If you think the employee might turn violent, arrange for security personnel and an escort for the employee.

☐ Make arrangements to have the employee's password and computer privileges turned off.

☐ If the employee has an assigned parking space, remove the employee's name from the list and reassign the space.

☐ Cancel the employee's company credit card and long-distance phone card.

☐ Collect company property from the employee.

☐ Identify someone to handle any mail that comes for the employee after his or her departure.

☐ Remove the employee's name from company lists, including routing slips, email lists, and telephone rosters. Also remove the employee's name from letterhead, if applicable.

Lessons From the Real World

Malcolm Bolton was a social work specialist at the Fergus Falls Regional Treatment Center, working with developmentally disabled people. He challenged the Center's decision to place a resident in a community group home. Based on this disagreement, Bolton was eventually fired.

Bolton sued the Center over his termination and lost on every count but one: that the manner in which he was fired damaged his reputation. On Bolton's last day, one of the directors of the Center walked Bolton to his office, stayed while he packed his belongings, and then marched him to the front door, in full view of Bolton's coworkers.

The Minnesota Court of Appeals found that these actions might constitute defamation, because they conveyed a negative message about Bolton every bit as much as a statement would have. And the message was "that Bolton was dishonest and was not to be trusted to leave the building unaccompanied." The Court allowed Bolton to present this claim to a jury.

Bolton v. Department of Human Services, 527 N.W.2d 149 (Minn. Ct. App. 1995).

Before Conducting a Layoff

As with firing one worker, laying off a number of workers requires an understanding of the most common mistakes companies make when letting workers go and how to avoid them. Here, we cover some issues to consider before deciding to lay workers off. (If you aren't in on the layoff decisions—that is, if your job is to carry those decisions out rather than to make them in the first place—you can skip this section.)

If your company is faced with the tough decision of whether to lay off workers—many of whom you may like and wish you could keep—you have a lot to consider. Your company's first priority is probably turning the business around—cutting costs to make the company more profitable. However, surveys have shown that downsizing doesn't always pay off in this way. According to the American Management Association, only a minority of companies that downsize report any increase in productivity or long-term gains in shareholder value.

Layoffs can be costly in other ways as well. Your company may have to pay for increased unemployment claims, severance packages, and outplacement services. And it will certainly risk declines in productivity and morale in the workers who remain—and possibly even lawsuits, depending on how the layoff is conducted. Given the risks, companies should carefully consider whether they really need to conduct layoffs and whether they can do so legally.

What to Consider Before Layoffs

Before your company can decide whether layoffs makes good economic sense, it must consider whether layoffs are legally justified and whether any special procedures or rules will apply when laying off workers. Consider the following questions:

- **Are there good business reasons for the layoffs?** Before handing out pink slips, consider why a layoff is necessary. Make sure there's a legitimate business reason for the layoff—such as a decrease in sales, overstaffing, changes in the company's direction, or technological changes that render some employees obsolete. If your company has a sound justification for the layoff, workers will have a more difficult time challenging the decision in court. However, if your company has illegal motives for laying off workers—such as a desire to get rid of older workers or retaliate against union supporters—it may find itself on the receiving end of a lawsuit.

- **Are alternatives to layoffs available?** Think about whether your company can achieve its goals with less drastic measures. Some less painful alternatives might include a freeze on hiring, promotions, or pay raises; cost cutting; or a freeze on filling positions left vacant when employees leave voluntarily. You might also consider pay cuts, asking employees to take time off, or reducing authorized overtime. Finally, some employers provide voluntary termination incentives to allow employees to decide whether to quit in exchange for a package of benefits. If your company considers or implements some of these alternatives before laying workers off, fewer workers will question whether the layoff was truly necessary.

- **Do the company's written personnel policies address layoffs?** Gather together your company's employee handbook, manual, or other written personnel policies. Do they discuss layoffs? If so, you will have to follow the company's guidelines or risk a lawsuit for breach of contract. Some companies lay down specific rules about when and how layoffs will be conducted, give workers bumping rights (the right to take the job of a worker with less seniority rather than be laid off), or promise severance pay to laid-off workers.

- **Do the company's actual policies or past practices limit its ability to lay workers off?** Even if your company's written policies don't deal with layoffs, it might have restricted its ability to lay workers off by actions or statements. For example, if the company president has announced that no one who is performing well will be fired, the company cannot lay off good performers. Or if your company has previously given severance pay to every worker fired for economic reasons, it may have to provide severance to workers who are laid off this time around.

- **Are layoff decisions limited by employment contracts?** If a worker has an employment contract, that contract might limit the company's right to fire the worker. (See "Firing Employees With Employment Contracts," above.) For example, a worker whose contract says that he or she can be fired only for serious misconduct cannot be laid off for economic reasons. Or if a contract gives the worker bumping rights or promises severance pay if the worker is laid off, you will have to abide by that agreement.

- **Is the workplace unionized?** If so, check the collective bargaining agreement for any limitations on the company's right to lay workers off. Workers may be entitled to bumping rights, to be retained according to seniority, or to be paid severance. Also consider whether the company will have to negotiate with the union over how layoffs are conducted. (See "Collective Bargaining" in Chapter 8.)

- **Will the company offer severance or other termination benefits?** Even if severance is not legally required (see "Severance" in Chapter 13), providing it can be a very good idea. By giving laid-off workers something to tide them over until they find another job, you show them that the company values their contributions and is concerned for their welfare. This will

only improve the company's standing in the eyes of the laid-off workers, the remaining workforce, and the public.

Making the Cut

Once your company has decided that layoffs are necessary, it's time to figure out who gets the axe. If the company is getting rid of an entire department or outsourcing particular work tasks, the answer will be obvious. However, if you need to make cuts across the board or simply reduce staff in some areas, there will be some tough decisions to make. Here are some tips:

- **Decide what the company will need going forward.** Before deciding whom to cut, the company will have to think about its future direction. Is the company shrinking in some areas? Expanding in others? Is the corporate focus shifting? What are the essential positions that must be filled for this plan to succeed? The decision makers should meet to hash out these issues. Once you figure out the functions the company will require in the future, you'll know what jobs can safely be cut.

- **Figure out which departments or positions will be cut.** Now that you know your company's goals, you will be able to figure out which areas need to be scaled back. For example, if the company is cutting back on direct sales to focus more attention on research and development, the sales department can be safely targeted for cuts. At this point, you should focus on jobs and positions, not on individual workers. At the end of this process, you should have a sense of which departments will face cuts and how many workers will have to be laid off from each.

- **Establish the criteria for layoff decisions.** Once you have a sense of what skills the company will need going forward, you can decide how to select workers for layoff. The safest course, legally, is to use objective criteria—like seniority, productivity, sales numbers, client base, and so on. After all, it's hard to argue with numbers that can be double checked and agreed upon. However, many companies want to include subjective considerations in deciding whom to lay off—factors such as quality of work, skills, ability to supervise, willingness to learn new tasks, communication, leadership skills, or team spirit. If you will consider subjective qualities, make sure everyone applies these criteria consistently.

- **Make a list.** After the criteria are set, apply them to the workers in the targeted departments to come up with an initial layoff list. Some companies choose to rank or rate their workers according to how well they meet the criteria and then weed out those with the lowest scores.

- **Check it twice.** Once the initial list is finished, look it over for potential problems. Consider the demographics of the workforce before the layoff and after. If you lay off the workers on your list, will the company be getting rid of a disproportionate number of women or minority workers? If so, the company could face a disparate impact discrimination lawsuit. (See Chapter 3 for more information about discrimination claims.)

- **Keep enough people to do the work.** Make sure the workers who are left will be able to do the work that remains—and don't get rid of anyone who is essential to the business. Even after the layoffs, the company still has to function. Workers who remain will quickly begin searching for new jobs if they are asked to do twice as much work to make up the shortfall. If the company makes drastic reductions in its workforce, you will also have to reduce the workload you expect the remaining workers to handle.

Conducting a Layoff

Layoffs are stressful for everyone. The workers whose jobs are cut will face unemployment, job searches, money worries, and possibly worse. The workers who remain will feel uncertain about their future with the company. And the managers who have to break the news will dislike having to be the bad guys.

There is nothing you can do to make layoffs pleasant for everyone—after all, it's undeniably a bad situation for the entire company. But you can take a few steps to make sure that layoffs are handled respectfully, with full recognition of workers' concerns and contributions to the company.

Before Announcing the Layoffs

Realistically, by the time the pink slips get passed around, most of the workforce will know that layoffs are coming. Why? Because layoffs are an open secret. Workers will likely have some inkling of the reasons for the layoff, whether job cuts are required by declining profits, changes in the marketplace, or the elimination of a product line. Savvy employees may have noticed the closed-door management meetings, the human resources department working overtime, or the stress on the faces of their supervisors.

Because news of layoffs often leaks out, some experts advise employers to take the initiative by announcing that reductions might be necessary—even before layoff plans are finalized. If your company chooses to go this route, a company officer or manager should gather the employees together and let them know that the company is considering job cuts. Explain why the cuts may be necessary, when decisions will be made, and how the layoffs will be handled (for example, whether severance will be offered, whether employees will be given incentives to quit, and so on). And be sure to talk about any

actions the company is taking to try to tighten its belt—workers are more likely to cooperate in cost-cutting efforts if they know that layoffs could be next.

Of course, other experts advise employers to keep their lips sealed until all of the layoff plans have been hammered out. The aim of this approach is to keep things confidential for as long as possible and prevent workers from leaving like rats fleeing a sinking ship.

If you're in on this decision, you'll have to consider what makes sense for your company. Consider how many people will be involved in the layoff planning, how likely it is that others will find out about the layoffs, and how the company has handled communications with employees in the past. Consider also your company's philosophy on worker involvement—if it places a high value on open communication and group decision making, keeping layoffs a secret might do serious damage to the company's credibility with its workers.

Breaking the News to Laid-Off Workers

We have all heard layoff horror stories: groups of employees herded into conference rooms to be canned en masse, workers fired by email, staff marched out of the office by armed security guards, and so on. Each of these actions illustrates a callous disrespect for employees and their contributions to the company. And employers reap the negative consequences, by creating legions of hurt ex-employees whose righteous anger at the way they were treated fuels their march to a lawyer's office.

The lesson to be learned from these fiascoes is clear: Be respectful when you lay workers off. Remember that they have made valuable contributions to the company, often for many years, and are suffering a significant loss—and act accordingly. Here are a few tips to help you keep things positive:

- **Involve the top brass.** Layoffs are a major event and should be handled by top company executives. Employees may not expect every layoff to be conducted personally by the CEO, but higher-ups should show their faces at meetings and make sure laid-off employees don't feel unimportant or ignored.

- **Give advance notice.** A federal law, the Workers Adjustment and Retraining Notification Act (WARN), requires larger employers to give workers 60 days' notice before a plant closing or mass layoff. (To learn more about the WARN Act, contact the U.S. Department of Labor. Many states have similar laws; see "State Plant Closings Laws," at the end of this chapter.)

- **Don't lay off workers in a group.** Whenever possible, take the time to inform workers individually that they will be laid off. Hold the meeting confidentially, allow enough time to answer the worker's questions, and give any necessary information. Don't rush through the meeting or make the worker feel like one stop on the layoff express.

- **Explain the decision.** Tell the worker why layoffs were necessary—and why he or she was chosen to be laid off. Also discuss whether the worker will be eligible for recall or will have any bumping rights to take the position of less senior workers.

- **Be gracious.** Unlike a firing for cause, in which you are getting rid of an employee who has caused some problems, a layoff hits workers who have done a good job for the company. Be sure to express your gratitude for the worker's contributions—and your sympathy about the termination.

- **Discuss what will happen next.** If the company will offer severance, explain the package. Tell the worker when his or her last day will be and what will happen in the meantime. And give the worker the name of someone in the company to contact with questions.

Handling Security Concerns

One reason why some companies treat laid-off workers disrespectfully is that they fear violence or sabotage. And these are legitimate concerns: According to a survey of 186 companies by the Computer Security Institute and the FBI, disgruntled workers caused their former employers

$378 million worth of damage in the year 2000 alone.

So how can you protect your company without treating workers like criminals? First, bring in security personnel only if you legitimately fear violence. If workers are resentful or have made threats, or if the situation seems particularly volatile, consider having extra security on hand for the layoffs. But don't ask them to guard the doors, escort workers out, or use any strong-arm tactics unless things really get out of hand.

Protect your company's computer system by turning off employee email and disabling passwords. The best time to do this is during the termination meeting itself. Do it too early and the employee will be left wondering what's going on; do it too late and you leave yourself open to sabotage. Also, make sure to collect company property—keys, credit cards, cell phones, laptop computers, and so on—on the worker's last day. And once the layoffs are through, most companies take the extra step of changing locks and security codes.

Dealing With the Rest of the Workforce

No one would dispute that the workers hit hardest by a layoff are those who lose their jobs. But a layoff is no picnic for the workers who avoid the axe either. They are likely to feel wary about their employment prospects—and quite possibly resentful of the company for firing their coworkers. At the same time, they will likely be expected to work harder, take on new responsibilities, and pick up the work done by their former coworkers. Here are a few things you can do to ease the burden:

- **Provide training.** Unless your company is eliminating an entire product line or company service, the work that used to be done by the laid-off workers still has to get done. This means that remaining employees might have to take on new jobs or added responsibilities. Consider providing some job training to these employees, so they will have an opportunity to learn their new roles. Training can reduce the frustration and anxiety employees feel after a layoff—and keep the business running more smoothly.

- **Avoid burnout.** Employees burn out when they are asked to do more work than they can handle. Remember, if the company is getting rid of a significant number of employees, it is not enough simply to cut those jobs. You must also cut the workload required of the new, streamlined workforce. If you expect remaining employees to simply pick up the slack and do all the work that used to be done by a much larger group, those employees will quickly move on to greener pastures.

- **Retain the employees you keep.** One unfortunate consequence of a layoff is that your company may even lose the employees it chooses not to lay off. After all, the best of these employees are likely to be able to find work elsewhere and may not want to stick around to see how things shake out after the layoffs. To keep these employees, reward good performance. Recognize employees who do well with positive performance evaluations, merit increases, and promotions.

- **Boost morale.** After a layoff, workers will likely have questions and concerns. You and other managers should be available to provide answers—including the reasons for the layoff. While you should not make promises that the company can't keep, you can tell workers about the company's future plans and expectations. Assure workers that you value their contributions and you appreciate them staying on in this difficult time.

- **Share the pain.** If your company laid off workers to save money and increase profitability, the yearly management team retreat to Aspen isn't going to go over well with the remaining workforce. Employees want the company to turn around financially, but they also want to know that management- and executive-level employees are in the same boat and feel their pain. Now is not the time to order fancy new office furniture or throw a big expensive party.

Lessons From the Real World

According to the *New York Times*, one company's firing practices might have cost it millions of dollars in damage to its computer system.

The employer, a chemical company in New Jersey, laid off 50 people in February 2001. One of the unfortunate pink slip recipients was the company's manager of information management systems—a guy with the inside scoop on the company's computer network. After he was fired, he used another executive's password to tap into the computer system and delete important inventory and personnel files, costing the company $20 million in damages and postponing indefinitely a public stock offering.

Why did he resort to sabotage? In an anonymous letter he wrote to the company president, he gave some clues about the source of his anger: "I have been loyal to the company in good and bad times for over 30 years … I was expecting a member of top management to come down from his ivory tower to face us with the layoff announcement, rather than sending the kitchen supervisor with guards to escort us off the premises like criminals. You will pay for your senseless behavior."

Eve Tahmincioglu, "Electronic Workplace Vulnerable to Revenge," *The New York Times*, Aug. 6, 2001.

Legal Dos and Don'ts: Firing and Layoffs

Do:

- **Document everything.** We can't say it enough: You should have a written record to back up your reasons for firings and layoffs.
- **Plan layoffs carefully.** Surveys have shown that layoffs often cost more than they are worth—companies cut too deep, lose critical performers to post-layoff attrition, or have to hire contract workers to pick up the slack. And layoffs are fraught with potential danger, including lawsuits. The lesson for the savvy manager is to think long and hard before undertaking layoffs—and make sure the layoff plan is legally and practically sound.
- **Fire only for good cause.** Although your company has the right to fire an at-will worker for any reason that is not illegal, you shouldn't exercise that right very often. If you fire only for legitimate business reasons, you give workers an incentive to perform well and follow workplace rules. And your company will gain a reputation for being fair and reasonable, which will help in recruiting new workers, retaining employees, and fighting off wrongful termination lawsuits.

Don't:

- **Disrespect workers on the way out the door.** The way in which you fire or lay off workers is hugely important for many reasons. Remaining workers will judge you and the company by these actions. And your actions will play a major role in determining whether the fired worker decides to sue over the termination.
- **Take workers by surprise.** A firing or layoff should not come as a complete surprise to the employee who gets the bad news. A worker fired for cause should have been on notice that his or her actions or performance were unsatisfactory and might lead to termination. In a layoff situation, workers should know of the company's efforts to cut costs in other ways and of the reasons why layoffs are necessary.
- **Play the heavy.** Don't march fired workers out under armed guard or prevent them from saying goodbye to coworkers unless you have a very good reason (like threats of violence). By treating former employees like criminals, you encourage acts of revenge.

Test Your Knowledge

Questions

1. An at-will employee can be fired for any reason. ☐ True ☐ False

2. If an employee has an employment contract, he or she can be fired only for good cause. ☐ True ☐ False

3. As long as an employee works at will, you don't need to bother reviewing the personnel file before you fire him or her. ☐ True ☐ False

4. It's a good idea to explain in detail the reasons why an employee is being fired. ☐ True ☐ False

5. An employee's direct supervisor should always be the one to do the firing. ☐ True ☐ False

6. Layoffs are a great way to save money. ☐ True ☐ False

7. Companies should decide which departments or positions will be cut before deciding which particular employees will be laid off. ☐ True ☐ False

8. Companies should try to use objective criteria when deciding who will be laid off. ☐ True ☐ False

9. Workers may be entitled to advance notice of a layoff. ☐ True ☐ False

10. Before laying workers off, a company should try to cut costs in other ways. ☐ True ☐ False

Answers

1. False. At-will employees cannot be fired for reasons that are illegal, such as discrimination or retaliation.

2. It depends on the contract. Many contracts (and virtually all implied contracts) require good cause for termination, but some contracts may impose different requirements—for example, that the employee can be fired only for committing a crime or for serious financial mismanagement.

3. False. A terminated employee's personnel file should support the reasons for firing, if possible. An employee who is fired for persistent performance problems or misconduct should have been on notice that the problems could lead to termination.

4. False. Although you should tell an employee why his or her employment is being terminated, you should not get into details. This will only encourage arguments.

5. It depends on the relationship between the employee and the supervisor. If the relationship is generally good, the supervisor should handle the firing. If there is friction, however, another manager might be better suited to the task.

6. False. Studies show that most companies that downsize don't realize any increases in productivity or long-term gains in shareholder value. Also, the company will be losing workers in a layoff, so, to realize a net gain, the costs it saves will have to at least make up for the lost productivity, sales, and/or other contributions of those workers.

7. True. A layoff should target the company's problem areas, not its problem employees. If the company is using layoffs as a way to get rid of certain workers, it might face a lawsuit claiming that the layoff was just an excuse for an illegal firing.

8. True. Although companies are allowed to consider subjective factors when deciding whom to lay off, the safest plan is to use objective criteria. This will make it harder for workers to argue that they were improperly targeted for layoffs.

9. True. The WARN Act gives employees the right to advance notice of a layoff, if a large number of workers will lose their jobs or the company is closing an entire plant. Many states have laws that provide similar protections.

10. True. Workers are more likely to accept layoffs if they believe that the company is really trying to reduce expenses and that layoffs were used as a last resort.

State Laws That Control Final Paychecks

Note: The states of Alabama, Florida, Georgia, and Mississippi are not included in this chart because they do not have laws specifically controlling final paychecks. Contact your state department of labor for more information. (See "Departments of Labor" in the appendix, for contact list.)

State	Paycheck due when employee is fired	Paycheck due when employee quits	Unused vacation pay due	Special employment situations
Alaska *Alaska Stat. § 23.05.140(b)*	Within 3 working days	Next regular payday at least 3 days after employee gives notice	Yes	
Arizona *Ariz. Rev. Stat. § 23-353*	Next payday or within 3 working days, whichever is sooner	Next payday	Yes	
Arkansas *Ark. Code Ann. § 11-4-405(b)*	Within 7 days from discharge date	No provision	No provision	Railroad or railroad construction: day of discharge
California *Cal. Lab. Code §§ 201 to 202, 227.3*	Immediately	Immediately if employee has given 72 hours' notice; otherwise, within 72 hours	Yes	Motion picture business: if fired, within 24 hours (excluding weekends and holidays); if laid off, next payday Oil drilling industry: within 24 hours (excluding weekends and holidays) of termination Seasonal agricultural workers: within 72 hours of termination
Colorado *Colo. Rev. Stat. § 8-4-109*	Immediately (within 6 hours of start of next workday, if payroll unit is closed; 24 hours if unit is off-site); employer decides check delivery	Next payday	Yes	
Connecticut *Conn. Gen. Stat. Ann. § 31-71c*	Next business day after discharge	Next payday	Only if policy or collective bargaining agreement requires payment on termination.	
Delaware *Del. Code Ann. tit. 19, § 1103*	Next payday	Next payday	No provision	

State Laws That Control Final Paychecks (continued)

State	Paycheck due when employee is fired	Paycheck due when employee quits	Unused vacation pay due	Special employment situations
District of Columbia *D.C. Code Ann. § 32-1303*	Next business day	Next payday or 7 days after quitting, whichever is sooner	Yes, unless there is express contrary policy	
Hawaii *Haw. Rev. Stat. § 388-3*	Immediately or next day, if timing or conditions prevent immediate payment	Next payday or immediately, if employee gives one pay period's notice	No provision	
Idaho *Idaho Code §§ 45-606, 45-617*	Next payday or within 10 days (excluding weekends and holidays), whichever is sooner; if employee makes written request for earlier payment, within 48 hours of receipt of request (excluding weekends and holidays)	Next payday or within 10 days (excluding weekends and holidays), whichever is sooner; if employee makes written request for earlier payment, within 48 hours of receipt of request (excluding weekends and holidays)	No provision	
Illinois *820 Ill. Comp. Stat. § 115/5*	At time of separation if possible, but no later than next payday	At time of separation if possible, but no later than next payday	Yes	
Indiana *Ind. Code Ann. §§ 22-2-5-1, 22-2-9-2*	Next payday	Next payday; if employee has not left address, then 10 days after employee demands wages or when employee provides address where check may be mailed	Yes	
Iowa *Iowa Code §§ 91A.4, 91A.2(7)(b)*	Next payday	Next payday	Only if required by employer's policies	If employee is owed commission, employer has 30 days to pay
Kansas *Kan. Stat. Ann. § 44-315*	Next payday	Next payday	Only if required by employer's policies	
Kentucky *Ky. Rev. Stat. Ann. §§ 337.010(c), 337.055*	Next payday or 14 days, whichever is later	Next payday or 14 days, whichever is later	Yes	
Louisiana *La. Rev. Stat. Ann. § 23:631*	Next payday or within 15 days, whichever is earlier	Next payday or within 15 days, whichever is earlier	Yes	

	State Laws That Control Final Paychecks (continued)			
State	**Paycheck due when employee is fired**	**Paycheck due when employee quits**	**Unused vacation pay due**	**Special employment situations**
Maine Me. Rev. Stat. Ann. tit. 26, § 626	Next payday or within 2 weeks of requesting final pay, whichever is sooner	Next payday or within 2 weeks of requesting final pay, whichever is sooner	Yes	
Maryland Md. Code Ann., [Lab. & Empl.] § 3-505	Next scheduled payday	Next scheduled payday	Yes, unless employer has contrary policy	
Massachusetts Mass. Gen. Laws ch. 149, § 148	Day of discharge	Next payday; if no scheduled payday, then following Saturday	Yes	
Michigan Mich. Comp. Laws §§ 408.474 to 408.475; Mich. Admin. Code R. 408.9007	Next payday	Next payday	Only if required by written policy or contract	Hand-harvesters of crops: within 1 working day of termination
Minnesota Minn. Stat. Ann. §§ 181.13 to 181.14	Immediately	Next payday; if payday is less than 5 days from last day of work, then following payday or 20 days from last day of work, whichever is earlier	Yes	Migrant agricultural workers who resign: within 5 days
Missouri Mo. Rev. Stat. § 290.110	Day of discharge	No provision	No provision	
Montana Mont. Code Ann. § 39-3-205	Immediately if fired for cause or laid off (unless there is a written policy extending time to earlier of next payday or 15 days)	Next payday or within 15 days, whichever comes first	No provision	
Nebraska Neb. Rev. Stat. §§ 48-1229 to 48-1230	Next payday or within 2 weeks, whichever is earlier	No provision	Yes	
Nevada Nev. Rev. Stat. Ann. §§ 608.020 to 608.030	Immediately	Next payday or 7 days, whichever is earlier	No provision	
New Hampshire N.H. Rev. Stat. Ann. §§ 275:43(III), 275:44	Within 72 hours; if laid off, next payday	Next payday, or within 72 hours if employee gives one pay period's notice	Yes	

State Laws That Control Final Paychecks (continued)

State	Paycheck due when employee is fired	Paycheck due when employee quits	Unused vacation pay due	Special employment situations
New Jersey N.J. Stat. Ann. § 34:11-4.3	Next payday	Next payday	No provision	
New Mexico N.M. Stat. Ann. §§ 50-4-4 to 50-4-5	Within 5 days	Next payday	No provision	If paid by task or commission, 10 days after discharge
New York N.Y. Lab. Law §§ 191(3), 198-c(2)	Next payday	Next payday	Yes	
North Carolina N.C. Gen. Stat. §§ 95-25.7, 95-25.12	Next payday	Next payday	Yes, unless employer has a contrary policy	If paid by commission or bonus, on next payday after amount calculated
North Dakota N.D. Cent. Code § 34-14-03; N.D. Admin. Code R. 46-02-07-02(12)	Next payday or 15 days, whichever is earlier	Next payday	Yes	
Ohio Ohio Rev. Code Ann. § 4113.15	First of month for wages earned in first half of prior month; fifteenth of month for wages earned in second half of prior month		Yes	
Oklahoma Okla. Stat. Ann. tit. 40, §§ 165.1(4), 165.3	Next payday	Next payday	Yes	
Oregon Or. Rev. Stat. §§ 652.140, 652.145	End of first business day after termination	Immediately, with 48 hours' notice (excluding weekends and holidays); without notice, within 5 days (excluding weekends and holidays) or next payday, whichever comes first	Only if required by policy or contract	Seasonal farm workers: fired or quitting with 48 hours' notice, immediately; quitting without notice, within 48 hours or next payday, whichever comes first
Pennsylvania 43 Pa. Cons. Stat. Ann. § 260.5	Next payday	Next payday	Yes	
Rhode Island R.I. Gen. Laws § 28-14-4	Next payday	Next payday	Yes, if employee has worked for 1 full year	

State Laws That Control Final Paychecks (continued)

State	Paycheck due when employee is fired	Paycheck due when employee quits	Unused vacation pay due	Special employment situations
South Carolina S.C. Code Ann. §§ 41-10-10(2), 41-10-50	Within 48 hours or next payday, but not more than 30 days	No provision	Only if required by policy or contract	
South Dakota S.D. Codified Laws Ann. §§ 60-11-10 to 60-11-14	Next payday (or until employee returns employer's property)	Next payday (or until employee returns employer's property)	No	
Tennessee Tenn. Code Ann. § 50-2-103	Next payday or 21 days, whichever is later	Next payday or 21 days, whichever is later	Yes	Applies to employers with 5 or more employees
Texas Tex. Lab. Code Ann. §§ 61.001, 61.014	Within 6 days	Next payday	Only if required by policy or contract	
Utah Utah Code Ann. §§ 34-28-2, 34-28-5	Within 24 hours	Next payday	Only if required by policy or contract	
Vermont Vt. Stat. Ann. tit. 21, § 342(c)	Within 72 hours	Next regular payday or next Friday, if there is no regular payday	No provision	
Virginia Va. Code Ann. § 40.1-29(A.1)	Next payday	Next payday	No provision	
Washington Wash. Rev. Code Ann. § 49.48.010	End of pay period	End of pay period	No provision	
West Virginia W.Va. Code §§ 21-5-1, 21-5-4	Within 72 hours	Immediately if employee has given one pay period's notice; otherwise, next payday	Yes	
Wisconsin Wis. Stat. Ann. §§ 109.01(3), 109.03	Next payday or 1 month, whichever is earlier; if termination is due to merger, relocation, or liquidation of business, within 24 hours	Next payday	No provision	Does not apply to managers, executives, or sales agents working on commission basis
Wyoming Wyo. Stat. Ann. §§ 27-4-104, 27-4-507(c)	5 working days	5 working days	Yes	

Current as of February 2005

State Plant Closing Laws

Alabama

Ala. Code § 25-3-5

When law applies: Substantial layoff or closing of any plant or industry.

State assistance for employees: Commissioner of labor to provide seminars to unemployed or underemployed employees on legal rights regarding debts. To lessen the financial burden of closure or layoffs, commissioner may meet with management and with labor or other organizations, may facilitate communication with creditors, and may set up programs to provide financial assistance. No employer or employee group may be required to contribute to or participate in these programs.

Alaska

Alaska Stat. § 23.15.635

State assistance for employees: Department of Labor offers employment and training programs to workers who are liable to be displaced within 6 months because of reductions in workforce or job elimination.

California

Cal. Unemp. Ins. Code §§ 15076 to 15077.5

When law applies: Permanent closing or substantial layoff at a plant, facility, or other business enterprise.

State assistance for employees: Private industry councils and the Employment Development Department and its dislocated worker unit shall provide training and assistance for workers who have lost their jobs or received a notice of termination.

Colorado

Colo. Rev. Stat. § 23-60-306

When law applies: Plant closings; workers displaced by technological changes.

State assistance for employees: Workers who have lost their previous jobs because of plant closings are eligible for retraining for new jobs through customized training programs provided by the State Board for Community Colleges and Occupational Education.

Connecticut

Conn. Gen. Stat. Ann. §§ 31-51n, 31-51o

When law applies: Permanent shutdown or relocation of facility out of state.

Employers affected by requirements: Employers with 100 or more employees at any time during the previous 12-month period.

Severance requirements: Employer must pay for existing group health insurance coverage for terminated employee and dependents for 120 days or until employee is eligible for other group coverage, whichever comes first.

Exceptions: Facility closure due to bankruptcy.

District of Columbia

D.C. Code Ann. §§ 32-101, 32-102

When law applies: When a new contractor takes over a service contract.

Employers affected by requirements: Contractors and subcontractors who employ 25 or more nonprofessionals as food service, health service, or janitorial or building maintenance workers.

Severance requirements:

- Within 10 days after a new contract is awarded, previous contractor must give new contractor names of all employees. New contractor must hire all employees who have worked for past 8 months for a 90-day transition period. After 90 days must give each employee a written performance evaluation and retain all employees whose

State Plant Closing Laws (continued)

performance is satisfactory.
- Contractor whose contract is not renewed and who is awarded a similar contract within 30 days must hire at least 50% of the employees from the former sites.

Florida

Fla. Stat. Ann. §§ 288.972, 370.27, 446.60

When law applies: Job loss or displacement due to industry changes.

State assistance for employees:
- Department of Labor and Employment Security establishes Workforce Florida, which provides counseling, training, and placement services to displaced workers in the defense industry and local telecommunications exchange workers.
- State agencies must give priority hiring to anyone who loses full-time employment in the commercial saltwater fishing industry because of the constitutional amendment limiting the use of nets to harvest marine species.

Hawaii

Haw. Rev. Stat. §§ 394B-1 to 394B-13

When law applies: Permanent or partial closing of business; relocation of all or substantial portion of business operations out of state.

Employers affected by requirements: Employers with 50 or more employees at any time during the previous 12-month period.

Severance requirements: Employer must provide 4 weeks' dislocated worker allowance as a supplement to unemployment compensation; amount is the difference between the weekly former wage and the unemployment benefit. Employers who do not follow notice and severance requirements are liable to each employee for 3 months of compensation.

Notification requirements: Employer must provide each employee with written notice 60 days in advance of closing or relocation.

State assistance for employees: Dislocated workers' program in Department of Labor and Industrial Relations provides assistance and training for workers who have lost their jobs or received a notice of termination.

Illinois

820 Ill. Comp. Stat. 65/1 to 65/99

When law applies: Mass layoff, relocation, or employment loss.

Employers affected by requirements: Any business enterprise that employs 75 or more full-time employees or 75 or more employees who in the aggregate work at least 4,000 hours per week (not counting overtime).

Notification requirements: Employer must give 60 days' written notice to affected employees and representatives of affected employees, and to both the Department of Commerce and Economic Opportunity and the chief elected official of each municipal and county government within which the employment loss, relocation, or mass layoff occurs.

Exceptions: Employer seeking capital in good faith; completion of explicitly temporary project; unforeseen circumstances; strike or lockout; physical calamity or war.

Penalties: Up to 60 days of back pay and the value of benefits for that time. Up to $500 per day civil penalty, unless employer pays the back pay within 3 weeks of announced layoffs; federal penalty payments count toward state penalty.

Kansas

Kan. Stat. Ann. §§ 44-603, 44-616

State Plant Closing Laws (continued)

When law applies: Employers involved in:
- manufacture, transportation, or preparation of food products or clothing
- fuel mining or production
- public utilities, or
- transportation

must apply to state Secretary of Labor for approval before limiting or discontinuing business operations.

Louisiana

La. Rev. Stat. Ann. §§ 23:1842 to 23:1846

When law applies: Job loss related to state environmental protection laws.

State assistance for employees: Workers who have lost jobs because employer has relocated to another state to avoid compliance with state environmental protection laws or instituted technological changes because of laws are eligible for services through the Displaced Worker Retraining Program administered by the Department of Workforce Development.

Maine

Me. Rev. Stat. Ann. tit. 26, § 625-B

When law applies: Discontinuation or relocation of business operations at least 100 miles from original location.

Employers affected by requirements: Employers with 100 or more employees at any time during the previous 12-month period.

Severance requirements: Employer must give severance pay of one week for each year of employment to all employees who have worked for at least 3 years; pay due within one regular pay period after employee's last full day of work.

Notification requirements: Employer must give employees at least 60 days' advance notice in writing before relocating a plant. Employer must

also notify the director of the Bureau of Labor Standards and municipal officials where the plant is located.

Maryland

Md. Code Ann. [Lab. & Empl.] §§ 11-301 to 11-304

When law applies: Shutdown of workplace or a portion of the operations that results in layoffs of at least 25% of workforce or 15 employees, whichever is greater, over any 3-month period.

Employers affected by requirements: Employers with 50 or more employees who have been in business at least one year.

Severance requirements: Employers are encouraged to follow Department of Labor voluntary guidelines for severance pay, continuation of benefits, and notification.

Notification requirements: 90 days whenever possible.

Exceptions: Bankruptcy, seasonal factors common to industry, labor disputes, temporary workplaces, or construction sites.

State assistance for employees: Department of Labor will provide on-site unemployment insurance bulk registration (when more than 25 workers are laid off), retraining, job placement, and job-finding services.

Massachusetts

Mass. Gen. Laws ch. 149, §§ 179B, 182, 183; ch. 151A, §§ 71A to 71I

When law applies:
- Permanent cessation or reduction of business operations which results or will result in the permanent separation of at least 90% of the employees within 6 months.
- Sale or transfer of ownership of a business with 50 or more employees.

State Plant Closing Laws (continued)

Employers affected by requirements:
- Employers receiving assistance from state business financing or development agencies.
- Employers with 50 or more employees who sell or transfer control of a business.

Severance requirements:
- Employers receiving state agency assistance must make a good faith effort to provide 90 days' group health insurance coverage for employees and dependents, at the same payment terms as before plant closing.
- When a company with 50 or more employees is sold or changes hands, new owner must give severance pay of 2 weeks' compensation for every year of service to employees who have worked at least 3 years. Employees terminated within 2 years of the sale are due severance within one regular pay period after last day of work; employees terminated within one year of sale are due severance within 4 pay periods after the sale.

Notification requirements:
- Employers receiving state agency assistance are expected to provide 90 days' notice.
- Employers with 12 or more employees must notify the Director of Labor and Workforce Development when business changes location.
- New owner of business with 50 or more employees must provide written notice of rights to each employee and to any collective bargaining representative within 30 days of completion of sale.

State assistance for employees:
- Reemployment assistance programs which provide counseling, placement, and training are available through the employment and training division of the Department of Workforce Development.
- Employees who have worked for a company for at least one year are eligible for up to 13 weeks of reemployment assistance benefits.

Michigan

Mich. Comp. Laws §§ 450.731 to 450.737

When law applies: Permanent shutdown of operations at any establishment with 25 or more employees.

Notification requirements: Department of Labor encourages businesses that are closing or relocating to give notice as soon as possible to the Department, the employees and any organization representing them, and the community.

State assistance for employees: Department of Labor may study the feasibility of the employees establishing an employee-owned corporation to continue the business.

Minnesota

Minn. Stat. Ann. §§ 116L.17, 116L.976

When law applies:
- Plant closing: Announced or actual permanent shutdown of a single site.
- Substantial layoff: Permanent reduction in work force (not due to plant closing) at a single site which results in job loss for at least 50 full-time employees during any 30-day period.

Notification requirements: Employers are encouraged to give 60 days' notice to the Department of Trade and Economic development. If federal WARN Act requires notice, then employer must report to state commissioner of employment and economic development the occupations of workers being terminated.

State assistance for employees: Department of Trade and Economic Development offers rapid response assistance to employees and businesses through the dislocated worker program. May include on-site emergency

State Plant Closing Laws (continued)

assistance, information about state and other agency resources, and help in setting up an employee-management committee.

Missouri

Mo. Rev. Stat. § 409.516(5)

When law applies: Any company making a business takeover offer.

Notification requirements: Company making offer must file a registration statement with the state securities commission disclosing any plans to liquidate, merge, or consolidate the target company; sell its assets; or make any other major change to its business, corporate structure, management, or employment policies.

New Hampshire

N.H. Rev. Stat. Ann. § 421-A:4(IV)

When law applies: Any company making a business takeover offer.

Notification requirements: Company making offer must file a registration statement with the secretary of state and with the target company disclosing any plans to liquidate, merge, or consolidate the target company; sell its assets; or make any other major change to its business, corporate structure, management, or employment policies.

New Jersey

N.J. Stat. Ann. §§ 34:1B-30, 52:27H-95

When law applies: Potential plant closings.

State assistance for employees: Department of Labor and other agencies mandated to assist workers who want to establish employee ownership plans to save jobs threatened by plant closure. If plant closure would cause significant employment loss to an economically distressed municipality, the Commissioner of Commerce

may fund a profitability study of an employee stock ownership plan.

New York

N.Y. Lab. Law §§ 835 and following; Pub. Auth. Law §§ 1836-a to 1836-9; Bus. Corp. Law § 1603(5)

When law applies:

- Plant closing: Permanent or temporary shutdown of a single site or one or more facilities or operating units within a single site which results in job loss for at least 25 full-time employees during any 30-day period. (If shutdown causes job losses at other sites, they also count toward the 25.)
- Substantial layoff: Reduction in workforce (not due to shutdown) at a single site which results in job loss for at least 33% full-time and 50 part-time employees or 500 full-time employees during any 30-day period.
- Any company making a business takeover offer.

Notification requirements: Company making offer must file a registration statement with the attorney general's New York City office and with the target company disclosing plans for plant closures or major changes in employment policies.

State assistance for employees:

- The Department of Labor, in coordination with the Department of Economic Development and the dislocated worker unit, provides rapid response services after a plant closure, including: on-site intervention within 48 hours; basic emergency readjustment services; information about retraining, unemployment insurance, and technical assistance.
- The Job Development Authority encourages employees of plants that are about to be closed or relocated to continue to operate

State Plant Closing Laws (continued)

them as employee-owned enterprises; state assistance is available.

Ohio

Ohio Rev. Code Ann. §§ 122.13 and following

When law applies: Permanent shutdown of operations at a business with at least 25 employees; relocation of all or substantial portion of operations at least 100 miles from original location.

State assistance for employees: Department of Development has an employee ownership assistance program that provides technical assistance and counseling; will conduct a feasibility study for workers who want to establish employee ownership plans to continue running a business threatened by plant closure.

Oklahoma

Okla. Stat. Ann. tit. 71, § 453(F)(3)

When law applies: Any company making a business takeover offer.

Notification requirements: Company making offer must file a registration statement with the state securities commission disclosing plans to close or relocate facilities or to make major changes in employment policies.

Oregon

Or. Rev. Stat. §§ 285A.510 to 285A.522, 657.335 to 657.340

When law applies
- Plant closing: Permanent or temporary shutdown of a single site or one or more facilities or operating units within a single site which results in job loss for at least 50 full-time employees during any 30-day period.
- Mass layoff: Reduction in work force at a single site not due to shutdown which results in job loss for at least 33% of the workforce

and 50 full-time employees, or for 500 full-time employees during any 30-day period.

Employers affected by requirements: Employers with 100 or more full-time employees.

Notification requirements: Employers must notify the Department of Community Colleges & Workforce Development of plant closings or mass layoffs.

State assistance for employees: State assistance and professional technical training available to dislocated workers. Workers who are in training are entitled to unemployment compensation and related benefits.

Pennsylvania

43 Pa. Cons. Stat. Ann. §§ 690a.1 to 690a.6; 70 PCSA §§ 74(1), 75(4); 73 PCSA §§ 2905 to 2909

When law applies:
- Current or projected plant closures.
- Any company making a business takeover offer.

Notification requirements: Company making offer must file a registration statement 20 days in advance with the state securities commission, the target company, and the collective bargaining agent. Must disclose plans for closing down the target company, making major changes in employment policies, or changing any collective bargaining agreements.

State assistance for employees: Workers dislocated by plant closures are eligible for customized job training program through the Department of Labor & Industry and are eligible for assistance to support them while in training.

Rhode Island

R.I. Gen. Laws § 27-19.1-1

When law applies: Involuntary layoff; permanent reduction of workforce.

State Plant Closing Laws (continued)

Severance requirements: Employees and dependents are entitled to at least 18 months' continuation of health care coverage at own expense; premium rate must be the same as the one offered under the group plan. (Length of coverage cannot exceed time of continuous employment.)

South Carolina

S.C. Code Ann. § 41-1-40

Employers affected by requirements: Employers who require employees to give notice before quitting work.

Notification requirements: Employers must give same amount of notice they require of employees or at least 2 weeks' warning. Notice must be in writing and posted in every room of the work building. Employers who do not comply are liable to every employee for any damages that result from failure to give notice.

Tennessee

Tenn. Code Ann. §§ 50-1-601 to 50-1-604

When law applies: Closing, modernization, relocation, or new management policy of a workplace or a portion of the operations which permanently or indefinitely lays off 50 or more employees during any 3-month period.

Employers affected by requirements: Employers with 50 to 99 full-time employees within the state.

Notification requirements: Employer must first notify employees who will lose their jobs due to a reduction in operations and then notify the Commissioner of Labor and Workforce Development. Must give circumstances of closing and number of employees laid off. Toll-free telephone line established to encourage employer compliance.

Exceptions: Construction sites; seasonal factors common to industry.

Texas

Tex. Gov't. Code Ann. §§ 2310.301 and following; Tex. Util. Code Ann. § 39.906

When law applies: Industry restructuring or plant or facility closing.

Employers affected by requirements: Private employers who contract with Department of Defense or whose business is directly affected by defense-related economic factors.

State assistance for employees:

- Through defense readjustment projects, state provides funding to communities, programs, and businesses that assist or hire dislocated defense workers.
- Public Utility Commission allows employers to recover reasonable transition costs for severance, retraining, early retirement, outplacement, and related expenses for employees affected by electric utility industry restructuring.

Utah

Utah Code Ann. § 67-1-12

When law applies: Defense industry layoffs.

State assistance for employees: Workers in defense or defense-related jobs who are laid off may apply to the Office of Job Training for assistance in retraining or reeducation for job skills in demand.

Washington

Wash. Rev. Code Ann. §§ 50.04.075, 50.12.280, 50.20.042, 50.20.043, 50.70.030 to 50.70.050

When law applies: Employees who have been terminated or received a notice of termination and are unlikely to return to work at their principal occupations or previous industries.

State Plant Closing Laws (continued)

State assistance for employees: The Department of Employment Security offers special training and counseling programs for dislocated workers in aerospace, thermal electric generation, and forest products industries in addition to any regular unemployment compensation.

Wisconsin

Wis. Stat. Ann. §§ 106.15, 109.07

When law applies:

- Business closing: Permanent or temporary shutdown of an employment site or of one or more facilities or operating units at a site or within one town that affects 25 or more employees.
- Mass layoff: Reduction in work force that is not the result of a business closing and that affects at least 25% or 25 employees, whichever is greater, or at least 500 employees.
- Employees who have worked at least 6 of the previous 12 months and who work at least 20 hrs/week.

Employers affected by requirements: Employers with 50 or more employees in the state.

Notification requirements: An employer who has decided upon a business closing or mass layoff in Wisconsin must give at least 60 days' written notice to:

- the Dislocated Worker Committee in the Department of Workforce Development
- every affected employee
- the employees' collective bargaining representative, and
- the highest official of the municipality where the business is located.

Employer who does not comply is liable to employees for pay and for the value of benefits employee would have received if closing or layoff did not take place, from the day that notice was required to the day notice was actually given or business closing or mass layoff occurred, whichever is earlier.

Wyoming

Wyo. Stat. §§ 27-13-101 to 27-13-103

When law applies: Workers unemployed due to plant closings or substantial plant layoffs.

State assistance for employees: Department of Employment, in conjunction with the Department of Education, the University of Wyoming, and the Community College Commission, offers occupational transfer and retraining programs and services for displaced workers.

Current as of February 2005

13

Departing Workers

Whether an employment relationship is good or bad, odds are it will end one day—and perhaps sooner than you think. Employment statistics show that the days of an individual staying with a company until retirement are long gone: According to 2004 study by the U.S. Bureau of Labor Statistics, workers spend an average of only four years with a company before moving on.

Observing legal rules is especially important at the end of the employment relationship. Departing workers (especially those who are leaving involuntarily) may be unhappy, angry, or dissatisfied with the way they've been treated by your company. If you show respect to departing employees, and make sure you observe all of their legal rights, you have a much better chance of averting lawsuits and other problems.

In this chapter, we look at some common issues you'll face when workers depart, paying special attention to trouble spots. Regardless of why a worker leaves—whether he or she was fired, laid off, or quit—you'll face many of the same issues as the employment relationship winds down. These issues include how to give references, whether to extend health benefits, whether to dispute unemployment benefits, and whether to give severance.

Frequently Asked Questions About Departing Workers

■ **Do we have to give references for every worker who leaves?**
No. No law requires employers to give a reference for a former employee, just as there is no law that prohibits telling the truth about a former employee. However, there are some steps you should take to make sure you don't create unnecessary legal problems when you provide a reference. (For more about this issue, see "References," below.)

■ **What should we say to our remaining workers when an employee leaves?**
It depends on why the employee is leaving. If the employee is separating on good terms, you can let other workers know where and when the employee is going. For employees who are fired, however, you should probably be less forthcoming. (See "What to Tell Coworkers When an Employee Leaves," below, for more information.)

■ **Do we have to continue to pay a former employee's health insurance premiums?**

No. Although your company may have to offer continuing health insurance benefits to workers who leave, you are not required to pay any of the costs. Even if you pay the premiums for current employees, you can pass those expenses on to former employees who opt to continue their benefits. (For more information, see "Health Insurance," below.)

■ **Are we legally required to pay severance?**

Probably not. Unless your company has led employees to believe that they are entitled to severance, there is no obligation to give it. (For more information, see "Severance," below.)

■ **Is there anything we can do to protect the company from lawsuits by former employees?**

Yes. You can ask employees to sign a release in which they agree not to sue the company over the termination. Some companies routinely ask employees to sign a release as a condition of receiving a severance package. (For more about this, see "Releases," below.)

■ **Are all departing workers entitled to unemployment compensation?**

No. The unemployment laws vary from state to state, but generally workers who quit for ordinary reasons or who lose their jobs because of gross misconduct are not entitled to receive benefits. Workers who are laid off, who quit for compelling reasons, or who are fired for conduct that isn't very serious can receive benefits. (For more information, see "Unemployment Benefits," below.)

References

Whenever an employee leaves, your company will have to decide what to say to other employers who call for a reference. The decision is pretty straightforward if the employee left on good terms: You and the former employee can come up with a mutually agreeable statement to explain the departure. Or, you can simply tell the whole glowing truth to any prospective employer who calls for a reference. But if the employee was fired, you face a more difficult task.

Defamation

If you are not careful in your statements about former employees, your company might find itself defending a defamation lawsuit. And, because defamation is a personal injury claim that can be brought against individuals as well as organizations, you could even be sued personally for your comments.

To prove defamation, a former employee typically must show that company representatives intentionally damaged his or her reputation by making harmful statements about the employee that they knew to be false.

At first glance, it might seem like only the most spiteful manager would get caught in this trap. But, if you make an unflattering statement that you don't absolutely know to be true, it could happen to you. Let's face it: Most reasons for firing make the employee look bad. And managers often cannot prove what they strongly believe to be true—that an employee is stealing from the company, is incompetent, or lied about job qualifications, for example. A manager who makes such statements about a former employee could get into trouble. Your best policy is to say as little as possible and stick to facts you can prove.

Rules for Giving References

When a potential employer calls for a reference, you may feel trapped between wanting to tell the truth and fearing a lawsuit if you say anything unflattering. Unfortunately, this fear is not unfounded. The number of defamation lawsuits filed over negative references is growing all

the time. And, even if a former employee can't successfully prove that you defamed him or her, your company and/or you will have to spend precious time and money fighting the allegation.

Here are some tips to help you avoid problems:

- **Warn a difficult employee that your reference won't be good.** Yes, the employee should know this already. But you can avoid problems at the outset by stating the obvious: "I cannot provide a positive reference for you."

- **Keep it brief.** Some companies adopt a policy of only giving out dates of employment, job title, and final salary to prospective employers. If your company chooses to tell more, keep it to a minimum.

- **Stick to the facts.** Now is not the time to speculate about a former employee's bad qualities or to opine on the reasons for his or her failure to perform. Limit your comments to accurate, easily documented information.

- **Don't be spiteful.** Many states offer some protection for former employers called upon to provide a reference. These laws generally provide that your company will be shielded from defamation lawsuits as long as you provide information in good faith. This is a fairly nebulous legal standard, but it surely does not cover nasty or mean-spirited gripes.

- **Don't give false flattery.** If you had to fire a real bad egg (for example, a worker who was violent in the workplace or threatened coworkers), don't lie about it. You may choose to give only name, rank, and serial number, but, if you give a more expansive reference, don't hide the bad news. Your company could also end up in legal trouble for failing to warn the new employer about these serious problems.

- **Designate one person to give references.** Choose one trusted person in the company to be responsible for all references, and tell employees to direct inquiries to that person. Make

sure that your company keeps a record of every request for a reference and every response, in case of later trouble. Some companies provide only written references, to make sure they have proof of exactly what was said.

- **Insist on a written release.** To make absolutely sure your company is protected against lawsuits, require former employees to sign a release—an agreement that gives you permission to provide information to prospective employers (and promises not to sue over the information you provide).

Lessons From The Real World

Randi was a female student at a California middle school when she was called into the vice principal's office one day in 1992. Later, she claimed that the vice principal, Robert Gadams, sexually molested her while she was in his office.

As it turned out, the school hired Gadams after receiving positive recommendations from another school district where Gadams had worked. Even though supervisors in his former school district knew that Gadams had been accused of sexual misconduct and impropriety with students, it failed to mention these claims when the new middle school asked for a reference. In fact, the former district gave letters of recommendation for Gadams that contained unconditional praise. One

letter recommended Gadams "for an assistant principalship or equivalent position without reservation."

When Randi sued Gadams's previous school district, the district claimed that she had no legal grounds for suit. After all, it argued, it didn't have any sort of obligation to her, a student in a different district. The California Supreme Court disagreed. It said that Randi could sue because the school district had a duty to not misrepresent the facts when describing the character and qualifications of an employee to a prospective employer—in this case, the middle school that Randi attended.

Randi W. v. Muroc Joint Unified School District, et al, 14 Cal. 4th 1066, 60 Cal. Rptr.2d 263 (1997).

What to Tell Coworkers When an Employee Leaves

Before a departing employee walks out the door, sit down and discuss what you will tell coworkers about the situation. If the employee is leaving on good terms, this decision should not be difficult. You'll probably want to thank the worker for his or her service, tell coworkers where the worker is going, and express high hopes for the worker's future.

You'll need to take extra steps if a worker is fired, however. Imagine how other employees will feel when they learn that a coworker—perhaps a friend—has been fired. Not only will they want to know why that person was fired, but they may also start to fear for their own jobs. Rumors will circulate. Morale may drop. This is especially true if you're terminating a popular employee or someone who's been with the company for a number of years.

You may be tempted to say nothing to other workers about the termination. Although this instinct is understandable, it's not a good one. Employees are not going to ignore or forget about the termination—no matter how much they may have wanted the employee gone. Every employee secretly fears being fired, so it is unsettling at best when it happens to a coworker.

So what should you do? You can keep other workers informed, boost morale, and avoid any legal missteps by following these tips:

- **Call a meeting.** Consider calling a meeting with employees to announce the termination so you can acknowledge the event on behalf of the company and encourage workers to move past it.
- **Relay the facts.** At the meeting, tell them who has been terminated and as of what date. Do not explain why the employee was fired.
- **Keep it neutral.** Do not express anger or relief. Be professional and calm. Tell workers that you can't go into details because you must respect the fired employee's privacy.

Of course, this doesn't mean managers can never discuss the reasons for termination with anyone. If there is a compelling business need to tell an employee why a coworker was terminated (for example, an employee is taking on the terminated worker's projects and needs to know what the worker did wrong), then do it one on one, in a private and confidential setting. Instruct the employee not to reveal anything you say to anyone else in the organization.

Health Insurance

With the astronomical increases in the costs of medical care, health insurance has become a coveted—if not essential—employee benefit. The importance of health care coverage means that this will be one of the first issues a terminated employee will ask about.

Many companies offer to foot the bill for continued insurance coverage—at least for a while—as part of an employee's severance package. Often, this benefit helps give former workers peace of mind and makes them feel more kindly disposed toward a former employer. (See "Severance," below, for more about this issue.)

Warm fuzzies aside, there are also federal and state laws that may require employers to make continued coverage available to former employees, even if your company isn't required to pay for it.

Federal Law

A federal workplace law, the Consolidated Omnibus Budget Reconciliation Act (COBRA), 29 U.S.C. § 1162, applies to companies that have 20 or more employees and offer a group health care plan. Among other things, it requires companies to offer former employees the option of continuing their health care coverage for up to 18 months if they quit or are fired for any reason other than gross misconduct. Companies must also make this opportunity available to the employee's spouse and dependents.

The employee must pay for continuing coverage under COBRA, including both the company's and the employee's share of the premiums. Your company can charge the employee 1–2% of the monthly premium cost—using the extra 2% to cover administrative costs. COBRA applies to HMO and PPO plans in addition to more traditional group insurance plans. COBRA also covers all other types of medical benefits, including dental and vision care and plans under which your company reimburses employees for medical expenses.

To learn more about COBRA, including your company's responsibilities under the law, refer to the website of the U.S. Department of Labor, at www.dol.gov.

State Laws

Most states also have laws that give former employees the right to continue group health insurance after they leave a job—and your company must comply with both state and federal law. In other words, complying with COBRA may not get your company off the hook if state law requires more. State protections are generally more detailed and more generous to workers than COBRA. In addition, even small businesses (fewer than 20 employees) that escape COBRA may have to comply with state laws.

To learn more about your state's law, see "State Health Insurance Continuation Laws," at the end of this chapter.

Severance

Many employers assume they have to offer a severance package—some combination of money and continuing benefits—to fired employees. In most cases, however, a company is not legally required to pay employees severance. (A few states require some employers to pay a small amount of severance when they lay off a significant number of workers at one time—see "State Plant Closing Laws," in Chapter 12, for more information.)

The law requires a company to provide severance to former employees only if it led them to believe they would receive it by:

- signing a written contract agreeing to pay severance
- promising employees severance pay in an employee handbook or personnel policy
- historically paying severance to other employees in the same position, or
- verbally promising severance to the employee.

Even so, many employers routinely give severance packages to long-term employees, unless the employees are terminated for serious misconduct. Many employers do this to soften the blow of being fired or laid off and to buy a little insurance against lawsuits. A severance package may help sweeten the sour grapes workers feel about losing their jobs. As a general rule, a happier former employee is a less litigious former employee.

If your company decides to pay severance, the most important rule is to be consistent. The amount of severance can vary depending on how long the employee has worked for the company and on the employee's job category. But be sure to treat employees equally. A company that is evenhanded and uniform in paying severance is less likely to face claims of discrimination (for example, that men received higher severance pay than women).

What to Include in a Severance Package

There are no hard-and-fast rules about what constitutes a severance package. The idea is to ease the burden on the soon-to-be-jobless employee. You might consider including any or all of the following benefits:

- **Pay.** Realistically, this is what is most important to employees. Many employers pay a set amount—a week or two of salary—for every year of employment.
- **Insurance benefits.** Some employers offer to pay for continuation of insurance coverage for a period of time after an employee is fired. Although COBRA requires most employers to offer their employees the opportunity to continue their health insurance, it does not require employers to foot the bill. (For more about COBRA, see "Health Insurance," above.) An employer may also want to continue other benefits, such as life or disability insurance.
- **Uncontested unemployment compensation.** Fired employees can apply for unemployment benefits if they were fired for reasons other than serious misconduct. After an

employee applies for benefits, the employer has the opportunity to contest the employee's claim. By agreeing not to contest an employee's claim, a company makes it more likely that the employee will receive benefits. (For more information about how unemployment works, see "Unemployment Benefits," below.)

- **Outplacement services.** Outplacement programs help employees find new jobs. They may offer counseling on career goals and job skills, tips on resume writing, leads for potential jobs, practice interview sessions, and help in negotiating with potential employers.

- **References.** You might agree to come up with a mutually agreeable letter of reference for an employee to use in job hunting. But proceed with caution here: Giving references carries with it some possible risks.

(For more about this issue, see "References," above.)

- **Other benefits.** Certain benefits or items may be particularly important to a departing employee. If possible, have an honest discussion to find out what the worker would like in a severance package. You might want to consider allowing the employee to keep advances or money paid for moving expenses, giving the employee equipment such as a cell phone or computer, or releasing an employee from contractual obligations, like a covenant not to compete.

As you can see, severance means more than money. If you think creatively and communicate with the employee, you should be able to come up with some valuable benefits that won't break the bank.

Checklist: Collecting Company Property

Before a departing worker walks out the door for the last time, you'll need to disable the employee's passwords and security codes so the employee will no longer have access to the company's computers, telephone system, and workplace. You'll also need to get back any company property in the employee's possession—and it's much easier to do this before the employee leaves than to try to track the employee (and the property) down later. Here are some of the things you may need to collect:

- ☐ company car
- ☐ keys and security cards that allow access to the workplace
- ☐ company credit card (you should also call the credit card issuer to cancel the account)
- ☐ computer password
- ☐ long-distance calling card (you should also call the provider to cancel the account)
- ☐ confidential files, client lists, manuals, and other company documents
- ☐ laptop computer, and
- ☐ cell phone.

Releases

Firing or laying off a worker is never pleasant. But sometimes, it's actually risky. Perhaps the employee is one who complains a lot or stirs trouble in the workplace. Or maybe you have made some mistakes in your management of the employee and have reason for concern if a judge or jury later reviews your decisions.

Either way, if your company is worried about a lawsuit, you might want to ask the employee to sign a release—an agreement not to sue the company in exchange for receiving certain benefits. Some employers routinely ask employees to sign a release as a condition of receiving a severance package. Others ask for releases only from employees who might have a legitimate legal claim against the company or who seem especially motivated to sue.

Because some states have specific requirements about what language must go into a release, you should consult an attorney for help in crafting a legal agreement that will meet your needs. Here are some general considerations to keep in mind:

- **Give the employee something in exchange for the release.** You are asking the employee to waive the right to sue the company, and that right is worth something. This means that if your company offers severance packages to employees who don't sign releases, it will have to give something extra to employees who do sign. Specify the additional benefits in the release.

- **Be clear about the rights the employee is waiving.** The release might state that the employee is waiving any right to sue for claims arising out of the employment relationship, including the termination of that relationship. In any case, make sure the agreement is specific enough to prevent employees from later claiming that they didn't know what rights they were giving up.

- **Give the employee plenty of time to decide whether to sign.** It is reasonable for an employee to take a week or two to decide whether to give up the right to sue. You might even suggest that the employee consult with a lawyer to review the agreement.

- **Avoid any hint of coercion.** An employee must sign the release voluntarily or courts will not enforce it. Don't threaten or talk tough with employees to convince them to sign; a release that gets thrown out of court won't do your company much good.

- **Special rules apply to older workers.** If the employee is 40 years of age or older, a federal law—the Older Workers' Benefit Protection Act (OWBPA)—dictates what language must be included in a release. Among other things, these employees must have a longer period of time to review the release; be able to revoke the agreement (change their minds) for a limited time after they sign; and be advised, in writing, to consult with an attorney.

Unemployment Benefits

Not everyone who's out of work is entitled to unemployment benefits. There are a couple of factors that dictate whether a former employee will receive unemployment: the circumstances of the employee's departure and whether his or her former employer decides to contest the employee's claim. This means your company has a lot of power over whether the worker will receive unemployment benefits.

Employee Eligibility

Employees are eligible for unemployment benefits only if they are out of work through no fault of their own. This rule works differently depending on whether the employee quit, was laid off, or was fired.

If an employee quits. An employee who quits or resigns from a job will be eligible for benefits only if he or she did so for what is called "good cause." A good reason for quitting a job is not necessarily good cause. The law requires the reason to be "compelling"—that is, the worker would have suffered some sort of harm or injury by staying. Put another way, the reason must be the sort that would have made any reasonable person leave.

For example, leaving a job because it doesn't offer opportunities for career advancement is a good reason, but it won't make a worker eligible for unemployment benefits. Similarly, simple job dissatisfaction is a good reason that does not amount to good cause.

If an employee leaves the job because of intolerable working conditions (such as being sexually harassed) or because he or she was offered the opportunity to quit in lieu of being fired, most states would allow the worker to collect unemployment. Similarly, leaving a job because it poses a serious threat to the worker's health or safety is usually good cause.

If an employee is laid off. An employee who loses a job through a layoff or reduction in workforce is eligible for benefits.

If an employee is fired. Fired employees can claim unemployment benefits if they were terminated because of financial cutbacks or because they were not a good fit for the job for which they were hired. They can also receive benefits if the employer had a good reason to fire but the infractions were relatively minor, unintentional, or isolated.

In most states, however, an employee who is fired for misconduct will not be able to receive unemployment benefits. Although you may think that any action that leads to termination should constitute misconduct, the unemployment laws don't look at it that way. Not all actions that result in termination are serious enough to qualify as misconduct and justify denying benefits to the terminated worker.

What qualifies as misconduct? Generally speaking, an employee engages in misconduct by willfully doing something that substantially injures the company's interests. Revealing trade secrets or sexually harassing coworkers is misconduct; simple inefficiency or an unpleasant personality is not. Other common types of misconduct include extreme insubordination, chronic tardiness, numerous unexcused absences, intoxication on the job, and dishonesty.

Common actions that often result in firing—but do not constitute misconduct—are poor performance because of lack of skills, good faith errors in judgment, off-work conduct that does not have an impact on the employer's interests, and poor relations with coworkers.

It is important to remember that what qualifies as misconduct is a matter of interpretation and degree. Annoying one coworker might not be misconduct, but intentionally engaging in actions that anger an entire department even after repeated warnings might be.

Should Your Company Contest the Claim?

Your state's unemployment office—not your company—will ultimately decide whether the former employee can receive unemployment benefits. You do, however, have the option of contesting the employee's application, and that option gives your company a great deal of power. In California, for example, the unemployment board presumes that a terminated employee did not engage in misconduct unless the employer contests the claim. Thus, in California, all terminated employees who claim unemployment benefits receive them unless the former employer intervenes.

Remember, there is no reason—and there are no grounds—to contest an unemployment claim if the employee was laid off. There are also no grounds to contest the claim if the employee did not engage in misconduct but was fired—for instance, for sloppy work, carelessness, poor judgment, or inability to learn new skills.

Even if an employee does engage in misconduct, your company might want to give up its right to contest an unemployment insurance claim as part of a severance package. This is especially true if the fired employee seems likely to sue. (See "Severance," above, for more about severance packages and unemployment insurance.)

Your company should contest a claim only if it has grounds to do so—that is, if the employee engaged in serious misconduct or quit without a compelling reason. And even then, your company should also have a good, practical reason to contest. Employers typically fight unemployment claims for one of two reasons:

- They are concerned that their unemployment insurance rates may increase. After all, the employer—not the employee—pays for unemployment insurance. The amount the employer pays is often based in part on the number of claims made against the employer by former employees.
- They are concerned that the employee plans to file a wrongful termination action. The unemployment application process can be a valuable time to

discover the employee's side of the story, and it can also provide an excellent opportunity for gathering evidence—both from the employee and from witnesses.

If your company plans to contest an unemployment compensation claim, proceed with extreme caution. These battles not only cost time and money, but they also ensure that the former employee will become an enemy. The employee might even file a wrongful termination

lawsuit that otherwise could have been avoided. If the fired worker has friends who remain on the job, they too may doubt and distrust your company's tactics.

Before making any decisions, you might want to do some research by contacting your state's unemployment office for specific information about the law in your state. This office can tell you what effect a successful claim will have on your company's rates. If it's relatively small, backing off might be a good idea.

Anatomy of an Unemployment Compensation Claim

Although the unemployment compensation system varies in each state, some general principles apply in most cases. An unemployment claim will typically proceed through the steps described below.

Step 1: Claim filing. The process starts when the former employee files a claim with the state unemployment program. Your company receives written notice of the claim and can file a written objection.

Step 2: Eligibility determination. The state agency makes an initial determination of whether the former employee is eligible to get unemployment benefits. Usually there's no hearing at this stage.

Step 3: Hearing. Your company or the former employee can appeal the initial eligibility decision and have a hearing before a referee—a hearing officer who

is on the staff of the state agency. Normally conducted in a private room at the unemployment office, this is the most important step in the process. At the hearing, the company and the former employee each has an opportunity to speak. In addition, you are entitled to have a lawyer there and to present witnesses and any relevant written records, such as employee evaluations or warning letters.

Step 4: Administrative appeal. Either your company or the employee can appeal the referee's decision to an administrative agency, such as a board of review.

Step 5: Judicial appeal. Either side can appeal to the state court system, but this is rare.

Adapted from *The Employer's Legal Handbook*, by Fred S. Steingold (Nolo).

Legal Dos and Don'ts: Departing Workers

Do:

- **Fight fair.** As a practical matter, it makes sense to contest an unemployment claim only in limited circumstances, such as when you know the employee plans to file a lawsuit (your company can use the information you gather at the unemployment hearing to help build a defense). Otherwise, let it go: Pursuing a vendetta against a former employee will only take up time and money—and could convince the employee to sue.
- **Negotiate creatively.** If you can offer a fired or laid-off worker something—anything—to ease the pain of losing a job, you will reduce the risk of a lawsuit. You don't have to break the bank to offer a meaningful severance package; the employee may want something that you hadn't considered, such as keeping a company laptop.
- **Show respect for departing employees.** Even if an employee leaves on bad terms, you shouldn't trash the employee to other workers or prospective employers. Bad-mouthing a former employee can lead to defamation lawsuits—and it will give remaining workers a sour taste of what they might expect should they ever leave the company.

Don't:

- **Ask every employee who leaves to sign a release.** There's a big downside to using releases: Some employees who otherwise wouldn't consider a lawsuit might start thinking about it when faced with a document that asks them to give up their legal rights. Reserve releases for employees whom you suspect might sue—or situations in which your company's conduct has been questionable.
- **Play favorites.** You might be tempted to treat some departing workers better than others. However, treating workers differently can lead to resentment—and to lawsuits. Make sure you have legitimate, business-related reasons for your actions.
- **Make life difficult for terminated employees.** If you treat former employees fairly, they are much less likely to sue your company. Remember this simple rule when deciding whether to contest an unemployment claim, give an angry reference, or deny a fired employee a simple benefit or two, such as paying for a couple of months of continued health insurance.

Test Your Knowledge

Questions

1. Your company can be sued for giving an honest but negative reference about a former employee, if the reference prevents the employee from getting another job. ☐ True ☐ False

2. The best reference policy is to say only positive things, even if a former employee was truly dreadful. ☐ True ☐ False

3. Managers should not go into detail when telling workers that an employee has been terminated. ☐ True ☐ False

4. Companies must continue to pay for health insurance for former employees for up to 18 months. ☐ True ☐ False

5. Employers are legally required to pay one week of severance for every year an employee has worked for the company. ☐ True ☐ False

6. A company may have to pay severance to a fired employee if it has always paid severance to employees who held that position in the past. ☐ True ☐ False

7. A company can refuse to pay an employee severance unless he or she signs a release agreeing not to sue the company. ☐ True ☐ False

8. A release is valid only if the employee has talked to a lawyer before signing it. ☐ True ☐ False

9. Employees who are fired cannot collect unemployment benefits. ☐ True ☐ False

10. Companies should always contest unemployment claims. ☐ True ☐ False

Answers

1. False. To sue for defamation, an employee must be able to prove that your statements were false. As long as you are honest and aren't motivated by malice or ill will towards the employee, a defamation lawsuit will fail.

2. False. If you give a detailed reference (that is, you go beyond name, salary, and position) for an employee who was dangerous, violent, or otherwise posed a risk to others but you omit that information, the prospective employer may have a legal claim against you if that employee goes on to cause harm. If you choose to be expansive, you must give the bad news as well as the good.

3. True. The safest course is simply to say that the employee has been terminated and explain who will be responsible for that employee's projects going forward.

4. False. Although some companies may be required to give departing employees the option of continuing their health insurance benefits, the company is not required to pay for it.

5. False. Except for the few states that require employers who conduct mass layoffs to pay a small amount of severance, employers are not legally required to pay severance—unless they lead employees to believe that they would receive it.

6. True. If your company has always paid severance to employees who are fired from certain positions, an employee could argue that this is company policy—and that your failure to adhere to it constitutes a breach of contract or discrimination.

7. It depends on your company's severance policies. If employees at your company are already entitled to receive severance, you cannot require them to sign a release to get it. If, however, an employee is not entitled to receive severance, you can condition a severance package on the employee's agreement not to sue.

8. False. In some circumstances—for example, if your company is firing an older worker or your state's law requires it—you may have to advise workers of their right to talk to a lawyer before signing a release. However, if the worker decides not to heed this advice, the release will still be valid.

9. False. A worker who is fired for serious misconduct is probably not entitled to benefits, but workers who are fired for poor performance or poor fit are.

10. False. In fact, there are very few situations when it makes sense to contest an unemployment claim. Fighting an employee's effort to collect unemployment will take time and money—and could convince the employee to try to get money out of your company through a lawsuit.

State Health Insurance Continuation Laws

Alabama

Ala. Code § 27-55-3(4)

Coverage: 18 months for subjects of domestic abuse who have lost coverage they had under abuser's insurance and who do not qualify for COBRA.

Arizona

Ariz. Rev. Stat. §§ 20-1377, 20-1408

Employers affected: All employers who offer group disability insurance.

Length of coverage for dependents: Insurer must either continue coverage for dependents or convert to individual policy upon death of covered employee or divorce or legal separation. Coverage must be the same unless the insured chooses a lesser plan.

Time employer has to notify employee of continuation rights: No provisions for employer. Insurance policy must include notice of conversion privilege. Clerk of court must provide notice to anyone filing for divorce that dependent spouse entitled to convert health insurance coverage.

Time employee has to apply: 31 days after termination of existing coverage.

Arkansas

Ark. Code Ann. §§ 23-86-114 to 23-86-116

Employers affected: All employers who offer group health insurance.

Eligible employees: Continuously insured for previous 3 months.

Length of coverage for employee: 120 days.

Length of coverage for dependents: 120 days.

Time employee has to apply: 10 days.

California

Cal. Health & Safety Code §§ 1373.6, 1373.621; Cal. Ins. Code §§ 10128.50 to 10128.59

Employers affected: Employers who offer group health insurance and have 2 to 19 employees.

Eligible employees: Continuously insured for previous 3 months.

Qualifying event: Termination of employment; reduction in hours.

Length of coverage for employee: 36 months.

Length of coverage for dependents: 36 months.

Time employer has to notify employee of continuation rights: 15 days.

Time employee has to apply: 31 days after group plan ends; 30 days after COBRA or Cal-COBRA ends (63 days if converting to an individual plan).

Special situations: Employee who is at least 60 years old and has worked for employer for previous 5 years may continue benefits for self and spouse beyond COBRA or Cal-COBRA limits (also applies to COBRA employers). Employee who began receiving COBRA coverage on or after 1/1/03 and whose COBRA coverage is for less than 36 months may use Cal-COBRA to bring total coverage up to 36 months.

Colorado

Colo. Rev. Stat. § 10-16-108

Employers affected: All employers who offer group health insurance.

Eligible employees: Employees continuously insured for previous 6 months.

Length of coverage for employee: 18 months.

Length of coverage for dependents: 18 months.

Time employer has to notify employee of continuation rights: Within 10 days of termination.

Time employee has to apply: 31 days after termination; 60 days if employers fails to give notice.

State Health Insurance Continuation Laws (continued)

Connecticut

Conn. Gen. Stat. Ann. §§ 38a-538, 38a-554, 31-51o

Employers affected: All employers who offer group health insurance.

Eligible employees: Continuously insured for previous 3 months.

Length of coverage for employee: 18 months, or until eligible for Social Security benefits.

Length of coverage for dependents: 18 months, or until eligible for Social Security benefits; 36 months in case of employee's death or divorce.

Time employer has to notify employee of continuation rights: 14 days.

Time employee has to apply: 60 days.

Special situations: When facility closes or relocates, employer must pay for insurance for employee and dependents for 120 days or until employee is eligible for other group coverage, whichever comes first. (Does not affect employee's right to conventional continuation coverage, which begins when 120-day period ends.)

District of Columbia

D.C. Code Ann. §§ 32-731 to 32-732

Employers affected: Employers with fewer than 20 employees.

Eligible employees: All covered employees are eligible.

Length of coverage for employee: 3 months.

Length of coverage for dependents: 3 months.

Time employer has to notify employee of continuation rights: Within 15 days of termination of coverage.

Time employee has to apply: 45 days after termination of coverage.

Florida

Fla. Stat. Ann. § 627.6692

Employers affected: Employers with fewer than 20 employees.

Eligible employees: Full-time (25 or more hours per week) employees covered by employer's health insurance plan.

Length of coverage for employee: 18 months.

Length of coverage for dependents: 18 months.

Time employer has to notify employee of continuation rights: Carrier notifies within 14 days of learning of qualifying event (employer is responsible for notifying carrier).

Time employee has to apply: 30 days from receipt of carrier's notice.

Georgia

Ga. Code Ann. §§ 33-24-21.1 to 33-24-21.2

Employers affected: All employers who offer group health insurance.

Eligible employees: Employees continuously insured for previous 6 months.

Length of coverage for employee: 3 months plus any part of the month remaining at termination.

Length of coverage for dependents: 3 months plus any part of the month remaining at termination.

Special situations: Employee, spouse, or former spouse who is 60 years old and who has been covered for previous 6 months may continue coverage until eligible for Medicare. (Applies to companies with more than 20 employees; does not apply when employee quits for reasons other than health.)

Hawaii

Haw. Rev. Stat. §§ 393-11, 393-15

Employers affected: All employers required to offer health insurance (those paying a regular

State Health Insurance Continuation Laws (continued)

employee a monthly wage at least 86.67 times state hourly minimum—about $542).

Length of coverage for employee: If employee is hospitalized or prevented from working by sickness, employer must pay insurance premiums for 3 months or for as long employer continues to pay wages, whichever is longer.

Illinois

215 Ill. Comp. Stat. §§ 5/367e, 5/367.2, 5/367.2-5

Employers affected: All employers who offer group health insurance.

Eligible employees: Employees continuously insured for previous 3 months.

Length of coverage for employee: 9 months.

Length of coverage for dependents: 9 months (but see below).

Time employee has to apply: 10 days after termination or reduction in hours or receiving notice from employer, whichever is later, but not more than 60 days from termination or reduction in hours.

Special situations: Upon death or divorce, 2 years' coverage for spouse under 55 and eligible dependents who were on employee's plan; until eligible for Medicare or other group coverage for spouse over 55 and eligible dependents who were on employee's plan. As of 7/1/2004, dependent child who has reached plan age limit or who was not already covered by plan also entitled to 2 years' continuation coverage.

Indiana

Ind. Code Ann. § 27-8-15-31.1

Employers affected: Employers with at least 3 employees.

Eligible employees: Employed by same employer for at least one year and continuously insured for previous 90 days.

Length of coverage for employee: 12 months.

Length of coverage for dependents: 12 months.

Time employer has to notify employee of continuation rights: 10 days after employee becomes eligible for continuation coverage.

Time employee has to apply: Must apply directly to insurer within 30 days after becoming eligible for continuation coverage.

Iowa

Iowa Code §§ 509B.3 to 509B.5

Employers affected: All employers who offer group health insurance.

Eligible employees: Employees continuously insured for previous 3 months.

Length of coverage for employee: 9 months.

Length of coverage for dependents: 9 months.

Time employer has to notify employee of continuation rights: 10 days after termination of coverage.

Time employee has to apply: 10 days after termination of coverage or receiving notice from employer, whichever is later, but no more than 31 days from termination of coverage.

Kansas

Kan. Stat. Ann. § 40-2209(i)

Employers affected: All employers who offer group health insurance.

Eligible employees: Employees continuously insured for previous 3 months.

Length of coverage for employee: 6 months.

Length of coverage for dependents: 6 months.

Time employee has to apply: 31 days from termination of coverage.

Kentucky

Ky. Rev. Stat. Ann. § 304.18-110

Employers affected: All employers who offer group health insurance.

State Health Insurance Continuation Laws (continued)

Eligible employees: Employees continuously insured for previous 3 months.

Length of coverage for employee: 18 months.

Length of coverage for dependents: 18 months.

Time employer has to notify employee of continuation rights: Employer must notify insurer as soon as employee's coverage ends; insurer then notifies employee.

Time employee has to apply: 31 days from receipt of insurer's notice, but no more than 90 days after termination of group coverage.

Louisiana

La. Rev. Stat. Ann. §§ 22:215.7, 22:215.13

Employers affected: All employers who offer group health insurance and have fewer than 20 employees.

Eligible employees: Employees continuously insured for previous 3 months.

Length of coverage for employee: 12 months.

Length of coverage for dependents: 12 months.

Time employee has to apply: Must apply and submit payment before group coverage ends.

Special situations: Surviving spouse who is 50 or older may have coverage until remarriage or eligibility for Medicare or other insurance.

Maine

Me. Rev. Stat. Ann. tit. 24-A, § 2809-A

Employers affected: All employers who offer group health insurance.

Eligible employees: Employees continuously insured for previous 3 months.

Length of coverage for employee: One year (either group or individual coverage at discretion of insurer).

Length of coverage for dependents: One year (either group or individual coverage at discretion

of insurer). Upon death of insured, continuation only if original plan provided for coverage.

Time employee has to apply: 90 days from termination of group coverage.

Special situations: Temporary layoff or work-related injury or disease: Employee and employee's dependents entitled to one year group or individual continuation coverage. (Must have been continuously insured for previous 6 months; must apply within 31 days from termination of coverage.)

Maryland

Md. Code Ann., [Ins.] §§ 15-407 to 15-410

Employers affected: All employers who offer group health insurance.

Eligible employees: Employees continuously insured for previous 3 months.

Length of coverage for employee: 18 months.

Length of coverage for dependents: 18 months upon death of employee; upon change in marital status, 18 months or until spouse remarries or becomes eligible for other coverage.

Time employer has to notify employee of continuation rights: Must notify insurer within 14 days of receiving employee's continuation request.

Time employee has to apply: 45 days from termination of coverage. Employee begins application process by requesting an election of continuation notification form from employer.

Massachusetts

Mass. Gen. Laws ch. 175, §§ 110G, 110I; ch. 176J, § 9

Employers affected: All employers who offer group health insurance and have fewer than 20 employees.

Eligible employees: All covered employees are eligible.

State Health Insurance Continuation Laws (continued)

Length of coverage for employee: 18 months; 29 months if disabled.

Length of coverage for dependents: 18 months upon termination or reduction in hours; 29 months if disabled; 36 months on divorce, death of employee, employee's eligibility for Medicare, or employer's bankruptcy.

Time employer has to notify employee of continuation rights: When employee becomes eligible for continuation benefits.

Time employee has to apply: 60 days.

Special situations: Termination due to plant closing: 90 days' coverage for employee and dependents, at the same payment terms as before closing.

Minnesota

Minn. Stat. Ann. § 62A.17

Employers affected: All employers who offer group health insurance and have 2 or more employees.

Eligible employees: All covered employees are eligible.

Length of coverage for employee: 18 months; indefinitely if employee becomes totally disabled while employed.

Length of coverage for dependents: 18 months for current spouse; divorced or widowed spouse can continue until eligible for Medicare or other group health insurance. Upon divorce, dependent children can continue until they no longer qualify as dependents under plan. Upon death of employee, dependent children can continue for 36 months.

Time employer has to notify employee of continuation rights: Within 10 days of termination of coverage.

Time employee has to apply: 60 days from termination of coverage or receipt of employer's notice, whichever is later.

Mississippi

Miss. Code Ann. § 83-9-51

Employers affected: All employers who offer group health insurance and have fewer than 20 employees.

Eligible employees: Employees continuously insured for previous 3 months.

Length of coverage for employee: 12 months.

Length of coverage for dependents: 12 months.

Time employer has to notify employee of continuation rights: Insurer must notify former or deceased employee's dependent child or divorced spouse of option to continue insurance within 14 days of their becoming ineligible for coverage on employee's policy.

Time employee has to apply: Employee must apply and submit payment before group coverage ends; dependents or former spouse must elect continuation coverage within 30 days of receiving insurer's notice.

Missouri

Mo. Rev. Stat. § 376.428

Employers affected: All employers who offer group health insurance.

Eligible employees: Employees continuously insured for previous 3 months.

Length of coverage for employee: 9 months.

Length of coverage for dependents: 9 months.

Time employer has to notify employee of continuation rights: No later than date group coverage would end.

Time employee has to apply: 31 days from date group coverage would end.

Montana

Mont. Code Ann. §§ 33-22-506 to 33-22-510

Employers affected: All employers who offer group disability insurance.

State Health Insurance Continuation Laws (continued)

Eligible employees: All employees.

Length of coverage for employee: One year (with employer's consent).

Time employee has to apply: 31 days from date group coverage would end.

Special situations: Insurer may not discontinue benefits to child with disabilities after child exceeds age limit for dependent status.

Nebraska

Neb. Rev. Stat. §§ 44-1640 and following, 44-7406

Employers affected: Employers not subject to federal COBRA laws.

Eligible employees: All covered employees.

Length of coverage for employee: 6 months.

Length of coverage for dependents: One year upon death of insured employee. Subjects of domestic abuse who have lost coverage under abuser's plan and who do not qualify for COBRA may have 18 months' coverage (applies to all employers).

Time employer has to notify employee of continuation rights: Within 10 days of termination of employment must send notice by certified mail.

Time employee has to apply: 10 days from receipt of employer's notice.

Nevada

Nev. Rev. Stat. Ann. §§ 689B.245 and following, 689B.0345

Employers affected: Employers with fewer than 20 employees.

Eligible employees: Employees continuously insured for previous 12 months.

Length of coverage for employee: 18 months.

Length of coverage for dependents: 36 months; insurer cannot terminate coverage for disabled, dependent child who is too old to qualify as a dependent under the plan.

Time employer has to notify employee of continuation rights: 14 days after receiving notice of employee's eligibility.

Time employee has to apply: Must notify employer within 60 days of becoming eligible for continuation coverage; must apply within 60 days after receiving employer's notice.

Special situations: While employee is on leave without pay due to disability, 12 months for employee and dependents (applies to all employers).

New Hampshire

N.H. Rev. Stat. Ann. §§ 415:18(VIIg), (VII-a)

Employers affected: Employers with 2 to 19 employees.

Eligible employees: All insured employees are eligible.

Length of coverage for employee: 18 months; 29 months if disabled at termination or during first 60 days of continuation coverage.

Length of coverage for dependents: 18 months; 29 months if disabled at termination or during first 60 days of continuation coverage; 36 months upon death of employee, divorce or legal separation, loss of dependent status, or employee's eligibility for Medicare.

Time employer has to notify employee of continuation rights: Within 15 days of termination of coverage.

Time employee has to apply: Within 31 days of termination of coverage.

Special situations: Layoff or termination due to strike: 6 months' coverage with option to extend for an additional 12 months. Surviving, divorced, or legally separated spouse who is 55 or older may continue benefits available until eligible

State Health Insurance Continuation Laws (continued)

for Medicare or other employer-based group insurance.

New Jersey

N.J. Stat. Ann. §§ 17B:27-30, 17B:27-51.12, 17B:27A-27

Employers affected: Employers with 2 to 50 employees.

Eligible employees: Employed full time (25 or more hours).

Length of coverage for employee: 18 months; 29 months if disabled at termination or during first 60 days of continuation coverage.

Length of coverage for dependents: 18 months; 29 months if disabled at termination or during first 60 days of continuation coverage; 36 months upon death of employee, divorce or legal separation, loss of dependent status, or employee's eligibility for Medicare.

Time employer has to notify employee of continuation rights: At time of qualifying event employer or carrier notifies employee.

Time employee has to apply: Within 30 days of qualifying event.

Special benefits: Coverage must be identical to that offered to current employees.

Special situations: Total disability: Employee who has been insured for previous 3 months and employee's dependents entitled to continuation coverage that includes all benefits offered by group policy (applies to all employers).

New Mexico

N.M. Stat. Ann. § 59A-18-16

Employers affected: All employers who offer group health insurance.

Eligible employees: All insured employees are eligible.

Length of coverage for employee: 6 months.

Length of coverage for dependents: May continue group coverage or convert to individual policies upon death of covered employee or divorce or legal separation.

Time employer has to notify employee of continuation rights: Insurer or employer gives written notice at time of termination.

Time employee has to apply: 30 days after receiving notice.

New York

N.Y. Ins. Law §§ 3221(f), 3221(m)

Employers affected: All employers who offer group health insurance and have fewer than 20 employees.

Eligible employees: All covered employees are eligible.

Length of coverage for employee: 18 months; 29 months if disabled at termination or during first 60 days of continuation coverage.

Length of coverage for dependents: 18 months; 29 months if disabled at termination or during first 60 days of continuation; 36 months upon death of employee, divorce or legal separation, loss of dependent status, or employee's eligibility for Medicare.

Time employee has to apply: 60 days after termination or receipt of notice, whichever is later.

North Carolina

N.C. Gen. Stat. §§ 58-53-5 to 58-53-40

Employers affected: All employers who offer group health insurance.

Eligible employees: Employees continuously insured for previous 3 months.

Length of coverage for employee: 18 months.

Length of coverage for dependents: 18 months.

State Health Insurance Continuation Laws (continued)

Time employer has to notify employee of continuation rights: Employer has option of notifying employee as part of the exit process.

Time employee has to apply: 60 days.

North Dakota

N.D. Cent. Code §§ 26.1-36-23, 26.1-36-23.1

Employers affected: All employers who offer group health insurance.

Eligible employees: Employees continuously insured for previous 3 months.

Length of coverage for employee: 39 weeks.

Length of coverage for dependents: 39 weeks; 36 months if required by divorce or annulment decree.

Time employee has to apply: Within 10 days of termination or of receiving notice of continuation rights, whichever is later, but no more than 31 days from termination.

Ohio

Ohio Rev. Code Ann. §§ 3923.38, 1751.53

Employers affected: All employers who offer group health insurance.

Eligible employees: Employees continuously insured for previous 3 months who are entitled to unemployment benefits.

Length of coverage for employee: 6 months.

Length of coverage for dependents: 6 months.

Time employer has to notify employee of continuation rights: At termination of employment.

Time employee has to apply: Whichever is earlier: 31 days after coverage terminates; 10 days after coverage terminates if employer notified employee of continuation rights prior to termination; 10 days after employer notified employee of continuation rights, if notice was given after coverage terminated.

Oklahoma

Okla. Stat. Ann. tit. 36, § 4509

Employers affected: All employers who offer group health insurance.

Eligible employees: Employees insured for at least 6 months. (All other employees and their dependents entitled to 30 days' continuation coverage.)

Length of coverage for employee: Only for losses or conditions that began while group policy was in effect: 3 months for basic coverage; 6 months for major medical at the same premium rate prior to termination of coverage.

Length of coverage for dependents: Only for losses or conditions that began while group policy was in effect: 3 months for basic coverage; 6 months for major medical at the same premium rate prior to termination of coverage.

Special benefits: Includes maternity care for pregnancy begun while group policy was in effect.

Oregon

Or. Rev. Stat. §§ 743.600 to 743.610

Employers affected: Employers not subject to federal COBRA laws.

Eligible employees: Employees continuously insured for previous 3 months.

Length of coverage for employee: 6 months.

Length of coverage for dependents: 6 months.

Time employee has to apply: 10 days after termination or after receiving notice of continuation rights, whichever is later, but not more than 31 days.

Special situations: Surviving, divorced, or legally separated spouse who is 55 or older and dependent children entitled to continuation coverage until spouse remarries or is eligible for other coverage. Must include dental, vision, or

State Health Insurance Continuation Laws (continued)

prescription drug benefits if they were offered in original plan (applies to employers with 20 or more employees).

Rhode Island

R.I. Gen. Laws §§ 27-19.1-1, 27-20.4-1 to 27-20-4.2

Employers affected: All employers who offer group health insurance.

Eligible employees: All insured employees are eligible.

Length of coverage for employee: 18 months (but not longer than continuous employment). Cannot be required to pay more than one month premium at a time.

Length of coverage for dependents: 18 months (but not longer than continuous employment). Cannot be required to pay more than one month premium at a time.

Time employer has to notify employee of continuation rights: Employers must post a conspicuous notice of employee continuation rights.

Time employee has to apply: 30 days from termination of coverage.

Special situations: If right to receiving continuing health insurance is stated in the divorce judgment, divorced spouse has right to continue coverage as long as employee remains covered or until divorced spouse remarries or becomes eligible for other group insurance. If covered employee remarries, divorced spouse must be given right to purchase an individual policy from same insurer.

South Carolina

S.C. Code Ann. § 38-71-770

Employers affected: All employers who offer group health insurance.

Eligible employees: Employees continuously insured for previous 6 months.

Length of coverage for employee: 6 months (in addition to part of month remaining at termination).

Length of coverage for dependents: 6 months (in addition to part of month remaining at termination).

Time employer has to notify employee of continuation rights: At time of termination must clearly and meaningfully advise employee of continuation rights.

South Dakota

S.D. Codified Laws Ann. §§ 58-18-7.5, 58-18-7.12, 58-18C-1

Employers affected: All employers who offer group health insurance.

Eligible employees: All covered employees.

Length of coverage for employee: 18 months; 29 months if disabled at termination or during first 60 days of continuation coverage.

Length of coverage for dependents: 18 months; 29 months if disabled at termination or during first 60 days of continuation coverage; 36 months upon death of employee, divorce or legal separation, loss of dependent status, employee's eligibility for Medicare.

Special situations: When employer goes out of business: 12 months' continuation coverage available to all employees. Employer must notify employees within 10 days of termination of benefits; employees must apply within 60 days of receipt of employer's notice or within 90 days of termination of benefits if no notice given.

Tennessee

Tenn. Code Ann. § 56-7-2312

Employers affected: All employers who offer group health insurance.

State Health Insurance Continuation Laws (continued)

Eligible employees: Employees continuously insured for previous 3 months.

Length of coverage for employee: 3 months (in addition to part of month remaining at termination).

Length of coverage for dependents: 3 months (in addition to part of month remaining at termination); 15 months upon death of employee or divorce.

Special situations: Employee or dependent who is pregnant at time of termination entitled to continuation benefits for 6 months following the end of pregnancy.

Texas

Tex. Ins. Code Ann. Art 3.51-6(d)(3), 3.51-8

Employers affected: All employers who offer group health insurance.

Eligible employees: Employees continuously insured for previous 3 months.

Length of coverage for employee: 6 months.

Length of coverage for dependents: 6 months.

Time employee has to apply: 31 days from termination of coverage or receiving notice of continuation rights from employer or insurer, whichever is later.

Special situations: Layoff due to a labor dispute: Employee entitled to continuation benefits for duration of dispute, but no longer than 6 months.

Utah

Utah Code Ann. §§ 31A-22-722

Employers affected: All employers who offer group health insurance.

Eligible employees: Employees continuously insured for previous 6 months.

Length of coverage for employee: 6 months.

Length of coverage for dependents: 6 months.

Time employer has to notify employee of continuation rights: In writing within 30 days of termination of coverage.

Time employee has to apply: Within 30 days of receiving employer's notice of continuation rights.

Vermont

Vt. Stat. Ann. tit. 8, §§ 4090a to 4090c

Employers affected: All employers who offer group health insurance and have fewer than 20 employees.

Eligible employees: Employees continuously insured for previous 3 months.

Length of coverage for employee: 6 months.

Length of coverage for dependents: 6 months.

Time employee has to apply: Within 60 days (upon death of employee or group member); within 30 days (upon termination, change of marital status, or loss of dependent status) of the date that group coverage terminates, or the date of being notified of continuation rights, whichever is sooner.

Virginia

Va. Code Ann. §§ 38.2-3541 to 38.2-3452; 38.2-3416

Employers affected: All employers who offer group health insurance.

Eligible employees: Employees continuously insured for previous 3 months.

Length of coverage for employee: 90 days.

Length of coverage for dependents: 90 days.

Time employer has to notify employee of continuation rights: 15 days from termination of coverage.

Time employee has to apply: Must apply for continuation and pay entire 90-day premium before termination of coverage.

State Health Insurance Continuation Laws (continued)

Special situations: Employee may convert to an individual policy instead of applying for continuation coverage (must apply within 31 days of termination of coverage).

Washington

Wash. Rev. Code Ann. § 48.21.075

Employers affected: All employers who offer and pay for group health insurance.

Eligible employees: Insured employees on strike.

Length of coverage for employee: 6 months if employee goes on strike.

Length of coverage for dependents: 6 months if employee goes on strike.

West Virginia

W. Va. Code §§ 33-16-2, 33-16-3(e)

Employers affected: Employers providing insurance for at least 10 employees.

Eligible employees: All covered employees are eligible.

Length of coverage for employee: 18 months in case of involuntary layoff.

Wisconsin

Wis. Stat. Ann. § 632.897

Employers affected: All employers who offer group health insurance.

Eligible employees: Employees continuously insured for previous 3 months.

Length of coverage for employee: 18 months (or longer at insurer's option).

Length of coverage for dependents: 18 months (or longer at insurer's option).

Time employer has to notify employee of continuation rights: 5 days from termination of coverage.

Time employee has to apply: 30 days after receiving employer's notice.

Wyoming

Wyo. Stat. § 26-19-113

Employers affected: Employers not subject to federal COBRA laws.

Eligible employees: Employees continuously insured for previous 3 months.

Length of coverage for employee: 12 months.

Length of coverage for dependents: 12 months.

Time employee has to apply: 31 days from termination of coverage.

Current as of February 2005

APPENDIX

Resources

· ·

Internet Resources

www.disabilityinfo.gov

This government website provides resources designed specially for small businesses and employers on how to comply with disability rights laws.

www.epinet.org

The Economic Policy Institute provides information on state and county living wage laws. From the home page, click on "Issue Guides: Living Wage" to get to the living wage information.

www.esgr.org

The National Committee of Employer Support of the Guard and Reserve explains employers' legal obligations to employees in the military. This site also gives employers tips on helping their employees balance military service with employment.

www.nationalpartnership.org

The National Partnership for Women and Families (then called the Women's Legal Defense Fund) was instrumental in drafting the federal Family and Medical Leave Act. Check out their website for information on the FMLA and similar state laws.

www.statelocalgov.net

This handy website offers a frequently updated directory of links to government-sponsored and -controlled resources on the Internet. If you are searching for a state or local agency or information about state laws, this is the place to start.

www.privacyrights.org

The Privacy Rights Clearinghouse offers helpful fact sheets on worker privacy issues.

www.findlaw.com

This website offers a library of helpful information for employers and small businesses. Under the "Legal Professional" heading, click "Legal Subjects," then "Labor & Employment Law" for a list of articles.

www.noworkviolence.com

The Workplace Violence Research Institute gives valuable tips on avoiding and handling workplace violence.

www.lambdalegal.org

The Lambda Legal Defense and Education Fund provides a state-by-state list of anti-discrimination laws that apply to gay and lesbian employees.

www.toolkit.cch.com.

This website provides helpful articles, tips, sample policies, and much more on a variety of employment issues.

Federal Agencies That Enforce Workplace Laws

U.S. Equal Employment Opportunity
  Commission
1801 L Street, NW
Washington, DC 20507
Phone: 202-663-4900
To be connected with the field office closest
to you: 800-669-4000
www.eeoc.gov

U.S. Department of Labor
200 Constitution Avenue, NW
Washington, DC 20210
Phone: 866-4-USA-DOL (866-487-2365)
www.dol.gov

U.S. Department of Justice
950 Pennsylvania Avenue, NW
Washington, DC 20530
Phone: 202-514-2000
www.usdoj.gov

Internal Revenue Service
U.S. Department of Treasury
1500 Pennsylvania Avenue, NW
Washington, DC 20220
Live telephone assistance for businesses:
  800-829-4933
www.irs.gov
www.treasury.gov

Departments of Labor

U.S. Department of Labor

Washington, DC 20210
202-693-4650
www.dol.gov
You can find a list of regional offices
of the Wage and Hour Division at the
Department of Labor's website at:
www.dol.gov/esa/contacts/whd/america2.
    htm
and a comprehensive list of state labor
resources at:
www.dol.gov/dol/location.htm

State Labor Departments

Note: Phone numbers are for department
headquarters. Check websites for regional
office locations and numbers.

Alabama

Department of Industrial Relations
Montgomery, AL
334-242-8990
www.dir.state.al.us

Alaska

Department of Labor and Workforce
    Development
Juneau, AK
907-465-2700
www.labor.state.ak.us

Arizona

Industrial Commission
Phoenix, AZ
602-542-4411
www.ica.state.az.us

Arkansas

Department of Labor
Little Rock, AR
501-682-4541
www.state.ar.us/labor

California

Department of Industrial Relations
San Francisco, CA
415-703-5050
www.dir.ca.gov

Colorado

Department of Labor and Employment
Denver, CO
303-318-8000
www.coworkforce.com

Connecticut

Labor Department
Wethersfield, CT
860-263-6505
www.ctdol.state.ct.us

Delaware

Department of Labor
Wilmington, DE
302-761-8000
www.delawareworks.com

District of Columbia

Department of Employment Services
Washington, DC
202-671-1900
http://does.ci.washington.dc.us

Departments of Labor (continued)

Florida
Agency for Workforce Innovation
Tallahassee, FL
850-245-7105
www.floridajobs.org or www.MyFlorida.
com

Georgia
Department of Labor
Atlanta, GA
404-656-3011
877-709-8185
www.dol.state.ga.us

Hawaii
Department of Labor and Industrial
Relations
Honolulu, HI
808-586-8865/8844
http://dlir.state.hi.us

Idaho
Department of Labor
Boise, ID
208-334-6112
www.labor.state.id.us

Illinois
Department of Labor
Chicago, IL
312-793-2800
www.state.il.us/agency/idol

Indiana
Department of Labor
Indianapolis, IN
317-232-2655
www.in.gov/labor

Iowa
Iowa Workforce Development
Des Moines, IA
515-281-5387
800-JOB-IOWA
www.iowaworkforce.org/labor

Kansas
Department of Human Resources
Office of Employment Standards
Topeka, KS
785-296-4062
www.dol.ks.gov

Kentucky
Department of Labor
Frankfort, KY
502-564-3070
www.kylabor.net

Louisiana
Department of Labor
Baton Rouge, LA
225-342-3111
www.ldol.state.la.us

Maine
Department of Labor
Augusta, ME
207-287-3787
www.state.me.us/labor

Departments of Labor (continued)

Maryland

Department of Labor, Licensing, and Regulation

Division of Labor and Industry

Baltimore, MD

410-767-2236

www.dllr.state.md.us/labor

Massachusetts

Department of Labor and Workforce Development

Boston, MA

617-727-6573

www.state.ma.us/dlwd or www.mass.gov/dlwd

Michigan

Department of Labor and Economic Growth

Lansing, MI

517-373-3034

www.cis.state.mi.us or www.michigan.gov/cis

Minnesota

Department of Labor and Industry

St. Paul, MN

651-284-5005

800-342-5354

www.doli.state.mn.us

Mississippi

Department of Employment Security

Jackson, MS

601-321-6100

www.mesc.state.ms.us

Missouri

Department of Labor and Industrial Relations

Jefferson City, MO

573-751-4091

573-751-9691

www.dolir.state.mo.us or www.dolir.mo.gov

Montana

Department of Labor and Industry

Helena, MT

406-444-2840

http://dli.state.mt.us

Nebraska

Department of Labor

Labor and Safety Standards

Lincoln, NE

402-471-2239

Omaha, NE

402-595-3095

www.dol.state.ne.us

Nevada

Division of Industrial Relations

Carson City, NV

775-684-7260

http://dirweb.state.nv.us

New Hampshire

Department of Labor

Concord, NH

603-271-3176

www.labor.state.nh.us

Departments of Labor (continued)

New Jersey
Department of Labor
Labor Standards and Safety Enforcement
Trenton, NJ
609-292-2313/2323
www.state.nj.us/labor

New Mexico
Labor and Industrial Division
Department of Labor
Santa Fe, NM
505-827-6875
Albuquerque, NM
505-841-8993
www.dol.state.nm.us

New York
Department of Labor
Albany, NY
518-457-9000
www.labor.state.ny.us

North Carolina
Department of Labor
Raleigh, NC
919-807-2796
800-625-2267
www.dol.state.nc.us or www.nclabor.com

North Dakota
Department of Labor
Bismarck, ND
701-328-2660
800-582-8032
www.state.nd.us/labor

Ohio
Division of Labor and Worker Safety
Department of Commerce
Columbus, OH
614-644-2239
www.com.state.oh.us/ODOC/laws/
   default.htm

Oklahoma
Department of Labor
Oklahoma City, OK
405-528-1500, ext. 200
888-269-5353
www.okdol.state.ok.us or www.ok.gov

Oregon
Bureau of Labor and Industries
Portland, OR
503-731-4200
www.boli.state.or.us

Pennsylvania
Department of Labor and Industry
Harrisburg, PA
717-787-5279
www.dli.state.pa.us

Rhode Island
Department of Labor and Training
Cranston, RI
401-462-8000
www.dlt.state.ri.us or www.det.state.ri.us

Departments of Labor (continued)

South Carolina

Department of Labor, Licensing, and
   Regulation
Columbia, SC
803-896-4300
www.llr.state.sc.us

South Dakota

Division of Labor and Management
Pierre, SD
605-773-3681
www.state.sd.us/dol/dlm/dlm-home.htm

Tennessee

Department of Labor and Workforce
   Development
Nashville, TN
615-741-6642
www.state.tn.us/labor-wfd

Texas

Texas Workforce Commission
Austin, TX
512-463-2222
www.twc.state.tx.us

Utah

Labor Commission
Salt Lake City, UT
801-530-6801
800-222-1238
www.labor.state.ut.us

Vermont

Department of Labor and Industry
Montpelier, VT
808-828-2288
www.state.vt.us/labind

Virginia

Department of Labor and Industry
Richmond, VA
804-371-2327
www.dli.state.va.us

Washington

Department of Labor and Industries
Olympia, WA
360-902-5800
800-547-8367
www.lni.wa.gov

West Virginia

Division of Labor
Charleston, WV
877-558-5134
304-558-7890
www.labor.state.wv.us

Wisconsin

Department of Workforce Development
Madison, WI
608-266-3131
www.dwd.state.wi.us

Wyoming

Department of Employment
Cheyenne, WY
307-777-6763
http://wydoe.state.wy.us

Current as of February 2005

Agencies That Enforce Laws Prohibiting Discrimination in Employment

Alabama

EEOC District Office
Birmingham, AL
205-212-2100
205-212-2112
http://eeoc.gov/birmingham/index.html

Alaska

Commission for Human Rights
Anchorage, AK
907-274-4692
800-478-4692
www.gov.state.ak.us/aschr/aschr.htm

Arizona

Civil Rights Division
Phoenix, AZ
602-542-5263
www.attorneygeneral.state.az.us/civil_
    rights/index.html

Arkansas

Equal Employment Opportunity
    Commission
Little Rock, AR
501-324-5060
www.eeoc.gov/littlerock/index.html

California

Department of Fair Employment and
    Housing
Sacramento District Office
Sacramento, CA
916-445-5523
800-884-1684
www.dfeh.ca.gov

Colorado

Civil Rights Division
Denver, CO
303-894-2997
800-262-4845
www.dora.state.co.us/Civil-Rights

Connecticut

Commission on Human Rights and
    Opportunities
Hartford, CT
860-541-3400
800-477-5737
www.state.ct.us/chro

Delaware

Office of Labor Law Enforcement
Division of Industrial Affairs
Wilmington, DE
302-761-8200
www.delawareworks.com/
    industrialaffairs/welcome.shtml

District of Columbia

Office of Human Rights
Washington, DC
202-727-4559
http://ohr.dc.gov/ohr/site/default.asp

Florida

Commission on Human Relations
Tallahassee, FL
850-488-7082
800-342-8170
http://fchr.state.fl.us

Agencies That Enforce Laws Prohibiting Discrimination in Employment (continued)

Georgia

Atlanta District Office
U.S. Equal Employment Opportunity
    Commission
Atlanta, GA
404-562-6800
800-669-4000
www.eeoc.gov/atlanta/index.html

Hawaii

Hawai'i Civil Rights Commission
Honolulu, HI
808-586-8636 (Oahu only)
800-468-4644 x68636 (other islands)
http://dlir.state.hi.us/divisions/hcrc

Idaho

Idaho Commission on Human Rights
Boise, ID
208-334-2873
www2.state.id.us/ihrc

Illinois

Department of Human Rights
Chicago, IL
312-814-6200
www.state.il.us/dhr

Indiana

Civil Rights Commission
Indianapolis, IN
317-232-2600
800-628-2909
www.in.gov/icrc

Iowa

Iowa Civil Rights Commission
Des Moines, IA
515-281-4121
800-457-4416
www.state.ia.us/government/crc

Kansas

Human Rights Commission
Topeka, KS
785-296-3206
www.ink.org/public/khrc

Kentucky

Human Rights Commission
Louisville, KY
502-595-4024
800-292-5566
www.state.ky.us/agencies2/kchr

Louisiana

Commission on Human Rights
Baton Rouge, LA
225-342-6969

Maine

Human Rights Commission
Augusta, ME
207-624-6050
www.state.me.us/mhrc/index.shtml

Maryland

Commission on Human Relations
Baltimore, MD
410-767-8600
800-637-6247
www.mchr.state.md.us

Agencies That Enforce Laws Prohibiting Discrimination in Employment (continued)

Massachusetts
Commission Against Discrimination
Boston, MA
617-994-6000
www.state.ma.us/mcad

Michigan
Department of Civil Rights
Detroit, MI
313-456-3700
800-482-3604
www.michigan.gov/mdcr

Minnesota
Department of Human Rights
St. Paul, MN
651-296-5663
800-657-3704
www.humanrights.state.mn.us

Mississippi
Equal Opportunity Department
Employment Security Commission
Jackson, MS
601-961-7420
www.mesc.state.ms.us

Missouri
Commission on Human Rights
Jefferson City, MO
573-751-3325
www.dolir.state.mo.us/hr

Montana
Human Rights Bureau
Employment Relations Division
Department of Labor and Industry
Helena, MT
406-444-2884
800-542-0807
http://erd.dli.state.mt.us/HumanRight/
    HRhome.asp

Nebraska
Equal Opportunity Commission
Lincoln, NE
402-471-2024
800-642-6112
www.nol.org/home/NEOC

Nevada
Equal Rights Commission
Reno, NV
775-688-1288
http://detr.state.nv.us/nerc/NERC-index.
    htm

New Hampshire
Commission for Human Rights
Concord, NH
603-271-2767
http://webster.state.nh.us/hrc

New Jersey
Division on Civil Rights
Newark, NJ
973-648-2700
www.state.nj.us/lps/dcr

Agencies That Enforce Laws Prohibiting Discrimination in Employment (continued)

New Mexico

Human Rights Division
Santa Fe, NM
505-827-6838
800-566-9471
www.dol.state.nm.us/dol_hrd.html

New York

Division of Human Rights
Bronx, NY
718-741-8400
www.nysdhr.com

North Carolina

Employment Discrimination Bureau
Department of Labor
Raleigh, NC
919-807-2796
800-NCLABOR (625-2267)
www.dol.state.nc.us/edb/edb.htm

North Dakota

Human Rights Division
Department of Labor
Bismarck, ND
701-328-2660
800-582-8032
www.state.nd.us/labor/services/human-
    rights

Ohio

Civil Rights Commission
Columbus, OH
614-466-5928
888-278-7101
www.state.oh.us/crc

Oklahoma

Human Rights Commission
Oklahoma City, OK
405-521-2360
www.youroklahoma.com/ohrc

Oregon

Civil Rights Division
Bureau of Labor and Industries
Portland, OR
503-731-4874
www.boli.state.or.us/BOLI/CRD/index.
    shtml

Pennsylvania

Human Relations Commission
Philadelphia, PA
215-560-2496
www.phrc.state.pa.us

Rhode Island

Commission for Human Rights
Providence, RI
401-222-2661
www.state.ri.us/manual/data/queries/
    stdept_.idc?id=16

South Carolina

Human Affairs Commission
Columbia, SC
803-737-7800
800-521-0725
www.state.sc.us/schac

Agencies That Enforce Laws Prohibiting Discrimination in Employment (continued)

South Dakota

Division of Human Rights
Pierre, SD
605-773-4493
www.state.sd.us/dcr/hr/HR_HOM.htm

Tennessee

Human Rights Commission
Knoxville, TN
865-594-6500
800-251-3589
www.state.tn.us/humanrights

Texas

Commission on Human Rights
Austin, TX
512-437-3450
888-452-4778
http://tchr.state.tx.us

Utah

Anti-Discrimination and Labor Division
Labor Commission
Salt Lake City, UT
801-530-6801
800-222-1238
http://laborcommission.utah.gov/
    Utah_Antidiscrimination_Labo/utah_
    antidiscrimination_Labo.htm

Vermont

Attorney General's Office
Civil Rights Division
Montpelier, VT
802-828-3171
888-745-9195
www.state.vt.us/atg/civil rights.htm

Virginia

Council on Human Rights
Richmond, VA
804-225-2292
www.chr.state.va.us

Washington

Human Rights Commission
Seattle, WA
206-464-6500
www.wa.gov/hrc

West Virginia

Human Rights Commission
Charleston, WV
304-558-2616
888-676-5546
www.wvf.state.wv.us/wvhrc

Wisconsin

Department of Workforce Development
Madison, WI
608-266-6860
www.dwd.state.wi.us/er

Wyoming

Department of Employment
Cheyenne, WY
307-777-7261
http://wydoe.state.wy.us/doe.asp?ID=3

Current as of February 2005

State OSHA Laws and Offices

If a state has a health and safety law that meets or exceeds federal OSHA standards, the state can take over enforcement of the standards from federal administrators. This means that all inspections and enforcement actions will be handled by your state OSHA rather than its federal counterpart.

So far, 21 states have been approved for such enforcement regarding private employers. They include Alaska, Arizona, California, Hawaii, Indiana, Iowa, Kentucky, Maryland, Michigan, Minnesota, Nevada, New Mexico, North Carolina, Oregon, South Carolina, Tennessee, Utah, Vermont, Virginia, Washington, and Wyoming. You can find an up-to-date list, along with contact information, at www. osha.gov/fso/osp.

Connecticut, New Jesey, and New York also have OSHA-type laws, but they only apply to government employees. Other states are considering passing OSHA laws—and some of the above states are considering amending the coverage and content of existing laws.

If your business is located in a state that has an OSHA law, contact your state agency for a copy of the safety and health standards that are relevant to your business. State standards may be more strict than federal standards, and the requirements for posting notices may be different.

■

Index